Stawiski Memorial Book (Poland)

Translation of *Stawiski; sefer yizkor*

Original Yizkor Book

Edited by: I. Rubin

Published by Stavisk Society, 1973

Published by JewishGen

**An Affiliate of the Museum of Jewish Heritage - A Living Memorial to the Holocaust
New York**

Stawiski Yizkor Book

Stawiski Memorial Book (Poland)
Translation of *Stawiski; Sefer Yizkor*

Editor: I. Rubin
Translation Project Coordinator: Jan Meisels Allen
Primary Translator: Jerrold Landau
Layout: Rabbi Helen Cohn
Image Editor: Jan R. Fine
Cover Design: Rachel Kolokoff Hopper

Published by JewishGen, Inc.
An Affiliate of the Museum of Jewish Heritage
A Living Memorial to the Holocaust
36 Battery Place, New York, NY 10280

Printed in the United States of America by Lightning Source, Inc.

Library of Congress Control Number (LCCN): 2015937413
ISBN: 978-1-939561-32-9 (hard cover: 406 pages, alk. paper)

Front and Back Cover Images: From the original Yiddish book.
Cover Background: Excerpts from the poem "My Shtetl of Stawiski" by
Chemda from the Yizkor book. Image designed by Rachel Kolokoff Hopper.

JewishGen and the Yizkor-Books-in-Print Project

This book has been published by the **Yizkor-Books-in-Print Project,** as part of the **Yizkor Book Project** of **JewishGen, Inc.**

JewishGen, Inc. is a non-profit organization founded in 1987 as a resource for Jewish genealogy. Its website [www.jewishgen.org] serves as an international clearinghouse and resource center to assist individuals who are researching the history of their Jewish families and the places where they lived. JewishGen provides databases, facilitates discussion groups, and coordinates projects relating to Jewish genealogy and the history of the Jewish people. In 2003, JewishGen became an affiliate of the **Museum of Jewish Heritage - A Living Memorial to the Holocaust** in New York.

The **JewishGen Yizkor Book Project** was organized to make more widely known the existence of Yizkor (Memorial) Books written by survivors and former residents of various Jewish communities throughout the world. Later, volunteers connected to the different destroyed communities began cooperating to have these books translated from the original language—usually Hebrew or Yiddish—into English, thus enabling a wider audience to have access to the valuable information contained within them. As each chapter of these books was translated, it was posted on the JewishGen website and made available to the general public.

The **Yizkor-Books-in-Print Project** began in 2011 as an initiative to print and publish Yizkor Books that had been fully translated, so that hard copies would be available for purchase by the descendants of these communities and also by scholars, universities, synagogues, libraries, and museums.

These Yizkor books have been produced almost entirely through the volunteer effort of researchers from around the world, assisted by donations from private individuals. The books are printed and sold at near cost, so as to make them as affordable as possible. Our goal is to make this important genre of Jewish literature and history available in English in book form, so that people can have the personal histories of their ancestral towns on their bookshelves for themselves and for their children and grandchildren.

A list of all published translated Yizkor Books in the project with prices and ordering information can be found at:
        http://www.jewishgen.org/Yizkor/ybip.html

Lance Ackerfeld, Yizkor Book Project Manager

Joel Alpert, Yizkor-Book-in-Print Project Coordinator

JewishGen
Yizkor Book Project

This book is presented by the
Yizkor Books in Print Project
Project Coordinator: Joel Alpert

Part of the
Yizkor Books Project of JewishGen, Inc.
Project Manager: Lance Ackerfeld

These books have been produced solely through volunteer effort
of individuals from around the world. The books are printed and
sold at near cost, so as to make them as affordable as possible.

Our goal is to make this history and important genre of Jewish
literature available in English in book form so that people can have
the near-personal histories of their ancestral towns on their bookshelves for themselves and for their children and grandchildren.

Any donations to the Yizkor Books Project are appreciated.

Please send donations to:
Yizkor Book Project
JewishGen
36 Battery Place
New York, NY 10280

JewishGen, Inc. is an affiliate of the
Museum of Jewish Heritage
A Living Memorial to the Holocaust

Hebrew Title Page of Original Yizkor Book

ס ט ב י ס ק

ספר זכרון

הוצאת אירגון יוצאי סטביסק בישראל
תשל"ג — 1973

Translation of the Title Page of Original Yizkor Book

Stawiski

Memorial Book

Published by

The Organization of Former Residents of Stawiski in Israel

1973

Yiddish Title Page of Original Yizkor Book

סטאוויסק

יזכור־בוך

ארויסגעגעבן דורכן סטאוויסקער לאנדסלייט־פאראיין אין ישראל
תשל״ג — 1973

Foreword for the Translation

Stawiski is the ancestral town of my maternal grandfather, Jacob Flower. We don't know his original name as no records were preserved in Stawiski—at least at the time of this publication in 2015, neither the Polish State Archives (PSA), the PSA Lomza Regional Archives or the Stawiski Municipal offices have found any civil records. I undertook the role of Stawiski Yizkor Book Project Coordinator project to have this Yizkor Book translated in the hope that I might find my family mentioned and learn about their lives. Unfortunately, I did not find my family mentioned but I did learn about the town, its people and history. On page 352b the Yizkor Book did include a photograph of my grandfather's sister, Ester Malka Kreplak, who died in the Shoah, along with one of her daughters and that daughter's husband and four of their five children. Today, that photograph in the Yizkor Book is the only surviving photograph of Ester Malka. When I first met with one of Ester Malka's granddaughters in Israel in 2004, she had the original photograph and went to have a copy made for me, but the photo shop lost the photograph. The preservation of the photographs within the Yizkor Books is one of the many special attributes for preserving these treasures by JewishGen for all to read and keep.

When I first decided to become the Stawiski Yizkor Book Translation Coordinator, the first task was to acquire a copy of the Yizkor Book —a daunting task because at that time it was not yet digitized on the New York Public Library website. An Israeli cousin whom I first met through genealogy, was able to provide me a copy of the book. Before any translations could begin we had to fund raise among those who are interested in Stawiski. Using the JewishGen family finder for those who listed Stawiski as a family town was how I first found other "Stawiskites". The first fund raising letter was sent out in May 2000 and the last translation was completed in February 2003.

Jan Meisels Allen
January 30, 2015

Acknowledgements

Over the almost three years it took to translate this Yizkor Book, it was the thirty-two people who collectively donated $3,371, each donation between $15 to $250, regardless of amount is important. These thirty-two people made this translation possible. I also want to thank Jerrold Landau who did translated most of the articles in this book. His scholarly input adding footnotes to further explain what was being translated added to the richness of this translation and speaks to the quality of his erudition, excellence in translation and Judaic and genealogical knowledge.

Additional materials translated by Yael Chaver.

Thanks too to Morris Whitcup for his efforts.

Special thanks to the National Yiddish Book Center in Amherst, Massachusetts and the New York Public Library for supplying the high resolution images used in this book.

Dedication For the Translation

To those who lived in Stawiski, their children, grandchildren and great-grandchildren are forever grateful. To those Stawiski residents who survived or lost their lives in the Shoah, we dedicate this translation so that today's generation and the generations to come have a better understanding of who we are and where we came from due to their lives which were tragically changed or cut short solely because they were Jewish.

BALTIC SEA

LITHUANIA

RUSSIA

Vilnius ●

POLAND

STAWISKI

BELARUS

● Sierpc

GERMANY

● Poznan   Warsaw ●

● Lodz

● Prague

CZECH REPUBLIC

● Krakow

UKRAINE

SLOVAKIA

⊨══════════════════⊨ 250 miles
0

⊨═══════════════════════ 500 Km
0   250 Km   500 Km

STAWISKI

POLAND - Current Borders

Map Stawiski in Poland

Geopolitical Information:

Stawiski is located at 53°22' North Latitude and 22°09' East Longitude

Alternate names: Stawiski [Polish], Stavisk [Yiddish], Staviski [Russian]

Today Stawiski is situated within Kolno County, in Podlaskie Voivodeship, approximately 16 kilometres east of Kolno and 74 km west of the regional capital Białystok. Stawiski is the administrative seat of Gmina Stawiski.

Period	Town	District	Province	Country
Before WWI (c. 1900):	Stawiski	Kolno	Łomża	Russian Empire
Between the wars (c. 1930):	Stawiski	Kolno	Białystok	Poland
After WWII (c. 1950):	Stawiski			Poland
Today (c. 2000):	Stawiski			Poland

Nearby Jewish Communities:
Jedwabne 8 miles SE
Kolno 10 miles WNW
Radziłów 11 miles ENE
Wąsosz 12 miles NNE
Piątnica 13 miles S
Łomża 13 miles SSW
Nowogród 15 miles SW
Wizna 15 miles SE
Szczuczyn 15 miles NNE
Zbójna 17 miles WSW
Gać 20 miles SSE
Rutki 22 miles SSE
Trzcianne 22 miles E
Czarnia 23 miles WSW
Grajewo 23 miles NNE
Śniadowo 24 miles SSW
Zawady 26 miles SE
Goniądz 26 miles ENE
Zambrów 27 miles S
Tykocin 29 miles ESE
Kadzidło 30 miles WSW

History of the Town

Compiled by Jan Meisels Allen

Stawiski is situated within Kolno County, in Podlaskie Voivodeship today, but from 1946 to 1975 it belonged administratively to Białystok Voivodeship, and from 1975 to 1998 to Łomża Voivodeship. The town is situated on the Dzierzbia River. It was a secondary market between Lomza and Szczuczyn and was a trade route which led from Prussia in the northeast.

Established between 1407–1411, Stawiski was a village in northern Mazowia, on the Dzierzbia River. Stawiski belonged to many owners over the years but it started with Prince Janusz I Mazowieki in 1407 and ended in the twentieth century with Kisielnicki. The town received city rights around 1688 due to Count Fortunato Zamoyski, another town owner. He also renamed the town from Stawiski to Fortunatowo-but the name did not remain and reverted back to Stawiski. The town did not have any civic rights from 1870-1921.

Napoleon was in Stawiski during his March across Europe to Russia. The town was destroyed by fire in 1812 during that campaign, and rebuilt again, to become a trades and commercial center known for its furs, fabrics and hats in Congress Poland. Fire again destroyed Stawiski during the Russian–Prussian war of 1915, before the re-establishment of the Republic of Poland- or interwar Poland (1918–1939). During the Polish-Soviet War (1919-1921), Stawiski was a site of a conflict between the Polish army and the Bolsheviks.

Jewish Stawiski

The independent Jewish community was founded in 1808, numbering about 1,200 members. The Great Synagogue of Stawiski- a brick building built in early 1739 was destroyed in 1942 during World War II. Today, the synagogue is a cinema and a fire station. A second synagogue opened in 1871. By the end of the 19th century the Jewish population measured 2,500.

By 1932, over 50 percent of the local population was Jewish, numbering approximately 2,000.

Annihilation of the Jewish Community During World War II

On September 17, 1939 Stawiski came under Soviet occupation. The Soviets left in June 1941. The Germans seized control of Stawiski and the surrounding area on June 27, 1941. In early July 1941, Germans set fire to the synagogue. They soon established a ghetto but began killing the remaining Jews almost immediately. The ghetto was liquidated in November 1942.

During the week of July 15, 1941 the Nazis made the Jews go to the forest outside the city and there is a mass grave where 700 Stawiski Jews are buried. A memorial is in the forest dedicated in 1964.

In August 1941 over 900 Jews perished in an anti-tank ditch outside Mściwuje village. It was a Nazi execution site for Jews of Kolno also.[2]

After the massacres there were 60 people remaining.[3]

The remaining Jews were taken to the transport camp Bogusze, where the conditions were wretched. Those surviving the camp were transported to Auschwitz when the camp was liquidated in December 1942. (The Stawiski City site says the residents were sent to Treblinka[4]. It might be that those sent to Treblinka were sent to Auschwitz once Treblinka was liquidated or that when Boguze was liquidated the surviving Stawiskites were divided and sent to both termination camps).

The Jewish Historical Institute in Warsaw has testimony from a survivor that the local Polish residents were encouraged by the Nazis to ambush and kill the Jews they found.

The cemetery located outside of the city limits was also destroyed during World War II.

The most famous Jewish resident was Akiba Rubinstein one of the world's famous chess players.

Today, no Jews live in Stawiski. The government in 2012 counted the total population as 2,419 inhabitants.

---

[1] http://en.wikipedia.org/wiki/Stawiski
[2] Encylopedia of Camps and Ghettos 1933-1941 Vol. II Ghettos in German-Occupied Eastern Europe Past A page 961 USHMM Washington DC 2011
[3] http://www.sztetl.org.pl/en/article/stawiski/16,accounts-memories/28736,losy-zydow-ze-stawisk-w-relacji-fajgel-golabek/
[4] http://www.stawiski.pl/index.php?k=11

Notes to the Reader:

Within the text the reader will note "{34}" standing ahead of a paragraph. This indicates that the material translated below was on page 34 of the original book. However, when a paragraph was split between two pages in the original book, the marker is placed in this book after the end of the paragraph for ease of reading.

Also please note that all references within the text of the book to page numbers, refer to the page numbers of the original Yizkor Book.

The original Yizkor Book can be found on line at the New York Public Libaray site: http://yizkor.nypl.org/index.php?id=1199

<u>Translator's Notes :</u>

1. Family names and first names are translated from the Hebrew annotations in the Stawiski Yizkor Book, therefore, the spellings may not be exact. We tried to spell them the way they would have been spelled in Poland at the time, and not how the names may be spelled today, or how they might have been spelled in countries other than Poland.
2. If the Hebrew letter "vet" is used in a name it is translated as a "v".
3. The use of Hebrew letters "vuv, vuv" as a transliteration of the letter "w" was common in Israel at the time the Yizkor Book was published (1973), as the Hebrew alphabet does not contain a "W". If a single "vuv" appears in a name as a consonant, it was translated as "W", the spelling probably closest to the Polish.
4. All captions are also translated within the text of the Yizkor Book.
5. If a page number is given with the annotation "a'"or "b", it means that a page number was not assigned to it in the Yizkor Book, but followed the indicated page number.
6. Photographs without actual captions are indicated by an asterisk *.
7. Descriptions of these photos are taken from the accompanying articles.
   If the term "murdered" is used, it implies murdered by the Nazis.

Table of Contents

Between the Two World Wars

Happenings and Personalities

During the Days of the Holocaust

Eulogies

Stawiski Yizkor Book

{17}

History of Stawiski

Facts About Stawiski
Translated by Jerrold Landau

Stawiski is a settlement, including a town and surrounding land that is on the Bierbza River, a tributary of the Narew. It is situated on hills on the route from Lomza to Szczuczyn. The distance between it and Kolno, the regional city is 24 wirwost. (A wirwost is slightly more than a kilometer.) The distance from Stawiski to Lomza is 21 wirwost, and to Warsaw, 168 wirwost. Its institutions include a district church, 2 synagogues, a public school, cheders, a district courthouse, a town council and a post office. It contains 181 houses, and has a population of 4,140 people (1,930 men and 2,210 women). It covers an area of 3,530 morag. (A morag is approximately 5 dunam.[1]) In the surrounding lands, there is a liquor distillery, flourmills, and a brick kiln. Some of its residents work in tanning. In an earlier time, Stawiski had factories for cloth, hats, and dyes (it is unclear to which time frame these facts are referring).

Stawiski developed due to its location. It was situated along a trade route, which led from Prussia in the northeast. It also served as a commercial center between Lomza and Szczuczyn.

There are no definitive facts about the timeframe of the founding of Stawiski. According to Karel Czirhoffer in "Names of Settlements in Northern Mazowia" which was published in 1957, Stawiski was recognized as an urban settlement in 1426. In 1697, Zamowski, the owner of the estate, built the Franciscan monastery and the Miec church. Later, a church was built out of bricks, and between the years 1790-1818, the large church which still exists today was built.

Around 1813, all of the houses of the town burnt down. The portion of the church that survived the fire was attached to the Porita church.

In the 8th century, the lands were in the possession of the noblemen of the Karmkowski family, and later in the possession of the noblemen of the Kiszlaniczki family.

In 1886, the lands of Stawiski included the estates of Smolnik and Sokolocha, which had an area of 3048 morag, including wheat fields, pastureland, forests, and irrigated land.

In the latter years, the population of Stawiski reached 8,163 people, and covered an area of 19,182 morag. It had schools, liquor stills, 2 brick kilns, 5 flourmills, and an oil-press. The community of Stawiski included the town as an urban center, 14 estates, and 13 villages.

(18} { same as page 17 , but in Yiddish rather than Hebrew.}

{19}

History of Stawiski
by Tzvi Liberman
Translated by Jerrold Landau

The Jewish Settlement

Even though the existence of Jewish settlements in northern Mazowia is mentioned for the first time in the annals of the Council of the Four Lands with respect to the community of Titian in the 17th century, it is possible to establish definitively that Jewish settlers reached this area many years previously. They played pioneering roles in the development of the land, they forged the trade routes, and set up the foundation of the manufacturing in the areas of agriculture and various trades. They came from higher civilizations, and brought with them great knowledge in the manufacturing of metal products, cloth, oil, drinks, and tanning of hides. According of the testimony of B. Mark, a stream of Jewish immigration came from a variety of places: from Krim and Reisin (in White Russia), western Poland, Germany, and also Bohemia and Moravia. The reason for this immigration was generally the poor situation of the Jews in these lands. Krim and Reisin suffered from Mongol invasions; Germany suffered from the crusades, and at a later time, Bohemia and Moravia suffered from the Husite invasion.

As things turned out, there were various factors that caused Jews from various lands to seek refuge in Mazowia. After a certain time, the new communities took on a similar style and character, however each community was slightly different from its neighbor. The differences were expressed in the architectural styles of the synagogues, in local customs, etc. The different styles between each town were also evident in the Christian population, in the various Gothic styles of the churches that had a special character in each settlement.

The entire region used to belong to the nobleman Zamowski, a descendent of the Mazowian princes. He built the first church in Stawiski, as well as the Franciscan monastery named after the Holy Antoninios in 1697. Until this day, there is a tablet in the church with his name engraved upon it. After some time, the lands of the region, or part of them, were passed on to noblemen of the Kiszlaniczki family, whose graves are found in this church, and whose palace was built to the west of the city, surrounded by a giant garden of fruit trees.

The town was built next to the lands of the Squire Kiszlaniczki. One of his ancestors valued the benefits that Jews would bring to the place, and granted them the right of protection, and supported their economic endeavors. Thanks to this protection, Stawiski turned into an urban settlement with most of its inhabitants being Jews. It is important to remember that during the days of the feudal government, which lasted all of the days of the Polish kingdom until the partition at the end of the 18th century, most of the residents were subjects of the squires, and depended on their good graces. After the agricultural reform in the latter days of independent Poland, well to do Jews received tracts of land for pasture near the forests, and the Christians received estates and the permission to acquire land from the noblemen. Thus, in the 18th century, the town took on the form in which we knew it. In this time frame, the main road from Lomza to Suwalki, which traversed the town, was paved. This road was knows as the Petersburg-Warsaw road. It was paved n 1841. In 1844, the great Prince Alexander Nikolowice traveled along this road. Later, Kaiser Alexander the Second, who freed the farmers who were oppressed due to their being subjugated by the noblemen, traveled along this road. The notable Moses Montefiore traveled this road on his way to Russia to intercede in front of the Czar for the benefit of the large Jewish population of that vast country. Napoleon traveled that important strategic route on his way to invade Russia in 1812.

In the book of properties, Stawiski is noted as a private urban settlement – Odasa (estate). Only in 1919 did the town obtain the status of Miasto (city). As a small town, it had only few institutions, including: a town hall, a post office, a police station, a school, and a courthouse.

As was customary, Jewish life was conducted in a separate manner from the rest of the population. In order to fulfil the religious, social, and economic needs, the Jews established and supported many institutions, including: synagogues, Beis Midrashes (houses of study), and cheders (elementary schools). There was also a Yeshiva in Stawiski for a period, and later there was a modern Hebrew school. There was also a library, a bank, charitable organizations, mutual help organizations, an organization for the visiting of the sick, a loan organization, a charitable organization for poor brides, Zionist gathering places, and other such communal organizations.

With respect to the economic situation, aside from the shops and workshops that were in the town, there were biweekly market days as well as six annual fairs. Merchants also traveled to fairs that took place in nearby towns, such as Jadowno and Kolno.

Synagogues and Study Halls

There was an old synagogue in Stawiski, which was built at the beginning of the 18th century. Its structure was unique. Its walls were very thick, like a fortress, and apparently, it was planned that it would serve as a place of refuge for the Jews in times of trouble. Its white arches were 12 meters high, and between them, there were boards inlaid which were painted greenish-white. The Holy Ark rose the entire height of the hall, and was finely crafted. The artistic wooden doors depicted many traditional Jewish themes, such as the twelve tribes, Moses and Aaron, the tablets of the covenant, the Leviathan and wild ox[2], the seven species for which the Land of Israel is known, as well as various other species of the Land of Israel. The colors were very fine. There was no more beautiful synagogue in the entire area.

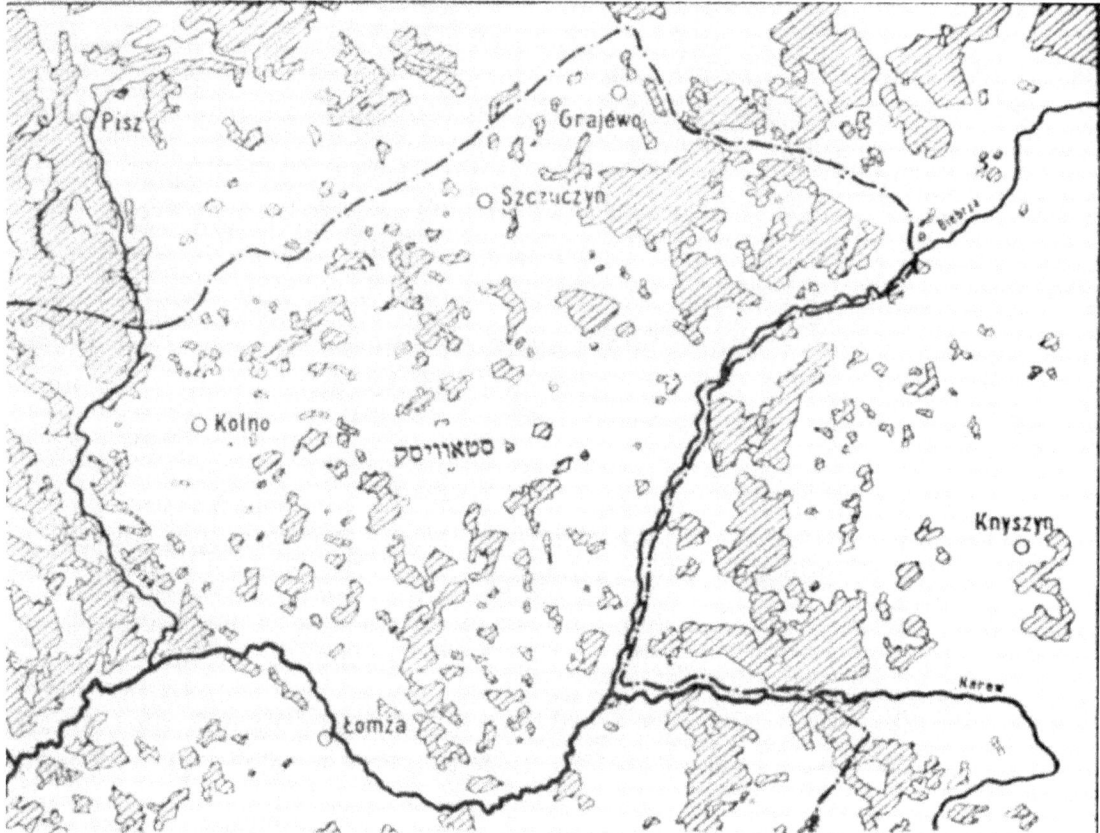

Map of Stawiski and vicinity

The region of Stawiski, with Stawiski in bold letters near the center, Kolno to the west (left), Knyszyn to the east, Szczuczyn and Grajewo to the north (top), and Lomza to the south, and Pisz to the northwest. The Narew River is to the south, and the Bierbza River to the north.

Next to it was the large Beis Midrash, and three other smaller houses of prayer and Torah. On Sabbaths, various prayer quorums took place in them, with more of the common folk, who would not have had the means to merit a Torah honor (aliya) in the larger synagogues and Beis Midrashes.

The synagogues and Beis Midrashes always served as a place of meeting for the adults, as well as on occasion, the youth. The communal life of the town was centered within their walls; there the simple folk heard the news about what was going on in the world at large. Local gossip also found an attentive audience there. In Stawiski, there were always a few people who read the Hebrew newspapers, such as "Hamelitz", "Hamagid", and "Hatzfira", and other people knew the vernacular language and would read Russian newspapers. The synagogue served as the center of transmission of news about what was transpiring in the outside world, both Jewish and gentile. Merchants and communal workers who would travel for business or communal matters to large cities in Russia or even Germany would relate their experiences and impressions to the population, who in general spent their entire lives in the vicinity of the town and its surrounding area. It is true that even "stormy" debates took place within the walls of these meeting places, regarding events that were taking place in their world, and in the general Jewish world.

Ups and Downs

The development of the town was not incremental. Just the opposite, during various timeframes, there were ups and downs. From various documents that were preserved, it can be determined that at one time Stawiski was heavily involved in various manufacturing endeavors, including: woven materials, felt, dyes, hides, hats, brushes, wine presses and beer distilleries, etc. One of the reasons for the various downturns was the fires that afflicted the town on occasion. In 1813, a large fire broke out which destroyed the majority of the homes of the town, most of which were built out of wood. After a short period, the residents reestablished themselves and rebuilt the town. Various factors helped in this, including: insurance money, donations from neighboring towns and estate owners, who provide wood from their large forests. Since fires were a common occurrence during that time period, communities would often help neighboring communities when disaster struck. Nevertheless, after a large fire, the population of a town would generally diminish for an extended period.

According to the facts which we have access to, in 1813, prior to the large fire, Stawiski had 3,146 residents, including 2,775 Jews. After the fire, the population was reduced to about 2,000 people. The manufacturing in the town which existed until that time was also not reestablished, for the most part. One possible reason for this was the development of neighboring towns. Another reason for the reduction of the Jewish population was the stream of emigration oversees which had begun at the end of the previous century, and continued until the Second World War. Stawiski Émigrés live in North and South America, Western Europe, and Israel.

In Free Poland

Stawiski was a small town, and it did not have any Yeshivas or high schools. Therefore, many of the youth left for places of Torah and Haskalah. Most were children of poor people. Yeshiva boys ate their meals on a rotation basis at tables of strangers, and found lodging in cheap inns. Those that studied in gymnasias also lived under very difficult conditions. It is no wonder then that most of them did not succeed in completing their course of studies, and returned to the town without a certificate and without a degree. The inability to satiate the thirst for knowledge left a scar upon the soul. Many found salvation in communal activism and in devouring books on sociology, philosophy and literature in order to self-educate themselves. In the 1920s, debates were often arranged by the youth about Hegel and Marcus, Spinoza and Borochov, even though it is doubtful that most of them understood their works, and were able to delve into their depths. However the fact that the youth debated and deliberated about these topics testifies to the drive for knowledge and wisdom which was in the hearts of the Jewish youth. It is no wonder that the Jewish youth joined up with all sorts of ideologies, and were very active in the various factional organizations that actualized these ideologies. Some became enthralled with the Zionist idea, and others, due to the pressures of the times, became attached to the misleading lightning flash of communism. Many joined up with communism in 1921, when the Bolsheviks invaded Poland, and our town was under their rule for a period. I remember that when they entered our town, the faithful of the revolution, who were mostly Jews, went out to welcome them. Many of the Jewish young people were very proud when Golda the daughter of the teacher Hertzke Kolinski stood at the helm of the "Rebkum" (town council). The Rebkum consisted mainly of young people in their twenties. Golda was a proud and capable girl, and Hertzke, the brother of Chaim Kadish, had the characteristics of a leader, sure of himself and quick to make decisions. In the battles that took place between the Red Army and the Polish Army, a general of the Red Army was killed, and the activists of the communist movement in our town made him a state funeral. Golda and Herzke walked at the front of the procession, with black armbands on their sleeves and red flags in their hands, and the band played revolutionary music. We children followed after the funeral procession until it reached the military cemetery. If my memory is correct, Perlman carried the main red flag. We were children and did not understand anything about the ideology, however we were proud that Jews had reached such greatness. With the retreat of the Red Army, the communist activists fled with the army, went to Russia, and there were lost track of. Their lot was the same as the lot of many other revolutionaries who were burnt in the flames of the revolution.

With the retreat of the Red Army in Poland, the communist enthusiasm dwindled in Stawiski, and most of the Jewish youth became involved the various pioneering movements. Many merited to make Aliya to the Land of Israel, and to be numbered among its builders. Others who saw no future under in anti-Semitic Poland emigrated, some to the United States, some to Western Europe, and others to South America. Their lot improved, and they were not present in Poland when the holocaust took place. Today we can find them in Jerusalem, Tel Aviv, Balfouria, Geva, New York, Los Angeles, Paris, and London. These are the survivors of Stawiski, who together with a number of those who managed to survive the Valley of the Shadow of Death, bear with love and devotion the memory of the thousands who were slaughtered by our

Polish neighbors, and who were gassed in the gas chambers of the death camps. May these lines serve as a modest monument to their memory.

———

Translator's Footnotes:

1. A dunam is 1,000 square meters, about ½ acre.

2. Two mystical animals, the Leviathan being a sea monster, and the wild ox being a very large bovine. In Jewish mystical thought, these animals are to form part of the meal that will be partaken of by the righteous in the World To Come.

———

{29-35}

My Shtetl of Stawiski
by Chemda
Translated by Yael Chaver

In winter my shtetl stands
bent, cold, and white,
and at the bridge the stream
is frozen with ice.
Snow lies, brand-new,
fresh from the night,
glittering as if with fire,
the white glory is dazzling.
Over every roof and window
hang pieces of ice like candles,
eyes sparkling from the wind,
all faces aflame.
Tiny white-washed houses
buried deep in snow,
nearby young white saplings
are standing in a row.
With its paintbrush, frost has
painted every window and glass
with slender trees, long branches,
delicate flowers, soft grass -
And when a warm breeze blows
white snow becomes muddy;
drops fall from the roofs,
dripping like sadness -
***
The road winds through
all down the shtetl,

running along the cemetery,
meeting up with the path.
The untouched snow lies
over the broad, free fields,
gleaming and sparkling like a carpet
decorated with stars.
Wrapped as though in a holiday robe,
as still and cold as stone,
sunk in deep dreams
as though bewitched - stands the forest.
The moon's delicate paleness
peers through thick branches,
her sad smile
drops into the secretive silence.
A song sings from somewhere far,
a melody tugs somewhere into a valley
and disappears in quiet yearning,
waking long-ago dreams -
***

As soon as spring arrives
the solemn mood is gone.
Buds open,
trees and flowers bloom,
bringing life to the avenues;
fields far and wide
bedeck themselves, holiday-like,
with soft green velvet.
Trees with fresh perfumes
spread through the forest,
a magician's hand sowed
tiny green shoots along the trails.
The throng of youngsters
rushed to the forest,
their laughter reverberating,
their song chiming.
The years flowed quietly
like the river in the valley
weaving a Jewish life
in my shtetl, once upon a time -
***

Once upon a time? It wasn't long ago,
and the market and road

and the long narrow alleys -
they're Jewish, familiar.
Jewish is the pain, the sorrow,
the poverty, the need;
you swallow the hot Jewish tears
with the meager bites of bread;
Jewish is the suffering,
silent sadness and weeping;
Jewish is every joy here,
touchingly familiar, full of charm.
The holy Sabbath is upon us,
--God's beloved, precious gift -
mothers bless the candles,
radiating holy fire.
Mothers' pale lips murmur
a quiet prayer from the heart:
"send us, God, your good angel,
and, may it never happen, do not forsake us - - "
***
The sun has just set
on the far horizon.
Fathers and children go
to welcome the Sabbath queen
in the synagogue and Bet Midrash -
two holy buildings
with the small synagogues where
Jews prayed in the early morning -
although so many years have passed,
who can forget how
they stood opposite each other
in the quiet back street?
How much joy and tears
were gulped between their walls,
and devout melodies rose up
on Sabbath and holidays;
generations drew
so much strength and courage
from the small letters
as from a deep spring;
From "Kol Nidre" and "Unesaneh" [1] --
who can forget the trembling
that overcame the congregation
and shook the community;

They beat their breasts
for uncommitted sins
and begged "hear our voice"
"accept our prayer" --
waiting, deeply yearning
to hear Messiah's shofar
and for the age-old hope
to come true very soon -
***
At dusk in the house of study
learned men sway
over the broad, open books
with a sweet Talmud melody
arguing smartly
about the Mishna and its teachers
quoting heaps of explanations
by generations of scholars;
Children in "cheders" [2] sat learning from early morning,
went home at night
by lantern light.
Some learned their a-b-c's,
others studied Torah and Rashi, [3]
young men immersed themselves
in a deep, baffling problem,
studied a difficult page
of Talmud, persevering,
sharpening their minds
with law and lore;
rich ark hangings,
Torah-scroll coverings -
sewn out of finest fabric
by delicate Jewish daughters.
All this existed then,
in our youthful years;
now – woe – only ruins remain
of my Jewish home.
When the slaughterer cut the throats
of old and young, and babies in cradles -
the world and God's emissaries
were silent, cruelly religious -- -- --
Over twitching bodies,
gangs went wild,

galoshes full of blood and dust,
sharing out the loot,
settling into the houses
-- the "inheritors" of my Jewish shtetl.
Where's the grave of the martyrs?
Where a sign? Where a marker?
No memory remains
of those taken, bound, to slaughter,
of the suffering, the choking -
of a whole Jewish community.
The wealthy, the leaders,
observant women in their wigs;
cart-drivers, smiths, porters,
laboring, crooked backs;
sooty craftspeople
from the small back streets;
the burial-society, schoolchildren
and dreamy young men;
a rabbi with his helpers;
ten fervent Hassids
(in this sober-minded shtetl
they were a rare sight);
community figures, talmudists,
interpreters of Marxism;
a bunch of Hebraists,
immersed in Zionism;
and the silken young people,
modest wives and daughters,
tiny innocent children -
only God knows the reason
why his murderous rage -
apparently because of the supreme sin
of bearing the name of Jew with pride -
flung you all to the hangmen -- --
***

The sun shone like always
and went on its way,
when Jewish blood flowed
like rivers without banks;
the skies did not split open
with the pain and sorrow of the martyrs;
no outcry thundered
from the throne high above,

the heads of murderers -
the emissaries of God's wrath,
executioners of his people, Israel, for generations -
were not torn apart.
The stars did not go out
in that dreadful night
when my Jewish shtetl
suffered and was annihilated -- --

Footnotes:

1. The phrases in quote marks are excerpts from the Yom Kippur service.

2. "Cheder" was the school for small boys.

3. Rashi was one of the greatest biblical interpreters.

Community Council

Standing from right to left: The shammas of the synagogue, Meir Leib; Chaim Kadysz-Kolinski; Yitzchok Indurski; Yisrael-Eli Szapira; Chana Jeleniewicz; Sitting from right to left: Meir-Yankel Koplowicz; Imiyal Rabbi Wasserman; Moshe Ladelski; Moshe-Zeev Bramzon; the boy (ed.note: standing leftmost in the front row) the son of Rabbi Wasserman. In the window: Yisraelke Morus; Kiwajko. (Trans. Note: Moshe Ladelski's name added in errata page that accompanied the Yizkor Book.)

The relief agency for refugees from World War sponsored by the Hatechiya (Trans: Revival) organization (Trans.: the bottom photograph is also accompanied by a Yiddish caption which reads: Relief for our refugees in Stawiski in first World War). Standing from right to left: Sarah Szimonowicz (murdered); Chaim Leibl Lewinowicz (lives in the United States); Melita Salotzka (murdered); Moshe Goelman, of blessed memory; Sarah Remigolski (murdered); Itzwowiski (murdered); Sitting: Sarah Mondensztejn nee Morus, Yosel Mondensztejn (both in the U.S.)

The Talmud Torah of Stawiski

The students and their teachers (in the middle, Rabbi Wasserman)
(Trans. Note: the photo is also accompanied by a Yiddish caption which
reads: "The students and their teachers, in the middle sits Rabbi Wasserman")

{36}

My Birthplace in the Past and Present
by Chaya Kolinski of Blessed Memory [1]
Translated by Jerrold Landau

Photograph of unnamed girl may be that of Chaya Kolinski, author of accompanying article.

My town of Stawiski is 21 kilometers from Lomza. Stawiski is a quiet and clean town, surrounded by forests, mountains, ponds and rivers. Its population is small: in total 592 families live there, of which 332 are Jewish and 260 are Christian. The town is surrounded by 35 villages, which barely have any Jews.

In the center of the Market Square stands a memorial plaque that was erected to commemorate the liberation of Poland in 1918. On the outskirts of the market are a church and a monastery that were built in 1697 by the Baron Ferdinand Zamoski. Not far from the church is a strip of stores (belonging to the Jewish community) put up in 1781 by the builder Zvi Gnida. A road passes through the center of the town. On the route leading to Lomza is a thick forest, containing a big rock that the Russian Czar Alexander the First ordered to be erected on his way from Petersburg to Warsaw. The road is called "The Warsaw-Petersburg Road".

There is no exact data as to when the town was established and when Jews started settling there. Some say that Stawiski is a very old town. The oldest wall in the town is about 170 years old. Jews from nearby settlements were buried in the cemetery of Stawiski. The oldest tombstone is about 200 years old.

The construction of the synagogue was completed in 5573 (1813). A Christian man from the descendants of the estate owner Kiszlaniczki donated the stones. The elders of the generation related that the foundation of the synagogue was so wide and solid that the philanthropist Kiszlaniczki rode on it with his horses hitched to his chariot. The Beis Midrash was built 85 years ago. A spring flowing with fresh, cold water was beside the Beis Midrash. The Germans discovered the spring in 1915. The waters of the spring flow constantly, however the flowing eventually ebbs.

The religious organizations in the town were: the Mishna study group; Poale Zedek, which is the committee for welcoming guests; the organization for purchase of books; the midnight group [2]; the Chevra Kadyza (burial society); and the group that recites Psalms. The group that recites Psalms had existed for 150 years, and the burial society had existed for 300 years. There were also charitable organizations such as: Gemilus Chasadim, Bikur Cholim (group for visiting the sick), and Lechem Laaniyim (organization for providing food for the poor).

Business flourished before the war (World War I), especially businesses devoted to exporting merchandise, such as garments, furs, silk scarves, curtains, fabrics, and all kinds of wheat, woods, and poultry. Industry in Stawiski flourished as well: leather processing, manufacturing of matches, beer, candles, oil, soap, wine, vinegar, seltzer, and more. The Jews of Stawiski were generous and did not skimp, particularly when it came to educating their children. Even the poor would sell the pillows under their heads to pay tuition fees. When the son would finish his studies at Cheder (religious elementary school), his parents would send him to learn Torah at Yeshiva. There were, therefore, many great Torah scholars, rabbis and pious people in Stawiski.

Many of the pious people of the generation are buried in the Stawiski cemetery. Among them are: Rabbi Abraham the son of Dov, Rabbi Fishele, Rabbi Aryeh Rakowski, Rabbi Meir Noah, Rabbi Sokolower, the righteous Rabbi Chaim Aryeh the son of Rabbi Aaron Joseph Myszkowski, Rabbi Rotenberg, Rabbi Yehoshua Lang, and Rabbi Aaron Dworski. Prior to and during World War I, Rabbi Binyamin Remigolski served as the rabbi of the town, followed by Rabbi Reuven Kac, who was the author of the book "Degel Reuven". Rabbi Reuven Kac lived in the United States for a certain period of time, and now serves as the chief rabbi of Petach Tikvah.

With the outbreak of World War I, business and industry deteriorated drastically. Many Jews who were considered to be among the affluent lost their possessions. The cessation of foreign trade undermined the livelihood of many families who were dependent on it. The situation improved slightly with the entrance of the Germans in 1915, when trade involving eggs, poultry, butter and sugar was revived. On the other hand, the situation of families whose heads were in America worsened significantly, and due to of the breakdown of the shipping lanes the monthly support that they used to receive stopped. These families suffered greatly and they earned their sustenance by gathering seeds and potatoes in the fields. The women would do any kind of work in order to provide their children with coarse-meal bread. Only as time passed did they start to receive a small amount of support through the "Organization of Assistance for the Jews of Germany". When the war ended, they joined their husbands in America.

During the years of 1915 and 1916, many of the boys that studied in the Yeshivas returned, among them teachers and leaders. Several of them became outstanding speakers. They all knew the Hebrew language and were committed to the Zionist idea that struck deep cords in the Jewish community, and awakened the town from the deep sleep in which it was entrenched. These boys established the Hatechiya (The Revival) movement and set up evening courses in the Hebrew language, Jewish history, Bible, etc.

A library was founded next to Hatechiya, and new books were obtained monthly. There were gatherings on Sabbath evenings, where lectures on various topics of importance to the Jewish people were presented. The youth read and studied a great deal. Every event which took place at that time in Jewish life was discussed and explained within the wall of Hatechiya. After some time, a few of the founders of Hatechiya became involved with anti-Zionist ideas. They left the Zionist organization and organized groups along the style of Bund. The two factors, the Zionists and Bundists, ran evenings of debates where each side attempted to convince the other of its ideology. During the 1920s, some of the Zionist youth began to go out to places of Hachsharah [3], and many made aliya to the Land of Israel.

During the years of the war, the town was shaken up economically. There was also bloodshed in the suburbs of the town on the route to Lomza. Cannonballs were shot onto the town. A few of them hit the center of the town. Mrs. Lewkowicz was killed near the entrance to the town, as she was going to bring food to her young son who was studying in Cheder. Henia Epstein was shot to death near the forest. Our lives were in danger. The believers from among us said that, due to the merit of the righteous people who lie in their eternal rest in the Stawiski cemetery, the town was saved from complete destruction. On the route to Lomza, there are communal graves of soldiers who fell at that place during the First World War. The monuments are inscribed: "Here, 100 Russians fell". "Here, 30 Germans fell", etc.

Our town was well known for the famous people who came from it, including writers, doctors, rabbis, teachers, lawyers, artisans, and wonder workers. The most famous were the wonder worker Reb Kadyz the elder, Reb Moshke Chiewo the Kabbalist, the well known chess player Akiva

Rubensztejn, the writers Jakobowicz and Meir Rabinowicz, Zelig Bzostowiecki who lives in Belgium, Dr. Koppel Lieberman who wrote the Yiddish book "The History of the Jews of Belgium", Chaim Grenet (Bzostowiecki) who lives in America, and the sculptor Brandenburg who is well-known for his statue "the prophet".

The sculptor, Yosef Brandenburg

In the final years, under the anti-Semitic Polish regime, business and industry declined greatly. Many Jewish stores closed, and Polish stores opened in their place. The stream of emigration removed the best of the youth from the town. Due to the fact that there was little employment, the town was emptied of the best of its sons. In former years, the market days were bubbling with life. The farmers of the region brought their agricultural products to town, and the sales were more than the purchases. Now, there is very left of these signs of life. The farmers make their purchases in the stores of the Christians. Anti-Semitism increases daily and its signs were recognizable all over. The Jewish traveling merchant who up to that time earned his livelihood by his business in the neighboring villages is no longer able to go to those towns on account of the danger to his life. The ruffians planted a bomb in the Jewish building near the church, and the fear was great. The youth grow up without Torah, and without modern education. Desperation is prevalent, for there was no future. The sources of livelihood of the Jews of Stawiski dried up, and many families suffer from hunger.

Written in Stawiski, 1937

Translator's Footnotes:

1. There is a footnote at the bottom of the page which reads as follows: This article was published in the Hebrew weekly "Baderech" on the 20th of Tevet 5698 – December 24, 1937. The weekly was published in Warsaw by A. L. Jakobowicz. It can be surmised that Chaya Kolinski of blessed memory gleaned her historical facts about Stawiski from the annals of the community and the Chevra Kadyza.

2. Apparently, a group which meets at midnight for prayer and/or study.

3. Hachsharah (literally preparation) refers to a program of agricultural training in preparation for aliya to the Land of Israel.

{43}

In the Paths of the Fathers
by Zelda Edelsztejn
Grandfather Reb Kalman Itzele and Grandmother Esther Kejla
Translated by Jerrold Landau

In the town of Stawiski, which was known for its rabbis, righteous people, and scholars, there lived about 150 years ago a teacher of children, who was scholarly, righteous, and of pleasant mannerisms. This was Reb Kalman Itzele. His wife Esther Kejla, was a woman of valor, was descended from a family of Admorim (Hassidic leaders) from the city of Wyszogrod, near Warsaw.

As was customary among Torah scholars in those days, the husband would sit in the tents of Torah and the wife would support the family. Esther Kejla excelled in business as well as in the traditional tasks of a woman, such as sewing, weaving, and knitting. Her main business was making head coverings for married women. She had great expertise in the making of head coverings for weekdays, as well as for Sabbaths and festivals. The head coverings for weekdays might have been made from simple linen; however for Sabbaths and festivals, she fashioned them from velvet and silk, often adorned with flowers of crimson and lace. These head coverings had a special name – Chipik. For the High Holy Days, Esther Kejla would make Chipiks of white linen, as it says: "if your sins be like scarlet, they will be turned to white" [1].

Esther Kejla did not only make Chipiks. She also made children's hats, women's aprons, and birthing shirts.

The aprons were made in the same fashion as the head coverings. The weekday aprons were made of simple linen, and the aprons for Sabbaths and festivals were made of black silk, with borders of colored lace, each one made according to the request of the purchaser.

Reb Kalman Itzele and Esther Kejla had two girls and a son named Akiva. The girls, the eldest Liba and the youngest Malka, learned from their mother.

Aside from picking up her good traits, they also learned the art of sewing and embroidery, and worked diligently and quickly, to the point where Esther Kejla could give over to them the tasks of preparing the goods, whereas she herself spent most of her time conducting the business. For even though the mother and daughters worked hard, the family made a meager living. When Esther Kejla was freed from the sewing and embroidery, she had the chance to take the merchandise – the handicrafts of her daughters – and travel to the fairs, where she sold her merchandise. This income was able to help sustain the household.

Reb Kalman Itzele did not skimp on his holy work. To his students, who were among the choicest boys of the town, he taught Torah with dedication and faithfulness. Many of them became outstanding Torah scholars. Each evening, when Reb Kalman Itzele concluded his lessons with his students, he would hurry to the Beis Midrash to study with a partner. The two of them were expert and sharp, and they studied with great depth, often continuing their studious deliberations until a late hour of the night.

Esther Kejla waited patiently for her husband to return from the Beis Midrash in order to serve him a warm meal. If he was still not pondering the study portion that he was studying with his partner, they would discuss household affairs, even though he never took an active role in household matters or in the tribulations of child rearing. These types of affairs had always been in the domain of Esther Kejla. He would also turn over the tuition fees he earned from his students to his wife, after taking off the relevant tithes for charity. She would then deal with this money appropriately according to her ability.

One evening, on a long winter evening, when Reb Kalman Itzele concluded the grace after meals, Esther Kejla opened her mouth and said:

"My dear husband, I wish to have you participate in the same work that the Holy One Blessed Be He engages in Himself."

Reb Kalman Itzele responded: "Why do you ask? I also have an important matter to discuss with you."

She replied: "You are correct, my husband. You should commence first."

Reb Kalman Itzele began speaking, and said: "For some time, I have being paying attention to a young man who is studying in the Beis Midrash, who is called by everyone "the diligent Leibele". This young man is diligent with his studies day and night, and he is also externally like a cedar: strong of body, and handsome."

Reb Kalman Itzele had not even finished his words, when his wife Esther Kejla interrupted him and said: "Myself as well, when I traveled the last time to the fair in a carriage packed with people, including scholars, I attempted to sit near them in order to hear their words of Torah as well as general conversation, for the general conversation of a scholar is like words of Torah. I heard of them speaking in the praise of the young man, the diligent Reb Leibele, and all of them praised his sharpness and expertise in Torah as well as his pleasant manner among people. At that time, as I heard their words, I also decided, that with the help of G-d, when I returned in peace to my home, I would ask you to make a marriage proposal between our daughter and this excellent young man. Thank G-d, we have an appropriate dowry for her, as befits even wealthy people, and she also excels in her fine character. It is a sign that this matter came from G-d, in that you also came to the same conclusion, and I hope that this praiseworthy young man will agree to be our son-in-law."

The next day in the Beis Midrash, after the morning prayers, Reb Kalman Itzele approached the marriage broker who deals with the well-to-do families. He requested that he that he speak to the parents of Reb Leibele regarding this match. The marriage broker was a diligent and vigilant man, and that very day he went to the parents of the young man, and proposed the match for their son with the eldest daughter of Reb Kalman Itzele and Esther Kejla.

Reb Leibele and his Wife Liba, and their Children

The parents of Reb Leibele agreed to the match. The contract was drawn up, and after a short time the wedding was celebrated with great glory and fanfare.

For two or three years, the young couple was supported by Liba's parents, and then they went out on their own. Liba was like her mother. She took upon herself the yoke of livelihood, so that her husband could continue his uninterrupted occupation with Torah.

Reb Leibele had gained a reputation as being great in Torah. Some of the important and wealthy householders approached him and asked him to teach their children Talmud and commentaries, on the condition that he would not take on too many students. In return, they promised to be generous with their tuition payments, so that he would be able to support his family with honor. Reb Leibele, whose entire interest was in the study and spreading of Torah, agreed to this condition, and for all his days he taught young men up to their point of marriage.

Liba bore eleven children, but only two girls survived: Zelda and Dina. When Zelda reached marriageable age, her parents decided to marry her off to a young man who would be able to bear the burdens of livelihood, so that their refined and pampered daughter would be freed of the yoke of livelihood.

In Stawiski, there was a scholar, Reb Yekutiel, who died before his time. His wife Chana supported the family by selling earthenware vessels. They had two sons and two daughters. Yitzchak Tzvi was the eldest. Yitzchak Tzvi was diligent in his Torah studies, and he had the reputation of being one of the geniuses of the Beis Midrash students. When he turned seventeen, Reb Leibele looked toward him and chose him as a husband for his daughter Zelda.

The young man Yitzchak Tzvi, aside from his wide knowledge of Talmud and legal responsa, also excelled in Hebrew writing and grammar, and his style was clear and pure.

After the wedding, Yitzchak Tzvi was not supported by his father-in-law, as was customary in those days; but rather, he invested his dowry money in the cotton and pig hair business. He would send the merchandise to Lipsia (Leipzig) in Germany. His fortune was good, he succeeded in his business, and after a short time, he became wealthy.

When he reached the age of 21, he had to appear before the army committee regarding Russian army service. Since he did not want to serve the Czar for six consecutive years, he had to give over all of his money and property as redemption.

When he was exempted from Russian army duty, worries of livelihood overtook him. In order to begin any enterprise he needed a sum of money, which he did not possess since he gave over all of his money to pay the bribe to the army. His wife Zelda stood at his right side, and she took off her expensive jewelry and gave them over to her husband. Yitzchak Tzvi gave the jewelry as a pledge to the lender, and with the money he borrowed, he began business again. He went to the marketplace and bought all types of merchandise. However, his fortune was not good this time, and he almost lost all of his money. Yitzchak Tzvi walked around worried and crushed, and once again, his wife Zelda came to his aid. She bought a bag of flour and started to bake bread for sale. She sustained her household in a meager fashion; however, the children never wanted for bread.

After some time, a hide tanning workshop opened up in Stawiski, and Yitzchak Tzvi, who was expert in this profession from his earlier business, was offered a job in this factory for a fitting salary. Yitzchak Tzvi hoped that now he would be able to live in peace and dedicate himself over to his household. However, one day, his beloved wife took ill suddenly, and before he could bring a doctor from Lomza (in those days, there was no doctor in Stawiski), Zelda passed away when she was only thirty years old.

Yitzchak Tzvi was left with four young children, three boys and a girl. The oldest Ezriel Zelig Noach was only ten years old when his mother died.

Yitzchak Tzvi worked for many years in that factory. He amassed an appropriate amount of money and attempted to try his luck in business again. This time, he set up a partnership with an established merchant who cheated him. After a short time, he left his business denuded and without anything. After his business failures, he turned to teaching. He was barely able to meet his needs, and he lived in poverty and want until the end of his days.

My Revered Father Reb Ezriel Zelig Noach Koszlowski of holy blessed memory

My holy father was born in Stawiski in the year 5627 (1867) to his father Reb Yitzchak Tzvi and his mother Zelda. As related above, he was ten years old when his mother died. He studied in the Talmud Torah of Lomza with Reb Baruch Obelbeker until he was thirteen years old. There, he began to write Torah novella on the Talmudic tractate Avoda Zarah [2], which served as the first material for his book "Levush Adanim".

When he reached the age of Bar Mitzvah, he left his father and wandered afar, to a place of Torah in the city of Szczuczyn. He was shy, and he was not brazen enough to turn to the famous Yeshivas, even though he would have been able to be accepted in a high Yeshiva due to his vast knowledge of Talmud and Jewish law. He lamented this all his life, and applied to himself the adage: "The shy person does not learn"[3].

After much wandering, he arrived at his desired destination of Szczuczyn. He went to visit a distant relative of his father. They received him graciously and offered him some food – a plate of grits and bread – and they also invited him to spend the night.

A few days passed in this manner. One day, when he returned from the Beis Midrash after the morning service, they did not invite him for breakfast. It became clear that they also subsisted on meager means, and the paltry meal that they served him was kept from their own mouths.

He returned to the Beis Midrash, took a Gemara and engrossed himself in study. He sat all day and did not eat. That day, he subsisted on water alone. The next day, after the morning prayers, he sat down to study, as he was wont. In order to distract himself from the hunger that was afflicting him, he tried to concentrate on what he was studying. He continued in that manner until the afternoon. Suddenly, weakness overtook him. His head became dizzy and a cold sweat covered his face. He nearly fainted.

His neighbor on the bench, Reb Tovia, noticed the whiteness of his face and asked him: "Young boy, why are you so pale? Your face is not like it was on previous days. Tell me the truth, did you eat today?"

Ezriel Zelig answered him: "I did not even eat yesterday."

He said: "Arise, make haste to Reb Yosef who lives at the corner of the marketplace, and is in charge of the charitable fund. If there are any kopecks left in his box, he will certainly give them to you and you can buy some food."

On weak legs, the boy ran to the house of Reb Yosef, however to his dismay, the box was empty.

When he left the house of Reb Yosef, a very strange and interesting thing occurred. A woman, who owned a textile store, sat in her store eating lunch. There was a loaf of bread next to her, on the table. A dog ran into the store, grabbed the bread with his teeth, and escaped without the storeowner noticing.

Two men who were passing by in the street began to chase after the dog in order to remove the bread from his mouth. When the dog reached the alley between the two synagogues, Ezriel Zelig appeared on the other side of the alley. The dog stopped, dropped the loaf of bread, and disappeared.

Ezriel Zelig was so engrossed in his thoughts that he did not see what happened next to him. In the meantime, the two Jews who chased after the dog asked him: "Young boy, did you not see that a dog tossed a loaf of bread at your feet?" He answered: "No, I don't have any bread..."

The two Jews said: "It is appropriate to give it over to the Yeshiva boy, and we will merit in the good deed (mitzvah)."

Ezriel Zelig heard their words and said: "If you do not find the owner of the loaf of bread and you want to give it to a Yeshiva boy, give it to me, for I am also a student of the Beis Midrash."

The Jews said: "You are correct, we now realize that the dog was the emissary to feed you bread."

He saw this as a wonderful thing, and from that day, Ezriel Zelig was no longer hungry.

Ezriel Zelig studied for a few years in the Beis Midrash of Szczuczyn. He was very diligent, and became an expert in the Talmud and its commentaries, both in breadth and depth. The thirteen-year-old boy grew up to be a tall, thin man. When he had satiated himself with Talmud and was ready to appear before great sages, he decided to travel to the famous Yeshiva of Volozhyn. However "there are many thoughts in the heart of man, but the will of G-d will prevail" [4]. He suddenly became ill with a severe intestinal disease, and had to forgo his desire to study in Volozhyn.

Once again, it was Reb Tovia who saved him from his straits. He brought him to the doctor. After examining him, the doctor ordered him to go to a place where the air was good and clear, to the pine forest. Through the intercession of Rev Tovia, Ezriel Zelig was hired as a teacher and spiritual leader in a village where there were about fifteen Jewish families.

The village was about ten kilometers from Szczuczyn, and the route to it was through the forest. The travel through the forest already had its positive influence on Ezriel Zelig.

Ezriel Zelig reached the village near the evening, and even before he descended from the carriage, the villagers surrounded him and greeted him with honor and affection.

Ezriel Zelig refused to be put up in a private house, and requested that the villagers arrange a place for him in the Beis Midrash. His desire was fulfilled. In a gathering of the villagers that took place, they decided that each one of them would provide for his needs for a week according to a rotation system. They would bring his food, including a hot dish, directly to the Beis Midrash.

Under the influence of good, fresh, food and clear air, he quickly regained his strength and recovered. He filled his role as teacher and spiritual leader with faithfulness. Every day, toward evening, between the afternoon and evening services, all those who attended the Beis Midrash studied Ein Yaakov [5] with him. On Sabbaths, he expounded the weekly Torah and prophetic portion (Haftarah).

The working, G-d fearing villagers revered and honored their young teacher and called him "Rabbi". His sermons in the village served as a good experience for the days to come, when he became well known as a preacher. The notes that he took on the weekly prophetic portion served as a basis for his book "Ein Tzofim".

After he recovered and regained his strength completely, he decided to travel to his birthplace Stawiski to visit his father and his family, whom he had not seen for many years.

After he visited his father, he decided to again fulfill the adage "exile yourself to a place of Torah" [3]. This time, he chose the city of Augustow, 80 kilometers from Stawiski. The choice of Augustow was due to the following two reasons:

a. Friends and relatives of his lived there;

b. The city was surrounded by thick forests and the air of the forests was necessary for the maintenance of his health, even though he had been completely cured.

In Augustow, he established his place of study in the synagogue that was known as Yetke Kloiz, which had previously been called the Hassidishe Kloiz due to the fact that its founders and worshippers were Hassidim.

Reb Ezriel Zelig wanted to live in peace and occupy himself in Torah; however the tribulations of the Russian army came upon him. He was called to appear for army induction examinations. He was sure that he would be freed since he was the firstborn male in the family, for according to Russian law, firstborn males and only children benefit from special privileges. If the quota of draftees was filled, firstborn males and only children are freed from the army.

Since Ezriel Zelig had the necessary qualifications to be freed, he made no effort at all to free himself through other means... To his bad luck, when he presented himself before the army medical examiners, he was found to be fit for service. All efforts to exempt himself were for naught.

When the time of his induction drew near, he went to Stawiski to bid farewell to the rabbi of the town, Reb Chaim Leib the famous Tzadik. At the time of his parting, Reb Chaim Leib said to him: "Don't worry my son, I am sure that everything will be for the good. G-d will help you, and salvation will come soon."

The induction camp was in Lomza. From there, the draftees were sent to various places in the breadth of Russia. Ezriel Zelig was sent to Poltava.

After a difficult journey that lasted for several weeks, he arrived in Poltava with the rest of the inductees.

Stock certificate of the Peoples Bank in Stawiski in name of Rabbi Szymon Kac (Katz)

He was fortunate in that the commander of his regiment as well as of his squadron were both liberal men. Unlike most of the Russian army captains, they were free of the venom of anti-Semitism. Furthermore, the secretary of the squadron was a Jewish young man, who was a Chabad Hassid, married with two children. They quickly became friends, and the secretary helped and supported the new recruit at all times. During their free time, the two of them would discuss Torah, Hassidism, and character improvement.

With the help of the Chabad Hassid, Ezriel Zelig was given the opportunity to eat his meals with other Jews, and in such a manner he was able to refrain from eating the army food. He received a hot meal every day from the Poltava community, including on Sabbaths and festivals.

However, the immunity did not last forever. Ezriel Zelig's fortunes took a turn for the worse, and both the captain of the regiment and of the squadron were switched. Instead of liberal captains, others came who were reactionary Jew haters. At first, he had permission to leave the barracks on Sabbaths and festivals in order to partake of his Sabbath and festival meals with the Jews. The new commanders revoked this privilege, and Ezriel Zelig was forced to subsist on hard bread and water in order to avoid defiling himself by eating non-Kosher food. His situation was difficult, and at times it seemed as if he could not take it any more; however he always remembered the parting blessing of the rabbi and Gaon of Stawiski, and he did not despair.

One evening, he went out for guard duty. He took up his position with his gun over his shoulder, and uttered chapters of Psalms with great devotion. Suddenly, he heard a voice calling to him:

"Soldier Koszlowski, you are free. Tomorrow, you travel home."

"Blessed is He who frees the prisoners" was the response of Ezriel Zelig.

On what merit was he freed? It was the law in the Russian army that on occasion they would cast lots among those who had the credentials for being freed. This time, Reb Ezriel Zelig won the lottery.

He served in the army for five months in total.

When he was freed from the army, Ezriel Zelig returned to Augustow. There he married Sara, the daughter of Reb Yehuda. Reb Yehuda owned a large hide workshop. After his wedding, he continued to diligently study Torah, and his wife opened a store for shoe products. After some time, he joined the Kolel for married men [6] in Eishyshok, which was founded by the Gaon Rabbi Yitzchak Elchanan, the Rabbi of Kovno [7]. He spent four years there. He only returned to his home and family for festivals.

Even though he was great in Torah and had rabbinic ordination, he never agreed to accept a position of a rabbi. Nevertheless, after some time, when the judge of the rabbinical court of the city died, after much urging he agreed to serve as rabbinical judge. When the rabbi of the city, Rabbi Kasriel Nathan, died, the running of the entire community fell to him.

During the Second World War, the holy community of Augustow was wiped out by the Nazis along with other Jewish communities in Europe. On December 8, 1943, the remnants of the Jewish community were sent out to be murdered. Men, women, and children were sent by train to the gas chambers of Treblinka.

In the stifling cars of the death train, the last group of Jews of Augustow was squished in, surrounding their old, beloved rabbi, who trusted in the mercy of G-d until the last moment. Being close to him was their final comfort. His strength ran out, and he died on the train.

May G-d avenge his death.

{Photocopy page 47a – Stock certificate of the Peoples Bank in Stawiski in name of Rabbi Szymon Kac (Katz).}

{Top photo page 48a – The children's health colony sponsored by the organization Santos.}

{Bottom photo page 48a – Kaminski, of blessed memory. A refugee from Russia in the first World War, served in education in Stawiski.}

Translator's Footnotes :

1. A verse from the Book of Jeremiah, which is often quoted in the High Holy Day liturgy, and is the source of the custom of wearing of white on those days.

2. The Talmudic tractate dealing with laws regarding the prohibition of idol worship.

3. A statement in the Mishnaic Tractate of Ethics of the Fathers (Pirke Avot).

4. A quote from the Book of Psalms.

5. A compendium of the Aggadaic (story like as opposed to legalistic) sections of the Talmud.

6. A Kolel is a high level Yeshiva for married men who continue their studies after their marriage.

7. This is Rabbi Yitzchak Elchanan Spector. Incidentally, the rabbinical school of Yeshiva University in New York is named after him.

The children's health colony sponosored by the organization Santos

Kaminski, of blessed memory. A refugee from Russia in the first World War, served in education in Stawiski (Trans.: the photo is also accompanied by a Yiddish caption which reads: "A refugee from Russia in the first World War")

{50}

Pesach Kaplan [1]
The material about Pesach Kaplan was collected and compiled
by Mr. Moshe Cynowicz
Translated by Jerrold Landau

Pesach Kaplan was born in Stawiski in 1870, where his father Reb Binyamin Nachum was a cantor and shochet. Reb Binyamin Nachum was a great-grandson of Reb Kasriel, the Torah reader at the synagogue of the Vilna Gaon. Like the diligent students of that era, he studied in the cheders of Stawiski for twelve years. In the 13 th year, his father left the town of Stawiski and traveled around as a cantor and a preacher, until he settled in Gorodishche in the Kiev Gubernia. Between the age of thirteen and seventeen, Pesach studied in the Yeshivas of Korycin, Ruszczany, and Zelwa. Pesach arrived in Warsaw in 5647 (1887), where his father took on the position of cantor at Reichman's synagogue.

During those years, he was overtaken by the Haskalah [2] winds. He read Hebrew literature, and studied German, Russian, and a little English on his own. When he was nineteen years old, he wrote his first article in Hamelitz. From Warsaw, he went to Bialystok, where he was a Hebrew teacher for several years. While living in Bialystok, he wrote many articles in the Warsaw "Hatzefirah" newspaper. He was a fighter for the Hebrew language, and an active member of the "Lovers of the Hebrew Language" organization.

In 1904, he published his first Yiddish poem, "Di Velgerke" ("The Vagabond") in the Petersberger Teg. After that, he often wrote in the Yiddish newspapers "Teg" and "Friend", and later in "Heint" and "Moment". In the year 1914, he edited "Das Bialystoker Vort", which was at first a weekly and later a daily newspaper. After the First World War, he founded the "Das Neie Leben" ("The New Life") newspaper in Bialystok. This was one of the best provincial newspapers in Poland. Almost every day, he wrote columns, reviews, commentaries, and works of fiction. Among everything else, he wrote memoirs of his birthplace of Stawiski. These articles were published under the name "Chranik Family", and a few are published in this book.

Kaplan was also a lover of music, and translated a "Song Book" into Yiddish – which was a collection of classical songs with music of Mendelssohn, Schubert, and Schumann. He also published such books in Hebrew, "Sefer Hazemirot" and "Shirei Zimrah". He composed songs for Jewish children's homes, and composed his first Hebrew songs called "Nevel Asor". He also translated from German, Russian, and Hebrew. Pesach Kaplan edited the Bialystok Jewish newspaper "Unzer Leben" until his death during the Second World War.

———————

Translator's Footnotes :

1. Pesach Kaplan (1870-1943) was the founder and president of the Jewish People's Party. He was a correspondent for the American Jewish Daily Forward. He died in the Bialystok ghetto in 1943.

2. Haskalah (literally enlightenment) refers to the opening up of traditional European Jewish life to modernity during the 18 th century and beyond. This was often accompanied by a break with traditional Orthodoxy. Adherents to the Haskalah are called Maskilim (singular, Maskil).

{51 - 53}

Long Forgotten Images
by Pesach Kaplan
Translated by Yael Chaver

As I am travelling in my current town, sitting on a bus, looking out at long, narrow, blinding white highways, I close my eyes for a while and, like magic, long forgotten images of my native town come to mind.

Rachel Leahke's image comes up, who ran off with Antek the sheketz (gentile). The previous day, her father beat her with a rope for talking to the sheketz. Despite the fact that it was the Sabbath, the rabbi, the Tzadik, permitted horses and wagons to be hitched up in order to look for her. Saving a Jewish child from apostasy was considered to be a matter of life and death, and therefore pushed aside the Sabbath. Approximately a week later, they found her in Lomza and brought her back home.

She was locked up in her home for a month. Afterwards, when she went out on the street, the entire shtetl would stand by the windows and stare with curiosity at her proud, princess-like gait.

About a half year later, the entire shtetl danced at her high-class wedding with a young man from Bialystok.

The Tzadik Reb Chaim Leib arrived as rabbi of Stawiski on one bright, warm day in Elul [1]. Everybody went outside the shtetl to greet him. People went by foot for a distance of four vorst [2] until the station. When the rabbi's coach arrived, they lead him into the station for a brief rest. The appearance of his tall figure, with blond hair covered with a sable streimel, as he looked over a crowd of several hundred people, still remains before my eyes. The procession into the town was solemn. The musicians accompanied the procession with joyous music.

Now it was the first night of Rosh Hashanah. We prayed the festive evening service. The rabbi stood for a long time reciting the Shmone Esrei [3]. The entire congregation had already gone home, and the rabbi was still reciting the

Shmone Esrei. When we had already finished eating, someone told us that the Tzadik was still in the middle of the Shmone Esrei. Tzadok the Shamash (sexton) remained in the synagogue and waited. We stood away from the synagogue, and saw how the tall figure was bowed down, twisting around, as he was lost in a river of tears. The synagogue was full of curiosity. The rabbi remained reciting the Shmone Esrei for almost two hours...

The Tzadik conducted the rabbinate with a high hand. People were afraid of him.

Matia died. He was a tall, yellow Jew with a white face. He did not obey the rabbi, and did not guard the excise payments. He threatened that the town would lose a portion of its livelihood through this. The Tzadik warned Matia one time, and a second time. When Matia feigned ignorance, he was excommunicated in the synagogue to the light of black candles.

I remember how Matia went about town, actually like a corpse. Nobody would talk to him. People would leave his four cubits. His face grew more pallid by the day. He did not hold out for more than a month, and he submitted. He died a short time later.

Now, I will discuss the personality of Akiva Aharon Leizers. He was a young man with black, curly hair, a white, clear face, and shiny boots. He was a scholar, and the son-in-law of a wealthy man. He would go to the neighbor to drink milk from the cow every morning and evening. People would shake their heads about his outbursts; he is only a guest in the world...

I went with the entire town to his funeral. I went to worship in the house of mourning for the entire Shiva period [4]. I noticed that the young widow, Reizl went around with a big belly... A few months later, Reizl gave birth. I went to the recitations of Shir Hamaalot [5]. The newborn child was given the name Akiva the son of Akiva.

This was the famous chess player Akiba Rubinstein.

Life in the town was poor, gloomy, monotonous, and cut off from the outside world. At that time, we still lived under old-fashioned conditions. A bit of refreshment and excitement would come through the city from time to time when border guards would appear suddenly for a search. On one occasion, they circled the town, and nobody was allowed to enter or leave. They conducted a rigorous house to house search. It was a Friday, when we children were free from cheder. I ran, along with my friends, behind the soldiers, and was therefore present when they tore out the large floorboards of the Great Synagogue and found the large cellar where they kept the sheimos [6]. There was no other contraband. For us children, this was a spectacle; however the hearts of so many Jews were filled with terror! Finally, the cordon was lifted, and they left in shame, without being able to take any trophy with them.

{Photo page 53: The Stawiski market.}

Once upon a time, I stood there by the river, looking out over the alabaster-clear water flowing over the white pebbles. This water had been flowing for perhaps thousands of years, and yet did not was away the sand...

Thus do long gone images fly by in my memory, images of the dead and fallen. They once more live and thrive as I bring myself near to my shtetl.

––––––––

Translator's Footnotes :

1. Elul is the Hebrew month that falls in August / September. It is the month prior to Rosh Hashanah.

2. An obsolete Russian unit of distance.

3. The 'Shmone Esrei', literally 'eighteen', meaning 'eighteen benedictions, is the fundamental part of any prayer service. During Shacharit (morning service), Mincha (the afternoon service), and Mussf (the additional service of Sabbaths, New Moons and Festivals) it is recited silently by the congregation and then repeated by the prayer leader. At Maariv (the evening service), it is only recited silently by the congregation, and not repeated. Particularly pious people, and especially Hassidic Rebbes, recite this silent prayer very slowly and intently, taking a long time. Generally the congregation waits for them to conclude before continuing with the service, but if they take an especially long time, the service might continue while they are still reciting this prayer. Incidentally, the prayer never has eighteen benedictions. On weekdays, it has nineteen, as an additional one was added in the first century of the Common Era. On Sabbaths and festivals, there are only seven benedictions (except for Rosh Hashanah Musaf, were there are nine). Yet, the name 'Shmone Esrei' is still the term used for this prayer on all occasions. Alternatively, and more accurately, it is known as the 'Amida' (i.e. the standing prayer).

4. Shiva (literally seven) is the seven-day mourning period for direct relatives following the funeral.

5. Sections of Psalms recited on various occasions, including before a bris (circumcision) ceremony.

6. Sheimos (literally 'names', a reference to names of G-d), are holy objects and books that have become worn out and unusable. It is forbidden to throw these out, so they are collected in certain places, and on occasion buried in a cemetery.

––––––––

The market in Stawiski

{54}

Visit to Stawiski
by Pesach Kaplan of blessed memory
Translated by Yael Chaver

a.

From childhood, after which I never saw my birthplace Stawiski, it would appear to me in a strange expressionist vision: a long line, in the back as straight as a violin string, in the front bellying out; above the large belly a high bosom, then a small straight neck topped by a head.

The line is the straight road from Grajewo to Lomza that cuts through the shtetl. The belly in front – the rounded marketplace. The bosom – the church, from which two massive Gothic domes rose like two breasts, and so on up to the protective wall on the Lomza road – the head of the shtetl.

How lovely the brook along the Grajewo road seemed, in my imaginary vision, with its clear gurgling rivulets. Where I and the other boys, my friends, would stand under the bridge, stirring up the water with pebbles, while sneaking a look at the bare legs of the shiksas who came to do their laundry on the rocks there, rubbing and beating their linens...

And further along the way, the six walls: tiny, whitish, in a straight line, that hid the mysterious secrets and the goyim in their houses, pigs in their stalls. And the two paths that started from there: on the right – to the landowner's courtyard, and on the left – to the mill.

The area beyond the walls was considered out of town; we children were permitted to take a trip there only on Lag B'Omer, or some other vacation day.

On the other side of town, along the Lomza road, the last stop for us kids was the post office. Beyond that – far away from town – was the cemetery, where we would go only on Tisha B'Av or for a large funeral. Yes, we knew that the Sabbath Pale extended further, as far as the Lomza wood with its wonderful rock on which Napoleon spent a night with a landowner's wife... But I never went that far on my own, never saw that rock.

Often, in later years, I would remember the mysterious small cemetery in the middle of town: a fenced plot, four by four, next to a house, where according to legend a bride and her groom were buried after they both died on the day of the wedding. When this happened, who they were, we never knew. But our childish hearts would tremble with suppressed fear whenever we happened to pass by, especially in the evening, when the shtetl was sunk in profound darkness.

To the right of the center, in a small alley, the large, cold, walled synagogue loomed like a giant, like a large, stern mother in the middle of a gang of small children – the low wooden houses. Next to the synagogue – the large walled Bet Midrash, where the finest property owners in town would pray and study. Profound mystery surrounded a gravestone, with an inscription that was rubbed off, right up against the Bet Midrash. How did a gravestone come to be next to the Bet Midrash? What had been inscribed on it? No one knew; it was a secret that was passed down the generations and remained a secret.

On the cold winter Sabbath mornings, when the whole town was smothered in a thick darkness, I would creep, with my father and several other Jews, to the synagogue courtyard. Thick beams of bright light streamed through the large synagogue windows, and carried the study melodies of dozens of people studying Torah. I have never forgotten that beautiful picture.

And just as the synagogue was the giant among the hunched houses, there was one human giant among the hunched souls: Aaron-Leyzer the wealthy, whose treasure came to seventy-five thousand rubles, and who had been in Eretz-Yisroel three times.

b.

This was how I came to the shtetl. Not longing for the bygone pictures, but with a romantic imagination that bewitched me... Falling straight into the arms of quivering young lives and fresh problems, I was drawn to the old days as to an old mother.

I came to the synagogue courtyard through a small alley. The large old synagogue stood shabbily, its plaster falling off. I marvel at its size: how observant the shtetl must have been if, over a hundred years ago, they built a synagogue for a thousand worshipers.

In the courtyard I encountered a monument from a new, strange civilization: a nicely enclosed pump with an iron pipe, from which water flowed constantly without stopping. The enclosure wall was inscribed: "An artesian pump, in memory of the German occupation during the last war."

Jews take a reviving drink here, and if necessary – stick their hands under the pipe before going in to pray – a sink, as it were...

I go into the vestibule. I want to go right, towards the small "Bookbuyers" Bet Midrash, where I used to spend days and nights studying Talmud, but I hear the sound of prayers from there. I turn left to the small "Psalms Group" synagogue, where my father used to chant in front of everyone. It's empty. I stand alone, looking at the old "mizrach" next to the cantor's desk. and my heart trembles. I seem to see the hunched, downcast craftsmen sitting there, and my father's Torah chant floats above them. But the craftsmen are now called artisans, and last night they organized the theatrical performance of the Radzilow "troupe."

...I'm in the large synagogue. I stand before the cantor's desk as though beaten. It seems to me that I am once again an eight-year-old boy, standing here on Rosh Hashana hidden in my father's large tallis; he is praying emotionally, with heart-rending sighs, leading my pointing finger through his large Machzor.

A fair in the shtetl

Yes, it's the same desk. Everything has been preserved, frozen, as in the fairytale.

The Shames [1] leads me to a bench on the eastern side and shows me:

"Do you see this knife-cut? It was made by a boy, Eli Zelig, forty years ago. Now he's a rich American. A year ago he came to visit; when he saw the scratch, he dissolved in tears..."

And here I was in the "Bookbuyers" synagogue. Here is the table where I studied. The same table. Thick, unsmoothed, unpainted, with traces of wax. Why don't I feel the same impulse to weep as Eli Zelig did? The Shames tells me that the table is ninety years old; a Jewish village storekeeper moved to town and donated the table to the small Bet Midrash. I'm thinking that this might be a museum piece, but here they could have set a nicer, newer table.

I'm swamped by a sea of memories. Right here is where Reb Yisroel-Yankel the arbitrator used to sit; when he prayed, he would shake his broad beard strangely, right and left. Further along is the place of Leybel, Shepsel's son, who would catch me between his legs hold me fast while pushing me away with his hand: "Go, why are you standing here?" Some game. And this was the seat of the melamed [2], Reb Yankev-Zev, who, when I was leaving, followed the carriage and begged that I should not be taken away among the goyim, because I might curdle...

And the old Shames is the son of my Hebrew teacher, Moyshe-Mordkhe, who in later years would always appear to me like a handsome patriarch, with a white beard and soft, loving eyes. The son resembles the father like two drops of water, but an air of misery hangs over him. Too bad I'm not an American and can't give him a dollar.

In the large Bet Midrash I stand by the door. Apparently this is still the finest place in town. This is where the privileged and the scholars pray. But what a strange prayer! Several minyans of Jews dash back and forth, tallises on their shoulders, constantly talking with each other as though this were a market. Was it like this in the old days? Who remembers? Unrecognized, I leave quietly.

Now I was in the cemetery. The same as in the old days: here is a nice gravestone with colored letters that stab one's eyes. Who lies here? A simple, poor woman, who has a rich son in America.

A second gravestone, larger than the first but plainer, stands over the grave of a Tsaddik. [3] Why not granite, or marble? Why is there no structure over it? The town decided that, just as the Tsadiks of earlier times had no structures over their graves, he, too did not need one. Apparently, they feared him more during his lifetime...

A group of young scholars was in the cemetery with me; as we strolled between the rows of graves we talked about modern Jewish movements, about Jewish culture. Standing beside the Tsadik's grave, one summed up his thoughts: "Without Zionism it's not worth being a Jew."

c.

Fifty years later I found a totally different shtetl.

The shtetl had suffered two large fires over the years. Its old wooden houses had vanished in smoke, and in their place stood nice, neat walls, or even wooden houses, but handsome and new, pulsating with life. The shtetl hadn't grown, certainly it hadn't become richer, but culture had turned it into a beggar woman with ornaments. The long line to the right of the road had been overlaid with a new asphalt sidewalk, electric light smiles out of the windows, and the market is drenched in electric light, giving it a big-city look.

There is no trace of many of the Jews I used to know; barely anyone remembers them. The city council has several Jewish members, and there is a Jewish deputy mayor. There is a Jewish community organization; a man named Shapira is its secretary. The young students have ignore the community's culture. Most of them are influenced by radical Zionism. I was told that there are Bundists in the shtetl, but they have neither organization nor influence.

When the sun set, young couples sat on the sidewalk, short-haired girls in short dresses, clean-shaven young men wearing pressed suits. The sidewalk was crowded with strolling young people, exuding life and joy.

I stood there, fascinated, and thought: "My beloved home shtetl, how you have grown younger, prettier, and larger!"

Translator's Footnotes :

1. Shames is the sexton in the synagogue.

2. Melamed is a teacher.

3. Tsaddik is a pious person in general; especially, the leader of a Hassidic group. [Tzaddik – "righteous one" is a term of moral stature rather than scholarship; and is perhaps best known as the title of Hassidic leaders.]

{58}

Stawiski
by Azriel Liberman of blessed memory
Translated by Jerrold Landau

a.

Our city recently endured two fires. Many houses were burnt and two people were killed. Many families, who up to this point were supporters of fire victims from near and far, were left bereft of anything, and their eyes looked towards the help of generous people. The chief volunteers of this exalted enterprise were the following: the postmaster, the town physician, the pharmacist, the secretary of the government office, and Reb M. Z. Bramzon. All of them, with the exception of the latter, are citizens of the city. To our dismay, members of our community do not wish to join in the activities of this honorable organization, which has been designated to keep watch over the wellbeing and peace of the city.

For how long will the citizens of our city not learn their lesson? They should pay attention to the fact that, had there already been an organized fire brigade, the tragedy of two fires that caused two deaths would not have happened. People of means here have sealed their ears to the words of the above mentioned volunteers, who knock at their doors daily to ask them to give their donation to the coffers of this enterprise, while nobody takes heed. There is not even one person from amongst the young people numbered among the members of this enterprise. Is this not an embarrassment to you, all of you upright people!

The educational situation here is in complete disarray. There is no properly organized school, and there is no qualified teacher to educate our children in the ways of intelligence and knowledge. It would be fitting if the local Zionists take this breech into their hands, and found a school that runs in accordance with the spirit of the times.

The contribution to the army in our town ended in the best possible manner. All of the young people came on the designated day. Many of the holders of the higher lots returned clean to their homes.

Here I have opportunity to bless the following donors in the name of the members of our community: Reb Y. Kajmowicz, Reb M. Z. Witriol, and Reb Y. G. Morus – natives of our town who live in New York, America. They sent in their appropriate donations for the maintenance of the synagogue and the Talmud Torah fund. May G-d bless them.

Hatzefirah, December 1900.

b.

Zionism in our town is going strong! This is despite the spirit of the holy ones and the Hassidim [1] of whom we have no shortage of in our town, and who never miss and opportunity to speak negatively and arrogantly against he Zionist idea. They spew out fire and brimstone about the Zionist leaders, even going so far as to claim that it is permitted to uproot the entire Torah and to desecrate the Sabbath in public in order to oppose Zionism. This is just as one zealot of this ilk did, when he ran every Sabbath eve shortly before sunset to chase the people out of the bathhouse, the storekeepers from their stores, and the fisherman from the marketplace. In the synagogue, prior to the service of welcoming the Sabbath, a certain policeman read a "proclamation" from the rabbis and Gaonim in support of the activists. Furthermore, he was so brazen as to say in the name of the community and the congregation that the rabbis who signed the "proclamation" were like the ten sons of Haman [2]... May dust fall in his mouth! However the Zionists do not pay attention to such low and disgraceful people, and they get stronger every day. They sold many shares and gathered many shekels. They also founded a group to study Talmud every day. One of the Zionists who is capable of doing so teaches a class on "Ein Yaakov" every day, where he spices the Zionist idea with the works of our sages. He wins over the hearts of all his listeners with the sweetness of his lips.

Rabbi L. Lipkin, the head of the rabbinical court of Kottingen, was chosen as the rabbi of our community. May he be blessed in his arrival.

Printed in Hamelitz, 10 Iyar 5661, Number 40 (March 16, 1901).

Translator's Footnotes :

1. A note of sarcasm, with a derogatory tone, is detected in these two terms. The terms in used in Hebrew are "those who make things holy", and "those who make things Hassidic."

2. This is a reference to the sons of Haman, the viceroy who wished to destroy the Jewish people in the book of Esther.

{60}

Here Laid my Cradle
by Zalman Hirschfeld
(Memories from my childhood)
Translated by Jerrold Landau

I was born in the town of Stawiski. I was the youngest child of my parents Michael Yaakov and Sheina Sara Hirschfeld. Our family lived for many years in the Wilamowski home, in the neighborhood of the buckwheat grinder Shlomo Yechiel Mondensztejn. I remember that his son Elchanan, who studied in the Yeshiva of Volozhin, came home for the festivals with a short coat and a starched white collar. He also wore a tie, in the manner of the Maskilim. People would talk about him, and rumors spread that he had fallen into a bad crowd, G-d forbid... Nevertheless, he was not exceptional in our town, for at that time already the children of the rabbi of the city, Rabbi Dworcki, already studies in universities.

Later, we moved from the Wilamowski home to the upper floor of the home of Reb Zeinwil Blanksztejn. Blanksztejn lived in the center of town, in the marketplace, next to the road that divided the town in two. As was related to me, this road was the highway between Petersburg the capital of Czarist Russia, and Warsaw the capital of Poland.

From the time of my early childhood, I remember an unusual event that took place in those days. In 1911, an automobile race took place, and since Stawiski was located on the main road, we were able see with our own eyes the cars that sped through our town at the speed of lightning.

The entire town prepared itself in an exceptional manner for this great and important event. The marketplace was swept and the edges of the road that traversed the town were whitewashed with lime and covered with bright yellow sand. To enhance the splendor, a gate of honor was erected. It was covered with branches, and the flag of Czarist Russia fluttered on top of it. Three or four policemen stood at the edges of the road. They were "representatives" of the Czarist governor, and kept control over the residents of the town with a high hand. They stood erect and taught, and marched with a respectful and awesome gait. Their boots were polished and the buttons of their cloaks were shiny. As well, a half a dozen of the firemen of the town, wearing shiny copper helmets on their heads, added to the honor the great event. Men, women and children, both Jews and gentile, stood for long hours as they waited impatiently to see that automobiles pass through. Everyone was wearing festive clothes, for rumor had it that high-ranking captains and officials would be driving in these cars. Some people even said that the Czar himself along with his family including the young heir apparent would be among the drivers. Who knows? ... Lo and behold, the automobiles appeared, and passed through the road speedily in interludes of five to fifteen minutes. They stirred up clouds of dust that covered the entire town. The high officials that sat inside did not even notice us, and did not pay attention to the splendid reception that stormy and agitated Stawiski had prepared for them. This was an unforgettable event, which passed with the blink of an eye like a fleeting dream. The festive town again sunk into the grayness of its day to day life, as if nothing ever had taken place...

Even today, the night alarms of "Fire!" resound in my ears. Speedily and with panic, moveable belongings such as pillows, blankets, and anything that might come to hand were taken outside. Crying and frightened babies were placed on the haystacks as everyone made haste to extinguish the leaping flames that enveloped the town with tongues of reddish fire. Everyone became a firefighter: some with pails and others with basins, some by shouting alarms, and others by offering advice... everyone ran together toward the fire. Even the firefighters from neighboring villages were summoned to assist in fighting against the devouring fire. The red sky, the pillars of smoke and the fierce winds instilled fear upon the entire town, lest they, Heaven forbid, be wiped off the face of the earth.

The next day, when one went out onto the street, one would see the remnants of the burnt houses, scorched walls and charred household utensils – remnants that survived the fire. Here and there, a remaining flame or spark of fire would leap up from the mud, making a last attempt to take root again, and within a moment it would suddenly die down. The families whose homes had been destroyed would wander among the destroyed houses, with their trembling hands searching through the ruble, as perhaps they might find something that survived the fire... The day after, the wounded and forlorn town set back into the grayness of daily life.

My father of blessed memory was the "doctor" of the town (known as the feldsher in Yiddish [11]). He was the premier "doctor" in town. His expertise and experience in the field of medicine was obtained during his six-year stint of service in the Russian army. There he took a medic's course, and served in that capacity in an army hospital. There, in the hospital, he obtained no small amount of knowledge and experience in healing the sick. The elders of the town relate that my father, Reb Michael, was a fabulous "doctor", of pleasant disposition, who got along well with his fellowman, conducted himself modestly, was never concerned about the amount of money that the sick person brought with him in payment, and that all of his attention and focus was upon the suffering person and his ailments. It is no wonder that the women did not call him by his name Reb Michael, but rather Reb Refael [2]. On numerous occasions, I would hear a pain-stricken Jewish mother express her feelings of thanks to father for saving her child from the Angel of Death. She would tell him: "Reb Refael, may G-d give you the energy to continue in your good deeds. First there is G-d, and next to him is you – Reb Refael!"

On many occasions, a frantic knock would awaken our family from its sleep, and a desperate mother, without any other recourse, would cry out bitterly to my father: "Awaken Reb Refael, and hurry to save my child from the nails of death!"…

With deep concern, my father would hastily get up, take his "doctor's" bag, and hurry to one of the dark lanes where the desperate mother lived. Neither torrential rain, fierce wind nor a snowstorm would hold him back from providing healing, and at times even the saving of a Jewish life. Perhaps it was in no small part due to those harried night disturbances and alarms that his health was affected, his heart weakened, and he reached the grave at age 52.

The elders of Stawiski relate the following story: Once, an honorable man of the town became gravely ill. His family members summoned a famous doctor from Lomza, the regional capital. After Reb Michael explained to the famous doctor in great detail, both orally and by providing a written report, about the course of the illness, the care provided, and the drugs that he prescribed for him, the famous doctor said to the family: "Why did you bother me to bring me from Lomza when in your own midst there is such a wonderful experienced doctor like Hirschfeld?"

My father's friends and neighbors included: Reb Azriel the pharmacist, Reb Yehuda Hirsch Liberman and Reb Chaim Binyamin Chaver, who would come to our home in the evening hours and discuss politics, Zionism, and cultural affairs over a cup of tea. They would read the "Hatzfira" and "Hazeman" newspapers, and would discuss important matters, particular those that related to the Jewish people and the Land of Israel.

I remember that in my childhood I discovered something special about the blue and white box, the box of the Jewish National Fund, which stood in our home along with other charity boxes, such as that of Reb Meir Baal Haness, and other similar organizations. The box of the Jewish National Fund (Keren Kayemet Leyisrael) was not like the other boxes. In my eyes it was the epitome of beauty, like the beautiful embroidered parochet (ark cover) which would be placed over the Holy Ark on festivals in the Great Synagogue. One day I asked my father: "Why is this box different from other charity boxes in our house?" My father answered me: "The uniqueness and specialness of this box is that it is dedicated to redeeming land in the Land of our Fathers, and to settling Jews there in order to establish the Jewish kingdom!". "How?", I would ask. "is it possible to renew the Kingdom of Israel in the Land of our fathers prior to the coming of the Messiah?" "It is possible, it is possible", answered my father, and a bright smile quivered upon his lips, "and even if the redemption does not come in our day, the hope is incalculably important for our people in the Diaspora. You should know that this box breathes hope into the heart of the nation, hope for the redemption and the reestablishment of the Kingdom of Israel, which will come some day, and even if it is delayed, it will surely come! Know my son, that this hope is no small matter! It encourages the hearts of our Jewish brethren in the Diaspora, and lightens the yoke of the bitter exile from our people. Thanks to it, the nation of Israel which is suffering from tribulation and exile will become reestablished!" Oh my dear father, who can remove the dust from your eyes, and the eyes of others like you, so that you could see that your dreams and hopes have come true. Who would have ever thought that our generation would merit the fulfillment of the hopes inherent in that box, the blue box!

My first teacher was Reb Alter the teacher of blessed memory. He was a tall Jew, and a bright red beard adorned his pleasant face. I was a small child, and during the winter, when the days were biting cold and there were fierce snowstorms, Reb Alter would carry me upon his arms from his Cheder which was on the alley behind the street of the glass-blowers and bring me to the home of my parents, which was far away. I learned the Aleph Beit and the Hebrew language in a clear and pleasant fashion from Reb Alter. Many years later, when I made aliya and was accepted as an actor and narrator in the Hebrew theater, and I would be praised for my clear and sharp Hebrew diction, I would say to my friend: "I learned this from the "professor", the teacher of children Reb Alter from the holy community of Stawiski, which is found in the north-west corner of Congress Poland".

When I became older, I began to study secular subjects in the Russian public school. I studied Torah, Bible, and later Talmud and Jewish law from the friend of my father, the teacher Reb Chaim Binyamin Chaver of blessed memory. Reb Chaim Binyamin was not like any typical teacher from the older generation, teachers that would impart their lessons by direct translation into Yiddish "And he said – gezogt, and he spoke – geredt". For aside from being a learned Jew, he was also familiar with secular works. When he taught Torah and prophets, he was careful to impart the principles of grammar, such as the need to seek out the root of each word, to be careful about the conjugation and the root in all it details. The scoffers of the traditionalist generation, who did not have any appreciation at all for the nuances of the Hebrew language and its grammar, would mock him and give him the nickname "Pakod Pakadeti" [3].

In 1912, my father became ill with arteriosclerosis and my mother traveled with him to Koenigsberg (in East Prussia) [4] to visit a famous doctor. My father did not recover from his illness, and he died the same year that he was undergoing medical care in Koenigsberg. Our family, which had lost its head, left Stawiski and settled in Lodz. In Lodz, I continued my studies in the

Jeruzinski Talmud Torah school, and from there I went on to the Hebrew Gymnasia of Dr. Braude, where I finished my studies and matriculated in 1922. My teachers of Jewish subjects in the gymnasia were writers and pedagogues: Dr. Simchoni, Reb Chaim Yitzchak Bunin, Dr. Yirmiyahu Frankel, the poet Yaakov Cohen, and the writer Yitzchak Berkman – all of blessed memory. On numerous occasions, during the years that I lived in Argentina (30 years), one of my friends who was a teacher would ask me: "from where is your Hebrew?". Even here, in the Land, after I became a member of the Hebrew theater, I was asked that question by my fellow actors. I answered them all with the same answer: "I learned the Hebrew language from the mouth of Reb Chaim Binyamin the teacher, in the narrow, warm Cheder in his home located on a small lane in the small town of Stawiski.

"Do you know from where I inherited my poetry? In the home of my father there dwelt a lonely poet..." Chaim Nachman Bialik

On occasion I ask myself: I, a child of a small town, sleepy and forlorn, where in those days most of its inhabitants did not know anything about theatre, and perhaps had never even heard of its existence – how did the inclination and desire come to me for stage work? What strong power pushed me to give myself over to theater? In particular, from where did I gain the ability to act? (My readers will forgive me that I do not, in general, act strange – nor paint my eyes blue [5].) Furthermore, it was not only I who was the only one in our well-known family who devoted his life to work on the stage. My eldest sister as well, Tzila may G-d avenge her blood, was an actress in the Yiddish theater in Poland. Her theatrical pseudonym was Tzasha Sarna, and she was a superb actress. She excelled particularly in the following roles: Leah in "The Dybbuk" of Aniski; Meita in "Pundak Hashomem" ("The Desolate Inn") of Peretz Hirschbein; Natasha in "Yankel Hakfari" ("Yankel the Villager") of L. Kobrin; and Magda in "Hamered" ("The Revolt") of Dr. Tzipor.

The famous partisan actor Jonas Torkow, in his book "Kochavim Kvuim" ("Extinguished Stars"), volume II (162-170) wrote about the workers in the Jewish theater who perished in the holocaust, and dedicates a chapter to the life, activities, and theatrical abilities of my actress sister Tzasha Sarna, who was murdered by the Nazis in the Rzeszow ghetto of Galicia, the city where she lived during the time of the war.

I return to my question: from where and from whom did I inherit the inclination and ability for the stage? The answer is: from my mother of blessed memory. How? For our mother, like all the Jewish women, was an ordinary housewife and a mother dedicated to her children and husband. She certainly was not an actress.

Nevertheless, when I look back upon the days of my youth from the far recesses of my memory, when I see before my eyes our mother, her ways, her manner of speaking, her popular sense of humor, and the superb way in which she told us children stories, whether true or pretend; when I recall in my memory the atmosphere of the Sabbath, the twilight hours at the departure of the Sabbath, the dreary darkness which enveloped the house at the time that the extra soul disappears like a passing shadow [6], and the six workdays are at the threshold, our mother would sing to us in a sweet and glorious voice, with great enthusiasm, the songs and lyrics of Avraham Goldfaden, the father of the Jewish theater, "Rozhenkes mit Mandlen" ("Raisins and Almonds), or "Fariomert, Farklogt" ("In agony and sighing"), or the songs of Zion of Elyakim Tzunzer, the national poet; or she would entertain us with the funny stories of "Sana Habadchan" ("Sana the Joker") of her hometown of Bialystok. She would describe to us in an animated fashion his tricks and entertainment that he performed at weddings. She would tell us about her grandfathers and grandmothers and about men and women who are no longer with us, about their ways, their words, their lives and deeds. Each of her stories was peppered with humor, jokes, sweet popular sayings, and funny incidents – such that all of these people stood before us as if they were alive. As I think about all this now, with the perspective of more than fifty years, I come to the conclusion that that wise and intelligent woman was blessed with a superb acting ability, and that my older sister, and I, the young one, inherited our natural acting ability from her. Later on, when both of us, impelled by a force that was within our natures, became involved with the theater despite the objections of our dear mother – the prime force was the legacy that we received from her.

However it was not only the home and the direct influence of my mother which was the source of this inclination. The strong tendency toward theater was instilled within me from my childhood also from other places, in particular from the atmosphere of my town where the most important and honorable places were undoubtedly the synagogue and Beis Midrash. I remember on several occasions, as I returned home from the synagogue, I would cover myself in my mother's cloak or kerchief, in place of a tallis, and I would imitate the Baal Koreh Reb Nachman the tall, as he grunted the "pazer" or "shalshelet" during his reading[7]; or the hoarse prayer leader as he coughed; or the cantor who would wink his eyes as he chanted his melodies; or any other of the congregants, each in accordance with his movements and idiosyncrasies – and the members of my family would enjoy themselves and laugh as if they were watching the performance of a veritable comedian.

Various preachers and lecturers would often come to the Chevra Kass [8]. I, a young child, would listen with short breath and an open mouth to their lectures, which were woven with legends and stories that would take me in my imagination to the world of visions dreams, to Gehinnom [9], to the seven dwellings of G-d, to the Sambation River which would rest only on the Sabbath, to the Garden of Eden where the righteous bask in the Divine glory, to the days of the Messiah when the Holy One Blessed Be He in His glory will prepare a meal for the righteous from the flesh of the wild ox and Leviathan. I would return home emotional and stormy after these lectures, and when my spirit settled down, I would cover myself again in a kerchief, climb up on the table, and repeat the lecture of the preacher, almost word for word with his own unique style. My family members would surround me, as well as neighbors who would come to enjoy the "spirited pleasure". My audience would listen to me attentively, and would wink their eyes at me with expressions of love and thanks. I (the young artiste) would bask in my success. At the end of my "performance" there would not be applause and calls for encore, for in my town of Stawiski, they still did not know about applause. The main thing, even without applause, was that myself, young as I was, saw myself as a professional actor in the theater, performing before an appreciative audience, even though for me, theater and acting were still unknown words. Now, with the perspective of over fifty years, I know that these were my first performances as an actor.

The Great Synagogue built in the middle of the 18th century and destroyed at the time of the Nazis in July 1941

Weddings in our town were mass gatherings. Most of the residents of the town participated, and they took place outside. The groom, bride and their entourage – the parents, in-laws and the crowd of guests invited from both sides – were led by everyone to the chupa (marriage canopy) which was set up in the yard of the synagogue. The members of the local "band" played violins, drums, trumpets and flutes. Their melodies and popular tunes accompanied the festive procession, and the entire town was lit up from the hundreds of candles that spread light to the surroundings. The mischievous pranksters would sneak about and push their way through the large crowd in order to spray the bride and groom with various oils. The crowd would throw confetti (small pieces of multicolored paper) upon them. The jester would tell jokes in rhyme, to the best of his ability, to the bride, groom and in-laws. The joy and mirth were great, and the entire city was celebrating. As I recall these weddings in my memory, I ask myself: would any modern theater, even the best, be able to perform such a massive and glorious presentation, as my own forlorn town Stawiski was able to perform when there was a local wedding on a regular weekday?...

The hakafot (processions) on Simchat Torah [10] in the synagogue – what can be compared to them? In the eyes of my spirit, I see dozens of Jews passing by in procession, surrounding the bimah (synagogue podium) with their arms hugging Torah scrolls decorated with crowns and bells. All the children of the town had flags flying from their hands. Some of the flags were decorated with pictures of Moses and Aaron, others with the two tablets of the covenant, and still others with splendid priestly vestments. On top of the flags were soft red apples and burning candles. These children would accompany the people in the procession. All of them were singing and dancing with enthusiasm. The women and girls would look on, kiss the Torah scrolls as they passed by, and issue greetings of "congratulations!", "next year again!". The men and boys would answer back: "to you too!"..

And Hoshanah Rabba [11]! Hundreds of bearded Jews, as well as young people and children were standing in the synagogue, beating their Hoshanah bundles and calling out in a festive voice "Kol Mevaser Mevaser Veomer". The crowd of Jews, with their etrog in one hand and their lulav in their other hand would walk around the bimah seven times as their voices utter the eternal plea "Hoshanah"! As I returned from the synagogue I would gather my friends together. Each one would bring a stick and a potato. I, the "great ringleader" would conduct the rejoicing crowd.

Even though all of the festivals were joyous, Purim [12] was the most joyous of them all. For on Purim, it is permissible to let loose, and the community of Israel is full of joy and mirth. The graggers make a tumult of noise when the Megilla reader mentions the name of the evil Haman and his ten sons, from Parshandata to Vayzata. Every year, the oppressed Jews forget about the tribulations of the exile and the difficulties in earning a livelihood, and they celebrate without bounds. It is required to become drunk "until one does not know the difference between cursed is Haman and blessed is Mordechai". The boys and girls make haste around the town from home to home, delivering Mishloach Manot on plates covered with cloths, that hide from the evil eye delicacies, treats, pastry, hamantashen, raisins and almonds. In the center of the plate was the king of fruits – a sole orange surrounded by its family members. The Purim players would dress up as the figures of the Megilla – Achashverus the silly king, Vashti the queen with a horn growing from her forehead, the wicked Haman, and, to differentiate one thousand fold, Esther the queen and Mordechai the Jew. All of them went out in haste as the satraps of Media and Persia from house to house and from Purim meal to Purim meal. Their mouths were filled with laughter and their tongues with joy and mirth. All of them, the players and the householders, would sing together "Shoshanat Yaakov Tzahala Vesamecha" ("The Jews of Shushan were happy and joyous") or the popular Purim songs "Today is Purim and tomorrow is not, so give me a coin and get rid of me cheaply!", or "The wicked Haman licks dust, and Mordechai the Jew rides on a splendid and majestic horse!", or other such songs that were composed in honor of Purim. The tumult and uproar was great for that day was Purim.

When I remember all of these events, whether on festivals or on weekdays, during my childhood in the small town of Stawiski – I know that even though later I merited to hobnob with the performers of the large Yiddish theaters, and I was able to learn from them, my first school in acting was my own town of Stawiski, in the grayness of it mundane times and it splendid festivals.

Translator's Footnotes :

1.   In my Yiddish / English dictionary, by Max Weinreich, this word translates as 'old time barber-surgeon'.

2.   A play on the meanings of these Hebrew names. Michael means "Who is like G-d?", and Refael means "G-d is the healer". Incidentally, these are two of the four protective angels that are said to surround a person (Michael at the right, Gavriel at the left, Uriel at front, and Refael behind).

3.   This phrase, made up of a repeated root (pkd) in two different forms, is a reference to the visitation of Divine wrath.

4.   Today, Kalinigrad.

5.   I do not understand the meaning of this sentence.

6.   According to Jewish lore, a Jew obtains an additional soul ("Neshama Yeteira") on the Sabbath.

7.   A Baal Koreh is the man who reads publicly from the Torah in the synagogue. The Torah is chanted according to various cantillation notes, which define the accenting and the melody. The pazer and shalshelet are among the most ornate of the cantillation notes. The shalshelet is very rare, occurring only four times during the yearly Torah reading cycle.

8. The name of a synagogue, literally "The society for the purchase of books".

9. Gehinnom (literally the Valley of Hinnom, a valley in Jerusalem where Molech worship used to take place in ancient times), has become synonymous in Jewish lore with Hell. The rest of this sentence refers to various aspects of Jewish belief and eschatology, which cannot be done justice in a short footnote.

    Simchat Torah (the Rejoicing of the Torah) is the ninth day of Sukkot (actually, the eighth and ninth days are considered a separate holiday – the eighth day being Shemini Atzeret, and the ninth day being Simchat Torah). On Simchat Torah, the yearly cycle of Torah readings is concluded and begun again. The festivities include processions around the synagogue with the Torah scrolls, known as hakafot.

10. Hoshanah Rabba is the seventh day of the Sukkot Festival, the last intermediate day before the full festival days of Shemini Atzeret and Simchat Torah. On Hoshanah Rabba, there are seven processions made with the lulav and etrog (the palm frond, citron, myrtle and willow which the Torah commands to be used as part of the Sukkot celebrations). A special bundle of willow twigs (known as the Hoshanah bundle) is beaten on the floor. There are many special hymns that accompany the processions and the beating of the Hoshanah. These prayers (which are also recited during the single procession that takes place on each of the first six days of Sukkot) are accompanied by the refrain "Hoshanah" ("Please save"). The final of these hymns looks forward to the advent of the Messiah. It starts and concludes with "Kol Mevaser Mevaser Veomer" ("The voice of the herald heralds and says").

11. Purim is a Jewish holiday that occurs in February or March, commemorating the events described in the Book of Esther. It is celebrated by the public reading of the Book of Esther (the Megilla). During this reading, when the name of the villain Haman is read, the congregation makes noise with special noisemakers, called graggers. During the day, gifts of food are sent to friends (Mishloach Manot), gifts of money to the poor (Matanot Laevyonim), and a festive meal is held, accompanied by drinking. Hamantashen is the name of a special three-cornered Purim pastry.

{79}

Rabbis and Personages

Eminent Rabbis of Stawiski
by Pesach Kaplan of blessed memory
Translated by Jerrold Landau

a.

I wish to present here to the younger generation a brief characterization of several rabbis of Stawiski, as they remain in memory.

Reb Fishele (Makower) was the rabbi in Stawiski prior to my birth. As is related, he was an upright pious Jew.

After him, the renowned Gaon Reb Leibele Plockier occupied the rabbinical position. (Rakowski, the father of the Maskil and writer Avraham Abba Rakowski, the grandfather of the writer Puah the daughter of Mendel Rakowski, the great-grandfather of the young man of letters from Bialystok, Marek Rakowski. [11]) On account of his being a Misnaged (opponent of Hasidism), Reb Leibele was not beloved in Stawiski, and they looked for a pretext to dismiss him.

Many years later, when I was a young child, I heard the following story in my home:

In the year 1864, after the Russians had already suppressed the Polish revolt, a letter came to Stawiski from the governor of Lomza on Rosh Hashanah, stating that Reb Leibele must immediately leave the city, or else he would be beaten, shackled, and thrown into prison.

The letter was a forgery, in order to assist in getting rid of the rabbi. The letter was read in the synagogue, and the rabbi fled from the town at the conclusion of Rosh Hashanah.

Reb Meir Noach Lewin came in his place. He was later the Maggid (preacher) of Vilna and the head of a Kollel (institute of advanced Talmudic study) in New York. He was also not liked in town. Being Lithuanian, he was regarded as a simple person. Once, a Jew saw through the window how the rabbi was lying on the sofa and looking at a book. In the meantime, the rabbi's yarmulke fell off. The rabbi did not realize it, and he continued looking into the book bareheaded. For that particular mistake, the rabbi had to leave Stawiski.

Many years later, my father at home would often relate, with great bitterness, about the bad deeds that the town did to these two rabbis, whom our family loved and supported greatly.

After Reb Meir Noach, Rabbi Yoel Abelson (from Sokol) became the rabbi. He was a tall, blond man with red eyes, which I can still remember. He was weak in character, not cold and not warm. They neither loved nor hated him in Stawiski. The town was very demoralized during his time. Therefore, when he went as a rabbi to Odessa, they brought in the Tzadik Reb Chaim Leib from Zaludok in order to clear away the humiliation from the Stawiski garden.

Reb Chaim Leib, a strong personality, served for a blessed period of time, about which will be related in the following chapter.

b.
The Tzadik Reb Chaim Leib studies Gemara in the Tavern.

The Tzadik Reb Chaim Leib conducted the rabbinate with a strong hand. If he did not succeed by gentle means, he would impose strong means upon sinners. Often, he would not only reprove the violator vary strongly, but he would also issue a ban of excommunication.

However, he did not always need to resort to strong means. Often as well, with the help of his deep astuteness, he was able to bring the violator to repent. I wish to describe such a story in the following lines.

Baruchke the tavern keeper (I have not used his real name here) was perhaps the only Jew in Stawiski who would trim his beard a little. Certainly, Baruchke never missed reciting the afternoon service (Mincha) with the congregation. Certainly there was a kosher kitchen in his Jewish home. However, in the Beis Midrash, he was looked down upon. He sat behind the Torah reading platform. He loved to snatch a nap when a preacher was speaking, he would always receive a second rate aliya [2], and he never became involved in communal affairs. However, in his home and in the tavern, he was vivacious and talkative. There he was always busy with something, unloading packages, talking idly, helping with the serving, and grabbing a shot of liquor or a bite with the group [3]. His guests were mainly characters from the "underworld". At his tavern, people planned their "expeditions" to the border. At his place, they unloaded merchandise. At his place, they sealed all kinds of dark transactions.

Baruchke already had no wife at the time. His assistant, the waitress for the secretive guests, was his daughter Gruntsha, a girl already in her upper twenties. She had a bold, manly face, a high bosom and healthy hands. Her sleeves were always rolled up past her elbows. When she would give a guest a friendly tap over the shoulder, everyone would double up from enjoyment...

Gruntsha was the only "old maid" in the town. Everyone considered her to be not particularly modest...

As Baruchke competed with the business of the other taverns, it is needless to say that he was not liked in town, and one dark rumor after another regarding his home and his conduct was spread about. No other girl was friendly with Gruntsha. When the girls of the town used to stroll along the highway to Lomza on Sabbath eves, Gruntsha would sit in her tavern with her rolled up sleeves and unkempt hair and look out the window with jealousy and hatred...

When Reb Chaim Leib heard that Baruchke's tavern serves on the Sabbath, that all taverns were locked on the Sabbath but Baruchke's was open; and that even though he hired a gentile woman to stay behind the counter and serve, Gruntsha wandered around and even on occasion dealt with the money with her own hands, the rabbi sent for Baruchke, and warned him in the following words:

"You sheketz [4], why do you do this type of sin? You deserve to be stoned!... [5]".

"Livelihood, rabbi! What will a Jew not do for livelihood?"

"You are speaking like a brazen person! Be silent, you and she must not violate the Sabbath again!"

The Tzadik make an uproar and sharply reproved and threatened Baruchke that he must not violate the Sabbath again. Baruchke was bent and downtrodden as he left the rabbi, but it did not help. He conducted business in his tavern on another Sabbath. The front door was indeed closed, but people could come in through the back door. In the town, people murmured and talked about a ban of excommunication, but the Tzadik had an entirely different plan.

The following Friday, the city sexton (shamash) [6] went to Baruchke and informed him that the rabbi requested that he not turn off the heat in the tavern. Towards evening, Tzadok returned to the tavern and brought with him a large volume of Gemara and a small lantern by which the Tzadik would sit for the entire night in his house and study. Tzadok hung the lantern on the wall, and placed the Gemara on a table. Baruchke and Gruntsha asked about the significance of this. Tzadok answered briefly: "tonight, the Tzadik is coming to study in the tavern".

The bizarre news quickly spread through the town. Indeed, on Friday night after the Sabbath meal, Tzadok went to the rabbi's house and accompanied him to Baruchke's tavern.

There, the father was already dressed in his Sabbath kapote (cloak) and the daughter had a kerchief over her thick, black hair.

"Gut Shabbes" [7] – the rabbi greeted Baruchke and his daughter.

"Gut Shabbes, gut yahr, rabbi", Baruchke answered as his teeth shook.

"Did you eat already, Baruch?"

"Yes, Rabbi."

"I want to study my from my book a little bit here. Baruch, you can do what you wish. I want to see how a Jew violates the Sabbath. I have never seen this before."

Baruchke did not answer. At the same moment, he noticed that there were curious children standing at both windows of the tavern. He ran to chase them away. Gruntsha went to block the door, but the rabbi stopped her.

"Daughter, you do not need to do so. Let anyone who wishes enter. I wish to indeed see the Jews who make purchases on the Sabbath. Don't be bothered, girl, I will answer those who come in."

Gruntsha went away and the Tzadik sat down and opened the Gemara. Nobody came in. The entire town already knew that the Tzadik was sitting in the tavern. Gruntsha was not seen for the entire evening, and Baruchke went from time to time to drive the children away. On occasion, he stuck his head through the back door in order to steal a glance at what the rabbi was doing.

The rabbi buried his head in the Gemara and studied. He seemingly forgot where he was and for what reason he had come. His quiet, sweet Gemara melody [8] cut through the air of the tavern, and pages turned one after another.

Late at night, they came to call for the Tzadik. That is what they had probably agreed upon. Baruchke again stuck his head through the door.

"Come here Baruch!", the Rabbi said, as he lifted up the Gemara, "I am going home now, and tomorrow, I want to come back."

"No rabbi! Why should I trouble you further? I will no longer run the tavern on the Sabbath. I swear by my Jewishness."

"Call in the girl", the Tzadik said quietly. Gruntsha then stood beside her father before the rabbi, and he said to her:

"Listen, girl! You are a Jewish girl, and you should know that violating the Sabbath is one of the worst sins. Tell me that you will not do it again."

She stammered a few words, and the rabbi left.

From then on, no customers came to Baruchke in the tavern on the Sabbath.

———

Translator's Footnotes :

1. I am not sure of the implication of this sentence in parenthesis. My guess is that Rakowski is an alternate name for Plockier – perhaps Plockier being a name given to him due to his place of origin.

2. An aliya is a synagogue honor of being called up to the reading of the Torah. Of course, there are more prominent and less prominent aliyas.

3. I was not able to translate this sentence with complete accuracy, but the meaning is correct.

4. A derogatory term for a non-Jew, here referring to one who acts like a non-Jew.

5. The biblical penalty for willful violation of the Sabbath is death by stoning. The practicalities surrounding the laws of capital crimes in the Torah make the sentence very difficult to carry out, yet the punishment is on the books. In times when the Temple is not functioning, and the central Sanhedrin (court of Jewish law) in not functioning, the penalty is impossible to carry out.

6. Probably the emissary of the rabbinical court.

7. A Sabbath greeting: "Good Sabbath". The response "Gut Shabbes, gut yahr", means "Good Sabbath, good year".

8. Talmud is often studies to a plaintive melody.

———

{83}

Rabbi Chaim Leib Myszkowski of Blessed Memory and the Yeshiva of Lomza
by Dr. Yom Tov Lewinski
In memory of my friend from the Yeshiva of Lomza, Chaim Leibele Goelman of blessed memory
Translated by Jerrold Landau

In the year 5643 (1883) after the death of Rabbi Yisrael of Salant of holy blessed memory, the father of the Mussar movement of the Lithuanian Yeshivas [1]), his expert student Reb Eliezer Shuliewicz, who became known as Reb Leizer, decided to found a Yeshiva in Poland along the style of the great Lithuanian Yeshivas, which included Mir, Telz, Radin, etc. Reb Leizer chose the city of Lomza, a district capital that is located on the Narew River. Reb Leizer was born in Kolno, in the region of Lomza, and during his childhood he lived in the village of Piontnica, which is on the other side of the Narew, and was generally regarded as a suburb of Lomza.

In the town of Stawiski, close to Lomza, Rabbi Myszkowski of holy blessed memory occupied the rabbinical seat. He was a childhood friend of Reb Leizer. When Reb Leizer though of the idea of founding a Yeshiva, he came to Stawiski to visit Rabbi Chaim Leib. He presented his plan to him and told him of his idea to establish a center of Torah and Mussar, according to the Lithuanian style, in the Mazowia region of Poland. Reb Chaim Leib became quite enthusiastic of the lofty idea, and told Reb Leizer, quite enthusiastically:

"Your people is my people, your G-d is my G-d, where you go, I will go..." [2]). The two of them hugged and kissed, and broke out in a dance in the room of the rabbinical court. It was late at night. People gathered below the window of the room of the rabbinical court and asked each other: "What is the cause of this joy?" The rabbi's wife understood that Reb Leizer had brought good news to her husband. She hurried and brought them some wine, cups, and cake leftover from the Sabbath as a snack.

The two of them sat all night and took council together. The next morning, hasty letters went forth, signed by Rabbi Chaim Leib Myszkowski, who was respected in the entire region, to several well-to-do people who were supporters of Torah study in the expanse of Russia and outside its borders. Within two or three months, the rabbi received letters of encouragement as well as several pledges of money for the Yeshiva. Reb Leizer added to these sums his own dowry that was in safekeeping with a Jewish merchant in Lomza. He added to this the interest, as well as a sum that was placed at his disposal by his friend Reb Zerach Brawerman to use for Torah works. Thus he succeeded in gathering together fifteen thousand Rubles, a significant sum in those days.

Rabbi Myszkowski arrived in Lomza, and along with Reb Leizer, they rented a premises for the Yeshiva, and sent out a notice to many rabbis and heads of neighboring communities. Together, they appointed expert teachers of Talmud, who were good at explaining lessons and would have foster a good relationship between the teacher and the students. However, their eyes looked far off, and in their vision they saw a large building standing upon its foundations, a building dedicated solely to the Yeshiva, which would be made up of young men studying Torah for its own sake.

After some time, they had the opportunity to purchase a property on the edge of Snatorska – the street upon which most of the Jewish communal institutions were located, including the Great Synagogue, the large Beis Midrash, the hospital, the Talmud Torah, the charitable organization, the organization for housing of guests, and others. The property consisted of a large house with a wide yard surrounding it. This place met with their favor, and with the favor of the Yeshiva activists in Lomza, so they purchased the house and the field for 10,000 Rubles. After the purchase was concluded, a meeting was called for members of the community, including those who volunteered to help set up the building to house a Yeshiva. One of them, Reb Asher Kopisker who was the owner of a brick factory, donated on the spot 30,000 bricks for the building. When his wife found this out, she became angry that her husband Asher had not included her in the Mitzvah. She came to the committee and donated another 25,000 bricks from her own money.

When the building was completed, Reb Leizer did not wish to register it in his own name, despite the fact that he was the chief activist and also the ordained head of the Yeshiva. He said that the entire honor came to him on account of the joint activity and dedication of the head of the rabbinical court of Stawiski. He desired that the house be registered in his name, as well as the government permit to set up a school for adults. Thus, for all the years, the house and all of the buildings that were connected to it were registered in the name of the rabbi of Stawiski, Reb Chaim Leib Myszkowski. Not infrequently, the Russian investigators bothered the rabbi when they suspected that the Yeshiva students were joining forces with the "Kramola" – the political organizations that were revolting against the Czarist government. On several occasions he was brought to Lomza for interrogation at the education office and the secret police headquarters.

For his entire life, the rabbi of Stawiski was the helper and faithful advisor of Reb Leizer in matters of the Yeshiva. During one of the years in the 1890s, the Yeshiva found itself in dire financial straits. This was in a year when there was a drought in Russia. Prices rose, the donations to the Yeshiva that were brought in from the emissaries all over Russia had shrunk, and the number of students who received weekly financial assistance to help them subsist in a modest fashion was growing. The debts grew. One matron who had lent the head of the Yeshiva 3,000 Rubles for the Yeshiva initiated litigation when the loan was not paid on time. The hands of Reb Leizer became weak, and he said: "How can I alone bear this heavy burden? After difficult tribulations, it was decided to close the Yeshiva at the end of the term, and to bring those students that were fitting, with some assistance from the Yeshiva coffers, to the Yeshivas of Mir and Telz. However, could any such thing be done without the advice and agreement of his friend, the rabbi of Stawiski? A special emissary was sent, and the rabbi was brought to Lomza for urgent consultations.

The rabbi came quickly. When he came to Reb Leizer, in his home that was in the main building of the Yeshiva, Reb Leizer poured out to him the bitterness of his heart, and broke out in bitter weeping: "Chaim Leib, the situation has become desperate, and I no longer have the energy to bear this heavy burden."

Reb Chaim Leib answered him with great deliberation: "I am tired from the journey and you are emotional and distraught, so let us put off our discussion until the evening." Reb Leizer wondered: "Is not the time for clear deliberation in the morning, after a good night's rest, as the prophet says: "Make your judgements in the morning." (Jeremiah 21, 12)." However, the words of the rabbi, which were uttered with seriousness and level-headedness, calmed him, and he waited until the evening.

After the evening service, the two of them ate supper in the home of Reb Leizer. Afterwards the two of them sat down, each from his own perspective, to study a book. During the entire time, the rabbi did not utter a single word. Reb Leizer got up, cleared his throat in order to attract the attention of the rabbi; however the rabbi was engrossed in his book and did not stop... It was 11:00 p.m. and the rabbi was still sitting there, bent over the book. Reb Leizer was not so brazen as to interrupt him, and he waited patiently. However, when the clock struck twelve, Reb Chaim Leib got up, kissed the book and closed it, and said to Reb Leizer: come my brother and let us go for a walk. The two of them went out without saying anything. The rabbi led him towards the Chevra Shas Beis Midrash. It was a dark night. Isolated stars twinkled from the sky, and the streets were quiet. There was nobody about. In Chevra Shas, there were always working people who would study until a very late hour of the night; however at that time, the Beis Midrash was already enveloped in darkness. Only the eternal light was flickering in the eastern side. From there, without saying a word, they walked toward the Great Synagogue, in whose foundations functioned two organizations for the spreading of Torah and good deeds: The Chevra Tehillim on the right and the Chevra Kadisha on the left. In the Chevra Tehillim, Reb Yoel Halevi Herzog, the father of Rabbi Yitzchak Izak Herzog [31]) of holy blessed memory, would lead a class in Talmud each evening until a late hour of the night. However the hour was already very late, and all of the students had returned to their homes. The two of them went silently to the large Beis Midrash, which was on the corner of SzaKolno Street. Even there they did not find anybody. The students and householders had already returned to their homes after they finished their daily page of Talmud. The rabbi lifted his eyes up to the second floor, where the rabbi of the city, Reb

Malkiel Tenenbaum, lived. Rabbi Malkiel would occupy himself in learning after the Sabbath. However, even the house of the rabbi was already dark, for it was now nearly 2:00 a.m., and even the rabbi had gone to sleep. The two of them set out for the Yeshiva building. They continued walking, and the darkness of the night enveloped the two pedestrians with a spirit of mystery.

As they passed the Talmud Torah building, Reb Chaim Leib stopped suddenly and asked Reb Leizer in a puzzled manner: "What is this sound that I hear in the middle of the night? What is this soft melody which penetrated the heart two hours after midnight?" [4L] Reb Leizer answered him in a fashion that had a taint of pride: "Is this not the voice of the students of our Yeshiva!". "If that is the case", said the rabbi, "Let us enter and see". The two of them entered the large building of the Yeshiva. They came through the gate and waited near the entrance. They stood near the open windows for a number of minutes. A thin light shone out from the window and spread rays of light onto the yard. The sound of the melody did not stop. It was heard as a quiet harmony of melodies merging together. The rabbi opened the door silently. They did not enter, they only stood at the entrance and glanced at what was going on inside. There were dozens of youths and young adults sitting each in front of his Talmudic volume, which was placed on the reading desks. There was a simple candle flickering on each desk, and the student seated next to it would shake in a rhythmical fashion to the melody, causing shadows to dance on the wall.

The rabbi asked, making as if he did not know the answer: "What are these people doing here? Does the day of study never stop?"

Reb Leizer answered: "These are the diligent ones, who keep "watch" one night a week, and occupy themselves with their study until daybreak."

"And an institution such as this you wish to close?", asked the rabbi with astonishment. Go forth and see, we walked the entire city. Every Beis Midrash is enveloped in darkness, for the students have gone home to give rest to their eyes. The gates of Torah are closed, and this large city, which excels in its Torah students, is enveloped in slumber. This is indeed the way of the world. However, here, in this holy place, the sound of Torah does not cease day or night. And you wish to close such an institution of Torah?"

"You have strengthened me", called out Reb Leizer, as tears choked his throat, "Reb Chaim Leibele, you have encouraged me."

"Let us go to sleep", said Reb Chaim Leib to him, "the hour is very late and we have much to do tomorrow…"

Suddenly, heartrending weeping was heard from the other side of the yard. The two rabbis were surprised and walked toward the voice. The voice was breaking forth from the cellar on the other side of the Yeshiva, where the elderly Mashgiach [5L] Reb Yisrael Leib Egielski gives his class in Talmud to his students. They looked through he window: there in the corner seated next to the oven, with a darkened face, was seated the emissary from Jerusalem, the Kabbalist Reb Zalman Rojtman, who was known as Reb Zalman Weinmacher since his wife used to make raisin wine for Kiddush and Havdalah [6]) and thereby support her family. Reb Zalman was seated in a corner reciting Tikkun Chatzot [7]).

"Lament Oh Torah for your glory has been desecrated, your crown has fallen from the day that your house was destroyed…"

Could Reb Zalman Weinmacher did not find a more comfortable place to recite Tikkun Chatzot than here in the basement of the Yeshiva? The rabbi asked. Reb Leizer answered: "The Yeshiva became the home of Reb Zalman on all the weekdays. There he studied all day, there his wife or one of his sons brought him his daily meals, and there he recited Tikkun Chatzot. Only on Sabbath eves did he go straight from the Mikva (ritual bath) to his home.

"And what would Reb Zalman Weinmacher do if you closed the Yeshiva?", asked the rabbi with a light smile.

Reb Leizer was silent. The answer was obvious.

The next day, toward evening, Reb Chaim Leib with the assistance and permission of the rabbi of the city Reb Malkiel, called an urgent meeting of the householders in the Chevra Shas Beis Midrash, where the wealthy people of the city worshipped. Reb Chaim Leib told them about the difficult situation of the Yeshiva, the pride of the holy community of Lomza. Reb Leizer described to them the difficulties of the poor students, from whom Torah will go forth. There on the spot they collected approximately 8,000 Rubles in cash and oral pledges. Reb Leizer breathed a sigh of relief and Reb Chaim Leib returned to Stawiski rejoicing and of good heart.

Several years later, when Reb Chaim Leib went the way of all living, Reb Leizer called his widow and two children, a son and a daughter, and provided them with a residence for all their lives in the main building of the Yeshiva. Reb Leizer also concerned himself with their sustenance for many years, for he loved Reb Chaim Leib dearly, and he remembered his good deeds for all his life.

Translator's Footnotes :

1. The Mussar movement stressed ethical and moral behavior within the Yeshiva world. It was founded by Rabbi Yisrael Salanter (of Salantai, Lithuania), around the beginning of the 1800s. Its influence set the tone and style of the Lithuanian Yeshivas from that time on, including in their present incarnations in Israel and the United States.

2. This is a quote from the Book of Ruth, where Ruth confirms her willingness to join the Jewish people to her mother-in-law Naomi. Here it is used as an expression indicating commonality of purpose.

3. Rabbi Yitzchak Izak Herzog was a Chief Rabbi of Israel. He died in 1959. His son Chaim Herzog later became the president of Israel.

4. Talmud is often studied using a simple melody.

5. A Mashgiach (literally supervisor), is the spiritual supervisor of a Yeshiva.

6. Kiddush (literally sanctification) is a blessing over wine made prior to the evening meal of Sabbaths and festivals, and again during the daytime meal. Havdalah (literally differentiation) is a blessing over wine made at the conclusion of Sabbaths and festivals.

7. Literally "The Midnight Rectification", a set of prayers recited in the middle of the night lamenting the destruction of the Temple. This ceremony is non-obligatory and generally recited only by especially pious people.

———

{92}

Words Studied from the Mouth of the Righteous
Gaon Reb Chaim Leib Myszkowski of Blessed Memory
Translated by Jerrold Landau

At the conclusion of the evening service on the eve of the Sabbath, it was silent in the Beis Midrash. The congregation was waiting for the rabbi to conclude his Shmoneh Esrei prayer [1]. Suddenly, someone came running into the Beis Midrash shouting: "Oh woe to what my eyes have seen, so and so the wagon driver has only just now returned from Lomza. This is public desecration of the Sabbath." [2]

Everyone waited for the words of the rabbi.

"Bring the wagon driver to the Beis Midrash", ordered the rabbi. In a few moments, the man was brought into the Beis Midrash. The wagon driver was a brave man, and many people had been scorched by the force of his arm, especially those who started up with him. However this time he walked with his head down toward the rabbi, embarrassed and humiliated.

"The rabbi ordered that I come, so I came", mumbled the wagon driver.

The man ascended to the rabbi's pulpit with the rabbi next to him. The wagon driver stood and confessed. His story was short. He had been waiting to receive his payment and did not realize that the hour was late and the sun was setting. "What could I do rabbi?", he asked, "Should I have remained in the forest during the Sabbath? Therefore I was a little late, for it is the Sabbath today."

However this late arrival was not his first. He was not careful to arrive at home on time on other Sabbaths as well.

The verdict of the rabbi was given on the spot. The rabbi commanded him to remain near the pulpit throughout the entire Sabbath. He was forbidden to move from his place, even to go to another part of the synagogue. He ate his Sabbath evening meal on the pulpit. Furthermore, he was required to remain on the pulpit in his weekday clothes that he had worn on the journey for the entire Sabbath night and Sabbath day. We children walked around the pulpit and chided him. We paid him back for all the fear he instilled in us at all times.

The Beis Midrash was full of people at all hours of the day. Apparently, people came from other houses of prayer to look at the "prisoner".

Only at the conclusion of the Sabbath was the wagon driver freed from his "prison" and allowed to return home.

This incident was the talk of the town. The "imprisonment" of the wagon driver who had desecrated the Sabbath instilled fear in all of those who treated the Sabbath lightly.

This vision from my youth accompanies me all the days of my life.

(Told by Moshe Zeev Goelman of blessed memory, and brought to print by his brother Elazar.)

The Incident with the "Pakentreger"
[3]

"Pakentreger" was a nickname for the merchant who carried on his shoulders holy objects for sale. These object included Mezuzahs, tzitzit, prayer books, tefillin, etc. [4]

He would set up his station with his merchandise in the synagogue, on a table near the oven on the western side, near the door. Those who entered the synagogue would purchase their required holy objects from him.

;The rabbi of the city approached his station and his eyes fell upon a bundle of secular books, which were regarded in that generation as books of heresy. The rabbi, who was known for his sharpness, never hesitated to fulfill the adage "excise the evil from amongst yourselves" [5]. He picked up the bundle of books and tossed them into the burning oven.

The owner of the stand complained: "My master the rabbi not only caused me a loss of three rubles, but has also spoiled my livelihood. Do I make enough money to purchase food for my family from the coins I earn from selling Mezuzahs or bundles of tzitzit? It is these books that are the main source of my livelihood.

The rabbi answered him in a whisper: "I will pay you from my own money for the burning books, but with regards to earning your livelihood – a person is not permitted to earn a livelihood from heretical books, and must search out another source of livelihood. If he cannot make a livelihood from this business, he is required to search out another position, and I, the rabbi, promise my help in this." When the merchant heard from the rabbi that he himself will help him attain a position that would earn him an honorable livelihood, he thanked him for his kindness, and decided that the next day, after the prayers, he would remind the rabbi about his promise.

The next day, immediately following the morning prayers, the merchant approached the rabbi at a time when he was engaged in a discussion with the Shamash (sexton) of the synagogue, and reminded him of his promise. The rabbi answered him that he has already started with this matter, and he told the Shamash to invite the priest to his house, for he has an important matter to discuss with him. He told the merchant that shortly, with his help, he would attain a fitting position.

"How", asked the merchant, "How can I be helped by the priest?".

The rabbi answered: "It is simple. A week ago, when I met the priest on the street, he told me that the gentile whose job it was to ring the bell of the church every morning died. He told me that if I could think of anyone, I should do him a favor and refer him to that position, and that person would earn a fitting salary."

The merchant was startled and said the rabbi: "Does my master the rabbi really think that in my old age, I should become an assistant to the priest and an accomplice of idol worship?"

The rabbi answered him: "Think for yourself – you refuse to ring a bell to awaken the gentiles to go to their house of prayer, but you are comfortable in selling heretical books to Jewish youth, and thereby encouraging them to go out to a bad crowd"

An Incident with a Bundle of Books

They asked the Gaon Reb Chaim Leib what was a fitting punishment for the bookbinder who purposefully bound a book of Russian parables together with a copy of the Book of Genesis in one volume.

The Gaon answered: "You are asking me about a bound set of books but why do you not rather ask me what should be done with the Yeshiva students who occupy themselves with secular studies, and in their minds bind together the Russian parables with the laws of the Torah and Talmudic discussions in one volume?... There is hope for that book, it is possible to loosen the glue, however what is the remedy for those who have made such bindings in their mind?"

An Incident with a Preacher

Once a preacher who was not acceptable to the rabbi came to Stawiski. As was customary, the preacher went to visit the rabbi. During their conversation, the preacher attempted to explain to the rabbi, that in this day and age there is no other way to arouse the community than though his manner of preaching, for otherwise, the community would not be willing to listen at all.

The preacher ignored the advice of the rabbi, who hinted to him not to deliver his lecture, and intended to do so nevertheless. The rabbi at that time was ill, and he did not worship in the Beis Midrash during the weekdays. However, on that day, he summoned up his strength and came to the Beis Midrash for Mincha (the afternoon service). After the service, he took out a volume of Talmud and sat down in his place to study. It is superfluous to say that the preacher was not brazen enough to ascend the pulpit and deliver his lecture while the rabbi was busy with his studies.

(From "Peulat Tzadik" – "The Deeds of the Righteous" – about Rabbi Ch. A. Myszkowski)

Compiled by Elazar Goelman

———

{94}

The Funeral of the Rabbi of Blessed Memory
by A. A. Rakowski
Translated by Jerrold Landau

Printed in the "Hatzefira" newspaper on the 10th of Av, 5658 (July 29, 1898)

We have recently returned from the field of weeping. There we buried one of the great renowned people, one of the few choicest people. There we buried the glory and honor of this city, its splendor and brilliance, the rabbi and Gaon, the Tzadik, the foundation of the world, Rabbi Chaim Aryeh Leib of holy blessed memory Rotenberg-Myszkowski, who passed away on the Sabbath at the age of 72, after having served in this city for about twenty years, and serving as a judge for the Jewish people for about forty years of his life.

It is not only this sorrowful city that is like a widow since the ark of G-d has been removed from it, but all of the nearby towns and far off place that was lit up by his name, all of them are cloaked in gloom, all our gathered together in darkness and are making a bitter mourning, for the late rabbi of holy blessed memory was a voice from the heavenly hosts, like a prince of G-d, and an honor in the midst of the people. Rabbi Chaim Aryeh of blessed memory was one of the remaining ones who were called "one of the older generation of rabbis" who remained with us in this orphaned generation. Even more than he was great in Torah and wisdom, he was wonderful in his deeds and his holy demeanor and in all other character traits that our sages enumerated.

He did not take any benefit from this world even with his little finger. He toiled in the tents of Torah and satisfied himself with a measure of carobs [6].

He hated remuneration in the full sense of the term. He spoke the truth in his heart, and whenever there was a disgrace to the honor of the Torah he played no favoritism and did what had to be done with swiftness and alacrity. He was modest, and he did not respond the the requests of the larger cities that wanted to bestow honor upon him and put their crown upon his head. However, wherever he saw that the breakers of the faith were increasing, he was the first to fight the battles of G-d with bravery and dedicate his soul to the battle.

He was like the foundation stone from which the great Yeshiva of Lomza spread out, from where Torah went out to hundreds of the children of the poor. He accepted with love the arrows and shots which were fired at him by the teachers who take honor in the disgrace of the Torah. He did not allow his followers and those who revered him to return their disgrace. However we should not think that all the praise of the late Gaon of blessed memory is simply gossip, and we should not think that the couch is too short for the person [7]. From the eulogies for this great man, we can see the great love that was bestowed upon him by all of our brethren who knew even a little about his ways. From all the towns near and far: Lomza, Zambrow, Szczuczyn, Grajewo, Kolno, Augustow, and others, all the heads and notables gathered together, from all the factions, in order to lament and weep about the tragedy. I give testimony as an eyewitness that as I was coming from Lomza to Stawiski, I met caravans of pedestrians, Yeshiva students and other people who honored and revered him, coming as evening was falling and in the midst of a heavy rainstorm, coming by foot to pay the final respects to the late rabbi of blessed memory who was to them like a holy man of G-d.

Thousands of people followed after his coffin. There was never such a large crowd as this in the town from the time of its founding. Rivers of tears were shed as the rabbis and Gaonim of Nowogrod, Kolno, Szczuczyn, Grajewo, Wasosz, etc. eulogized him in a fitting. Aside from these rabbis and Gaonim, The Gaon Rabbi Gavriel Mocz of Warsaw was also present. A telegram arrived from the Gaon Rabbi Eliahu Chaim Meisel, the head of the rabbinic court of the holy community of Lodz giving notice that he would come, but that they should not wait to greet him on account of the honor of the deceased [8].

The rabbis and Gaonim did their good deeds to the dead and the living, and they made sure that the widow and son of the rabbi of holy blessed memory, who were left without livelihood, would not go hungry. The community accepted and fulfilled everything that was decreed upon them. May G-d have mercy on his soul [9] and comfort all of his mourners, including myself, for I honored him during his life and I honor him after his death.

Translator's Footnotes :

1. The Shmoneh Esrei (literally 'eighteen', referring to eighteen benedictions), is the central part of all prayer services. It actually consists of nineteen benedictions on weekdays, as an extra benediction was added in the first century C.E. On Sabbaths and festivals, it consists of seven benedictions, however it retains the name 'Shmoneh Esrei'. It is also referred to as the 'Amida' (i.e. 'standing' – standing prayer).

2. This is presumably Hershel, the wagon driver of pages 272-273.

3. Literally "package dragger".

4. A Mezuzah is a box containing a scroll with sections of the Torah written on it that is to be posted on each door of a home. Tzitzit (literally fringes), refers to the fringes that are attached to the tallis (prayer shawl) or the tallis katan (four cornered undergarment). Tefillin are the phylacteries, black boxes containing parchment scrolls with sections of the Torah inscribed upon them. Tefillin are worn during weekday morning services.

5. A verse from Deuteronomy referring to the commandment to uproot idolatry, but here referring to uprooting anything evil.

6. A reference to the talmudic sage Shimon Bar Yochai who, according to legend, sustained himself on carobs for thirteen years as he hid in a cave from the Romans.

7. A expression meaning that the descriptions of the person are exaggerated.

8. It is considered an honor to the dead to conduct the burial as soon as possible.

9. Literally, his 'dust', but this idiom is not used in English.

———

{95}

Rabbi Avraham Stawisker and Peretz's Three Gifts
by Yeshayahu Berger, New York
Translated by Jerrold Landau

Our fellow native Betzalel Zwieback of California forwarded us a letter that he received from Mr. George Aronson of Brooklyn in which he makes note that the first gift of Peretz's famous story "Three Gifts" is bound up with Avraham Stawisker.

We bring here, with minor editing, the work of Yeshayahu Berger of New York regarding the above-mentioned topic, which was published in "The Golden Chain" number 56, 1966.

The Editor

– – – Menashe Ungar earlier pointed out the historical sources of the second and third gift. – – – Now the question is regarding the first gift. I am now prepared, perforce, to accept that Peretz' idea came from a small 40-page book that came into my hands a few years ago. This book contains eulogies of famous rabbis, and was printed about 100 years ago. After a few words, my eyes lit up, for I found the long sought source of the first gift.

In order to appropriately bring down the similarity between the source and the poem, we must cite the highlights of Peretz' creation in his own words:

"Robbers fell upon a wealthy man, robbers with masks over their faces. One holds a burning torch in his hands for light; a second the second holds a gleaming knife to the man's breast and looks him over: If you move, Jew, it will be your end! The tip of the knife moves around, and points to the other side! The Jew stands near the knife and looks casually at.... He looks around completely peacefully, as they open the last drawer of the last dresser and takes out sacks of gold and silver, sacks with jewelry and sundry utensils, and he is silent... And perhaps he has given up completely! But suddenly, as the thieves find the last hiding place and take out a sack, the last hidden object – he forgets himself, trembles, and with flaming eyes raises his right hand, as he shouts out: Don't move!

From the source of the shout, a red stream of smoky blood streams out – the knife did its work... This is the blood from the heart and it is spraying on the sack – this was the best, the most precious! They made a bitter mistake: the blood flowed for naught. There was no silver, no gold, and no jewelry in the sack; there was nothing that had any value in this world! There was a little bit of earth, earth from the Land of Israel to put in the grave, and this is what the rich man wished to save from foreign hands and eyes, even with at the cost of his own blood." [1]

And now I return to the little book. Its name is "Arrows", "Its arrows are arrows of fire, ignited by the lessons of the ark of G-d, the Gaon of our strength and the crown of our head, the righteous Gaon Rabbi Akiva Eiger, the head of the rabbinical court and head of the Yeshiva (the rabbi of the entire exile, our master and rabbi) of Poznan. The last one honors the Tzadik and modest man, the scholar of Israel and its Holy One, our Rabbi Eliahu, the head of the rabbinical court of Kalisz. My eyes, my eyes shed tears, etc. I am the man who is the author of this memorial book, Avraham of Stawiski."

At the end of the book, the place of printing is listed as Koenigsberg. There is no date, but Friedberg in his book "The Book Library" lists it for the year 5612 (1852).

The parable is brought down on pages 5-6, and reads as follows: "The author states that in the days of my youth I heard a powerful parable from the famous rabbi and preacher of Vilna, the late Tzadik Rabbi Kurser. He presents a parable about the final end of mortals who perish in their poverty, of thieves of the night who wander far off from their native city for many years. When they again return to their city, they recall that they left behind a noble man, a ruler and a very rich man, and they did not realize that he had already turned back ten degrees, that he is among those who go out to sea in great poverty (a play on Psalms 107, 23, "Those who go down to the sea in ships"). They decided together to murder that wealthy man, and that they would each receive one sack of goods. They remembered that this man had one office in which he had his treasury of all good things and precious stones. They decided to execute their plan specifically in that store. The evil people destroyed it down to its foundations and searched through it in the dark, but they found nothing (for he had already lost his belongings). They decided amongst themselves to search in the highest place in the room. They found one small sack bound up with a seal on the side. These men rejoiced, saying that it was certainly full of pearls and precious stones, and that they had in their hands the choicest of belongings of the owner. Due to their great fear that they would be pursued and caught, they fled all night, and escaped with all of their might. When they sat down in a certain forest to rest, an argument broke out among them. One said that half should belong to him alone, for if he had not sensed the value of the treasure by feeling it with his hand, they would have all withdrawn from it. The other said the same, and the first retorted. They began to hit each other until blood flowed. However when they sat down again to divide the treasure and opened the sack, they *found it full of earth, for they did not realize that this was all that the ruler had left from all of his valuables was the earth that he had prepared for himself for when he died, so it can be used for his burial,* for only this alone he would be able to take with him of all his belongings at his death. The object of the parable is self evident, regarding being caught up in the affairs of this world and its vanities, etc."

Here we have the first gift in its chief traits, and we can see it from its literary standpoint. It is in a clumsy Hebrew, with a few Yiddishisms. Peretz accentuates the dedication of the wealthy man, who does not stir at all when his gold and silver is taken. He only wants to save that which is most precious to him, the little bit of earth from the Land of Israel.

In the work "Arrows", the story demonstrates the foolish sacrifice for the vanities of this world, which will end up in a bit of earth…

Who is this "well known preacher from Vilna" Reb Moshe Kurser, whose power of imagination was able to build upon such wonderful material from Peretz' "Three Gifts"? I was unable to find his name in our Jewish encyclopedias and biographical lexicons. As well, in Rabbi Shimon Yaakov Halevi Glicksberg's "Homilies of Israel" (Tel Aviv, 5700, 1940) there is no mention of him at all. As well, I do not see him in Rabbi Sh. Y. Fine's "Faithful City" (Kirya Neemana) and in Hillel Noach Magid Steinschneider's "The City of Vilna" (Ir Vilna).

In any case, Reb Avraham Stawisker heard this parable from Reb Moshe Kurser in his youth. When he brings down the parable, he already refers to Reb Moshe Kurser as "The honorable late Tzadik". Since this small book was published around 1852, apparently the Vilna preacher would have used the parable in a sermon many years previously. The fact that the book "Arrows" is the first literary source of this parable is evident before the eyes. Since Reb Avraham Stawisker is proficient in the homiletic literature and in the words of the sages, this parable is certainly not a well-known story from known sources. A preacher such as Reb Avraham would have certainly known about it. Therefore, we can surmise that Reb Moshe Kurser is indeed the one who invented the parable, and Reb Avraham identifies him as the source from who heard this parable orally – "I heard a powerful parable from the famous rabbi and preacher of Vilna, the late Tzadik Moshe Kurser".

Did Peretz indeed see this parable in "Arrows"? It is entirely possible. Peretz searched and rummaged everywhere for material for his creations. He looked in books of ethics, storybooks, and indeed possibly in books of homiletics, especially in a book that was bound up with such a great halachist as Rabbi Akiva Eiger. Rabbi Avraham Stawisker, the author of "Arrows", traveled around to raise funds for his great book "Avnei Zikaron" (Memorial Stones) on halacha, and thereby befriended the rabbi and shochet of Luck, Rabbi Eliezer Lipman Zilberman, who indeed helped Reb Avraham publish the booklet "Arrows". He also included a dirge "Haga Vahi" (A Moan and Lament) for Reb Zalman Titkin, the rabbi of Breslau (Wroclaw). It is also possible to surmise that Reb Avraham left a number of copies with Rabbi E. L. Zilberman, and some of them might have ended up in the hands of various maskilim, writers of the newspapers, and others, and thereby "Arrows" may have moved throughout the years from one Maskil's house to another, and also to booksellers who dealt with Haskalah books. That is how it would have reached Peretz, despite the fact that he most probably read very few books of homiletics. The parable was possibly also brought down in other books, or was used by later preachers, and Peretz might have heard it once.

It is interesting that the year in which "Arrows" appeared, 1852 (according to what is brought down by Friedberg), was also the year in which Peretz was born.

Other bibliographers would advance the research into Peretz if they would be able to identify who were Reb Moshe Kurser and Reb Avraham Stawisker.

*

In the same letter from Mrs. George Aronson to Mr. Zwieback, Mr. Aronson also includes the following fact:

"A Jew by the name of Aharon Zvi Friedman (possibly a rabbi) lived in New York, not in your times, for it was in the year 1850. That Jew published a book on shechita (ritual slaughter), one of the first books [2]in America. That book was translated into English, German, and French. That Jew was from Stawiski (The History of the Jews in America, F. Wiernick, page 426.)"

Translator's Footnotes :

1. It is a custom to include some earth from the Land of Israel in a coffin of Jewish person.

2. Obviously meaning: one of the first Jewish religious books.

{99}

The Gaon Rabbi Binyamin Eliahu Remigolski of Blessed Memory
Introduction to the Halachic book (book on Jewish law) "Hadrat Binyamin" [1]
by Rabbi Binyamin Eliahu Remigolski of holy blessed memory
Translated by Jerrold Landau

Rabbi Remigolski

We are still downtrodden and brokenhearted due to the influence of the terrible loss that occurred in the taking from us and from our people of my father, the great Gaon, famous in all corners of the land, Rabbi Binyamin Eliahu Remigolski of holy blessed memory. Nevertheless, due to the magnitude of our duty and our desire to fulfill, without delay, the last wish of our father of holy blessed memory, we are hastening the publication of his many works that we possess as manuscripts.

The book "Hadrat Binyamin" is divided into two sections: Volume I, "Hadar Hamikdash" (The Splendor of the Temple) regarding the laws of Kodshim [2]; and Volume II "Hadar Hakodesh" (The Holy Splendor), consisting of discourses in a homiletic and didactic style. This book that we are now publishing is the first of sixty manuscripts that our father of holy blessed memory left us. They cover all areas of the Babylonian and Jerusalem Talmud, Midrash and Aggadah, early and later Halachic decisions, as well as responsa that he wrote in answer to queries that he received regarding the word of G-d, that is practical Halacha [3].

Approximately one year ago, our father the Gaon of holy blessed memory began to organize his novellae on the issues of Kodshim. These were the most precious to him. Until the day of his illness, he dedicated any free moment, during the day and the night, to organize this book, but he did not succeed in organizing all of the chapters of the book. His severe illness that overtook him suddenly on his way from Warsaw to Siemiatycze impeded him, and therefore we present the remaining chapters (the five final chapters of Hadar Hamikdash) as we find them in the manuscripts. The chapter regarding "The receiving of the blood of the guilt offering of the leper", which our father began to organize and did not complete, is published in both versions.

We also find it necessary to present a few sections on the origins and life of the author, the Gaon of holy blessed memory. Our father of holy blessed memory was born in the year 5631 (1871) in the city of Kedainai (Keidan) of Lithuania. He was a descendent of the great Gaon who was the author of "Knesset Yisrael". He excelled in his wonderful talents and his deep diligence already during his youth. When he was eleven years old, he already knew all of "Ein Yaakov" [4] by heart literally. He studied in Volozhin [5] when he was only 17 years old , and there he made a name for himself as one of the greatest scholars of the Yeshiva, and he became known as the "Genius of Riga" (his parents had left Kedainai and moved to Riga at that time). At that time, he already knew the entire Talmud with wonderful breadth and great depth. When he was about 20, he married our righteous mother, Fruma Rachel, may she live, the daughter of the well-to-do rabbi Reb Yehuda Leib Gordon of blessed memory of Baltermantz [6]. After he spent three years being supported by his father-in-law, while studying with strong diligence, he did not want to accept a rabbinic role at all.

Our mother tried her hand at business, and our father of holy blessed memory continued his holy work. He produced many novellae at that time, even before he was appointed as a rabbi. He received his rabbinical ordination when he was approximately 23 years old, From the Gaon Rabbi Shlomo of Vilna, who advised him to accept the mantle of the rabbinate. However our father chose to listen to the advice of his beloved, true friend, the Gaon and Tzadik Rabbi Moshe Daniszewski, the author of the work "Beer Moshe", and he went to learn in the Kolel of Rabbi Yitzchak Elchanan of blessed memory [7].

Rabbi Yitzchak Elchanan of blessed memory ordained him, and when he recognized his great worth in Torah and deeds, he influenced him to accept the mantle of the rabbinate. Aside from the greatness of his knowledge and his expertise in Torah, our father was also a man of character. He truly hated falsehood, and for all the days of his life, truth was his guiding light. When he was twelve years old, he took it upon himself never to utter any falsehood, and never to take an oath [8]. He never violated his commitment for all the days of his life. He was very modest, and he treated easy commandments with the same respect as difficult commandments. He would put on the Tefillin of Rabbeinu Tam discretely in his home every day [9], and nobody knew of this aside from his family. His love for his fellowman and his dedication to every Jew were boundless.

From the year 5669 (1909) he served in the rabbinate for more than 20 years in the communities of Troszyn, Stawiski, Griva, and finally in Siemiatycze. In all of those cities, he excelled in his dedication to his flock. In particular, he did a great deal of good for his community of Stawiski during the years of the difficult war. All the members of his community, young and old, were bound up with his soul due to his wisdom and kindness of heart. For example, the members of the Stawiski community did not let him leave when he received a request to serve as the rabbi of Bransk. The day that our father of holy blessed memory set out for Griva was a day of mourning in the entire city.

Even though he was constantly occupied with issues of the rabbinate, he excelled in his diligence in learning, and he occupied himself with Torah study during any free moment. He was also very wise in worldly matters, and his legal decisions regarding monetary matters became known even among the gentiles. In general, our father was, as many of the leaders of our generation have written, one of the prime Gaonim. He was a prime Gaon with regards to his wondrous breadth of knowledge of Talmud, both the Babylonian and Jerusalem versions, as well as the Mechilta, Sifra and Sifre [10]. No secret was hidden from him in any aspect of Torah, and he did not desist from learning until the day of his illness.

He excelled in his deep sharpness, to which more than sixty of his friends testified. He excelled also in the refinement of his heart, and in his love for his fellowman, both in the general and in the specific sense. Anyone who spoke with him from any stratum of the people, even well disposed gentiles, became his friends. He excelled also in his great and deep love for the Land of Israel. In many excellent sermons, he called out with fiery words to the Jewish people to concern themselves with their land and to fulfill their obligations toward the Land. Thus did this great Gaon toil with great enthusiasm for the benefit of Torah, teaching, love of his people, and love of his Holy Land. He toiled with eternal strength and lofty desire until he departed Heavenward on the holy Sabbath, the 25th of Sivan, of the current year 5690 (1930).

Written by the family of the Gaon who was the author of the book, of holy blessed memory. Siemiatycze, Av, 5690.

{101}
The Rabbi and Gaon Rabbi Reuven Kac of holy blessed memory
by Rabbi Zadok Hakohen
Translated by Jerrold Landau

Rabbi Kac

Our master, the Gaon Rabbi Reuven Kac of holy blessed memory, who was previously the rabbi of Stawiski and latter the chief rabbi, head of the rabbinical court, and Talmudic teacher in Petach Tikva [11], was one of the greatest rabbis of the previous generation. His methodology, his Halachic decisions, and his interpretations were based on the pillars of Torah, ethics, wisdom and knowledge.

He was one of the select group whose words had a recognizable influence upon the community, both within the Orthodox community and in the liberal community, including upon rabbis and the leaders of the people. His variegated personality, his extensive learning, his intuition and resoluteness along with the sharpness of his intellect all helped forge the image of the community of those that feared the word of G-d.

Whenever a difficult Halachic issue arose, when observant Jewry was caught up with problems and internal strife, or in strife between itself and the non-observant, they would turn to the rabbi of Petach Tikva to ask him to offer assistance, and solve the dilemma with his wisdom and understanding, so that he could present a clear, blessed solution.

He conducted his rabbinate with strength and rigor. Even during his old age, everyone would turn an ear to listen to the opinion of the "Rabbi from Petach Tikva" at rabbinical conventions and on the advisory council of the Chief Rabbinate of Israel.

He forged his path of life, not with storming and impetuousness, but rather through diligence, persistence, gradual development, and spiritual ascent step by step. His humble beginnings were upon the rabbinical seat of the small town of Sulevo, and his pinnacle was as one of the leaders of the previous generation.

His birthplace was the small town of Olshany in the Vilna region. There he was born on the first day of the New Moon [12] of Iyar 5640 (1870) to his father Rabbi Shimon of blessed memory, one of the local scholars who worked in business. It was already evident during his childhood that he was destined for greatness. When he was about eleven years old, he was already expert on the Tractates of Shabbat and Bava Kama [13], and was known as the Genius (Illui) of Olshany. His Bar Mitzvah speech, delivered when he was a student at the Yeshiva of Ivye, included didactics that astounded the local Torah scholars.

From Ivye he transferred to the Yeshiva of Mir, and when he was 15, he was accepted in the Yeshiva of the Chofetz Chaim of holy blessed memory in Radun [14]. After about one year, he went to the Yeshiva Knesset Yisrael of Slobodka, which was headed by Rabbi M. M. Epstein of holy blessed memory, and Rabbi Nosson Tzvi Finkel of holy blessed memory. In the year 5657-5658 (1887-1888) he was numbered among one of the initial fourteen students of the Yeshiva of Slutsk, founded by the Gaon Rabbi Isser Zalman of holy blessed memory [15].

In the year 5663 (1893) he moved to Vilna. There, the Gaon Rabbi Avraham Yitzchak Maskil Leeitan of holy blessed memory, the rabbi of Gicialaukia, chose him as the husband for his righteous daughter Reichel, may peace be upon her. She stood together with him as his partner in all of his activities until her last day upon the earth.

While living in his father-in-law's house, he became expert in practical Halacha, and was ordained by the leading rabbis of the generation. His first rabbinate was in the town of Sulevo in the Minsk region, and in the year 5669 (1899) he ascended the rabbinic seat of Amdur (Indura). He served as the rabbi of Amdur for fourteen years, and from there his net was spread out afar. As testimony of this was the request of him by the holy Gaon Rabbi Nosson Tzvi Finkel, who was known as the "Saba of Slobodka" [16] in the month of Adar of 5683 (1923) to our rabbi to go with him together with the head of the Yeshiva rabbi Moshe Mordechai Epstein of holy blessed memory on a special mission to the capital city of Petersburg in order to save the Yeshiva. According to words of the Saba, "the Yeshiva was floating between existence and disappearance, Heaven forbid". There was a special condition upon this mission, for the Saba pointed out: "it is obvious that we must specify that the matter must be a secret, and should not become known to any of the aforementioned people until after it is completed". There, he spent the years of the First World War with all of its tribulations: the Russian army police, the German occupation government, the transfer to Polish rule, and finally, the evil, cruel hand of the nationalistic Polish ruler. During these years of trouble, Rabbi Kac not only occupied himself with the discussions of Abaye and Rabba [17], but also with public activity. He protected the rights of the Jews with complete dedication with respect to the changing governments, and with the organization of self-defense. He saved thousands of Jewish souls from death. In the merit of his intercession, many difficult decrees were annulled, many people were saved, and many who had been accused were freed. He also did a great deal for the rehabilitation of refugees and those injured at war. He was the chairman of the local assistance bank, and the chairman of the "Joint" American aid committee in the Grodno region. During the time of transition from one government to another, when the hooligans increased in number and there were many attacks upon the Jews, he was strong enough to establish a unit of Jewish self defense, whose duty was the protection of the community. This organization assured the peace of the Jews of Amdur.

In the year 5682 (1922) he published his first book: "Questions and Answers Degel Reuven" [18], in which he demonstrated his expertise and sharpness in all areas of Halacha. He particularly displayed his ability to explain difficult and complex issues in a straightforward fashion. The book made an impression in the Torah world, and its publication was an important occurrence among the Yeshiva students, who saw the book as an aid to their studies. The publication of the book made a name for its author, and after a few months, he was invited to sit on the rabbinical seat in the city of Stawiski in the region of Lomza.

In Stawiski, he served as the rabbi of the city, taking the place of the Tzadik who was well known in his generation, the Gaon Rabbi Chaim Leib of holy blessed memory. He was known by all for his greatness, and all the residents recognized his greatness, on account of his deep knowledge, his righteousness, his boundless love of Torah, and especially his love of every human created in the image of G-d, in accordance with the trait of Aaron the priest the head of his family, who "loved peace, pursued peace, loved people, and brought them close to Torah" [19]. In every place that he lived, he established Yeshivas for the young and study groups in the synagogues to delve into the depths of Torah.

As in Amdur, in Stawiski as well he expended effort to strengthen the institutions of Torah and education, and to improve the economic situation of the city's Jews. Through his efforts, a "Kupat Malve and Gemilut Chasadim" organization was established in the city to grant loans to help sustain the craftsmen and small-scale merchants, who were becoming impoverished due to the burden of government taxes. He also made efforts to establish elementary Yeshivas in the neighboring towns. He was active in the Yeshiva committee that was founded by the Gaon Rabbi Chaim Ozer Grodzinski of Vilna [20].

In the year 5685 (1925), his second book was published. It was called "Dudaei Reuven" and dealt with homiletics and explanations on the books of Genesis and Exodus. This book was also accepted with esteem in the circles of rabbis and sermonizers.

During the period of his tenure in Stawiski, in the winter of 5689 (1928-1929), he was requested by the elder of the Gaonim of the generation, the author of the Chofetz Chaim, to embark on a mission to the United States in order to save the Yeshivas of Poland, in particular the Chofetz Chaim Yeshiva. The following letter, which was written by the holy hand of the Chofetz Chaim, is testimony to this.

"Blessed is G-d, the 9th of Cheshvan, 5689

To My friends the Gaonim and rabbis may you live long, and to the generous donors who love and respect Torah, the heads of the Jewish communities in America, may G-d be with you, and may you live.

I am hereby turning to you with a request for support for my holy Yeshiva, which currently, to my distress, finds itself in a situation of terrible pressure, burdened by deep debts that endanger it existence, G-d forbid. I have requested of my friend, the well-known rabbi and Gaon Rabbi Reuven Kac, may he live long, the head of the rabbinical court of the city of Stawiski, the author of the book Degel Reuven, that he take upon himself the great difficulty of travel to your country, in order to inspire the generous people of our nation to save the Yeshiva from its difficult situation, so that it can be set on its proper footing with the help of the Blessed G-d. I am requesting that you honorable people come to the assistance of the aforementioned Gaon in his holy work on behalf of he existence of the Yeshiva that has been spreading Torah for more than fifty years, for which I have toiled a great deal to ensure its existence, and in which more than three thousand young men, experts in

Torah and the fear of Heaven study at the present time. The merit of the great Mitzvah (commandment) of strengthening our holy Torah shall stand with all those who assist and offer support, and may G-d bestow upon you much blessing and success in all of your affairs, to them and to all that bless and honor them.

Yisrael Meir Hakohen, the author of the Chofetz Chaim and Mishnah Berura, from the city of Radun."

אישור נסיעת הרב כ"ץ לאמריקה

The permit of travel of Rabbi Kac to America. (Note by translator: In Hebrew script, and not clear.)}

The communal leaders of Stawiski took pride in the request of the leading rabbi of the generation, and authorized their rabbi, Rabbi Reuven Kac, to take a one-year leave, from November 1, 1928 until November 1, 1929. During the period of his absence, his son Rabbi Shimon was appointed to fill his place.

His mission to the United States was crowned with success. While he was winning over souls to strengthen Torah in Poland, he received an invitation from the Jewish community of Bayonne, New Jersey, to sit on their rabbinical seat. Rabbi Reuven Katz [21] accepted their invitation and received the position. In the United States, he very quickly found an honorable place among the rabbis of the country. He was active in the rabbinical union, and did a great deal to raise the stature of Judaism. A short time after his arrival, during the annual rabbinical convention held in Iyar 5691 (1931), he was chosen as vice president of the Rabbinical Union.

After the tribulations of 5699 (1938-1939) [22], he said the following during a eulogy to the victims of the cruel murder: "If it is indeed His will to grant the enemies of our soul a complete and eternal response, and also to avenge the spilled blood of our holy martyrs, it is our duty to arise and make aliya to our Holy Land, which has now received an additional dose of holiness by virtue of the blood of our martyrs. We must have mercy upon its soil, support those that have fallen during the course of its conquest, and stand at the right hand of its sons and builders."

He was not only a good speaker, but he acted upon his words. When he received in 5692 (1932) a request to serve as rabbi in one of the most important settlements in the Land of Israel, Petach Tikva, he left the United States and made aliya to the Land of his desire and his childhood dreams. Many of his friends attempted to dissuade him from this, however his wife, Rebbetzin Reichel, who was famous for her intelligence and common sense, stood at his right side and insured the decision.

Rabbi Reuven Katz, who served as the head of the rabbinical court of Petach Tikva, was one of the judges upon whose crown was inscribed three great qualities that are fitting for a judge: men of valor, fearers of Heaven, and haters of reward [23].

New vistas of activity opened up for him in the Land of Israel in all areas of communal life, the rabbinate and the spreading of Torah. Technically, he served as the head of the rabbinical court and chief rabbi of Petach Tikva and the area; however in actuality he did much more than this. A short time after his arrival in the Land, during the days that the mighty Gaon Rabbi Avraham Yitzchak Hakohen Kook of holy blessed memory served as the chief rabbi, the rabbinate of our rabbi already broke forth from the bounds of Petach Tikva, and shone upon all areas of the Land. He became one of the pillars of the chief rabbinate and Orthodox Jewry in the Land. He was a citadel of teaching and Halacha. Rabbis and Torah giants streamed to him from all across the Land.

אישור נסיעת הרב כ"ץ לאמריקה מטעם ועד קהילת סטביסק

המכתב של ה"חפץ חיים"

Top: The permit of travel of Rabbi Kac to America, issued by the communal council of Stawiski: (Note by translator: Also in Hebrew script – this appears to be a continuation of the permit on the previous page, and concludes with several signatures of members of the communal council. Not all are clear, but I can partially make out the following, without attesting to accuracy: Chaim Bolinski, Sh. Smaul – chairman of the communal council, Meir Lim, ?, Sh. Szapira – secretary).

Bottom: The letter of the Chofetz Chaim. (Translator's note: the text of which is included in full in the text above.)

Rebbetzin Reichel (Rachel) Kac of blessed memory.

His influence was great not only in his city and in the region, but in all spiritual and public matters in the country. He participated in all meetings to strengthen the situation. He was always chosen as a member of various delegations to speak to the ministers of the State of Israel regarding matters of Yeshivas and the strengthening of religion.

He was one of the founders of the committee for Yeshivas in the Land of Israel, and he served as a member of the managing committee of that organization. During his old age, when he became weak, the chief rabbis along with all members of the rabbinate would come to his house to conduct meetings of the chief rabbinate.

He disseminated Torah to his students during all his years, particularly in the Yeshivas of Petach Tikva. One of his prime students described him as follows: ".. In particular when he appeared before us in the hall of the Yeshiva to deliver his regular class in Halacha, when word spread that the rabbi was arriving to deliver the class, the atmosphere became electric. A deep feeling of sublimity, awe and honor enveloped all of the students of the Yeshiva, young and old together. We regarded the Rosh Yeshiva (Head of the Yeshiva) as a man of stature, as is befitting in the world of Yeshivas."

His multifaceted work in the rabbinate did not detract one drop from his dedication to his Yeshiva, the large Yeshiva, in which he saw the crowning role of his life, whether in the spiritual realm, in raising the level and character of his students, or in the physical realm in ensuring the existence of the Yeshiva, and in the meeting of the needs of the students. Indeed, the Yeshiva of Petach Tikva was not only the prime Yeshiva in the "mother of settlements" [24], but it was also the "mother of Yeshivas" throughout the modern settlements of Israel.

Our rabbi dedicated a great deal of time and effort to the issues of the religious education of elementary students. Already in the year 5693 (1933), one year after he arrived in the Land, a large meeting of all of the great rabbis and Rosh Yeshivas of the Land took place in Petach Tikva through his efforts. The deliberations focussed on the subject of religious education. At that meeting, a network of all of the Talmud Torahs throughout the land was established, which flourished as time went on and served as the basis for independent education [25]. He served as the chairman.

In the year 5700 (1940), he published the second volume of his book Degel Reuven. This volume contained several answers regarding practical Halachic issues of laws that relate to the Land, such as: the applications of orla, leket, shichecha, and peah in modern times [26]. In the year 5709 (1949) he published the third volume of this work, in which he elaborated upon various Halachic discussions with the Jerusalem Gaonim Rabbi Tzvi Pesach Frank, the rabbi of Jerusalem, Rabbi Yaakov Moshe Charlap the head of the Merkaz Harav Yeshiva, and other leaders of the generation. One responsa was regarding the issues of aguna [27] , was from the Gaon Rabbi Shlomo David Kahana of blessed memory, who was originally the rabbi of Warsaw, and served in glory in the old city of Jerusalem towards the end of his life. Rabbi Kahana asked about his opinion regarding women who became "agunas" during the years of Nazi murder. His fundamental understanding of issues surrounding this difficult problem astounded even the expert Halachic decisors who attempted to deal with it. This volume of Degel Reuven won the Rabbi Kook prize from the municipality of Tel Aviv, and has already been published in three editions.

In the year 5714 (1954) he published the second volume of his book Dudaei Reuven, with explanations and sermons on Leviticus, Numbers, and Deuteronomy. He appended the small work "Ohel Rachel" to this volume, which contained words of eulogy and appreciation for his wife the Rebbetzin Reichel, may peace be upon her, who died on the 20th of Shvat 5714.

With the establishment of the state, his duties increased as did his responsibility for dealing with difficult, thorny issues that had not been present prior to the establishment of the state. In particular, after the passing of the chief rabbi Gaon Rabbi Y. A. Herzog and the Jerusalem Gaon Rabbi Tzvi Pesach Frank, duties of Halachic decisions fell upon him. Our rabbi recognized his great responsibility to Heaven and also to the people in whose midst he dwelt. He would delve into the depths of the law in order to find reasons for leniency. This was not always possible, however whenever he found reasons for leniency, he rejoiced greatly that he was able to repair the bridge that connected the Land of Israel to the People of Israel through the Torah of Israel.

With his passing, honor departed from Israel.

Our rabbi and Gaon of holy blessed memory left behind the children: Rabbi Shimon Katz, who dealt with matters of agunas within his leadership duties in the rabbinic court system of Israel; Professor Dr. Avraham Yitzchak Katz, the president of Dropsie College in Philadelphia, U.S.A.; Rabbi Aharon Katz, a member of the regional religious court of Jerusalem; Nissan Katz, a manufacturer in the United States; Rabbi Eliezer Katz, the chief rabbi of Clifton, U.S.A.; Rabbi Yechiel Michael Katz, one of the heads of Yeshiva University in New York; Dina Harkavi, the wife of the writer Tzvi Harkavi; and Chasida Sorotzkin, the widow of Rabbi Yisrael Sorotzkin of blessed memory, who was a member of the regional religious court of Tel Aviv.

{109}

The Gaon Rabbi Nachman Shmuel Wasserman of Blessed Memory
by Yeshaya Wasserman
Translated by Jerrold Landau

My father of blessed memory was born in the year 5647-1887 in the town of Nobla in the region of Pinsk. This was a small town that was surrounded by bogs and ponds, with few neighboring settlements due to the difficulty of communication, which took place for the most part by boats on the pond.

The Jewish residents of Nobla were almost all poor – they were craftsmen and fishermen. When my father reached the age of Bar Mitzvah and there was no teacher in Nobla to teach him, his father, the shochet Reb Yaakov of blessed memory, sent him to one of the Yeshivas that was far from home. When he was seventeen years old, he was accepted into the Yeshiva of the Gaon Rabbi Baruch Dov Leibowitz of holy blessed memory in the town of Haluski[28]. His rabbi admired him greatly on account of his deep understanding, quick grasp, and pleasant mannerisms. He joined him up as a study partner with his expert student the Gaon Rabbi Shlomo Heiman of blessed memory, who later became a teacher in the Yeshiva of Baranovitch, along with the Gaon Reb Elchanan Wasserman of holy blessed memory, and then later became the Rosh Yeshiva of the Torah Vadaas Yeshiva of New York. Throughout his life, my father maintained his admiration for his rabbi, and the rabbi maintained his admiration for his student. I remember that when I went to study in the Yeshiva of Kamenets, which was headed by the aforementioned Gaon, and I mentioned the name of my father to him, his face lit up, he asked about his wellbeing, and he rejoiced greatly that the son of his beloved student was numbered among his students. Once when Rabbi Shlomo Heiman came to Bialystok during a time of a financial crisis in order to collect money for the Yeshiva, he asked my father, whom at that time was already a rabbi in Stawiski, to assist him. My father of blessed memory did not hesitate for a moment, he left his family and rabbinate for two weeks, traveled to Bialystok and dedicated all of his energy and efforts to the task that was placed upon him by his rabbi.

From Haluski, my father went to the famous yeshiva of Volozhin, which was at that time in its prime. There he was ordained into the rabbinate by the Rosh Yeshiva, the Gaon Rabbi Rafael of Volozhin of holy blessed memory. After a few years, he married the daughter of a respected, learned householder from the town of Korelicze (Karelitz), that is near Novaradok [29]. His father-in-law owned a textile store, and was considered a well-to-do man. His daughter, my mother of blessed memory, was the youngest of his six daughters, all of whom married scholars. She helped him in his store. He agreed that after the wedding, my mother could remain in her parents' home and continue to help in the store, while her husband can continue to occupy himself with Torah for a few years. After the wedding, my father went to the Yeshiva of nearby Novaradok, where he studied for two years under the Gaon Reb Yozel Horowitz of holy blessed memory – the Saba of Novaradok. He would go home only for the Sabbaths. These two years in proximity to the Saba were decisive in the life of my father, for under the influence of Reb Yozel, he strengthened in him self the trait of not recoiling from anything, and not fearing any person when he was defending something that he felt was right. Indeed, there were many incidents during his public life when he stood alone against many, knowing that the right was with him. He also learned the trait of faith from him, a trait which was his guiding light during the most difficult of circumstances.

Rabbi Wasserman

After the First World War, my father and his family settled in Novaradok, where he opened up a textile store. My mother, who was familiar with this line of work from her youth, ran the store. This enabled father to set aside times for the study of Torah and also to occupy himself in communal affairs. He founded a religious elementary school and later a small yeshiva. At night, he taught Torah to the working youth. The great depression that affected Jewish business in Poland during the 1920s caused my parents to sell the business in order to pay their debts to the middlemen. They liquidated the business. Left penniless, he was forced, with no other option available, to accept a rabbinic post.

At first he served as a rabbi in the town of Lipnishki Valnin, which was near the Polish-Russian border, and was cut off from the other towns of the area. At night, a constant curfew was imposed upon the town, and anyone who was not a permanent resident had to obtain a special permit to enter into its precincts. The isolation affected him, and when his friend Rabbi Moshe Szeckes of holy blessed memory, who in the interim had been appointed as the rabbi of Lomza, advised him to accept the rabbinate of Stawiski, he accepted the advice with joy; for the rabbinate of Stawiski was considered honorable since the time that the Tzadik Rabbi Chaim Leib Myszkowski of holy blessed memory, who was famous in all of Poland, served there. It is superfluous to state that there was no shortage in candidates for this important rabbinate. However, after father went a few times and delivered lectures, the matter was discussed among the honorable people of the city, and he was unanimously accepted as the rabbi of that community.

The rabbinate of Stawiski imposed a burden upon my father, a burden that he did not know in Lipnishki Valnin. Even though all of the residents of those towns had difficulty in their livelihoods, only very few were in need of actual assistance. The situation was not the same in Stawiski. Here, aside from a number of well-to-do residents and numerous small scale merchants and craftsmen who earned restricted livelihoods but did not require help, there was a large stratum of poor people, who satisfied themselves with a measure of carobs [30] during the week, but require assistance from the public coffers to obtain provisions for the Sabbath. Those people would come to father, and he would give them tickets for challah and meat, and sometimes even a little bit of cash. The charitable fund was meager. The donations came mainly from the "Organization of Stawiski Émigrés" in America, and also from the local wealthy people. In particular, the expenditures of the fund were great on two occasions of the year: a) as Passover approached, and the list of those in need because of the upcoming festival was very long, father and a few of the important householders would go out to collect "Maos Chittin" [31]. Most of the city's residents would participate in this; and b) after Sukkot, as the winter approaches, and there was need to supply fuel for the poor – wood and peat (the farmers would dig up peat – tarf – form it into the shape of bricks and dry it during the summer. Since the price of peat was cheaper than that of wood, it would be used as fuel primarily by the poor.) At that time, father would again go out accompanied by several members of the community in order to collect donations to provide fuel. The role of the Stawiski natives in America was large for both of those campaigns.

When I met Mr. Yaakov Elfenbaum, the secretary of the "Organization of Stawiski Émigrés in New York" who worked with dedication on behalf of the needy of our town, he showed me the accounting that father had sent to him for the Maos Chitin and fuel campaigns, along with a list of people to whom the money was distributed.

Over and above the constant yoke of supporting the poor, the burden of loans to small-scale storekeepers and artisans, who often required assistance from the charitable fund, also fell upon the shoulders of father. Since there were few guarantors, out of fear that they would need to pay the loans of the borrowers, the borrowers would often turn to the rabbi of the city, who never refused to sign himself as a guarantor for the Jew. Indeed, on more than one occasion he paid a lender out of his own pocket for such overdue loans.

During the course of the years, there was only one physician in Stawiski. He was a Pole, who like the majority of his fellow Poles, did not have special affection towards Jews. In addition, he was not greatly expert in his field. It came to the point that, during a meeting of the householders of the town, they decided to bring a Jewish doctor to town. A committee was set, up, chaired by the rabbi, in order to bring a physician from Warsaw. As was intended, all of the Jewish ill moved over to the new doctor. One night, after midnight, a sound of tumult was heard from the house of the rabbi. Large rocks were thrown intentionally into the bedroom in order to injure the residents of the house. Only through a miracle was nobody hurt. We knew that the hand of the Polish doctor was involved in this incident, that he hired some hooligans to break to windowpanes of the rabbi's house. The police came the next day "conducted an inquiry" and recorded notes. Even though the police informed them that they suspect that the hand of the Polish doctor was involved in this matter, no investigation took place against him.

Anti-Semitic activities increased in Poland during the 1930s, and the atmosphere was drenched with hatred toward Jews. News reached the Jews that on the next market day, when all of the farmers gather in town, they were preparing to destroy Jewish businesses and homes.

Father traveled to the regional leader in Lomza, brought the matter up with him, and requested that he send police reinforcements for the day that was set for the troubles. He not only requested, but he also reminded him of his duty to concern himself with the welfare of all of the residents of the region, including the Jews. Indeed, the regional leader sent reinforcements for the local police, who stood at the entrances to the town on the market day. The appearance of the police dampened the enthusiasm of the farmers to become rich from the wealth of the Jews, and the market day passed in peace.

Father's judgements were famous not only in the city that he served, but also throughout the entire region. Even when the litigants were not satisfied with the judgement, they accepted it in good spirit, for everyone knew that the rabbi does not play favorites, and that his judgement is a judgement of truth. Not only the Jews came to be judged before him, but even a Pole who had a dispute with a Jew would often say: let us go to the "rabbin", and whatever he says will be. On occasion, people from other towns would turn to father and request that he join together with other rabbis in judgment in complex cases.

Father greeted everyone pleasantly. When a troubled person would come to ask advice of father or to pour out the bitterness of his heart before him, he would leave the house of the rabbi encouraged and in good spirits.

A teacher in a Yeshiva in France, whom I met in New York, once had a conversation with me about a meeting with my father of blessed memory. When he heard that I was the son of Rabbi Wasserman of Stawiski, he related the following story to me: "My parents lived in a town near Stawiski. I was fourteen years old and studied in Yeshiva. I had relatives in Stawiski, and I went to visit them. In the morning, I went to the Beis Midrash to pray. I did not know anyone, and I stood behind the bimah (synagogue lectern). I did not have the courage to approach the rabbi after the prayers. As I was about to leave the Beis Midrash, the rabbi approached me, and, with a smile on his face, extended his hand to greet me, and asked me my name. He seated me next to himself and chatted with me in a friendly manner for quite a while. I will never forget that pleasant encounter." Father used to particularly enjoy the companionship of Yeshiva students. I once had the opportunity to spend seven days in Grodno with him. Father spent all of his free time at the Yeshiva of the Gaon Rabbi Shimon Shkop of holy blessed memory, engaged in Talmudic and legal discussion with the students, and felt himself as one of them.

The Second World War broke out. The Germans invaded Poland, and whoever could, fled. The enemy airplanes flew over the heads of those who were fleeing and bombarded them. My family was among those that fled. We traveled in a wagon. An eyewitness related to me: Every time that an enemy airplane would fly overhead, the travelers would bend over in panic, and only my father would sit in his place calmly. He said: "Every bullet has an address, and it will never hit a place that was not preordained". This adage of the Saba of Novaradok was actualized by my father during his life.

When Poland was partitioned between the Germans and the Russians, and the Soviets entered Stawiski, my father returned with his family to the city. At first, the Soviets did not become involved with the religious life of the Jews. The rabbi remained at his post. They did confiscate his home, but they granted him permission to rent another, smaller dwelling. However, they imposed heavy taxes upon him, and it was only with great difficulty that he was able to provide a meager amount of bread for his family. Father continued to teach his class in Talmud at the Beis Midrash. A few months passed, and the route to Vilna opened up. Masses of people streamed to Vilna, including many of the rabbis of the region, since they knew what awaited them under Soviet rule. Rabbi Szeckes of blessed memory told me that he asked father to leave Stawiski and move to Vilna. However, father refused, saying: Particularly in a small town everyone needs a rabbi, and how can I abandon them at such a time of tribulation? He sent my younger, fourteen-year-old brother to Vilna. Only my sister remained. She did not wish to leave mother and father alone. The situation worsened. A rumor spread that they were about to deport the rabbi and his family to Siberia. The route to Vilna was already closed off, and father continued along as always. The Soviets began to show their true colors, and people began to keep away from the Beis Midrash. In the last letters that I received from him prior to the Soviet invasion of Russia, he wrote: "It is very good with us, we stand in line and receive bread, stand in line and receive a glass of milk, and we only have to rely upon our Father in Heaven."

One of the Stawiski survivors who was saved, Mr. Kiwajko, told me that even after the Nazi invasion of Stawiski, father continued to go to the Beis Midrash, where he sat alone all day studying from a book. One night, the Nazis closed the Beis Midrash from the outside, set it on fire, and did not allow the Jews to rescue father or the Torah scrolls. One hunchback (I remember that he came for judgements with Jews to my father of blessed memory) endangered his life, and removed father from a back window as the Beis Midrash was becoming engulfed in flames. He then shaved father's beard, dressed him up in gentile clothes, and brought him to Lomza. Father lived his final months in the Lomza ghetto after the destruction of Stawiski. In the Lomza ghetto, he comforted and encouraged the poor Jews, and was their leader until the final hour, when the Jews of Lomza, with father among them, were taken out to be slaughtered on the 26th of Tevet. May G-d avenge his blood.

————

{114}
The Gaon Rabbi Chizkiahu Yosef Myszkowski of holy blessed memory
by A. Y. G.
Translated by Jerrold Landau

Rabbi Chizkiahu Yosef Myszkowski of holy blessed memory, "the rabbi from Krynki" was a multi-faceted personality, great in Torah and wisdom, with wide horizons, full of kindness, a pleasant man, of great activity and great insight – and more than anything he was the valorous man of salvation during the years that we witnessed evil, the years of the Holocaust and thereafter, through which he earned his place in the eternal world and inherited an eternal name for himself.

Rabbi Myszkowski.}

He became renown in a positive sense during the interwar years in Poland. He had an honorable position among the rabbis of the country, and he served as the vice-chairman of the "Rabbinic Council", to which belonged the lions of Torah and the finest scholars, exemplary in character and action. He put a great deal of effort into supporting traditional education, as well as into the struggle against the ban of shechita (ritual slaughter) in Poland. From the home of his holy father Rabbi Chaim Leib of Stawiski and from the house of his father-in-law, the Gaon of Torah and Mussar (fine character) Rabbi Yitzchak Blazer – he went out armed with a sensitive internal spirit and the traits of grace and kindness, to serve in the rabbinate and in public service in the finest tradition of the shepherds of the Jewish people from generations past.

"Everyone who saves one Jewish soul is as if he sustains the entire world" [32] – and how many Jewish souls did Rabbi M. save, and how many worlds did he sustain during the Holocaust and after it! The height of his activity and personal greatness came during the days of anger and tempest. Rabbi M. was one of the sublime people who concerned himself with saving people at any price and under all conditions. The tidings of Job from the vale of murder encouraged him in his rescue work – and he answered the call with all the warmth of his heart and of his aching and flaming soul. He became like an active institution in his rescue efforts. He established a committee for refugees in Russia and breathed a life spirit into the "Rescue Committee". He became the address for the Jewish people for matters of public salvation. He did not rest and was not silent – as he said: "It is forbidden to be lazy in matters of rescue, for at every moment, the issue of saving a Jewish soul is at stake." Due to his great dedication to the matter, he did not desist from his work for even one hour, and did not delegate the technicalities to anyone else. He even wrote with his own hand the hundreds of addresses to send packages to the refugees of the sword and captivity.

The writer of these lines was an eyewitness to the fact. It was an hour well past midnight, and Rabbi Ch. Y. Myszkowski was leaning over pages of addresses – that included thousands of names of rabbis, scholars, and public officials – written in his own handwriting. With indescribable haste, he wrote out the hundreds of addresses – in order to provide food and provisions and greetings to those in the depths of Siberia. Due to his haste, the pen dropped from his hand several times. He put his hand near his weak, broken heart and a heavy sigh issued from his throat. However, he only stopped the work for a tiny moment, and then he immediately continued with even greater haste and strength. This situation was repeated, not for one day or two days – but for many long months without a break.

When the flood of blood in Europe ceased, Rabbi Myszkowski went to his brothers in the camp to see their suffering and comfort them. He hastened to their aid, organized rescue and aid activities, helped the survivors in the camps, and went to America to awaken hearts. He labored and toiled to save in particular the young children from the strangers, and return them to the midst of the Jewish people. With trembling from the depths of his soul, he asked his oldest daughter to leave her family and her children, and to make haste to assist him in taking care of the young children who were being saved from the claws of apostasy. He said to her: "There in your home, you are the mother to your children alone. Here, you will be the mother of many children who through the fury of the oppressor have been deprived of the bosom of a loving mother and the hand of a caressing father. What is preferable?"

From the blood and tear drenched annals of the darkest period of Jewish history, the name of Rabbi Chizkiahu Yosef Myszkowski will shine out as one of the giants of rescue in the generation, and his memory will not be lost from us.

From Hatzofeh, 6th Tishrei 5527 – September 20, 1966 [33], at the conclusion of twenty years from the passing of the Gaon Rabbi Chizkiahu Yosef Myszkowski, of holy blessed memory.

Translator's Footnotes:

1. Literally, "The Splendor of Binyamin".

2. Kodshim is the fifth of the six tractates of the Mishnah. Its literal meaning is "Holy Things". It deals with laws of the Temple and sacrifices. It also includes sections on the laws of kashruth.

3. There are two editions of the Talmud. The Babylonian Talmud is about 200 years later than the Jerusalem Talmud, and is considered more authoritative. It is the version commonly in use today. However, the Jerusalem Talmud covers more tractates (particularly those dealing with agricultural laws of Israel) not dealt with by the Babylonian Talmud. Midrash and Aggadah are works of legends and homiletics from the Mishnaic period. Halacha (literally "the path") refers to the corpus of Jewish law. Responsa literature is written answers to questions that are posed to a specific rabbi. Many great rabbis wrote down their questions and answers, and this forms the body of responsa literature. Novellae (referred to in the subsequent paragraph – known as 'chidushim' in Hebrew) refers to innovative works and applications of Talmud, Jewish law, etc.

4. An anthology of the Aggadaic sections of the Talmud.

5. Volozhin was one of the most famous Lithuanian Yeshivas of the time.

6. I could not definitively identify a town with this name. Using JewishGen's ShtetlSeeker with Daitch-Mokotoff matching, Baltkarcai in Lithuania is the closest match. Using the Daitch-Mokotoff matching on JGFF, an entry for Baltermansk can be found.

7. A Kolel is a post-graduate rabbinical school for advanced Talmudic study. Rabbi Yitzchak Elchanan refers to Rabbi Yitzchak Elchanan Spector of Kovno (incidentally, the rabbinical school of Yeshiva University in New York is also named after him – the Rabbi Isaac Elchanan Theological Seminary).

8. Although the Torah permits taking an oath under certain circumstances, it is considered virtuous to avoid such, due to the risk of taking the name of G-d in vain.

9. The tefillin are the phylacteries warn by Jewish men each weekday during the morning prayers. There are two types of tefillin, which vary slightly in structural detail. Most people use on the Rashi tefillin. However, especially pious people have the custom of putting on the Rabbeinu Tam tefillin in addition for a brief period toward the conclusion of the prayer service. By doing so at home, the rabbi was fulfilling the stringency in law by putting on both pairs, but not making a public show of his piety by doing it in public.

10.   Mechilta, Sifra and Sifre are Halachic exegetical works on the Torah dating from the time of the Mishnah. The Mechilta is on Exodus, the Sifra is on Leviticus, and the Sifre is on Numbers and Deuteronomy.

11.   A suburb of Tel Aviv.

12.   The New Moon (Rosh Chodesh), is the minor festival observed at the beginning of each Jewish month. If the preceding month is 29 days, Rosh Chodesh is observed for one day, on the 1st of the next month. If the preceding month is 30 days, Rosh Chodesh is observed for two days, on the 30th of the preceding month and the 1st of the next month. Thus, the first day of Rosh Chodesh Iyar is the 30th day of Nissan, the preceding month.

13.   The Talmudic tractate of Shabbat deals with the laws of the Sabbath. The Talmudic tractate of Bava Kama is one of several tractates dealing with jurisprudence, torts, and monetary laws.

14.   The Chofetz Chaim, Rabbi Yisrael Meir Kagan (1838-1933), was recognized as perhaps the greatest rabbi of that generation. His works are used extensively in Yeshivas to this day. The name "Chofetz Chaim" literally means "He who desires life", and is the title of his book on the laws of interpersonal relationships, for which he is particularly famous. His other famous work is called the Mishnah Berurah, a commentary on the section of the Code of Jewish Law dealing with issues relating to day to day life and the cycle of the year. Incidentally, in the story related below, where the Chofetz Chaim sent the rabbi to America on a fundraising mission, the Chofetz Chaim was already a nonagenarian.

15.   Isser Zalman is Rabbi Isser Zalman Meltzer, another of the leading rabbis of that generation. The Yeshivas of Mir, Slobodka, Slutzk, and Radun are among the greatest Lithuanian style Yeshivas of the time.

16.   The Hebrew term here is the Saba of Slobodka. In Yiddish, he is often known as the Alter of Slobodka. The term means "the venerable old sage of Slobodka".

17.   Abaye and Rabba are two Talmudic sages who often debated with each other. The meaning here is that the rabbi did not only involve himself with Talmudic study.

18.   A book of responsa. Degel Reuven is a biblical quote, based on the rabbi's name.

19.   A quote from the Mishnaic tractate Pirke Avot (Ethics of the Fathers). Kac (Katz) is a name that is frequent among the priestly cast of Cohanim (Cohens) of the Jewish people. It is an acronym for Kohen Tzedek (righteous Cohen) Moses' brother Aaron was the first Cohen.

20.   Rabbi Chaim Ozer Grodzinski is another one of the leading rabbis of the pre-war period.

21.   At this point in the narrative, I am changing the spelling of his name from the Polish to the American version.

22.   I suspect that this is referring specifically to Kristalnacht.

23.   These are the traits that Moses' father-in-law Jethro described in a judge, when he recommended the appointment of judges to Moses in the desert in the book of Exodus.

24.   A term for Petach Tikva, one of the earliest areas of Jewish settlement (aside from the ancient cities) in the Land of Israel.

25.   "Chinuch Atzmai" (literally: independent education) is a network of independent religious schools in Israel, with a more intensive religious curriculum that the public religious Zionist school network "Mamlachti Dati" in Israel. Israel has two public school systems, a secular and religious Zionist network. Chinuch Atzmai is a third stream, not under direct supervision of the state.

26.   These are four areas of Jewish agricultural law that only apply in the Land of Israel. Orla is the prohibition of eating fruit of the first three years of a tree's life; leket is the law that mandates that one or two dropped sheaves from a harvest must be left for the poor (see the book of Ruth for a graphic illustration of leket); shichecha is the law that mandates that sheaves that were forgotten from the harvest be left for the poor; peah is the law that mandates that the corner of a field be left unharvested for the poor.

27.   The law of the "bound woman", which prohibits a woman from remarrying without definitive proof of the death of a husband. This was a common issue in the years following the war, when people often had no

definitive proof of the death of their spouse. Nowadays, it primarily refers to the issue of a woman who is "bound" in a marriage by a husband who refuses to grant a religious divorce (get).

28.   Haluski may be Glusk, Belarus (with the interchange of the G and H).

29.   Novaradok (officially Novogrudek, but known in traditional Jewish circles as Novaradok or Novharudok) is the home of one of the famous Lithuanian style Yeshivas. The Yeshiva of Novaradok stressed the lowliness of man, as opposed to the Yeshiva of Slobodka, which stressed the greatness of man. Like Slobodka, Novaradok had a 'Saba' or 'Alter' (see note 15). Both yeshivas followed along the path of the mussar (ethics) movement founded by Rabbi Yisrael of Salant.

30.   A reference to the Talmud of someone who satisfies themselves with very little food due to poverty.

31.   Literally "Money for wheat (i.e. for matzos)". This is a term for charity collected for poor people prior to Passover in order to enable them to purchase the needs of the holiday.

32.   A quote from the Mishnaic tractate of Sanhedrin.

33.   The date given here is 20.5.66, which is obviously incorrect from the Hebrew date. The date corresponds to 20.9.66. I suspect it is a typographical error.

{116}
My father-in-law Rabbi Shabtai Zeev Frydman of blessed memory
Translated by Jerrold Landau

Famous rabbis, who were people of stature and great in Torah and teaching, occupied the rabbinical seat of Stawiski, and in their merit, Stawiski became known as an important Jewish city.

During my youth, when I studied in the Beis Midrash in Stawiski, I heard a great deal about these Torah luminaries, their righteousness and generous characters. One of them was Reb Chaim Leib Stawisker, who was numbered among the greats of the previous generation. At that time, I also heard that the lion of the sages of our generation, the Chofetz Chaim [1], came to Stawiski as a young man, and studied Torah in a discrete fashion in the Beis Midrash of our city, in order to cleave to the dust of the feet [2]of Reb Chaim Leib of holy blessed memory, and to hear Torah from his mouth.

My mother of blessed memory told me a great deal about him. She would frequent his house, for during his time, her uncle Reb Yisrael Yaakov served as a rabbinical judge and teacher of righteousness in Stawiski. She would also recall my uncle with great reverence. He was known as a rabbi, halachic decisor, a sharp expert, as a unique individual – not only as an expert in Jewish law, but also as a person with a refined soul, who possessed fine character traits, was pleasant with his fellow man, modest, and fled from honor.

Everything that I know about Rabbi Chaim Leib Stawisker is from information and stories that have come my way. Nevertheless, I did know his son, who was great in his own right, Rabbi Ch. Y. Myszkowski of holy blessed memory. I remember him from my youth, when I studied in the Yeshiva of Lomza, and he was serving as a rabbi in Krynki at the time.

Already prior to the Second World War, Rabbi Myszkowski was renowned as one of the pillars of Torah Jewry in Poland, and as the right hand man of Rabbi Chaim Ozer Grodzinski of Vilna [3]. Rabbi Myszkowski arrived in the Land after the outbreak of the war and immediately dedicated his life to saving the remaining survivors of Polish Jewry. He was the first to organize assistance for hundreds of rabbis and Yeshiva students who fled from Poland to Soviet Russia. When Rabbi Herzog [4]went to Europe at the end of the war to support and encourage the Holocaust survivors, he went before him to lay the groundwork for his activities. He went to Rome and Paris, and when he saw what the enemy, may its name be blotted out, had perpetrated upon the Jewish people, he took seriously ill from the great tribulations and anguish, and died in the Land, approximately one week after returning from Europe. A high level Yeshiva was established in Israel in his name as a token of recognition.

Rabbi Shabtai Zeev Frydman of blessed memory

One of the great rabbis who occupied the rabbinical seat of Stawiski, whom I merited to befriend, was Rabbi Binyamin Remigolski. I became close to him already during my youth, and I was most fortunate to hear Torah from his mouth. I numbered among those who frequented his house. His young son Aryeh (Leibele), a person with a good heart just like his father, was my friend. We studied together at the Hebrew school that was founded by his father, the rabbi of the city. We began together to read Hebrew books when we were about ten or eleven years old. We continued our friendship in Vilna, where he studied in the Polish Gymnasia, and I studied in the Seminary for Hebrew Teachers. Our paths separated when we went abroad to continue our studies. At the conclusion of the Second World War, when I was already in the United States, the sad news reached me from Israel that Dr. Aryeh Remigolski died in his prime. Woe over such a fine person who was swallowed by the earth [5].

Since I was among those who would visit the home of Rabbi Remigolski, I had opportunity to get to know him from close and to witness his holy ways. He conducted the rabbinate with a strong hand, but he did not play favorites. He was upright in his ways and noble in spirit. He loved people, and brought everyone close to Torah. His home was a gathering place for the wise.

There was a general principal among the parnassim (communal administrators) of Stawiski: one ascends in holiness and does not decline [6]. When Rabbi Remigolski was appointed as the rabbi of Griva [7], he was replaced by Rabbi Reuven Kac, who had previously served in Indura (Amdor) near Grodno. Rabbi Kac was famous for his important books: the "Degel Reuven book of responsa; and "Dudaei Reuven", and "Shaar Reuven" – explanations on the five books of the Torah and articles on questions of Judaism and the state. Rabbi Kac occupied the rabbinical seat of Stawiski for approximately seven years. He worked very hard on behalf of the Jewish community there. Afterward, he was accepted as a rabbi in a large community near New York, and, upon making aliya, he became the chief rabbi of Petach Tikva.

A native of Stawiski also sat on the rabbinical seat of Stawiski; that is to say someone who was born and educated in that city. This was my father-in-law Rabbi Shabtai Zeev Frydman.

Rabbi Shabtai Zeev was the son of Rabbi Avraham Eliahu Frydman, who was himself great and eminent in Torah. My father-in-law excelled in his studies already in his childhood, and his name went forth as a genius, expert and sharp. He studied in the great Yeshivas of Poland and Lithuania, especially in the Yeshiva of Radun, which was headed by the Chofetz Chaim. He cleaved to the dust of his feet, drank his waters with thirst, and merited to be his private secretary.

Filled to the brim with Talmud, Reb Shabtai Zeev returned to his native city. There he married Sara Reizl, the daughter of Reb Yehuda and Chava Perlowicz. My mother-in-law was a fine woman, modest and refined. She loved Torah, and did good deeds for those both near and far. After the marriage, my mother-in-law, who was a woman of valor in the full sense of the term, took the yoke of livelihood upon herself and sent her husband off to continue occupying himself with Torah. Young Reb Shabtai Zeev took up his staff, sack, and Tallis and Tefillin bag, and went off to a place of Torah, to the town of Eishyshok (Pol: Ejszyszki, Lith: Eisiskes) near Radun. In the Kollel [8] there, he deepened his knowledge of Yoreh Deah and Choshen Mishpat [9], and when he returned to his native city, he was ordained as a rabbi by the heads of the Yeshiva of Volozhin. He was appointed as a rabbinical judge in Stawiski, and filled the place of Rabbi Reuven Kac during his absences from the city.

In his introduction to my father-in-law's book Tevuat Yaakov, Rabbi Reuven Kac writes, among everything else: "I knew the rabbi and Gaon Rabbi Shabtai Frydman as great and praiseworthy during the period that he served as rabbi of the city of Stawiski. He would fill my place in all matters of religion and jurisprudence during my absences from the city. He also involved himself in communal affairs, and aided and assisted anyone who required support and assistance.

During the era that my father-in-law served as a rabbi in Stawiski, the rabbi in a city of scholars as well as laymen who were great in Torah, he merited serving in a most honorable fashion despite his young age. He entered with full force into communal work, and dedicated himself with a full heart to any communal role that was placed upon him. He did everything without the aim of receiving reward.

I heard a great deal about his activities in matters of charity, good deeds, and support of religion. He was especially active on behalf of the Mizrachi movement and the redemption of the Land. He did great things in a trailblazing manner for Hebrew education. He was one of the founders of the Talmud Torah – a school for poor children whose parents were not able to afford the tuition fees of private teachers. He would visit this institution on regular occasions, examine the students, and take pride in the knowledge that they obtained within the walls of that institution.

His public activities did not impinge upon his diligent Torah study, which took place day and night. His name went forth in a praiseworthy manner as a rabbi and judge, who had a sharp intellect and a clear way of thinking. His expertise was especially great in the laws of monetary matters, and he was always chosen as an adjudicator in his city and in nearby cities.

When Rabbi Shabtai Zeev left Poland and traveled to the United States, he had the honor of serving in the large Neve Shalom synagogue of Brooklyn.

A new chapter of his life opened when he came to America. There he found a large field of activity for spreading the study of Torah and communal work. His external appearance also attracted the hearts of those that saw him. He had all of the fine traits mentioned with respect to a communal representative [10]: his beard was grown, his youth was well spent, and his voice was pleasant. His name went forth very quickly in America as one of the greatest halachic decisors, especially in the fields of divorce (gittin) and marriage laws. The rabbis of America posed to him their complicated questions regarding the realities of life in the United States. His responses were always well thought out and right on the mark. Within a brief period of time, he succeeded in penetrating the thickness of he wall of Jewish life in America. He was active on the rabbinical council of New York. I was an eyewitness to the effort and toil that he devoted to the great enterprise of "Ezras Torah", which was founded by his friend Rabbi Yisrael Rozenberg of Lomza. The aim of that institution was to offer assistance in an honorable manner to thousands of scholars and important people in the Land and in the Diaspora. His home was wide open to any person. Anyone with a problem on his mind found an attentive ear and an open heart (and also an open pocket...). His refined rebbetzin assisted him in these endeavors. She was pleasant to everyone.

I would sit with him for many hours during long winter nights, discussing ideas of Torah and the issues of the world. I never saw in him signs of fatigue.

He would stay up late at night, studying with diligence, despite the urgings of his rebbetzin that it was time to rest from the problems of the day. Due to our discussions, I realized that my father-in-law was also expert in Jewish history and Hebrew literature. He was a blend of an Orthodox rabbi and an enthusiastic Zionist.

In addition to his expertise in rabbinical decisions, he was also an accomplished orator. He enchanted the congregants of his synagogue in Brooklyn with his sermons.

He believed with full faith that "the religion could sustain itself in America only because of the sermons of the sermonizers, the speeches of the speakers, and the preaching of the preachers", and that "only thanks to their words, the Zionist idea continues to win over hearts, and strike deep roots within the people towards a great desire for the Land of Israel". "I reminded them often about the words of Rabbi Levi in the Midrash of the Portion of Kedoshim [11]: all good, blessing and consolations that the Holy One Blessed Be He will eventually bestow upon the Jewish people will only be through Zion". (Quoted from the introduction of his exegetical work "Mishan Mayim".)

There was no bound to his happiness at the founding of the State of Israel. During those days, he was like an overflowing well. During his sermons in the synagogue and his speeches at many gatherings, he never ceased to point out the strong connection between the Land of Israel, the Torah of Israel, and the people of Israel, as well as his love for the building of the Land.

My father-in-law not only spoke well, but he fulfilled properly his own words. He left the rabbinate in America in the year 1951, after having occupied the rabbinical seat of Neve Shalom for almost 25 years, and he made aliya with his wife to the Land. When he arrived in the Land, he was greeted with great honor by the rabbis of Israel, thanks to his reputation as a great scholar and a religious Zionist activist. He had three daughters and seven grandchildren in Israel, "Fruits of the Land". He set up his home in the Karkur Moshava with his daughter Tova.

He did not rest on his laurels in the Land. He prepared his books on halacha and aggadah (Jewish traditional lore) for print. In his preface to his first book "Yekev Zeev" that was already printed in New York in the year 5611 (1951), Rabbi Frydman apologizes for being brazen enough to publish his own novellae: "I realize my lack of worth, and I know myself that it is not my place to publish books. However, since many of my rabbinical friends and also my colleagues urged me to organize my novellae so that I could publish them, I gave in to them, and following their advice, I organized a few of the many in such a fashion that I would be able to publish them."

His first book "Yekev Zeev" that appeared a short time before his departure from America gained very positive reviews n the Torah world. Many of the rabbis of America published in the newspapers of New York words of praise for the book, which excelled in its presenting his clear thoughts and pleasant style.

After the publication of his first book, which merited great acclaim among those that study Torah, my father-in-law hoped that G-d would give him the strength to prepare and publish all of the following six books of his: "Mishan Mayim", "Tevuat Yaakov", "Imre Shefer", "Mili Dehespeda", "Mili Deavot", and "Amira Neima" [12]. However, he only merited to publish one of these books in his lifetime "Mishan Mayim" that includes sermons and speeches appropriate for each Sabbath and festival of the year. He called this book "Mishan Mayim" (Staff of Water) in accordance with the words of our sages in the Talmudic tractate of Chagiga, page 14: "Every Staff of Water – this refers to words of aggada (lore) that attract the hearts of people like water". This book is a comprehensive treasury of ideas and thoughts based upon the five books of the Torah, the prophets, and the words of the sages. This book also won great acclaim in the Torah world.

My father-in-law lived in Karkur for about four years, and he endeared himself greatly to the residents of the Moshava and the surrounding area. His strength did not fail and his eyesight did not dim until his final year. The study of Torah did not depart from his mouth. In his letters to us he wrote that he feels in his heart that any strength granted to him by his Creator comes to him because he merits to live in the Land of Israel with his daughters, sons-in-law and grandchildren. His joy of living in the Land of Israel only lasted a few years, for in his fourth year of living there, on the 5 th of Adar 5615 (1955), he returned his pure soul to his Creator, to the sorrow of his daughters, sons, sons-in-law and daughters-in-law, grandchildren and other family members, and to the sorrow of all of his acquaintances and friends.

After his death, his brother Rabbi Moshe Farber published his last book, called "Tevuat Yaakov". This book had the approbations of the Torah giants of Israel: the chief rabbi Rabbi Isser Yehuda Unterman; Rabbi Yechezkel Sarna, the head of the Yeshiva of the Chevron "Knesset Yisrael"; and of Rabbi Reuven Katz. In their approbations, the rabbis of Israel write the following in this third book of Rabbi Shabtai Zeev Frydman of blessed memory, among other things: "It is fitting and important that his words be received in the Beis Midrash, and as was his deeds with the first book, so it is with the third book – the fruits of thoughts about Torah with a great scope and delving into halacha" (Rabbi Unterman); "This book is a precious treasure of novellae and explanations built upon the foundations of thought and understanding" (Rabbi Reuven Katz). These three books should serve as a sign and testimony to a pure soul, great in Torah, in whose heart a holy flame of love of the people of Israel, the Land of Israel, and the Torah of Israel burnt all the days of his life.

May his soul be bound in the bonds of the lives of the pure pious people, who labor in Torah and good deeds.   New York

{120}

My Two Grandfathers of Stawiski
Yehoshua Maaravit
Rabbi Shabtai Frydman of holy blessed memory
Translated by Jerrold Landau

From my earliest childhood, my soul was attached to my grandfather Shabtai. I felt a special bond to him, as if he was attached to me. He is guarded within me in the place where I place him, and from where I will now bring him forth – from the inner chambers of my soul and the storehouse of my heart.

We had a wonderful relationship between us, a relationship without prying and investigation, without questions and answers. This was a relationship that was beyond time, beyond life and death. Even now, It is not clear to me from whence this relationship flowed. One thing I do know, it is guarded in my heart.

What was most wondrous about this is that I never saw my grandfather Shabtai with my own eyes. He made aliya a month before I was born, and when I was two years old, he died and was buried in the holy land [113].

Grandfather bequeathed to us three books that he wrote: "Yekev Zeev", "Mishan Chaim", and "Tevuat Yaakov" – all of them filled with pearls of wisdom and Torah. My mother likes to tell that grandfather dedicated his body and blood to them. He toiled greatly during his life, and these are the fruits of his efforts, treasures written on paper.

I recall that when I was a very young soul, I used to leaf through grandfather's books. I would say, "A day will come when I will know how to read clearly the language of the Torah that is necessary to study them".

Years went by. My period of youth passed, yet still being a youth, where is the study and the grasp of Torah?

Grandfather would forgive me, for he was a man of kindness and great love. Even though my dreams and wishes were not fulfilled in their entirety, his sublime character and memory are very dear to me, and his death did not separate us.

{121}

Elchanan Maaravit, may G-d avenge his blood

Grandfather perished in the terrible, frightful storm that descended upon the Jewish community of Europe. There is no monument over his grave, no remaining photograph, and no documents. The only thing that is left is his memory, which is very dear to me.

I thought a great deal about my father's father and his toil. He had sons and daughters. Torah was the path of his house, and labor had two meanings – the service of G-d and the work of the hands.

On more than one occasion I see in the eyes of my spirit the house in which my father grew up – an old, large house, full of life and bustling with children. I imagine before my eyes the image of grandfather: he loved his fellowman, and was beloved by everyone. I see him as a quiet man, immersed in thought and contemplation, carrying out his work with diligence and faithfulness.

An additional picture appears before the eyes of my spirit: Grandfather would return home towards the end of the day, and sit down with his sons and daughters to dine around the large, old table. They would discuss the issues of the day. Grandfather would dedicate the hours after work to the study of Torah, in order to fulfill the directive: "Make your Torah your steady occupation" [14].

Behold, when the darkness descended upon the town and the lights were put out in his house, grandfather would thank G-d for the fortune and happiness which He had blessed him with, and would request from the All Merciful to spread the canopy of peace upon him and the members of his household [15]. However, his prayerful request was not accepted. The dream was buried. The treasures of my heart no longer exist. Grandfather was murdered; grandmother was murdered. The town was destroyed and the community was exterminated. There is nobody other than my father who can tell about his father and what happened in his houses.

New York

{122}
The Prodigy of Stawiski – Rabbi Dr. Efraim Edelsztejn of blessed memory
Dr. Yom Tov Lewinski
Translated by Jerrold Landau

Reb Zanwil Edelsztejn was one of the most important householders of Stawiski at the beginning of the 19 th century. He was an honest merchant, G-d fearing and a great scholar. His wife, the daughter of Rabbi Aharon Yoel of Stawiski, was a righteous woman known for her good deeds. She was also the "magedet" in the women's gallery in the synagogue – that is to say, she would direct the women in matters of prayer, and read to them on Sabbaths from the book "Tzena Urena" [16], as was the custom of those days. They were charitable people. They gave of their bread to the poor, and supported poor scholars with their money. However, they had no children of their own.

The elders of the community would often relate: One day, a holy rabbi passed through Stawiski, and remained in town for the Sabbath. As was customary, he was hosted in the home of Reb Zanwil. When the rabbi and Tzadik saw their agony, he blessed them to have living and viable children. "The son which will be born to you", said the Tzadik, "will light up the eyes of people with his Torah". Indeed, as the year turned, they bore a son in good fortune, and called him Efraim.

Efraim displayed special abilities already in his youth. He started studying in cheder at age three, and within a short period of time, he knew how to worship as an adult. He started studying Talmud when he was six years old, and he astounded his teachers with his quick grasp and sharpness. He was given the name "The Prodigy of Stawiski" at age seven, and it was difficult to find a local teacher for him. When he was about ten years old, he would sit in the Beis Midrash and study Talmud himself, without a teacher. The rabbi of the city taught him every day for an hour or two Torah, rabbinical decisions, and responsa. He was effusive in his praise of the boy. Due to his great sharpness, he would disrupt the students in the Beis Midrash with his questions, and when they could not answered him, he would mock them. His father was saddened about this and took counsel with the rabbi: "What should we do with a lad who embarrasses the scholars?" The rabbi advised: "We have to enter him very soon into the burden of the ways of the world and find a wife for him. Then he will change his ways."

They married him off when he was thirteen years old. Reb Tevil Warsawer of Lublin, a wealthy merchant, gave him his only daughter as a wife and offered to support him at his table until he would grow in Torah and be accepted as a rabbi in one of the communities.

The youth sat in the Yeshiva of Lublin and studied all day. His father-in-law loved him very much, and predicted greatness for him. They called him "Efraim the Prodigy of Stawiski" at Yeshiva. He was ordained at age seventeen, when he was already the father of two children.

Suddenly, a different spirit overcame him. By chance, he found a small Hebrew book by the physician Reb Tovya the son of Moshe the Cohen, called "Maase Tovia" (published in Venice, 1708). This book dealt with metaphysics, astronomy, geography, and human science. The author wrote at length about the four foundations of nature: fire, water, wind and dust, and explained several things about the science of medicine. This book caused a change in the heart of the prodigy of Stawiski. He was especially influenced by the preface. In the preface, the author Reb Tovya the physician explains how he escaped together with a friend from the Yeshiva in Poland to Germany in order to acquire education. He did not rest and was not quiet until he was accepted to a university, where he studied natural sciences and medicine.

The prodigy of Stawiski decided to do so himself. Secretly and diligently, he began to study Polish, German, mathematics and nature. He did not abandon the Talmud, and he studied in the Beis Midrash daily. He would study the books of the Rambam (Maimonides), as he secretly advanced in his secular studies. He was granted the title of "Moreinu" (Our Teacher) when he was twenty years old, and his father-in-law got in touch with well-connected activists to help find him a rabbinical seat in one of the communities.

One day, Reb Efraim disappeared. He took the dowry with him that was hidden in a closet, abandoned his wife, left his children, and covered his trail. He left a note for his wife saying that she should not worry about him, for he went abroad to acquire knowledge. He said he would return to her when he reached his goal.

A few years alter, a merchant from Lublin returned from the fair in Vienna and told the people there that he met the prodigy of Stawiski, who was wearing short clothing like a German, had a trimmed beard, and without doubt has entered into a bad group, Heaven forbid. His father-in-law heard this and hurried to Vienna. He searched for his son-in-law and found him sitting in a university studying medicine. He pleaded with him in vain to return to his wife and children, promising to turn his business over to him. Efraim answered: "I will finish my course of study and return to my family." The father-in-law saw that it was impossible to convince Efraim to return home, so he advised him to grant a divorce to his wife, for he did not want a son-in-law who was an apikorus [17]. Efraim proved to him that he remained faithful to the commandments and orthodox in his religion, but the father-in-law did not want to listen. Unwillingly, Efraim agreed to send a get (bill of divorce) to his wife.

Reb Efraim was distraught for some time that he was forced to divorce his wife, however he slowly regained his composure and continued his studies in the university. He graduated as a doctor of medicine from the University of Vienna in 1835. He then returned to Poland, to his birthplace of Stawiski, being about 35 years old. The Polish authorities did not authorize him to practice medicine until he would pass a test in Warsaw, called "Nostriphysica". He was examined in Warsaw in 1836 and he received a license to practice medicine throughout Poland. There was no possibility of earning a living from medicine in Stawiski, for it was a small town and could not support an additional doctor over and above the regular Polish doctor. Therefore, he went to Lomza to find a position in a large city. First, he went to the "Chevra Shas" Beis Midrash, took a Talmud, and sat down to study. The students of the Beis Midrash were astonished. How could it be? A young man, shaven, wearing "German" clothing, with the face of a German nobleman – how could he be sitting and studying Torah? They began to investigate him and found that he was expert in Talmud, halachic decisions, commentators, and the Rambam. When they found out that he was a physician, the city was astonished.

After a short time, Dr. Efraim was invited to serve as a physician in the Jewish hospital. They set for him an appropriate salary, and they also fulfilled his request for a large advance, so that he could return to his ex-wife the dowry and the money of her marriage contract.

The young doctor became beloved in the city very quickly. The Jews appreciated him because he spoke to them in Yiddish and not Polish, as was the custom of the Jewish doctors. Furthermore, they liked him because he was observant of the commandments, for Efraim did not desecrate the Sabbath like the other doctors, and he set aside times to study Talmud in the Beis Midrash. On occasion, he would also ascend the pulpit and deliver a sermon like one of the rabbis. Therefore, they began to call him: "The Rabbi Doctor", or the "Doctor from Stawiski". The householders of Lomza did not let the doctor live as a bachelor. After he fulfilled his obligations toward his first wife, he married a second wife, an intelligent woman of a good family from the town of Jasionowka – Shoshana the daughter of the scholar Reb Eliezer Rozental.

His home was a gathering place for scholars, rabbis, and maskilim. He supported with his own money poor young men who wished to go to study in places of Torah and Haskalah. In the newspaper "Hatzefira" of the 1 st of Adar II, 5641 – 1881, when he was about 78 years old, he published an open letter to his friend and comrade Reb Chaim Zelig Slonimski, the editor, complaining that the progressive Jewish circles are allowing the elder researcher Reb Yakov Raifman of Sierbuczyn to suffer the indignities of hunger and want in his old age. He sent 50 rubles to the organization, the first donation to the fund to support the scholar Reifman, and expected that others would take note and follow suit. Slonimski the editor of Hatzefira praised the deeds of the "Rabbi Doctor", and recommended that other communities follow suit.

As has been said, the Rabbi Doctor would often lecture in the Beis Midrash. Furthermore, he also organized a group of young men in Lomza for the study of the Guide of the Perplexed of the Maimonides [18].

When the Polish revolt broke out in the year 1863 [19], Dr. Edelsztejn joined forces with his friends, the Polish physicians, and he was elected to the communal council on the side of the revolutionaries. He exchanged letters on this matter with the rabbi of Warsaw, Rabbi Dov Berish Meisels, who also stood on the side of the Polish revolutionaries, and attempted to influence the rabbis of the outlying cities to follow in his footsteps. The Polish revolutionaries required money and clothing to help care for the wounded and hospitalized. The Rabbi Doctor Efraim Edelsztejn gathered the Jewish community together into the large Beis Midrash, and invited members of the Polish top brass and notables of the city. He lectured in Polish and then in Yiddish about the common lot that unites the Poles sitting on their own land that has been pillaged, and the Jewish residents, who are sitting securely on the banks of the Wisla, while their eyes look towards the banks of the Jordan, toward their own pillaged homeland. He also quoted the words of the Polish historian Joachim Lelebel who called upon the Jews to enlist to help Poland in its war of independence. In return, they would receive complete rights of citizenship in the freed state of Poland. Furthermore, the Poles would also help them return to their historical homeland – the Land of Israel. With a heartfelt call in Polish: "Let there be brotherhood between the Jews and the Poles", and with the motto of the great exiled Polish poet Adam Mieckiewicz "Kochajmy sie" – let us love each other – the Rabbi Doctor concluded his patriotic speech in favor of an independent Poland. His words struck a chord in the hearts of the Jews.

The historian of the city of Lomza, Wladyslaw Szwedzki, writes in his book "Lomza" (page 68) that Dr. Efraim Edelsztejn, a physician from the Jewish hospital, was one of the heads of the Polish committee for the revolt, and organized a medical assistance depot for the wounded revolutionaries along with his Polish friend Dr. Wicikowski. To this end, Dr. Edelsztejn collected a large sum of money from the wealthy Jews and manufacturers. He organized a committee of Jewish women who gathered linen for sheets and bandages, as well as linens and clothing for the revolutionary fighters.

The Russians reconquered Lomza after the failure of the revolt. The Russian executioner Moraviov sent the cruel General Ganichki to Lomza to pillage the city and devastate it. About 150 honorable people of the city, Jews and Christians were imprisoned and beaten cruelly by the Russian soldiers. A delegation of representatives of the city, consisting of the Catholic priest Talarowski, the prosecutor of the judicial court Trocowski, Dr. Efraim Edelsztejn, the Jewish member of Sejm (the local government) and manufacturer Moshe Nowinski, and the town councilor and merchant Ticoczynski, presented themselves before the general and requested that he free the prisoners. Dr. Edelsztejn was the chief spokesman. The words of the delegation further incited the wrath of Ganichki, who commanded that these delegates also be imprisoned and publicly flogged. In the prison of Lomza, which had room for 200 people at the maximum, approximately 1,500 Jewish and Polish prisoners were crowded in. As a result of this, a typhus epidemic broke out in the prison, which infected the Russian army as well. There were no doctors, for most of the Polish doctors escaped from the city with the retreat of the revolutionaries, for fear of retribution. The Russians were forced to free Dr. Edelsztejn from prison and to place him at the head of the medical campaign in the city against the epidemic.

In the Jewish-Russian anthology "Yevreiskaya Starana" (volume 6, page 490, from the year 1913), it is written that Aleksander, the son of Dr. Efraim Edelsztejn, was among the Jewish revolutionaries who joined ranks with the Poles. He was a native of Lomza, a student of the University of Kiev and a student in the Medical Academy of Warsaw. Aleksander joined the anti-Russian demonstrations of 1861. He was wounded and healed. Later, he enlisted in the Polish revolutionary army, participated in battles and fell in battle near Ratkovo, while serving under the command of General Chmielinski.

Dr. Edelsztejn died at about age 80 on the 3 rd of Av, 5643 (1883) in Lomza. The day of his death was a day of deep mourning in the city. In Hatzefira (18 th of Av, 5643, number 31), the Hebrew teacher of Lomza, Akiva Binyamin

Smolinski, writes about the death. He writes that all citizens of the city, both Jews and Christians, joined the funeral procession. He was eulogized in the cemetery by the rabbi of the city Rabbi Eliezer Simcha Rabinowicz; the polish physician Michelowski on behalf of the physicians of the city and the Polish community; as well as several Jewish citizens. A 35 line obituary was written about him by Nachum Sokolow, the editor of "Haasif" (5645, 1885, number 135). Among everything else, he writes about him: "This man rose high above most of the physicians of our people, due to his life of service. He loved Torah and its students. He took great pleasure in joining with them at his table. He donated a great deal of money to the guardians of Torah and it students -- -- -- his greatest pleasure was to sit in the council of scholars and Maskilim, to discuss with them issues of Torah, the ways of the world, and Haskalah. – His adages and sharp wit are well known and pass from mouth to mouth..."

To our sorrow, none of his adages and sharp wit has reached us. As we have said, he excelled in this even in his youth, as we mentioned above. In his native town of Stawiski and his city of residence Lomza, several examples of his "sharp wit" circulated around. I only heard of one incident from Lomza, which was related in his name: Once he went to intercede for the freedom of Jewish prisoners, and to clearly prove their innocence. The general listened to his words with great interest, and finally said "Dielo po dielam – A sud po ustawie", that is to say: the issue is special and the judgement is according to the law – and he cannot do anything. When Dr. Edelsztejn presented a report of his mission, he mocked the words of the general: "Dielo po Dielam – A sod Kein Stawiski" [20]. This statement took on a life of its own, and I heard it approximately thirty years after his death, given the meaning: "You are correct – but such is the law".

For many years, the elders of the community of Lomza told about the genius of Stawiski, who later became the Doctor from Stawiski. We have added this article to remember his soul.

May his memory be blessed.

––––––––

Translator's Footnotes :

1. Rabbi Yisrael Meir Kagan of Radun, 1838-1933, arguably the leading rabbi of the pre-war generation. He is known as the Chofetz Chaim (Delighter in Life), due to his magnum opus on the laws of proper speech, based on the verse from the book of Psalms: "Who is the person who delights in life, loving his days and experiencing good? He who guards his mouth from evil, and his lips from speaking slander...".

2. An expression implying extreme devotion to a sage as a disciple.

3. Rabbi Chaim Ozer Grodzinski was one of the leading rabbis of pre-war Europe.

4. Rabbi Isaac Herzog served as the Chief Rabbi of Israel. His son Chaim Herzog served as the President of Israel (1983-1993).

5. A Talmudic style lament over the death of a fine person.

6. A statement used at various times in Jewish law to indicate that, when given the choice, we move from less holy to more holy. Here, it is used colloquially to indicate that one person was finer than the next.

7. Griva, Latvia, just north of the border with Lithuania. May possibly be Grajewo – it is not clear form the context.

8. Kollel is a center for advanced Talmudic study for married young men.

9. Two of the four sections of the Shulchan Aruch (Code of Jewish Law).

10. Here the term refers to a chazzan or prayer leader. These traits of the chazzan (known as a shaliach tzibur or the representative of the congregation) are listed in the Hineni prayer, recited by the chazzan prior to Musaf on Rosh Hashanah and Yom Kippur.

11. Kedoshim is one of the weekly Torah portions, from Leviticus. Midrash is a rabbinical exegetical work from Mishnaic times.

12. The titles of these types of books tend to be cryptic and full of euphemism, therefore I rarely translate them. However, for the sake of interest, the six books are as follows: "The Staff of Water", "The Wheat of Jacob", "Beautiful Sayings", "Words of Eulogy", "Words of the Fathers", and "Pleasant Statements". The first book "Yekev Zeev", is "Vineyards of Zeev".

13. From the above article, it is clear that Shabtai Frydman lived in Israel for three or four years, so the current author's statement that he was 2 years old when his grandfather died must be off by a year or two.

14. Implying that one should study Torah on a regular basis, devoting all of one's free time to it.

15. A paraphrasing of a passage from the evening service of Sabbaths and Festivals: "Spread over us the canopy of your peace...".

16. A book of lore from the weekly Torah reading, written especially for the study of women.

17. The Hebrew term, derived from the Greek philosopher Epicurus, for a heretic or non-believer.

18.   The Guide of the Perplexed (Moreh Nevuchim) is the major philosophical work of the Rambam (Maimonides).

19.   The text says 1963, but this is obviously a typographical error.

20.   The sound of the word Stawiski and ustawie are similar. The meaning of "A sod kein Stawiski" is that "the secret of Stawiski". I am not sure of the meaning of the nuance here.

{131}

My Parents' Home
by Nechama Bizounsky (nee Kotton)
Translated by Jerrold Landau

I cannot describe my parents' home without flashing back to an even older era, about which I heard from my mother, grandmother, and various family members.

My mother was Dvora Zelda of blessed memory, nee Ladelski, the daughter of Yosef Yeshayahu and Itka. Her family was rooted in Stawiski for generations. My grandmother's father, Reb Shlomo Zalman Kac, was also a native of Stawiski. He was a profound scholar, but he refused to make Torah the source of his livelihood [11]. He sustained himself with the work of his hands throughout his life. He had a dye shop, where he worked manually until the final years of his old age (he died at age 86).

My grandmother, his daughter Itka, went in the path of her father. Since my grandfather Yosef Yeshayahu toiled in Torah for all his days, she bore the responsibility of earning a livelihood – a task that she fulfilled with dedication and faithfulness.

Whenever I remember grandmother, she awakens in me memories of awe and honor of her unusually noble personality.

My grandfather Yosef Yeshayahu had two brothers in Stawiski – Moshe Ladelski and Nissan Ladelski. Both of them were scholars of Torah, and possessed vast general knowledge. Many people would come to them to take counsel regarding various matters. Moshe (Moshke) served also as an arbitrator.

They were Zionists who desired to make aliya to the Land. Nissan merited having his two daughters make aliya to the Land of Israel, where they established large families. No remnant remains of the family of Moshe Ladelski. They all perished in the Holocaust.

As opposed to his father-in-law, grandfather chose teaching as a profession. He started as a Talmud teacher in Stawiski, and later as a Rosh Yeshiva in Grajewo. He was admired by everyone. The family continued to live in Stawiski, and grandfather came home for festivals and special Sabbaths. From a practical perspective, it would have been easier for him perhaps to move his dwelling to Grajewo, but his roots were so deep in Stawiski that he did not want to be cut off from his native town and the birthplace of his ancestors under any circumstances. An interesting fact that sheds light upon grandfather of blessed memory is the fact that he taught his wife Torah, including Talmud, and she excelled in her learning, and even displayed a recognizable expertise in the issues of Abaye and Rabba [2].

Devora Zelda Kotton (nee Ladelski) of blessed memory

My mother, Devora Zelda, who was the eldest daughter, married my father Chaim Binyamin Chever-Kotton, who was not from Stawiski. My father was born in Lida, an important city in Lithuania, to his parents Yossele and Yocheved. His father, that is to say my paternal grandfather, was an ordained rabbi. His wife Yocheved died in her prime, when my father was very young child. Grandfather remarried and moved to Warsaw, where he served as a rabbi for many years. For various reasons I am not privy to, my father did not join grandfather when he moved to Warsaw, but he rather remained in Lida with relatives. There he studied as any Jewish child, at first in cheder, and later in yeshiva. He attained a wide and deep knowledge of Talmud and its commentaries, and he was considered to be an outstanding scholar with a phenomenal memory.

When he was still young, he thirsted for knowledge outside of Torah literature. Slowly but surely, along with his work in Torah, he began to study on his own initiative Hebrew as a living language, as well as general knowledge.

He had an unsettled soul. His birthplace caused him difficulties, and he began to wander from one place of Torah to the next. Thus he arrived at the Beis Midrash of Stawiski. My grandfather Reb Yosef Yeshayahu took note of the young stranger, and invited him to his home. After a short time, he married his daughter Devora Zelda. He set up his home in Stawiski after the marriage, and my mother opened up a haberdashery store in order to sustain the family. As I stated, my father was a restless person, and it was difficult for him to settle in one place. An occupation presented itself that satisfied his need for travel. He became a wandering agent for religious books. He wandered with his bundle of books from city to city, and he even reached Germany.

Due to his shaky state of health, father was forced to give up his occupation of distributing books. He opened up a "cheder metukan" [3] in Stawiski, where the language of instruction was Hebrew. Aside from the study of language, the prime subjects taught were bible, Jewish history, Mishna and Talmud.

Quickly, he became known as a wonderful teacher and pedagogue. Those who merited being his students remember his teaching fondly until this day. Indeed, my father was an exacting teacher, but the students accepted his teaching style with love, for they saw a blessing in it.

My father's love of Torah did not prevent him from being a fan of modern Hebrew literature. As far as I remember, over the years, father used his last savings to acquire a complete library. There was barely any new Hebrew book published that father did not obtain after its publication. Father did not only purchase books, but he also subscribed to the Hebrew newspapers of that era, such as Hatzefirah, and Hador, as well as various other publications that appeared in his time.

Many young people from the town would come to our house to borrow Hebrew books from father. He would provide them with a full heart, for he wished to spread knowledge and education among the Jewish youth. Furthermore, even many years after his death, the young people of Stawiski would come to our home, and mother would let them use whatever books they desired.

Father was not only a lover of books, but he was also an enthusiastic lover of Zion. He won over people in town to the Zionist idea, along with Dov

Szymonowicz of blessed memory, the father of Avraham Shimoni, a resident of the Balfouria Moshav.

I do not exaggerate when I state that the influence of father was so great, that many years later, after the Balfour declaration, when he was no longer alive, Stawiski was a strongly Zionist town. Many natives of Stawiski made aliya to the Land and settled there. Father also had the dream of making aliya to the Land and settling there, but he did not merit to do so, for in the interim, the First World War broke out, and father died in 1917. He was 43 years old at his death. Even though he himself did not merit to realize his desire, two of his sons did so, my brother Yitzchak Kotton and myself, the writer of these lines. Our mother of blessed memory also made aliya after me, in 1933.

From what has been said above, the portrait of my parents' home was of a home suffused with the spirit of Hebrew, Zionism, and traditional Judaism, which spread out from its own wellsprings outward.

For various reasons, my two brothers, Mordechai and Eliahu of blessed memory, did not merit to live in the Land. Father sent Mordechai to study in America when he was 15 years old. He studied in university there and graduated with a doctor of philology. Eliahu completed studies at the Hebrew seminary in Kovno and immigrated to America, where he completed his studies at an English teaching seminary. He taught Hebrew and English for several years. Mordechai enlisted as a volunteer in the American Army during the Second World War, and fell in Manila, the capital of the Philippines. My brother Eliahu died at age 50.

Had my two brothers remained alive, they surely would have made aliya to the Land, and actualized the dream of our father.

{134}

Reb Yehoshua Menachem Zilbersztejn of blessed memory
by Rabbi Baruch Zilbersztejn [4]
Translated by Jerrold Landau

{Note: This Hebrew chapter is equivalent with the following Yiddish chapter.}

Reb Yehoshua Mendel Zilbersztejn

My father, Reb Yehoshua Menachem the son of Reb Shraga the Levite, was born in the regional center of Szczuczyn in 1876. His father was a carpenter, and his mother was known as Chana the righteous. Everyone revered her, and she was like a mother to all of the yeshiva students of the city.

My father studied in the famous Telz Yeshiva, and also in the Yeshiva of Novhorodok. He married Necha Lejbik, the daughter of an old family from our town. After the wedding, he established his home in Stawiski, and tried his hand at various occupations. Finally, he became a merchant of forestry products. He conducted the forestry business in partnership with Yehuda Rubensztejn and with Wilamowski. Father was known as a wealthy man. I remember that in my youth, I was considered to be the son of a rich family. I remember that my parents spent a few days of vacation every summer in Bad Vermind in Germany. I also remember that my parents used to visit Warsaw several times a year, and when they returned home, they would enthusiastically describe their visits to the opera, to the theaters, and other places of enjoyment in the capital city.

My father Reb Yehoshua Mendel was one of the first Zionists in town, and he worked diligently for the renewal of the land and the revival of the Hebrew language. During the debates that broke out from time to time between the young Zionists and the opponents of Zionism, he always stood at the side of the Zionist youth. I remember the beautiful and memorable celebration that Reb Shabtai Frydman organized along with father in honor of the dedication of the Hebrew University in Jerusalem on April 1 st, 1925. The celebration and party that followed took place in the home of Bramzon, and I gave a brief speech in Hebrew. My eldest brother Yissachar was one of the first Chalutzim (Zionist pioneers) in town. He made aliya in 1925, and worked for a brief period in Ein Harod.

Reb Yehoshua Mendel Zilbersztejn was numbered among the leaders of the town, both in the Jewish community and the town council. He was the vice-mayor (the mayor was Polish) and the assistant to the judge. He was once sent to the regional center in Kolno as a delegate of the town council. When the Jews of Stawiski were searching for a fitting rabbi to take the place of Rabbi Remigolski of blessed memory, who moved to serve in Griva [5], they convened a special meeting for the scholars of the town: Reb Shabtai Frydman, Reb Meir Kac, and father, in order to examine various rabbis and visit various cities. Finally, they advised to invite Rabbi Reuven Kac of blessed memory to sit on the rabbinical seat of Stawiski.

Father loved very much to serve as a prayer leader in the large Beis Midrash on Sabbaths and festivals. He even led the Musaf service on the High Holy Days. It is self evident that he did not do this to receive any reward. His reward was the recitation of the Haftarah (prophetic reading) on the first day of Rosh Hashanah (I Samuel, chapters I and II)). This Haftarah is considered a good omen for a woman who has difficulty in childbirth [6], and is read at her bedside. I remember that on more than one occasion, father was called in the middle of the night to hurry to the home of a women in labor in order to read this Haftarah at her bedside.

When father served as a cantor, he loved to include the tunes of well-known operas that he was familiar with in the recitation of the prayers and hymns. The youth and younger generation enjoyed this, but it was met with fierce opposition by the adults.

Father looked positively upon modern Hebrew education. He often argued with the orthodox people and traditionalists, and proposed changes in the style of the old cheder. He sent his children to study in Hebrew-Polish high schools, including schools of the Tarbut and Tachkemoni network.

My father died in 1969, and my mother six years previous, in 1963.

Brooklyn, New York

Translator's Footnotes :

1. Literally "a spade to dig with", from a statement in the Mishanic Pirke Avot: "One should not make Torah a spade to dig with" – i.e. the source of one's livelihood.

2. Two Talmudic sages.

3. Modern style cheder.

4. In the title of the Yiddish chapter (page 135) the name appears as Reb Yehoshua Menachem [Shai Mendel] Zilbersztejn.

5. Possibly Grajewo, but probably Griva, Latvia.

6. As it deals with the birth of the prophet Samuel.

{137}

Aharon Eliezer Zack of Blessed Memory
by Moshe Goelman of blessed memory
Translated by Jerrold Landau

I confess that I am writing about this personality with awe and love [1]; however since there is no one else to perpetuate his name in our Yizkor book, I have taken this task upon myself. I hope that the readers will accept my words with favor.

My first meeting with Aharon Eliezer was in the summer of 1909, in the Yeshiva of the city of Krynki that was under the direction and supervision of the Gaon Rabbi Shlomo Zalman Sender Kahana Shapira of holy blessed memory, who served as the rabbi of Krynki for many years.

This Yeshiva was noted for its special learning style. Each of the students had to choose what tractate he wished to study, and the rabbi presented his lecture only once a week [2]. Most of the students were older than I, and their knowledge of Talmud was greater than mine. Salvation came to me from Aharon Eliezer, who took me under his protection by promising the supervisor of the Yeshiva that he would teach me the customs of the Yeshiva and help me advance in my studies. Therefore, thanks to him, I was able to remain as a student of the Yeshiva of Krynki for four years. As far as I remember, he left the Yeshiva after about one year. He did not go to another Yeshiva, but rather remained in Stawiski to assist his ill father in running the store. I met him again in our town during the years of the First World War.

While he was still in the Yeshiva, he amazed the students with his expertise, sharpness, quick grasp and phenomenal memory. He was able to review the lecture of the rabbi – which was a tapestry of sharpness, breadth of knowledge, and difficult and convoluted questions and answers – almost word for word to those students who had difficulty in understanding it as it was given.

During the first summer of my sojourn in Krynki, I entered not only its splendid Yeshiva, but also the world of in-depth study, not only of Gemara and Tosafot, but also of the other commentators of the Talmud [3].

It is interesting that Aharon Eliezer was not one of the diligent students. He did not sit attached to his bench and his open Gemara, as did the other students. He also was not present for most Mishmar (the all night study sessions) that took place each Thursday evening. He did not need this. It was sufficient for him to look into the text. He also studied quietly, without the traditional melodic hum of the students. After a short time, he was able to delve into the depths of the Talmudic section more so than the students who dedicated an entire day to their studies. He was regarded as one of the elder students of the Yeshiva, not due to his age, but rather due to his ability to explain matters of Gemara and Tosafot to those who had difficulty in their understanding.

Aharon Eliezer was one of the humble ones. He never set himself up with a place among the benches of the large Beis Midrash where the Yeshiva sessions took place. He particularly avoided the eastern wall, the place where the more experienced scholars sat. His place was next to the long table that stood at the edge of the Beis Midrash, next to the large bookcases. He was able to study by sitting, standing and walking in the Beis Midrash.

He was good hearted, had a fine character and a pure conscience. As he would pass by one of the students, he would glance at him, smile, and ask: "What is it? Is something difficult?" He would then immediately explain the subject matter clearly and go on to see other students. He knew which of the younger students were in need of help, and he did not wait until they would come to him to ask, as did the other senior students. Rather, he would pass by them as if by chance, tarry in front of any one of them who seemed to be having some difficulty, and explain the matter as best he could.

It is fitting to spend a bit of time discussing the origins of Aharon Eliezer. His father was Reb Zeev the judge, who served in the position of judge not to receive a reward, during the time that the Rabbi, Gaon and Tzadik Reb Chaim Aryeh Myszkowski of holy blessed memory served as Rabbi of Stawiski. He had a store that sold iron implements, run by his wife. He was a Torah scholar. He had a corner in the large Beis Midrash, where he sat and studied on his own. He founded the "Magen Avraham" organization, in which various well-known scholars such as Reb Meir Kac, Reb Mendel Lewinowicz, Reb Motka Shapira, my father, and others participated. They would gather on Sabbaths and festivals by the large table next to the entrance of the Beis Midrash, and study their lesson in Magen Avraham [4].

Aharon Eliezer's mother was a pure and modest woman, generous and pleasant to everyone. One of the things she kept busy with was Matan Beseter [5], which distributed charity to poor families prior to every Sabbath and festival. It is told that once a well-known person came to her and told her: "You should know that your son Avraham Eliezer does not put on his tefillin (phylacteries) and does not recite his prayers". She answered him in her simplicity: "This is impossible, for if that was indeed the case, how would he be able to eat his breakfast?". [6] She lived a long time after the death of her husband, and continuing running the store with the assistance of her son and daughter.

As is known, Aharon Eliezer was a good and swift chess player, and it was difficult to beat him. He inherited this skill from his ancestors. The famous chess player Akiba Rubinstein [7] was his uncle, and a native of our town. During the time of the war and before it, when Akiba would visit Stawiski, he would play simultaneous games with the chess players of Stawiski, in order to encourage them to particpate in this stimulating game.

I have already written about the activities of Aharon Eliezer with the youth during the First World War in the Hatechia organization, in a different part of this book under the chapter entitled "The Jewish Youth of the Town During the Years of the First World War and the Founding of Hatechia" [8]. However his influence was not only significant upon the youth, for adults and scholars as well would ask for his assistance in explaining a difficult issue, not only in the Talmud but also in the affairs of the world. In the landscape of people in Stawiski, it was common to see Reb Shabtai Friedman of blessed memory and Aharon Eliezer walking together in the marketplace, both of them so deeply engaged in conversation that they did not notice who was passing in front of them. The joke passed through our town: Why was the Christian church in the center of the marketplace built with a tall fence surrounding it? So that Aharon Eliezer and Reb Shabtai would know when to turn back, for if not for that, they would continue walking all the way to Lomza...

Aharon Eliezer Zack, along with his wife Frumka of the Silbersztejn family and their young son, perished in the Holocaust. May G-d avenge their blood.

Translator's Footnotes:

1. An Aramaic expression denoting deep respect, often used in reference to G-d.

2. The implication is that during the remainder of the time, the students would be studying on their own. In most Yeshiva curricula, all of the students study the same tractate at the same time.

3. Talmud is divided into two parts – the Mishna, which is the terser, older legal code, and the Gemara, which is the long, detailed commentary on the Mishna, replete with questions, discussion, and cross-examination of the contents. The Gemara also contains aggadaic material – stories, legends and vignettes. Gemara is also used as a generic term for Talmud. Rashi and Tosafot are the prime commentators that appear on a folio of Talmud.

4. The Magen Avraham (literally Shield of Abraham), is the pseudonym of one of the major commentators on the Code of Jewish Law.

5. Literally "giving of charity in secret", the name of an organization that distributed provisions for needy people without the recipients knowing who the specific donor was. In Jewish Law, it is considered a higher degree of charity to give charity when the donor is anonymous, and even more so when both the donor and recipient are anonymous, as that protects the feelings of the poor.

6. In Jewish law, it is considered inappropriate to eat breakfast, or even to eat anything, prior to reciting one's morning prayers.

7. See article on Akiba Rubinstein on page 144.

8. Page 157.

{141}

Dr. Aryeh Remigolski of Blessed Memory
by Moshe Goelman of blessed memory
Translated by Jerrold Landau

Apparently Aryeh Leib Remigolski

Aryeh Leibl Remigolski was the son of Rabbi Remigolski of blessed memory, born to him later in life [1]. He was born in Alita, Lithuania in 1908. He spent his childhood in the town of Tristina, where his father held his first rabbinical position, and later in Stawiski, where Rabbi Remigolski sat on the rabbinical chair for eight or nine years.

During his childhood, Leibele, as he was known to everyone, excelled in his sharp intellect, his quick grasp, and special sense of humor, which endeared him to everyone. He was beloved by the youth who used to frequent the house of the rabbi. All of them loved to chat with him and to hear his sharp answers to the difficult questions that they asked him. He was my student in Hebrew and Bible for many years, and he excelled greatly in these studies.

He received his general education from the Tachkemoni School and the Druskin Gymnasia in Bialystok. He completed his secondary education and received his matriculation in the Epstein Gymnasia of Vilna. He received his higher education from various universities. He attempted to study mathematics in Warsaw. From Poland, he went to Cologne in Germany, where he studied medicine, for Warsaw did not accept Jews in the faculty of medicine. From Cologne, he moved to Koenigsberg and from there to Bern and later Basle in Switzerland. He concluded his studies in Switzerland and became licensed as a physician.

He made aliya to the land in 1936. He spent some time in Tel Aviv and its vicinity. On account of the troubles that broke out in the summer of that year, it was difficult to become settled in that city, so he moved to Kibbutz Ayelet Hashachar with his wife and three children, who made aliya in 1938.

He did not work in agriculture. He received living quarters and sustenance on the kibbutz in return for his medical services to the kibbutz members. He also took care of the ill from the surrounding area. Dr. Remigolski was a physician who was dedicated to his patients. The residents of all the moshavim and kibbutzim of the Upper Galilee held him in esteem and loved him. During the eight or nine years that he lived in Ayelet Hashachar, his home was always filled with sick people, for he would tend to them at all hours of the day or night. His fame spread far and wide, even to the Druze and Arab residents in the Galilee and Huleh valley. He contracted tuberculosis during the course of his tending to the Arabs. This caused his death in 5708 – 1948 when he was only 40 years old. He was brought to eternal rest in Ayelet Hashachar.

Translator's Footnotes:

1. The Hebrew 'ben zekunim', literally means 'son of old age'. It refers to a youngest child, or a child that was born when the parents are already older. It is taken from the Genesis, where Joseph is described as the 'ben zekunim' of Jacob.

{144}

Akiba Rubinstein of Blessed Memory
by Akiva Fett [1]
Translated by Jerrold Landau

Akiba Rubinstein

Akiba Rubinstein was born in Stawiski in 1882. He was the fourteenth child in his family. He was born approximately eight months after his father died of tuberculosis, and he was named Akiba after his father.

His father was one of the outstanding students of Rabbi Shimon Sofer of Krakow. He was the son of Rabbi Yaakov Yonatan Rubinsztejn, the rabbi of Grajewo, one of the students of the Chatam Sofer [2] who received rabbinical ordination from him at the age of eighteen.

His mother Reizel was the second daughter of the well-known philanthropist Reb Aharon Eliezer Denenberg, who became rich through the forestry business and donated a great deal of his fortune to the benevolent societies of Stawiski. Reb Aharon Eliezer Denenberg visited the Land of Israel and built a synagogue in Jerusalem that stands to this day. Every Wednesday, sixty Yeshiva students ate at his table, in honor of the birth of his son who was born after three daughters.

When Akiba's mother became a widow, it was very hard for her to take care of her many children, who were weak. Indeed, most of them died in their childhood or youth. During his childhood, the Rubinsztejn family moved to Bialystok after his mother married Rabbi Heller, who was known as "The Genius (Illuy) of Pinsk". Akiba was educated in Bialystok along with Chaim, the son of the Illuy of Pinsk, who was the same age as him. Chaim was also a genius, who later became known as Professor Chaim Heller, a researcher into the sources of the bible in the traditional style. In his time, he was known as one of the spiritual leaders of Orthodox Judaism in the United States.

Due to his physical weakness during his childhood and youth, and out of fear for the tuberculosis that was prevalent at that time, he was not sent to Yeshiva as was customary in those days. During his many free hours that he had at his disposal, he played chess in one of the inns that was close to his home. He would often "play with himself", that is to say he would study detailed chess operations that would later bear fruit. Within a short period of time, he made a name for himself as an expert chess player. When the famous chess player of Lodz, a place known as an important chess center, visited Bialystok, Akiba presented himself before him. As the guest evaluated him, it was proven that the young Rubinstein was a gifted chess player, and the guest invited him on the spot to participate in the chess championships of Lodz. During that competition, Akiba beat the best chess players in the city hands down, and to the surprise of everyone, he won the chess title of Lodz. After this brilliant victory, Akiba Rubinstein became a well-known national chess personality. He was invited to competitions in other cities, and he continued progressing until he was invited to the Russian national chess championships in St. Petersburg in 1909, where the most experienced chess players in all of Russia participated, including the world chess grandmaster Dr. Emanuel Lasker. To the surprise of everyone, young Akiba Rubinstein tied for first place in this national competition along with Lasker, and became a known chess personality in the entire world. From that time on, he was invited to the most important international competitions.

During these competitions, he reached heights that very few people reached in the annals of chess. He won first place in the four largest international chess championships, as he brilliantly defeated the chess giants. Apparently, he reached the height of his success in the San Sebastian competition in Spain (1912).

His many fans raised his standings in the world chess championships. However, the world grandmaster, Dr. Emanuel Lasker, ignored the opinion of the international chess community and invited the chess expert Schlechter to compete against him for the world title. This refusal of Dr. Lasker to invite Rubinstein, who was regarded as one of the chess greats in those days, was never forgotten. When the world chess championships were reinstated after the Second World War, this incident was brought down by the grandmaster Botvinnik as a convincing reason to disallow the chess grandmaster from deciding who his competitor would be for the championship.

Akiba Rubinstein made many innovations in the theory of chess, and a collection of his plays that was published serve as educational material for chess players until this day. His brilliant games were included in the chess textbooks (e.g. in that of Dr. Euwe, a former chess grandmaster).

He married a woman from the Lev family of Szczuczyn during the First World War. He and his wife had two sons, Yonatan and Shlomo. He settled in Brussels, Belgium after the war. Many of the chess experts of the cities of the Low Countries were numbered among his students.

After the First World War, his health became shaky, and he began to suffer from headaches and nervousness. This affected his game. With the passage of time, his game suffered greatly, and he lost games of the second and third level. Despite this, even then he attained fine accomplishments as he played against great competitors, and he won prizes for the most sportsmanlike game.

He visited the Land of Israel in 1931. This was an uncommon event in the annals of chess in the Land. His health degenerated completely around the time of the Second World War, and he fell into depression. He became a loner, and withdrew from communal life. His economic situation also weakened, for he made a living from chess for all of his life. Chess institutions published his games in books, and he was supported from the proceeds.

During the Second World War, he was hidden in Belgium by his fans, and he remained alive. His youngest son was sent to a concentration camp, and survived due to his brilliant game, for the Nazi camp commander, who himself was a good chess player, did not want to forgo such a chess competitor.

His wife tended to him with boundless dedication, and took care of all of his needs. After her death, he entered an institution where he remained until the end of his life.

{146}

Akiba Rubinstein is No Longer With Us
by A. Cherniak
Translated by Jerrold Landau

With the death of Akiba Rubinstein, one of the last of the chess leaders of the world at the beginning of this century has passed from the scene. There are only two of these champions that remain alive: Dr. Bronstein and Professor Widmer. Rubinstein was born in 1882 in the Polish town of Stawiski, a scion of a rabbinical family. He became involved with chess when he was fifteen years old, and he quickly became an expert chess player. His first accomplishments included a victory in a duel with Silva, the third prize in the Russian chess championships in 1930, and a tie for first prize with Duras in a competition in Armenia in 1905 (first with Lasker) [3]. The year 1912 was the year of his most brilliant victories – three first prizes in international competitions. During this era, he was regarded as a serious competitor for the world grandmaster, and if not for the outbreak of the world war, he might very well have merited this.

Rubinstein visited Israel in 1931 and conducted a simultaneous game. During his visit, he wrote an article about chess in clear Hebrew, at the request of the editor of the "Chess" ("HaShachmat") periodical that was published at that time.

Rubinstein, a quiet and modest man, would leave the competition hall at the conclusion of the game without asking about the results of the other players, and without studying the changes that took place on the competition ledger. The prize did not attract him. In his eyes, the properness of the game, the correct ideas, and the exacting moves were what were important. When he spoke about his most brilliant games, he would customarily point out: "this was a logical game".

Rubinstein excelled in all aspects of the game. There is almost no opening move which does not bear the mark of some of his ideas: for example, the opening of the four knights, the Tarrasch move of the queen's gambit, several methods of the French defense, the Nimzovich defense, and others. However, he attained eternal fame in his endplays, which he conducted with virtuoso.

Rubinstein's two sons are counted among the best chess players of Belgium, and in accordance with Dr. Euwe: "Only the great name of their father disadvantages them".

From an article in "Haaretz", April 14, 1961.

{147}
The Engineer David Tovia (Dobrzyjalowski) of Blessed Memory
by Sarah Tovia
Translated by Jerrold Landau

Strong roots anchored him

Sent their vigor to his body and soul,

A very bright vigor.

The brilliant forehead of a genius

Shining and desirous of life.

Modest grace and pent up silence were the weights

For the heat of his temperament and his vigorous character,

And humbleness against pride

On the plates of the scale.

He sowed around him the light of wisdom

He went around in celebration in his world:

The world of a builder, a judge, and a friend

One of the righteous of the generations.

Justice and duty ennobled his character.

He was like Hillel [4] who controlled his character.

He needed nothing for himself,

He only loved his people, he loved this land

He loved his fellowman, near and far.

Translator's Footnotes:

1. There are many articles about Akiba Rubinstein on the world wide web. If you do a web search for Rubinstein & chess, you will find them. Three such pages are as follows:
   http://starfireproject.com/chess/rubinstein.html
   http://www.msoworld.com/mindzine/news/chess/rubinstein2000.html
   http://misc.traveller.com/chess/trivia/r.html

2. The Chatam Sofer, Rabbi Moshe Sofer (1762-1839), was one of the outstanding rabbinical leaders of the early 18th century. He was the rabbi of Pressburg (Bratislava) for 33 years, and was very zealous in defending Orthodoxy from the inroads of Reform.

3. There is something mixed up about this sentence, in that it names two people with whom he shared the first prize, the second one being in parentheses. Also, the word 'Armenia', is 'Arman' or 'Urman' in the Hebrew. I am not sure if Armenia was really intended, but I could not think of another major locale that matches that name.

4. A reference to the Talmudic sage Hillel, who was known for never getting angry.

———

{148}

Chaim Granit (Brzostowiecki) of blessed memory
Some lines about his personality
by Zelig Broshi
Translated by Jerrold Landau

My brother Chaim was born in 1900 in the town of Stawiski, close to Lomza. He received his general education from the Russian school. He also spent some time at the "Cheder Hametukan", and studied Torah from our revered father Reb Moshe Ari Brzostowiecki of blessed memory, who was known as a scholar and expert Talmudist.

M. Z. Goelman introduced him to the world of Hebrew literature. He revealed to his students the glory of the language of the prophets, developed their hearts with faith and inspired in them a thirst for reading.

Chaim was fortunate, in that even in such a forlorn town as this there was a library next to the "Hatechiya" organization, which collected the best of the poetic and prose works of Hebrew and Yiddish literature of those days.

My brother read with thirst everything that came his way: Brenner and Brszdaski, Berdichevski and Frischman, Kabak and Nomberg, Asch and Reizin, as well as many other writers who influenced him greatly.

At the time of the outbreak of the First World War, hunger and want fell upon the Jewish people. The town groaned under the yoke of the German conquerors, and the Jewish youth who were cut off from the ground dreamed about bread, work, peace, aliya to the Land of Israel, and going out to the wide world.

In 1917, at the time of the Balfour Declaration, a monthly called "Eglei Tal" was published, dedicated to literature, Zionism, and the issues of the day. The editors were Albos (the penname of Chaim), Niger (Y. Y. W., today a pharmacist in New York), and Z. B. who served as the secretary of the organization.

This monthly was written and edited in the living Hebrew language and served as an expression for the effervescent energies of the youth. It had a great influence upon the youth of the nearby villages due to its significant content and its pleasing presentation.

Chaim wrote poetry, lead articles, and stories. Aside from his work as editor of this monthly, he was active in the Hechalutz and Tzeirei Zion movements of Lomza.

He arrived in the United States in 1921. It was difficult to become acclimatized to the new country, however he slowly became accustomed to the new environment and conditions. He got his first job as a teacher in Gloversville. The first steps were difficult for this young Eastern European man who was not fluent in English. He arrived with an empty sack and a head filled with dreams, hopes, faith, and longing. The cruel reality was not favorable to him. His working conditions were difficult. Most of the parents of his students were German émigrés, who were not desirous of a Jewish education. Nevertheless, Chaim did not become discouraged. He decisively forged a path for himself in the community, he prepared the way, and started courses for adults. On festivals he would lecture in the synagogue, and with his heartwarming words spiced with homiletic interpretations and the words of our sages, he ignited hearts and won over souls to the national idea.

From there he moved to Jersey City, New Jersey, where he taught for eighteen consecutive years in the Ohev Shalom institution. He also taught in the Yeshiva of Rabbi Soloveitchik[1] and in the last seven years of his life he was the principal of "The University Heights Center".

He dedicated thirty years of his fertile life to Jewish education.

A special area of his energetic activity – not for the purpose of receiving a reward – was dedicated to the "teacher's union", which became part of his life. Thanks to his activity, the Yiddish newspapers began to discuss the problems of the Hebrew educator. There was not one week in which an article, did not appear – a review or an accounting of the happenings in the "union", something about educational styles, about the economic situation of teachers, their problems and struggles. In his articles, he delved into the professional life of Hebrew teachers, he raised their stature both personally and communally, and made the community aware of the physical and spiritual needs of teachers.

He also wrote evaluations of school books, people, literature, etc. in the "Morgan Journal" ("Morning Journal"), "Das Yiddishe Folk" ("The Jewish Folk"), "Eltern Un Kinder" ("Parents and Children", "Kol Hamoreh" ("The Teacher's Voice"), "Di Yiddishe Shtime" ("The Jewish Voice"), "Hadoar" ("The Post"), and "Shvilei Chinuch" ("Pathways of Education").

His enthusiastic connection to the Yiddish language inspired him to write two schools books in that language: a) "Di Ershte Trit" ("The First Step") for beginners, and b) "Funem Yiddishem Lebn" ("From Jewish Life"), under the influence of Kalman Witman of blessed memory.

Prior to his death, he was working on compiling a schoolbook in Hebrew for beginners. He passed away when the manuscript was ready for publication.

Chaim loved order and discipline. His books rested on long shelves, sorted by their content and type: poetry, science, and history. He would always say: "There is no thing which does not have a place" (Pirke Avot, 4, 3).

My brother was very careful regarding interpersonal matters, including with his own family. For example, if he arranged a meeting or was supposed to be somewhere, he would certainly show up – even if there was rain, snow, cold, or ice. He was never late even by one minute. On the contrary, he was always early, saying that it would be better that he wait rather than have others wait for him. He was disgusted by those who would trample those "simple" niceties with their heels.

He was meticulous in his dress, and was always very careful about his physical appearance. This was not due to haughtiness or coquettishness, but simply due to his natural tendencies. He gave expression to his well-developed sense of esthetics.

Sometimes this behavior seemed a bit strange to me: From where did he, a young man from a Polish town, have this sense of esthetics? Once I asked him:

"Reb Chaim, this meticulousness – why is it?"

He explained to me in detail:

"I could have answered you about this "strange" behavior with a quote from our sages. A scholar who has a wrinkle on his clothes...[2]. However, if I answer you in that manner, it would seem like haughtiness on my part. I will tell you that it is my opinion that every Jewish person – and even a poor person who goes begging at the doors – and how much more so a Hebrew teacher, is required to be meticulous in his dress, for in such a matter he raises his esteem and importance in the eyes of his pupils.

He approached the table upon which rested my slightly crushed hat, felt it and continued: "You should know that it is different with food, for I eat modestly. No person will look into my stomach to see what I "cooked upon the oven". However with clothing and garments – this should be no small matter to you."

"Nu, nu Reb Chaim, have you forgotten about the adage – 'one should check into one's food but not one's clothing'?"

He smiled, and concluded the conversation with great pleasure:

"Wonder of wonders, to you is due praise! However it appears to me as if there is also an adage 'one should check into one's clothing, but not one's food'."

We were accustomed to engaging in conversation together when we were in one place together. My brother used to take pleasure in linguistics, similes, learning new words, adages of the sages, and legends.

In general, we did not discuss issues of the teaching professions. To Chaim, the paths of Hebrew education were clear. He knew many teachers, he knew their situation, he remembered all of the schoolbooks that were published and all of the educational institutions that had closed or were about to close. He had what to talk about in this subject; however, apparently it was ingrained in our subconscious that there was a secret agreement between us not to enter into this stormy subject area.

However, I once overheard him engage in these matters.

It was the year after he left his job in New Jersey. We were walking together in one of the neighborhoods of the Bronx. Chaim was subdued. He walked with his head down, and shrugged his shoulders, weighing in his mind whether to open up a window to his soul.

We passed by a garage. A man covered in filth was lying on the ground inspecting the innards of an automobile.

Chaim stopped, pointed to that man, and said:

"Do you see this, Reb Zelig? This man will have remuneration for his activities after many years of toil and hard labor. And I, I have worked for eighteen years – eighteen years – in an educational school, and left without anything. I did not even save one penny. And now, you understand the difference between a Hebrew teacher and a mechanic.

After his heart attack, when he returned from the hospital, there was a definite change in him and his life. He separated himself from the group, and stayed within his own confines. He preferred to engage in solitary activities, as if he was depressed. His steps slowed and he began to watch himself closely. Some sort of constant fear filled his being.

One day, we had a conversation about "the psychological foundations of Midrash"[3]. My brother complained that the treasures of Jewish Aggada are still a locked up garden and sealed off well to the youth. They are not as well compiled and explained as the Halacha. He spoke about the vital need for such a compilation, which would serve as enjoyable reading material for students, starting in grade five.

Going from topic to topic, I purposefully mentioned the Midrash about G-d saying to King David: "You will die on the Sabbath". The Angel of Death struggled with him and had no power over him, since he, the psalmist, never interrupted his learning, until one day a wind came and rustled the trees in his garden. When the pleasant songwriter of Israel went out to see what had taken place – his soul left him...

"Reb Chaim", I continued, "if you wish, here is the opportunity to construct a wide variety of homiletic interpretations. It was the Sabbath – this means that work stops, there is inactivity, and calm in the life of the spirit. The Torah renews the person and states that as long as a person has a hold upon life, a purpose, an occupation, content – he is assured that he will remain in this world. However if he cuts off the cord that connects him to the present – there is no more rectification. On the Sabbath, the morbid spirituality brings with it physical destruction..." I opened up for him literary and educational content that could be expressed.

Chaim listened intently. I saw that my words pained him. His gaze looked as if he was looking for a point of exit. Finally, he said:

"By homiletic exegesis, one can explain any problem. You know that lately I have been working on compiling a book for study, but doubts have overcome me, and I cannot continue. Apparently, this is also vanity, and chasing after the wind[4]".

He rested for a moment and added:

"Our sages who looked into all the crevices and wrinkles of the soul explained the verse 'Jacob arrived whole' (Genesis 33, 18) – whole is his body, whole in his money, and whole in his Torah. That is to say, there is a threefold sense of wholeness: health, economic security, and cultural life. These are the urgent needs of man that are required for peace of the soul. However, how many Jacobs are there in the marketplace?"

"My wings are plucked, plucked – and I am silent –".

The feeling that "his wings are plucked", did not come upon him suddenly, at one time. In the last years – particularly after his illness – thin doubts began to seep into his subconscious, for "the day has declined", and an angst seeped into his soul and poured onto it drops of poison mixed with fear. This was not due to physical decline, but rather due to a dream, which was not realized and would never be realized. He must become accustomed to the idea that he was "only" a teacher. "Traveled and traveled but not a veteran", he used to say. Then I realized that days came upon Chaim for which he had no desire.

When he went on vacation during his final summer, I came to take leave of him. The conversation was choppy. He was in the midst of a flurry of activity. Chaim was taking measured steps from room to room, deciding what to pack and what to leave behind.

I suddenly realized that the first item that he put in his suitcase was his Tallit (prayer shawl). He folded it and caressed it. He yearned for it with devotion as would a pious Jew.

I followed after him, and from behind his back I asked him:

"Reb Chaim my brother, why did you see fit to pack your Tallit first?"

His face became serious.

"I will answer your query with a story that I read or heard: Once the Maggid of Kelm came to town. He entered one house and did not see anybody there. Behold, from one of the rooms he heard a gentle voice of quiet wailing. The Kelmer followed after the voice. Suddenly he saw that on a chair in the corner there was a Tallit. He leaned over it and whispered to it:

Tallit, Tallit, why are you weeping?

It answered:

My owner went abroad. He packed all of his precious belongings, including insignificant objects, but he forgot me.

When the Kelmer heard these words, he said:

Tallit, Tallit, take comfort! The day will come when your owner will leave everything behind and only take you[5]".

My brother spoke a very vibrant Yiddish, and he embellished this story with special language. He added his own style and special melody. With the expressions of his face and the movements of his hands, the Maggid of Kelm became alive, and with his trembling, emotional voice, it was possible to hear the bitter weeping of the Tallit.

He stopped. I always knew that Chaim would take a pause in the middle, and have something more to say. However, he did not add anything --- ---

Now that my brother is here no more, it seems to me that he walked through life as an experienced actor. I ask myself: these noble expressions with which he adorned himself and the external peace which flowed from his sublime face – were there not on them any sign of internal turmoil, covering up the storm and fire that were caught up in his heart, and eventually burned him with their coals?

Who can understand the struggles, setbacks, obstacles, hindrances, wounds and scars in the inner recesses of a person? Who can come and investigate into his soul?

The choppy words that came out of his mouth inadvertently, gave hints that the breech in his soul was larger than the solid part.

Chaim was burdened with a primitive sense of poetry and a somnolent expertise in literature. Hebrew and Yiddish walked side by side with him. His soul knew no bounds in his love for them. He collected books of poetry and read them with deep concentration, especially the classics, which imprinted their impression upon him.

His literary legacy included poems in Yiddish, articles on problems in education and personalities, as well as evaluations of school texts. He also translated some of the Poems of Cohen, Pichman, Tshernikovsky, Schneur, Katznelson, and Efrat, as well as the Hebrew words of G. Shufman.

However his soul played tricks upon him, in that he did not develop to his full potential and expertise. From here came the thirst, the longing, and blinding efforts to give expression to his restrained abilities. Thus did Chaim battle with his desires, and he overcame – but eventually fell in battle...

I sometimes think to myself that the fate of Chaim was not private, but rather general – the fate of many: a broken heart.

One rainy Sunday I accompanied him to his final rest. I did not believe, and I still do not believe that this was the last time. I am pained for you by brother Chaim! Your were very dear to me. My love of you was wondrous[6]. Rest in peace!

5713 – 1953.

Translator's Footnotes:

1. Yeshiva University.

2. A statement from the Talmud that a scholar should be careful about the appearance of his clothing, since people look to him as an example of the glory of the Torah.

3. Midrash is traditional Jewish legends and homiletic stories, often found in the Talmud and other collections. Midrash is otherwise known as Aggada. The legalistic material in the Talmud is known as Halacha.

4. An expression from the book of Ecclesiastes (Koheleth), describing futility.

5. Jewish men are placed into the coffin wrapped up in a Tallit.

6. A paraphrase of the elegy recited by David over the death of Jonathan and King Saul (II Samuel, chapter 1).

Between the Two World Wars

{157}

The Jewish Youth in the Town During the Years of the First World War, and the Founding of Hatechiya
by Moshe Goelman of blessed memory
Translated by Jerrold Landau

As was related in another place, our town was conquered twice by the Germans. The first occupation was in 1914, a few days prior to Rosh Hashanah, and continued until the eve of Yom Kippur. Two families, wheat merchants, suffered from this occupation, since the Poles informed on them, and the husbands were exiled by the Russians to Charbin. These families were the son of Kiwajko and Yeshaya Baruch Chmielewski. The informing was that they had sold wheat to the German infantry.

The second occupation, which lasted until the end of the war, started in March 1915. The Germans destroyed the large Beis Midrash and turned it into an army hospital. Those who were wounded on the front, which was very close to our town for seven or eight months, were brought there for first aid. Once, a cannonball shot but the Russians hit the Beis Midrash, and destroyed the roof and southeast corner.

The German authorities conscripted the youth for various tasks, such as paving and fixing the roads. Two main streets were paved at that time: One to Jedwabne and one to Kolno. Every morning, the townspeople arrived at the meeting place with spades over their shoulders, and from there they were sent by foot or wagon to the various workplaces. The women were conscripted for a different task, easier but less honorable, that of cleaning the houses and their residents. The Germans were very much afraid of contagious diseases, especially in the warm summer months. An army physician along with a translator came to the town at the beginning of the summer, and they investigated the sanitary condition of all the houses. When they found a problem in sanitation, they sent the residents of the house to the bathhouse, and they disinfected their clothes in a special oven which was set up for this purpose. Zusha Szapiro, who was a professional pharmacist, was conscripted for this job. Aharon Eliezer Zak, Pinchas Mark, and myself assisted him. We had to prepare baths with hot water, light the oven in the early morning, disinfect the clothes of the bathers, and return them via a small opening in the door. Due to the state of war, there was a curfew that extended from sunset to sunrise. In such conditions, there was no time for people to meet, except on Sabbaths in the synagogue during the hours of prayer.

I remember a significant experience during those days, whose impact was not erased through the long years. About two or three weeks before Passover, an army rabbi from Berlin, named Zonenfeld, came to town. He invited several young boys and girls to come with him, to organize a Passover Seder for the Jewish soldiers on the nearby battlefronts. He promised that he would concern himself with wine for the four cups, matzos, and haggadas, and we would concern ourselves with the meal – chicken, soup and dumplings. We accepted this task with great enthusiasm, and began to prepare. A day before the festival, we cleaned up the small synagogue of the Chevra K.S. We arranged two long tables, spread out white cloths, and brought candles and kosher for Passover dishes and cutlery. We provided enough kerosene to light the large lamps to light up the Beis Midrash.

It was the eve of Passover. At sunset, the Jewish captains and soldiers gathered in the Great Synagogue, and we recited the evening service for the eve of Passover together. After the prayers, we sat around the tables, and the Seder took place according to its statutes, but with a slightly different style from that which we were used to at home. An exalted atmosphere prevailed that evening. However one thing was improper. Hungry soldiers came to the Seder, and some of them took out a loaf of bread from their bag, broke it into pieces, and ate it [1]. The rabbi requested that we not publicize this, and attribute it to the hunger that prevailed during the time of war.

The soldiers worshiped with us in the synagogue the next day, the first day of Passover, however they only came to the Mincha (afternoon) and Maariv (evening) services. In the morning they were required to be at their stations on the front. The rabbi delivered a lecture to them. I remember that one Jewish captain who stood near to us asked us: "why do you shake at the time of prayer?" I answered him that this was due to the great enthusiasm, to fulfil the verse: "all of my bones shall utter his praises". My answer did not suffice him. David Leibel Dobrzalowski explained to him that this custom still survives from the time when there were no printing presses, and not everybody had a prayer book. Two or three people would pray from one prayer book, and in order to read the prayer book they would have to bend down. It turns out that the three people would bend down successively, one after another, and thus arose the custom to shake during prayer. This explanation made more sense to him, and he even told it to the rabbi after the prayers.

The soldiers of the German army once again gathered in the synagogue on the Shavuot holiday, at the time of Mincha, and Rabbi Zonenfeld delivered a lecture to them, and distributed drink and sweets to them after the prayers.

This gathering of Jewish youth during the Seder with the soldiers also spawned other meetings. After the conquest of Warsaw, Bialystock and Grodno in the fall of 1915, the front moved farther away from Stawiski and the soldiers left the city. A home guard arrived to replace the military governor. The commander was an older man, as were the police officials. The guard was more lenient, and civic matters were turned over to local residents. Chaim Zevulun Bramzon was appointed as Bergermeister (mayor). The curfew was shortened significantly. It now began from 9:00PM, and afterward from even later. A few people were permitted to go out even during the time of the curfew.

Paltiel (Pelet) Remigolski of blessed memory

The Jewish youth who wandered around with nothing to do began to meet and organize. At first a small group gathered in the room of Avraham Siemienowicz – today Avraham Shimoni who is a member of the Balfouria Moshav. This room was on the roof of Menashe Szapiro's house. These meetings took place in particular on Friday and Saturday evenings. At first these meetings did not have a set agenda. News was shared from German newspapers, and from the newspapers that arrived from Warsaw. On occasion we also arranged parties with music and games.

The number of meetings increased, and the small room was no longer large enough for these gatherings. We rented a large room in the yard of Moshe Zeev Bramzon, and we set up a hall for these gatherings. We brought in benches and a table, and we set up a library of books that we collected in the city. Later we purchased books from Lomza and Warsaw. We also gave a name to this hall: "Hatechiya", which was the same name of the Zionist youth hall in Lomza. From that time, we arranged gatherings and presentation every Sabbath eve. The first speakers were, Aharon Eliezer Zak, Pelet Remigolski (the son of the rabbi), David Leibel Dobrzalowski, the teacher Itzkowski from Radzilow, and this present writer. There were also recitals from the young people of their own songs and prose. I was given many tasks: I was the secretary, the collector of membership dues, the organizer of the presentations on Sabbath eves, and the one responsible for the upkeep of the meeting hall. At that time, Perec the businessman and other members of the club were financially successful, and covered the outlay from their own pockets. Fishel Cybulki also made a donation. The Germans granted him the permit to collect the pork tax in the entire area of occupied Poland, an enterprise that enriched the holders of the permit. The chess players from the towns of the lowland were among his pupils.

The word about the Hatechiya Hall reached the German officials in the city, who were lacking for entertainment, and they made a point to come to the hall and meet the youth. They became accustomed to understanding the content of the presentations, which were in Yiddish, and after some time a sort of camaraderie developed between them and the Jewish youth. We were hungry during the years of occupation, and there was a great deal of lack of food and clothing. We sewed clothing from colored sacks, but we were given complete freedom to pursue our cultural activities. This was a similar situation to that in other cities in our area, such as Kolno, Szczuczyn and Grabowo where the youth had a high intellectual level.On occasion, we would travel to visit them, and they would visit us, in particular for performances and "literary judgements" which were very popular in those days among the youth.

In the spring of 1916, the Germans conquered Baranowice and its environs, on the border of Lithuania and White Russia. For security reasons, they transferred the civilian population away from the front. On this journey, refugees from Baranowice, Pinsk and other cities joined us. We had to concern ourselves with finding shelter, some sort of employment, and food for these Jews. We organized a committee to care for the refugees, headed by Chaim Zevulun Bramzon. Older people, such as Orlinski (the son-in-law of Chaim Leib Bramzon) joined this committee. We collected money, clothing, bedding, kitchen utensils and food for them. For this purpose, with the permission of the Germans, we arranged a "flower day" on the streets of the city. Five or six couples went out to the streets and visited the houses, and the population responded with a generous hand, as much as was possible under the circumstances. The Polish population also helped out, and even more so the Germans. In the evening we gave over the money we collected to the treasurer Orlinski. The money was counted in his store, and a document was produced which was signed by all the couples who participated in the collection.

The most important event, which occurred in the Jewish life of the town, particularly for the youth, was the Balfour Declaration. The news of this declaration reached us late, in the month of December 1917, or January 1918.The enthusiasm of the youth and the elders was boundless. We were like dreamers, and we devoted a special time to read the books of Herzl "The Jewish State", and "Altneuland".We also read in depths the four volumes of "At the Crossroads" by Ahad Haam. We presented these topics in front of the community, and we discussed them even in the Beis Midrash with the adults, in particular with those who were members of the Mizrachi movement. These presentations were presented in the following fashion: a translation of an entire discourse or giving over the idea with long quotations. Obviously, the explanations were in Yiddish. Aharon Eliezer Zak particularly excelled in this, for he had a phenomenal memory, as if he had a camera in his brain. He was able to present and entire section just as it was written, in its original form and style, along with a very clear interpretation.

To mark the event, the committee decided to arrange a parade through the streets of the city, at night with torchlight. The parade started out from the hall, and went via the main street to Schmid Gas (the Street of the Smiths), and from there turned right toward the Beis Midrash. Needless to say, we received a permit from the German authorities for this, including for the use of torches and the Hebrew flag. The speakers included David Leibel near the hall; Pelet Remigolski near the Street of the Butchers; and Aharon Eliezer in the Beis Midrash. We erected two wooden podiums, one near the hall and the other in the corner of the street. The preparations took a great deal of time, for all of the members of the community intended to participate in the parade: the elderly and children, women and men all together. On that night, it was like the night of Simchat Torah in the Beis Midrash. Tears of joy and kisses expressed the enthusiasm that overtook the Jewish population. The parade took place on a snowy winter night, which added significantly to the impression of the torchlight and lit windows. To my sorrow, I was not able to participate in the parade, for that night I lay in bed with a cold, however the next day; I received a full account of the strong impression that was left upon all the participants.

This event brought a large percentage of the Jews toward the Zionist movement, and the youth toward the "Young Zion" group, which was spreading at that time very quickly in Russia, and from there transferred to Poland and other lands. Until that time, the Hatechiya Hall was considered non-partisan. Its most important role as in the spreading of culture and enlightenment, however from that year, we began to associate ourselves with the various factions of the Zionist movement. Many of us chose "Young Zion", and the hall officially became a branch of that movement.

In the spring of 1919, a regional convention of Young Zion took place in Lomza, in which I participated as a delegate from our branch. Delegates from nearby towns participated in that convention, from both banks of the Narew. The most important tasks were performed buy the committee and members from Lomza, who had a longer affiliation with the group that we did. The representative of Ostrowiec, Berl Kachan, also excelled. He was a sharp witty youth, who later immigrated to America. In Chicago, he and his two brothers played an important role in Young Zion, and in the local Jewish community.

The convention took place in the Hatechiya Hall of Lomza, and lasted three days and nights. All aspects of the ideology of Young Zion, which was beginning to take its first steps in Poland, were explained there.At that time, the "Chalutz" idea began to develop, even though this name was not yet known. Among the resolutions, which were accepted, the most important were the spread of the Hebrew language, and its use as a living language, as well as Hachshara (practical preparations) for aliya to the Land of Israel. At that time, I was invited by the representatives of Szczuczyn to serve as a Hebrew teacher for adults there. I studied throughout the summer with two groups there, the beginners and advanced groups. However, the youth of Szczuczyn were distant from the Zionist idea, which demanded realization. They were more like associates rather than practical Zionists.

The performance of David Pinski's play "Yankel Der Schmid" (Yankel the Smith) was a unique experience. The stage manager and chief actor was Chona Mondenstein. Since he worked outside of the city all week, all the rehearsals took place on Sabbaths. Therefore, the rehearsals and preparations for this performance took a long time. It was difficult to transform the large granary at the edge of the town into a performance hall. Other than four simple wooden walls and a roof, it had nothing else. We had to clean it, flatten the ground (it did not have a floor), and build a stage and dressing rooms. We did the work with diligence and great enthusiasm. We fixed up its appearance, brought benches for the audience that was expected from all segments of the population. All the hard work was worthwhile. The performance successful (according to the conditions of the time), and the entertainment was superb. People talked about this performance for several weeks thereafter, and it was discussed in every house in town. These types of performances were commonplace at that time in all of the towns of the area, and the presentation of "Yankel der Schmied" on stage raised our worth.

The idea of autonomy for minorities in the new nations, which arose on the ashes of the Austro-Hungarian and Russian empires, made waves also in Poland. In the winter of 1919, a Jewish delegation was called to Warsaw for that purpose. Representatives from all the cities and towns of the newly created Poland were part of that delegation. Two delegates traveled to this meeting from our town: Rabbi Remigolski, and Aharon Eliezer Zak, who represented the youth.I remember that a discussion about this meeting, presented by Aharon Eliezer Zak, took place in our meeting hall, and the crowd was so large that not everybody could fit in. Some people remained outside. His lecture was full of enthusiasm, vision, and faith. The audience stood up and applauded him.

I will never forget that meeting for the rest of my life. We saw in that the footsteps of the Messiah...

Very quickly a change took place in the attitude of the Polish government to the Jews, and whoever could leave Poland and emigrate anywhere did so. A few made aliya to the Land of Israel, while most went to the U.S.A., Canada, Cuba, Mexico, and the countries of South America. Slowly but surely, the town was emptied of its youth, and it was hard to even gather two dozen people for a meeting in our meeting hall.

The meeting hall was transferred to a small room in the attic on top of the bakery of Shlomo Yechiel. The library existed for many more years, and it even grew and developed. However, the meetings no longer took place, partly because of the difficulties in obtaining permits from the Polish authorities.

Our town of Stawiski remained Zionist. In my time, there were no Bundists of Folkists, and the small number of communists who were there left with the retreat of the Bolshevik army from our town in 1920 and immigrated to Russia.

When the news arrived about the authorization of the British Mandate, issued in San Remo in 1922, to set up a Jewish homeland, the Jews went out to the streets and wept from joy. The news reached us on a Sabbath eve, and on the Sabbath morning during the morning prayers, we read the full Hallel [2] in the Beis Midrash, verse by verse. Rabbi Remigolski of blessed memory ascended the lectern (bima) in front of the Holy Ark, and read the Hallel, and the congregation followed after him. I had never heard such a recitation of Hallel previously, and I never have thereafter.

Translator's Footnotes :

1. The eating of leavened bread is strictly forbidden on Passover by Jewish law.

2. Hallel is the psalms of prayers that form part of the service on Passover, Shavuot, Sukkot, Chanukah, and Rosh Chodesh. Nowadays they are recited in many congregations on Israel Independence Day and the day of the liberation of Jerusalem as well. Hallel is associated with miraculous events.

{162}

The First Zionist Activity in Stawiski
by Moshe Goelman of blessed memory

(Impressions and incidents from childhood)

{This Hebrew chapter is equivalent with the following Yiddish chapter – page 167.}

Stawiski was considered to be a town of Misnagdim [1]. Nevertheless, there were several Hassidim there, but their numbers weren't enough for a Minyan [2]. On Simchat Torah, for example, when the Hassidim would gather in a private home for the reading of the Torah and a Kiddush [3] in order to enjoy a Hassidic atmosphere, they would have to invite one or two lads to complete the Minyan. I don't remember exactly how many Hassidim there were in Stawiski, but in accordance with the word about the town, there were eight and a half. Who was the half? A Hassid who was unable to decide to which Admor he belonged: to Gur or Aleksander. Therefore, he was called a half Hassid.

Since most of the residents of Stawiski were Misnagdim, Jewish life in the town was dry. It lacked the Hassidic enthusiasm and effervescence. People were very strict about the observance of the commandments, both the easy and difficult ones, and they watched very carefully to ensure that the youth would not stumble in sin. I remember, for example, that during the youth groups, they would tell the following story (I am stating at the outset that I cannot take responsibility for its veracity). The forest on the road to Lomza was a vorst [4] or more far from town, that is to say, father than the Sabbath limit [5], which was 2,000 cubits. During the summer, the youth used to go on Sabbath afternoons for walks in the forest. When Reb Peretz the teacher found out of this, he would walk along the street up to the Sabbath limit, and make the walkers return. Nevertheless, the youth, who did not want to forego their Sabbath enjoyment, bypassed the street and went to the forest via the fields, in order to avoid meeting Reb Peretz. What did Reb Peretz do? He went and prepared an "Eruv Techumim" every Friday, in order to render permissible the walking to the forest on the Sabbath [6].

Our town had great and renowned scholars. I met two of them by chance. This was on the intermediate days of Sukkot 5683 (1922) when they sat in a hotel in Grodno and investigated Rabbi Reuven Kac of blessed memory, to determine if he is fitting to occupy the rabbinical seat of Stawiski. These two scholars were Reb Meir Kac and Reb Shabtai Frydman of blessed memory.

There were joyous occasions in our town, joy in mitzvot, when the singing of prayers and hymns would take place. However, the joy was restrained. As far as I remember, even on Simchat Torah in the large Beis Midrash, they would not dance with the Torah scrolls during the processions. Enthusiasm never broke out of its bounds, even after a cup of drink. They would sing songs between the processions [7], particularly at the conclusion of the seventh circuit, with the accompaniment of Reb Mordechai the carpenter, a strong baritone, who led the Shacharit (morning) services on the High Holy Days and on other festivals. However, as stated, the joy was restrained, in the manner of Misnagdim.

Chevrat Kass [8]

There was a small Beis Midrash in Stawiski, which had a different atmosphere. It was not strictly Hassidic, but it was full of vitality and enthusiasm. This small Beis Midrash was the locale of the Kass (Keniat Sefarim) organization. From the name "Purchase of Books", the different spirit of this Beis Midrash can be discerned. The walls of this Beis Midrash were filled with books. There were books on the shelves, and there were books in the closets on the eastern wall. I do not know the year that this small Beis Midrash was founded, or who were its founders, but I remember who worshipped there during my youth. The entire Chawa family worshipped there, that is to say Itza Chawes and his son Shebsel Chawes (Frydman), Abba Heler, Shachna Witkowski, Rubinsztejn, the Bramzons, the Liberman brothers (one of them was appointed as the rabbi), Michael the medic (Hirszfeld), the Szymonowicz, Chaim Binyamin Kotton, the three brothers Reb Yeshayahu, Reb Moshe and Reb Nissan Ladelski, and others.

How did the unique atmosphere of Chevrat Kass express itself? It did so in two ways: a) many of its members were readers of newspapers. They would discuss news, and even debate the news of the day. These included my Uncle Yoel, the brother of my mother, who read books and newspapers in Hebrew and Yiddish. Needless to say, he did not subscribe to newspapers himself, for subscriptions were expensive. Rather, he belonged to a group of readers who would take turns reading the newspaper. Often, I would be the messenger who would bring the newspaper to somebody, and go back to fetch it an hour or two later. When I was still a child, I learned my first songs of Zion from my Uncle Yoel. He would intersperse them with the Sabbath hymns. The following are the songs of Zion that were known in those days: "Raise a Flag and Banner to Zion", "The Place of Cedars", and others. I remember that I one brought to him the work of Mendele Mocher Sefarim, "Hasusah" along with the newspaper. He was so excited about the book that he kissed it, and gave me a few coins for candy.

Without doubt, there were also some readers of newspapers among the worshippers of the large Beis Midrash, but I never remember seeing a newspaper in the large Beis Midrash even once. Whereas in Chevrat Kass, I saw people reading the newspaper between Mincha (the afternoon service) and Maariv (the evening service), as well as people discussing and debating the issues of the day based upon what they read in the newspapers. I see the need to point out that in Chevrat Kass I felt a spirit of life and joy that I did not feel in other places of the town.

Simchat Beit Shoeva [9]

On one of the nights of the Intermediate Days of Sukkot, a Simchat Beit Shoeva would take place in the large Beis Midrash. They would sell the "Shir Hamaalot" Psalms with an auction, and whoever donated the most would recite the Psalm in front of the congregation. They would purchase drinks and snacks, which would be distributed among the congregation, whose hearts were merry from eating and drinking as well as singing. In Chevrat Kass, they would celebrate a Simchat Beit Shoeva with even greater festivity and esthetic pleasure. They would decorate the tiny Beis Midrash with colored paper lanterns and light candles in them, which added a special sprit to the festivity. The young people prepared the lanterns, and the adults of the Beis Midrash helped place them. These lanterns remained in place until the night of Simchat Torah, to increase the light and gaiety of the holiday that is completely joyous. In general, the small Beis Midrash was considered as a center of Haskalah and Zionism in Stawiski.

The Zionist Minyan on Simchat Torah

The Zionist Minyan on Simchat Torah took place in the home of Ezriel Liberman. Ezriel Liberman lived in the marketplace, in a mansion where the Wilamowski family later lived. He was a pharmacist by profession, and he owned a small factory for the production of vinegar and various spices. This factory had a door that opened into the marketplace, and when we would pass by during the summer, the strong smell that penetrated out would enter our nostrils. The large room was always filled with large glass bottles covered with straw, from which exuded strong odors. On Simchat Torah, the large room would be emptied from all of its products, and would turn into a prayer hall. Ezriel obtained a Torah scroll from Chevrat Kass, and the Zionists of the city, particularly the youth, gathered in his home for prayer and song. In the Zionist Minyan, they sold off "Atah Hareita" [7], and those called up to the Torah made pledges. All of the money collected went to the Keren Kayemet. After the festival it was sent to the Chovevei Zion committee in Odessa. It goes without saying that there were snacks – drinks and large apples, and that, along with the prayers and hymns of Simchat Torah, songs of Zion were sung. Furthermore, there were also Zionist lectures. I recall that on Simchat Torah, the daughter of the rabbi (I have forgotten her name) spoke. She studied in university in Germany, and came home for the festival. An enthusiasm for Zionism pervaded this Minyan, which made a great impression upon the children that came with their parents to celebrate the Festival of the Torah in the Zionist Minyan.

A Zionist Wedding

When our neighbor Moshe Chaim Kohen, who was numbered among the Zionists of Stawiski, got married, a Zionist wedding was arranged, which was an unusual event. We all recall the customs of a normative wedding during those days, which went more or less as follows: First there would be a reception in the home of the groom. If the groom was a Yeshiva student, he would deliver a lecture on Torah, and afterward receive wedding gifts, known as "Drasha Geshank" [10]. Afterwards, they dressed him with a kittel [11] under his outer cloak, and take him to the home of the bride for the veiling. From the bride's home, they went to the open area that was between the synagogue and the large Beis Midrash. There they set up the chuppa (marriage canopy) and conducted the marriage ceremony. The family and invited guests went to the home of the bride for the wedding reception with dancing, accompanied by the Klezmer band.

My uncle Yoel took me to the wedding of Moshe Chaim Kohen. (My father was not home at the time. At that time, he was an emissary [12] and only came home for the festivals). When we entered the reception at the groom's home, we heard Yisrael Eli Szapira delivering a lecture. Immediately at the conclusion of his speech, the youths went up to all of the invited guests, and pasted blue and white triangular stamps on their lapels. The donations were dedicated, obviously, to the Keren Kayemet. When we came to the home of the bride, we saw that most of the women, particularly the girls that surrounded the bride, already had these stamps on them. After the chuppa ceremony, when we went to the home of the bride, the youths surrounded the bride and groom and sang songs of Zion. There were also fireworks, a wonder that I saw for the first time in my life. People did not stop talking about this unusual wedding for many days, whether in praise or in denigration, each in accordance with his own outlook. As for me, this Zionist wedding left an indelible impression upon my heart.

My Teacher and Rabbi, Reb Moshe Ladelski of blessed memory

During my first five years as a student, I studied with four teachers: The first was Alter the melamed [13]. From him, I learned how to read from a Siddur from him, as well as the first portions of Chumash. From the cheder of Reb Alter, I graduated to Reb Peretz. I studied Chumash and Rashi, the Early Prophets, and my first chapters of Gemara. My third teacher was Reb Yeshaya Ladelski. I studied Gemara and the Latter Prophets with him. My final teacher in the town was Reb Moshe Ladelski, with whom I studied until I was 11. I continued my studies in an elementary Yeshiva that was run by my grandfather Reb Elazar in Jadowna, after the death of my mother of blessed memory. I wish to discuss in particular Reb Moshe and his style of teaching.

His first wife was the daughter of the cantor Kaplan of Stawiski. Her brother was Pesach Kaplan, the editor of the newspaper "Bialystoker Shtime". He was also known as a musician and composer. He composed many melodies for songs in Hebrew and Yiddish, and he also published a small songbook with his melodies. Pesach Kaplan particularly excelled in composing tunes for Yiddish operettas in the theaters of Vilna and other cities. His sister also loved song, and as she worked in the kitchen, she would sing with her sweet voice before the Rebbe returned from the evening prayers. We would come to the cheder of Reb Moshe after the morning prayers and breakfast. It is interesting that every student was free to worship himself in any synagogue that he chose, or at home. This independence that Reb Moshe granted increased our self-assurance, and we saw ourselves as adults.

The morning hours were dedicated to independent learning (machn aleinen in Yiddish). Even though this study was under the supervision of the Rebbe, its main purpose was independent study in private or in pairs. We returned home at noon. When we returned to the cheder, each of us had to tell over to the Rebbe the lessons that we had prepared in the morning. Then, Reb Moshe would add explanations, correct errors, and provide background discussion on the topic that we had studied on our own. On occasion, he would ask one student to correct the error of another student, which opened up the opportunity for debate between the students. I do not know the source from which Reb Moshe obtained this pedagogical style. Perhaps it was from intuition. The important thing was that it led us towards independent study in Yeshivas, and instilled in us self-assurance and great satisfaction.

Reb Moshe was taciturn in his speech, and on occasion we had to understand him through innuendoes. We learned how to grasp the issue before he finished a sentence. We would then finish the sentence, at time as a chorus. His style was simple and straightforward explanation, without sharpness and didactics, and without questions and answers. The examples that he brought to explain topics came for the most part from day to day life. The discipline was free, and he treated us light adults. First he asked to hear what we had to say, and only afterward did he add his own comments. A whip or rod – standard implements of the teachers of that time – were not found in the cheder of Reb Moshe.

We were free from our studies on Sabbath afternoons. Most of the students were examined at that time by their fathers or other examiners. One of them was Reb Chuna the baker (Chuna Hersh Leibes Wladkowski), who also served as the gabbai in the large Beis Midrash. I studied in the same class as his son Tzvi Aryeh of blessed memory. Since my father was for the most part not at home, I was examined by Reb Chuna along with his son.

There was another custom in the cheder of Reb Moshe Ladelski. Every Friday, the students would bring a sum of money to the cheder, each according to his means, some less and some more. This money was placed into a special box that was tied to the wall. At the end of the term, for a that time we learned in accordance with terms – From Pesach until Rosh Hashanah, and from Sukkot until Pesach – the Rebbe's wife would open up the box, take out the money, and arrange a feast of conclusion for the students. Our parents participated in this feast, and our mothers assisted with the preparations. I only remember one such meal at the end of the term, for this fine woman died the following winter. All of us, all of the students of Reb Moshe, felt ourselves as orphans after the death of the wife of our Rebbe, for she endeared herself to us in an exceptional manner.

Reb Moshe was numbered among the first of Chovevei Zion in our city. In those days, at the beginning of the 20 th century, Dr. Herzl founded the Colonial Bank in London. Zionists sold shares of this bank in all Jewish communities. Reb Moshe also purchased a share in this bank, which cost 10 rubles (a significant sum of money in those days). He paid for it in installments of 5 kopecks. I remember that two youths came to the cheder every Friday, took the payment, and gave him a triangular stamp as a receipt. Reb Moshe put the stamp into the volume of Talmud that was on the table. This volume of Talmud was, apparently, his ledger.

On one summer day in 1904, Reb Shalom the melamed appeared suddenly at our cheder (Reb Shalom was the shofar blower in the synagogue, and he also fixed shofars), and told our Rebbe the bad news of the death of Dr. Herzl. I recall that Reb Moshe, when he heard this news, put down his head, turned white, and appeared to be weeping silently. That day, we concluded our studies in the middle the day. This was not out of joy, as was customary for children on a day off. This time we left the cheder sad, even though we did not know whom this man was whose death caused our Rebbe such deep anguish.

After Reb Moshe married the widow Chaya Shoshka, who had a grocery store next to the church, he stopped teaching and earned his livelihood from the store. He set up his home in one of the dwellings in our home, and accepted a new position in our town – the job of arbitrator of monetary matters. He would at time sit in judgement together with Reb Shabtai Frydman, and sometimes he would adjudicate himself. This task of arbitrator that Reb Moshe accepted earned him great appreciation in the town. He maintained this position even in the years after I had left Poland.

May his soul be bound in the bonds of eternal life.

Finally – I wish to discuss the aliya of our friend Avraham Szymonowicz to the Land of Israel. Avraham merited being one of the first to make aliya from our town during the time of the Second Aliya and also the Third Aliya [14]. If you were to ask, how was this? The first time he made aliya, he worked in Hadera at the drying of swamps. He took ill with malaria, and was forced to leave the Land for a period. In the interim, the First World War broke out, and the Land was closed off and sealed. When the gates of the land opened at the conclusion of the war and the Third Aliya commenced, Avraham was once again one of the first to make aliya from our town. At that time, he was already married. He settled in the Moshav of Balfouria. The eldest son of Reb Chuna the baker, the son of Reb Motel Kaminski (the baker), as well as others were among those of our town who joined the Third Aliya.

Since we are discussing the family of Berl Szymonowicz of Stawiski, it is fitting to point out that his eldest daughter Sarake, Avraham's sister, was the first to travel to Warsaw to study in the school for kindergarten teachers. She was one of the first licensed kindergarten teachers in that time, but for various reasons, she did not actually practice this profession.

Translator's Footnotes :

1. Ideological opponents of Hassidism.

2. A quorum of ten male Jewish adults over the age of 13, needed to conduct a prayer service.

3. A prayer recited over wine at the beginning of the Sabbath and Festival meals. Here, it refers to a snack, accompanied by the recitation of Kiddush, after the morning services.

4. An obsolete Russian measure of distance.

5. The Sabbath limit (Techum Shabbat) is the boundary beyond which one is not allowed to walk outside a built up area on the Sabbath or festival. This limit is set at 2,000 cubits (roughly 3,000 feet) outside of the last built up area of a town.

6. Eruv Techumim (literally the intermingling of boundaries) is a technically detailed halachic device that allows the Sabbath boundary to be moved. Rather than have it extend 2,000 cubits to the right and 2,000 cubits to the left, it can be 'moved', for example, so that it would be 1,000 cubits to the right and 3,000 cubits to the left. This is accomplished by placing a token Sabbath meal, consisting of bread and wine, at the new outer limit, thereby establishing that point as place where one 'establishes' his Sabbath rest. By moving it in one direction, one detracts from the opposite direction, so one cannot move it more than an extra 2,000 cubits. This halachic device sounds like it is skirting a law – however, the 2,000 cubit limit on the Sabbath boundary is a rabbinically based (as opposed to Torah based) law, so the rabbis who set this law in the first place also set up a device to move the boundary, within limits, in cases of need.

7. On Simchat Torah, the festival of the Rejoicing of the Torah following the Sukkot holiday, seven circuits are made around the synagogue with the Torah scrolls, both at night and during the day. These processions are generally accompanied with much singing and dancing. Prior to removing the Torah scrolls from the ark for the processions, a selection of verses is recited, called "Atah Hareita". In many synagogues, it is customary to auction off the honor of reciting these verses, as well as other Simchat Torah honors.

8. Kass is an acronym for Keniyat Sefarim – Chevrat Kass is "The Organization for the Purchase of Books".

9. A joyous celebration of song and dance held on the nights of the Sukkot holiday. Literally "The rejoicing of the Water Drawing", reminiscent of the water drawing ceremony and celebration on Sukkot during the time of the Temple. A

Simchat Beit Shoeva often includes the recitation of Psalms 120-134, known as "Shir Hamaalot" – Songs of Accents. They are called so because they were recited on the steps of the Temple courtyard during the water drawing ceremony on Sukkot.

10.   Drasha is Hebrew (and Yiddish) for a Torah lecture, and Geshank is Yiddish for gifts.

11.   A white cloak worn by men during the wedding ceremony, and also during the prayers of Yom Kippur and the Pesach Seder. It is worn by the chazzan on other occasions, such as Rosh Hashanah, the Hoshanah Rabba service, the Prayer for Rain on Shemini Atzeret, and the Prayer for Dew on the first day of Passover.

12.   A Meshulach, one whose job it is to raise funds for an institution.

13.   A definition of terms used in this section: Melamed – a teacher of young children; Siddur – prayer book; Chumash – the Five Books of Moses; Rashi – The acronym for Rabbi Shlomo Yitzchaki, the classical commentator on the bible and the Talmud. Gemara – another term for Talmud. The Early Prophets include the books of Joshua, Judges, Samuel I & II, and Kings I & II. The Latter Prophets include the books of Isaiah, Jeremiah, Ezekiel, and the twelve minor prophets.

14.   The period of the Second Aliya was from 1904-1914, and the Third Aliya was from 1919-1923.

{173}

Paths in the Ashes
by Chemda Lewinowicz
Translated by Jerrold Landau
The Town and its Panoramas

The center of the town was a square plaza surrounded on all four sides by rows of houses. From this plaza, the streets and lanes spread out to the length and width of the town. The Jews lived in the center and in the nearby roads, while the Poles lived in the outer alleys. The Polish intelligentsia was for the most part concentrated around the roads adjacent to the road to Lomza, and around the courthouse and post office.

The town served as a business, cultural and religious center for the residents of the villages that surrounded it on all sides. On the regular weekly market days, villagers would stream into the city, some by wagon and some by foot (in the summer, the villagers would walk barefoot to the outskirts of the town, with their shoes tied to their backs so that they would not wear them out). They would bring bags of grain, produce of the chicken coop and cattle barns, firewood, peat and other such items, to sell to the Jews. They would purchase foodstuffs, cloth, household utensils, tools, etc. During the fairs, the market plaza and the nearby roads would be filled to capacity with wagons laden with agricultural products that were brought in by the villagers for sale. Merchants and salesmen would come from afar during the fairs with their variegated merchandise, and the market would be noisy and bustling.

During the summer months, wanderers would bring into the town a merry-go-round, which was set up in one of the corners of the market place. Beautiful wooden horses attached to two seated winter wooden wagons would circle around from the afternoon hours until late at night, accompanied by the sound of a noisy band. The merry-go-round was an attraction for the children, both Jewish and Polish. First and foremost, the gentiles of the villages would invite their girlfriends for a spin.

Aside from the children, the adult Jews would also try out this means of enjoyment. Only Reb Avraham Ber Kilinsky of blessed memory once broke this 'tradition'. The friends of my brother Yitzchak of blessed memory knew Reb Avraham Ber, who was an intelligent Jew and a lover of tricks, and they would jest and converse with him on occasion in our home. Once, when these boys were light of heart, they promised Reb Avraham Ber a specific prize if he would dare to take a spin on the merry-go-round. To their surprise, Reb Avraham Ber agreed, and the entire group accompanied him to the merry-go-round. Reb Avraham Ber mounted a horse, took hold of the reins, and to the cheers of the crowd made an entire circuit, and thus won his prize.

There were other attractions for the children. A man with a street organ that rested on a wooden pedestal would circulate through the streets. He would stop at every house and turn the handle of the organ, and a melody would play: "From Russia, Oh From Russia...". At a later time, a person came with a more advanced street organ, equipped with a large amplifier, which was able to play many melodies. The small children who faithfully accompanied the organ player would inspect the organ from all sides, place their heads into the amplifier, and search for the singer who was "hiding" inside...

The small monkey tied to a rope, which would dance to the order of its master, brought special enjoyment. Similarly, on occasion a troupe of youths who were practicing acrobatics would appear in the outskirts of the city, and present their routine to the children.

Each summer, a variety of vagabonds would come to town and pitch their tents in the nearby forests. The men would sell handmade copper vessels, and the women would go around from home to home to solicit fees for palm reading and telling of fortunes by cards.

The first radio that arrived in the town was far from perfect. It was barely possible to hear the broadcast through the pair of receivers that was attached to the device. However, due to the novelty, it gave rise to great curiosity in the community. In order to allow for a large group of people to see the wondrous device and to hear the voice coming from it, the small radio was brought to the library hall, where people would stand in line until the awaited moment arrived in order to listen to the broadcast. However, only a small period of time was allotted to each person, and even though it was only possible with difficulty to make out a word here and there, the people would leave satisfied, and describe with enthusiasm the wonderful device to those who did not merit to hear it.

Hershel Mark of blessed memory, a well-to-do man in town, was the first to acquire a large and functional radio, as functional as could be at that time period in any case.A large amplifier was attached to the side of the device. On summer nights, he would place his radio on the sill of his open window of his second floor residence. Since his house was near to the main street where many people would stroll along the sidewalk near the house in the evenings, many people would be able to listen to the tunes that blared into the street via the amplifier.

Stawiski was blessed with beautiful forests that were part of the property of the Squire Kiszlaniczki, a member of the Polish nobility. On the southwest side, about a kilometer and a half from the town, stood the Sokolocha flourmill, which the Squire leased to the Jewish miller Stolnicki. A gigantic wheel drove the mill through the power of the waterfall that was created from the waters of the nearby river. The river continued to flow through the depths of the forests, and there the women of the town would go to bathe in the summer. The route to the mill served as a shortcut for the path that led between the wheat fields. Particularly pleasant was the sound of the walking of bare feet upon this path while it was still soft from a summer rain which had fallen a day previously, and while it had now been warmed from the sun which shone when the clouds had dispersed.

During our childhood, we loved to visit this pleasant place. We would secretly go around the house that was in the center, and walk along the path to the mill. On occasion, we would succeed in hiding in the haystacks that were at the side of the road when we would see from afar Uncle Chaim of blessed memory walking along the path to the mill, in order that he would not find us and report at home that he had caught us in our "mischief". Our friends, the children of the miller, would greet us at the mill, and take us for a boat ride on the river, or we would go for a walk in the depths of the aromatic forest. When we got tired, we would rest in the valleys of one of the hills, and refresh ourselves with cold buttermilk and black bread, made by the wife of the miller.

There was a large forest of pine trees on the hills to one side of the mill. On the other side of the hills, the village Chmielewo was nestled among the trees of the forest. It spread out for a few kilometers on the sides of a dirt path, which led to the estate of the Jew Denenberg, the brother-in-law of Yisrael-Eli Szapira of blessed memory. On that estate, the "Hechalutz" youth group members would receive their agricultural training (hachshara) prior to immigrating to the Land of Israel. During the summer, the village of Chmielewo served as a vacation spot and spa for the residents of Stawiski and the towns in the area of Lomza, Szczuczyn, and others.

The scenery was amazing. Artists would come from afar to draw pictures of the landscape. The Squire Kiszlaniczki would invite his noble guests to the forest, near the flourmill, where he held parties during summer evenings. After some time, the Squire cultivated the forest, and the hills and valleys that were once covered with trees were now bare, and sadly bore witness to the beautiful landscape that once was and now is no longer.

There was a six-kilometer long forest along the sides of the road to Lomza. This forest served as a meeting place for the youth, who came there in droves primarily during Sabbaths and festivals. They would come alone or in groups, by foot or on bicycle (of course, only on a weekday). This forest had the splendor of creation, and it was saturated with its beauty and special charm during all seasons of the year. Its tall, erect coniferous trees looked as if their tops were kissing the heavens.

A spring flowed from the thickness of the forest, and would provide cold water for the thirsty hiker. During the summer, the children would spread out among the thick trees to pick berries and strawberries. On moonlight nights, a walk in the forest was like a walk in some far-off enchanted land, which was wide without end.

Destruction befell this forest as well during the Second World War. As is related, the trees of this forest served as building materials for the Soviets, who built a new city in that place.

In a cave in the forest, near an open field, stood the lone house of the guardian of the forest, who was also a skinner of carcasses. That gentile, who would mingle with the Jews, would greet our group pleasantly and allow us to use the seesaw that was in his yard. He would purchase his household goods from the Jews in our town. Once I saw him in the bakery of Meir Katz of blessed memory, he purchased a loaf a bread and said "Hamotzi lechem min haaretz, I want to eat like a squire" [1]– he laughed heartily and devoured an ample piece of bread with his healthy teeth.

There were gentiles, particularly young ones, who learned to speak Yiddish fluently due to their constant dealings with Jews. The horseman of one of the wagon drivers particularly excelled in this. He was sent on long journeys with his horse and wagon, including to the capital city of Warsaw. Once this young gentile was forced to spend the Sabbath in one of the towns. What did he do? He went to the synagogue, pretended he was a Jew, and, as was customary in those days, one of the Jews of that town invited him as a Sabbath guest to his home.

The church of Stawiski took up one entire corner of the market plaza.Even though it was not a low building by any stretch of the imagination, the priest decided to raise the spires so that it would not be lower than the Jewish synagogues, even though the synagogues were on one of the side alleyways, and did not "compete" at all with the church. The construction effort was done primarily by Christians from both the town and the villages. Christian girls also assisted in the construction effort by bringing building materials to the builders. Thus did the priest realize his wish, and the spires of the church were higher than anything else.

There was a large courtyard behind the church, which had in it a fruit orchard. On each Christian festival, the congregation of worshippers would exit through a large gate in the side of the building in order to make processions around the church. A long brick fence surrounded the east side of the church. In the center, near the door to the church, there was a tall, thick wooden pillar, upon which rested a large statue of the "holy mother" carrying her son Jesus in her arms.

On Sundays and Christian festivals, all the Jewish stores were closed.Only the grocery store, which was owned by one of the rich gentiles, remained open. Ironically, it was only that individual, a Christian, who was allowed to conduct business on Sundays and Christian festivals.

Another rich gentile purchased the inn in the center of the city from its Jewish owners. Thus did the Christians slowly encroach on the businesses that had been the sole domain of the Jews for generations, in an effort to increase their livelihood. This activity became more prevalent, overt and brutal during the latter years of the 1930s, when, with the rise of the Nazis in Germany, the Polish anti-Semites began to pillage the domain of the Jews.

There were Christian holidays that were the cause of practical jokes in the town. In addition to the prayers and confessions that took place in the church, the anti-Semitic priest injected a heavy dose of Jew hatred into the hearts of his flock. Many of the gentiles filled up the taverns after they left church, and as they left there drunk as Lot, they would often provoke the Jews. On such days, brave fearless Jews would stand on guard, and any drunk who would attack a Jew would merit to feel the full force of their power. This independent Jewish defense instilled fear upon the hotheaded anti-Semites.

There were Christian holidays when Jews avoided going out on the streets. Once such day was January 1st, the New Year of the Christians. On the eve of the holiday and during the following morning, their children and youths would roam about in groups in the town dressed up in a variety of costumes. The most prominent of these costumes were: the angel of death dressed in white, upon his head a gigantic styliform white hat, with a sickle in his hand; another costume was black, with long horns and a tail, with a whip in his hand; a third costume was a hunchbacked dwarf – symbolizing a Jew. If any such a group would come across a Jew, they would mock him and force him to bow down before them. Thus did the gentile take revenge on the Jew for the crucifixion of Jesus.

In the summer, on a particular Thursday, the "Green Festival" (the festival of the fields and the crops) would take place. There would be a religious procession which drew large crowds. This procession spread out all over the town plaza. Only after the conclusion of the religious ceremony, when the crowds returned to the church, would the Jews come out onto the streets.

The Jews did not live their lives in the town in comfort. From way back, Poland spread hatred and venom upon the Jews. Their babies imbibed this hatred from their mother's milk. A child who did not listen to his parents was threatened with the threat that "the Satanic Zhid (Jew) will come and snatch you". The Jews seldom entered the gentile alleys, especially so during evenings and nights, due to fear of Polish hooligans "shkotzim" [2], who would pelt them with stones and send their dogs toward them.

From my childhood, I remember one particular incident with a dog that scared my friend Gittel and myself as we returned in the evening from a walk in the forest of Lomza. A gentile whom we did not recognize walked behind us, and beside him was a gigantic hunting dog. When the gentile caught up with us and passed us, the dog fell upon us and frightened us.As it approached us we began to scream in fright.We thought that it would tear us to pieces. The dog backed off from us for a moment as we screamed, and then again fell upon us. This cruel game lasted the entire way from the forest to the entrance to the town. The gentile walked in front of us the entire time, as if he did not hear our screams.

From among the Polish intelligentsia, we remember fondly the teacher Helena Laskowska, and the justice of the peace, whose relationship with the Jews was liberal. The judge would customarily come, along with a number of other Christians, to the synagogue on Yom Kippur eve in order to listen to the singing of Kol Nidre. They would also come on Simchat Torah eve. The teacher

Helena described the final journey of the Jews of Stawiski in a letter to Dr. Yona Rubinsztejn, a native of our hometown who lives in Paris.

In those days, wide wagons were used for transportation. They were covered with thick cloth that was supported by semicircular iron bars. This protected the travelers from the sun, rain, and snow.Later, people would travel in a wagon that was harnessed to two horses, where eight travelers were squished in like sardines. With the passage of time, there was a radical change in the mode of transportation.People would travel from Grajewo to Lomza via Stawiski by bus. The young wagon drivers in our town could not compete for long with the modern mode of transportation.At one point they purchased a bus which would travel twice daily to Lomza and back. The bus was not new, however its red color caught the eye. When it would park in front of one of the inns in the center of the town, a group of curious onlookers would gather around to witness the wonders of modern technology. The bus was primarily an attraction for the children, who would gather around it and pat it lovingly. They did not leave it until it began to drive away.

It is related about one gentile farmer, that he stood and wondered how such an inanimate object could move by its own power. After he listened to the explanation, he pursed his lips and asked: "this all makes sense, but I still wonder how the bus can move without the aid of horses...".

I still remember an event that occurred to me in connection to the bus. One day, I was almost trampled by the hooves of horses. The event was such: When the driver moved the bus, I was in the middle of the plaza. Suddenly the horses became frightened from the sound of the horn and the engine, and began to panic as they were tied to the wagons. I made my way with difficulty among the horses that were fleeing in confusion. I ran with all my might, and my hands were spread out to all passers by in an effort to "stop" the horses. I was constantly shouting to them : Frrr!... Frrr!... Only by a miracle did I come out unharmed from this unexpected stampede.

During the Time of the First World War

A few weeks prior to the outbreak of the First World War, I began grade one in a Russian public school, since White Russia, like other areas of Poland, was at the time under the dominion of Czarist Russia. The school was housed in a large room on the second floor on one of the Chamilawski houses on the route to Szczuczyn. There were three classes in that room, one for beginners, one for more the more advanced, and one for older students, and one teacher taught all three. We did not have opportunity to learn much. One day, we heard the ringing of a bell outside. As was customary in those days, the town clerk would go about at a time of need, ringing a bell in different places to alert the residents and inform them of various announcements from the civic government. This time there was something out of the ordinary in the alarm of the bell, since we saw the teacher leave the room in a hurry, jump over the stairs and disappear. We never saw him again.That was the day that the First

World War broke out, and a short time later the Germans occupied Poland, that is to say, the part that belonged to Czarist Russia.

During the war, a few cannonballs landed in the town. One cannonball damaged the side of the Beis Midrash and destroyed a portion of the eastern wall. The Germans fixed it, and even decorated the windows that were part of the door of the Great Synagogue with stained glass. Another cannonball hit a woman who was carrying food to her son who was studying in the cheder and killed her on the spot. An additional cannonball fell near the smith shop that was at the edge of the city, in the direction of Jedwabne. At that time, I was walking from the market plaza to my home with a half a pail of water (I was not able to carry more than that). Suddenly I heard a frightening whistle. I recognized that this was a cannonball, and at that moment, I imagined that it was falling upon my head. In fright, I left the pail in the street and ran home with all my might as I was "shaking" off the cannonball from my head. A short time afterward, we, the children and older youths, ran toward the smith shop. Only through a miracle was the house saved from destruction and its inhabitants from death. To their good fortune, the cannonball fell on loose ground near the smith house, and did not explode.

At first, the German army garrison that was stationed in the city began to plunder anything that came to its hand – cloth from stores, barley, wheat, flour, sugar, and other provisions, and transferred them to Germany. In return for this plundering, the Germans gave a "receipt". Apparently, all of the receipts were written with the same text: "Giving on credit causes worry". They left a small amount of flour to bake black bread, which was distributed each day to the hungry population in small quantities. White sugar was not available, but on occasion they distributed portions of yellow sugar that was referred to as "horse sugar". Tea was made from Landrin candies [3], and dry cherry stems were used to make juice.

In those troubled days, my brother Yitzchak would go at night to the villages to purchase wheat from the farmers. Most of the time, he went with my Uncle Chaim. The trip to bring the grain to the Sokolocha flourmill, and to bring the wheat home was fraught with fear, lest this food fall into the hands of the Germans. Once my brother requested my help in bringing the flour from the mill. At the time, I was a young girl. He dressed me in a wide long dress, and placed a cloth on my head so that I would resemble a gentile, and my brother took me with him on a wagon to the mill. After they loaded up the sacks of flour, my brother seated me on top of them so that my long wide dress would cover the sacks. Thus we were able to traverse the entire journey, and bring the flour home without a problem.

We were not always that successful. As was customary in those days in the town, we raised chickens for our own use. From among all of the hens, I liked one in particular, which had very nice feathers. It was very fat, and "motherly" as she walked with her chicks. One morning, I found it dead in the yard. When I began to cry, my mother got angry and said: "is this what you cry for?

If the Germans, would take the flour, heaven forbid – you certainly would not cry". That afternoon, when my brother returned from the mill with a wagon laden with bags of flour and stopped near the house – German soldiers suddenly appeared and took everything.They did not even give a "receipt".

My mother was correct – I did not cry about the theft. I only had enough tears to cry about the beautiful hen that died.

It is important to point out that the Germans during the First World War were not the same as the Germans during the Nazi era. As they became acquainted with the residents, they related to them in a sympathetic manner, and made various improvements for the benefit of the population. They closed up the open pits, dug new wells and equipped them with pails for drawing water, in order that the residents would be able to draw good, clean water. The uncovered springs of water near the Beis Midrash, and hear the Sokolocha mill, which gave forth an ample supply of clear water.

The Germans also ensured that the town would be kept clean. They would arrange the cleaning of any dirty place. They would enlist youths for "hard labor". For this purpose, they would enter houses and find any young person who was young and able in order to do various jobs – in the winter for clearing snow from the paths and in the spring for cleaning the streets from the mud that remained after the snow melted. They put up large shelters in all open fields for the benefit of the residents, and placed benches in them. They placed benches around the old chestnut trees that were close to the post office so that the pedestrians and those who came to the post office could rest. In the evenings, the soldiers would sit on the steps of the house in the center of the city which served as the garrison headquarters, and they would play joyous marching tunes with hand held accordions, accompanied by percussion instruments.They loved children, and would give them sweets.

Nevertheless, I remember an incident that left a heavy impression on me. One day, a crowd of villagers entered the market plaza. They said that they were brought there because they did not provide the requested amount of grain to the Germans, and they did not know what was to happen with them.The villagers stood in the plaza in a square. The Germans ordered some of them to place down bags of sand in a few places. Suddenly, other villagers were brought there, and the Germans commanded them to lie on the bags of sand, and the thugs beat them on their backs until blood flowed. The site that we saw by peering out of the window was horrible. This incident took place in front of all of the villagers, so that they should see and be afraid. The screams of those that were beaten were heart-rending, however they did not move the hearts of those "good" Germans.

At the conclusion of the war, Poland was left with a great shortage of food and clothing. Salvation came from the United States, which sent large shipments of food to the hungry lands of Europe. Poland also received its share, and each city and town received an appropriate portion. Cloth for clothing was very expensive, and we used the American wheat sacks for that purpose. They were made of thick, fine cloth, which was appropriate for the sewing of clothes. First, mother would dye the cloth bright gray. After some time, our brother Nechemia who was in the United States sent large amounts of non-perishable food, as well as wonderful packages of clothing. Due to the unusually large size of the shipment, my brother Yitzchak had to travel to Czestochowa, a large distance from Stawiski, in order to bring them home. The package included clothing for men and women, shoes, sewing materials, soap, and many more such things – all new, straight from the factory. Friends and relatives came to see the array of fine things, and their mouths were full of praise for the dedicated son who was overseas.

The Bolshevik Invasion

The road that went through the city was known as the "King's Road" or the Warsaw-Petersburg Road. The Bolskeviks arrived via this road in 1920, when the Red army invaded Poland. The soldiers camped out in the market plaza for some time, with all of their utensils and weapons. The soldiers appeared forlorn in their poor clothing and their torn shoes. They did not give the impression of an orderly army, but rather as riffraff who had weapons in their hands quite by chance. They behaved sympathetically toward the population during their sojourn, and the gentiles also enjoyed their food.

The estate of Kiszlaniczki was on the side of the road that led to Szczuczyn. He lived there in a splendid palace with his family. It is told that his daughter was married to one of the wealthy oil sheiks of the Persian Gulf. After some time, she separated from him, and she went to live in her father's house with her child. They guarded the grandson of Kiszlaniczki very carefully. Rumor had it that the emissaries of the sheik were stalking her in order to kidnap the child and return him to his father's house. The daughter of the Squire would on occasion suddenly be seen driving along the main street in a splendid automobile. A private automobile, especially one driven by a woman was in those days in Stawiski one of the wonders of the world.

Near the entrance to the villa, on the other side of the road, stood a row of low two family houses, where the estate's employees lived. Some of them looked after the fruit orchards; another group took care of the fields near the villa that grew all types of vegetables. The wealthy Jews of the town would purchase the best of the fruits and pay top dollar for them. The remainder of the workers worked in the fields. During the time of the harvest, early in the morning, wagons full of groups of workers, male and female, would pass through the town. They would be on their way to the wheat fields that were behind the city, a few kilometers away. They would return at dark to their homes after a hard day of difficult labor.

The houses of the workers were small, poor and covered with soot. The foreman of the estate was hard hearted, and had no concern for the minimal needs of the workers. The working conditions in the estate were difficult, and the pay was poor. Strikes were not acceptable in those days, and the exploitation was terrible. It is no wonder that the hatred toward the rich Squire, who lived a life of excess and comfort, overflowed in their hearts.

When the news arrived that the Red Army invaded Poland, the Kiszlaniczki family fled to Warsaw. The last one who remained was the foreman of the estate, who did everything to save what could be saved, including among other things the large flock of cows which was transported on foot to Warsaw by a group of workers. After the Bolsheviks entered Stawiski and set up a local government, the workers of the estate were the first to rise up in revenge against their master, and many of the gentiles of the town joined them.

On one Sabbath, we went to the estate. We entered inside the courtyard and the palace. This was the first time that a Jew set foot there. The courtyard was quite large, and it had a variety of fruit trees. Surrounding the palace, there were shade trees and flower gardens. We entered the main palace, went up to the second floor – everywhere we turned there was ruin and destruction. The gentiles pillaged everything that they were able – they destroyed without mercy. This was the first time that we saw a bathtub in a home, for aside from in the bathhouse, there was no bathtub even in the homes of the wealthy people of the city. The bathtub had also been destroyed. Parts of books from the large library of the Squire rolled around the steps and the paths in the courtyard like falling leaves. Our gentile neighbors also enjoyed the loot, and they brought to their homes upholstered chairs, curtains, fine foodstuffs, bedding, expensive mirrors, etc. The revenge was thorough.

The leader of the local communists was the young man Hertzke Kolinski, the son of old age of Rev Avraham Ber. He was a fine young man, self-taught. He knew Russian fluently. The Polish authorities knew that he was an ardent communist, and persecuted him. He hid from them in granaries or attics.

When the government passed to the Bolsheviks, Hertzke stood at the head of the "Rebkum", the town council. He was strong willed and energetic. He would speak to his elders in an authoritarian manner. When he took control of the government, he treated harshly anyone who appeared to him as a counter-revolutionary, or who disobeyed his edicts. He did not show favoritism to anyone, whether he was a person of honor, or a family member.

Reb Yechiel Mondensztejn was one of the first of the bakers who was put in jail because he refused to accept Czerbonczim (the Bolshevik coin in those days) in payment for bread. The Jews had no faith in that currency, and treated it as a low value. After a few days, he also put my father in jail for the same crime. When I went to visit my father, I heard Hertzke's secretary tell one of the prisoners who looked at her longingly that Hertzke "almost shot a bullet into the head of Yechiel the baker". It is told that when Hertzke's mother, who was known as a valiant and sharp witted woman, came to Hertzke to request that he have mercy on the life of Reb Yechiel, he said to her": "Get out of here immediately, otherwise I will shoot a bullet into your head". His mother knew that her son was liable to carry out his threat – and she left as quickly as she came.

After the defeat the Bolsheviks suffered near Warsaw, the famous defeat that was known as "the miracle on the Wisla", they retreated via our town. They passed through the road in three rows for three consecutive days and nights. That was the first time that we saw a camel. It was the conclusion of the Sabbath, the final night of their retreat. Most of the local communists joined the last of those retreating. One of them, a gentile, came to us and tried to take the coat from my brother Yitzchak by force. My brother wrestled with him, and my mother and my sister assisted him. Suddenly the gentile quickly left the house, after his Jewish friend, who stood behind the door, warned him that someone was approaching.

This was not sufficient. In our neighborhood, there lived a Polish family. With their good anti-Semitic hearts, they incited a soldier of the Red army to enter our house, to go to the cellar and take anything good from there. They told them that they would find a bounty there. The claims of mother that we did not have very much were to no avail. The soldier went to the cellar. A Russian captain entered our house when he heard the loud argument. When mother explained to him what happened, the captain went to the soldier, who in the meantime came up from the cellar empty-handed, and scolded him: "You are a communist, are you not ashamed? What business do you have here?" The soldier left in haste. Mother thanked the captain. He comforted her, and told her to close the doors, to shut the blinds, and not to open up to anyone.

At the Time of the Polish Liberation Army

The next day, on Sunday, a tense quiet prevailed in the town. There was great fear about the future. There was a fear that the Polish army that would come on the heels of the retreating army would see every Jew as a communist. There would be no shortage of groups among the gentiles who would support this notion, in particular since the city government during the time of the Bolsheviks was almost all Jewish. Shots were heard all day, which were fired by the Polish army that was advancing along the road to Lomza, even though the last of the retreating Bolshevik army left the town in the middle of the night. The residents spent the day locked up in their homes. Some found refuge behind the inner walls, and others in the cellars of their houses.

As the Polish army hesitated to enter the town, lest they find remnants of the Bolshevik army in town, a delegation of Jews went out to inform them that the town was clear of the enemy.

The Polish army entered the town in the evening, and filled up the entire Market Square. According to an edict from the Jewish guard, all of the stores were opened wide, and the Jews welcomed the arriving army with joy, and gave them goods some of the goods that they had left. The soldiers behaved toward the Jews with great indignity. Soldiers requested from us pails from which to feed their horses. It is unnecessary to add that the two pails that they took were not returned. We did not become upset about this. We were happy that we were saved from "blood of revenge" in their anger.

At that time, garrisons of the Polish army visited the town at certain times. Among these were the troops of General Haller, whose soldiers were called after his name – Hallercziks, and garrisons from the Poznan region – Poznancziks. Both of these were known for their great hatred of Jews. Whether they spent a short period in town, or a longer period, the Jews were afraid, for they would pillage the Jews and treat them with cruelty. They would search the houses of the Jews, and take whatever they wished.

The head of the Poznancic garrison, who lived in our home for a long time, was certain that our silver and gold – for is there any Jew who did not own silver and gold? – was hidden in the thick plank that was in the ceiling of the large room. According to his imagination, it was manufactured for that purpose, due to the unusual dimensions of that plank. The soldier began to knock the plank with a stick. He thought that in that manner he would hear the sound of the clanging of the valuable objects, which his soul so desired, and he would be able to find the hidden door to this treasure. However all of his efforts were for naught, and his eyes became green with flames of anger. His eyes were able to freeze the blood in the veins. I was not at peace until that soldier left the town with his friend.

 One day an army garrison arrived in the city. There was a rumor that a group of Hallercziks was approaching. All the stores and homes were locked, and no Jew wandered in the marketplace. Unexpectedly, the garrison continued on and traveled to Szczuczyn, however the last of the soldiers of this garrison intentionally remained in town to pillage the Jewish homes. Suddenly, cries of "help" were heard from amidst the quiet with reigned in town. Members of the local government could not be found on the streets, as if the earth had swallowed them, and the cries for help of the Jews were like cries for help in a desert.

The soldiers entered our house as well through the back door. They searched until they found father's coat hanging in one of the corners of the room, with a sum of money in the inner pocket. When the soldier placed his hand in the pocket, mother rose from her place, grabbed the soldier's hand, and did not let go. He at first began to wrestle with her, but he was finally startled by her bravery and her words of admonition, and he left the house.

On another occasion, when we thought that all of the Hallercziks had left the town, were surprised to see behind the market plaza one of the soldiers on the back of his friend climbing the wall, grabbing onto the edge of the parapet of the second floor, and breaking into the home of Chaim Kolinski. We quickly closed the shutter of the door with a wide metal rode, but we did not know how to deal with the large window of the main room, whose frame had been given to the glazier one day previously for repair of its broken pane. The sight of the broken window frame which was near our house made the soldiers think that their friends who came previously had already done the job on that house, and they left the house without coming to us. Thus we were saved from their hands due to the broken windowpane.

Those soldiers had a particular interest in the elderly Jews. When they caught a Jew, they would pluck out or cut his beard with great enjoyment. Once they captured Uncle Chaim. He had an impressive beard, divided in half like the beard of Nordau [4]. They cut off one side of his beard in order to torture him. Uncle Chaim walked around with a bandage on his cheek for quite a while until his shorn beard grew again.

On May 3rd, the most significant Polish national holiday, national flags fluttered from all the houses from the early hours of the morning. Woe to any Jew who would forget to place a flag on his house early in the morning, or who would forget to remove it the next day. At noon on that day, a large crowd would enter the market plaza near the statue that was erected in the center in order to honor the independence of Poland, to hear speeches from the leaders of the city. At the conclusion of the ceremony, the firefighters band would play patriotic songs.

The conductor of that band was a gentile who was always tipsy. Without a drop, he would not do anything, and as he became more drunk, he would began to play the trumpet in fine fashion. Daily, during the afternoon, he would ascend the roof of the church, and play liturgical music from up there, which could be heard all over the town. The leadership of the church paid him a special salary for these songs.

That gentile became attracted to communism. Since he was the head of the firefighters, and was also the bandleader, the communal leaders needed him more than he needed them, and he was not afraid of expressing his political views. One year, as May 3rd approached, he made an agreement with his employer the major that he would perform with his band on the national holiday, if he would permit he and his band to also perform on May 1st, the workers' holiday. The mayor had no choice. Therefore the band played on May 1st at the "International" workers' gathering, and after the main speech, which was delivered by one of the chief communists from Lomza, and after the words of the head of the local communists, the band played happy tunes. On May 3rd, the gentile did not fulfil his word, and he refused to perform with his band. Threats and persuasions were to no avail. To the distress of his supervisors, and to the joy of many of the residents, he stood his ground. His supervisors were not brazen enough to punish him.

Slowly, Zionist activity was renewed among the youth in the city. The majority of the youth were Zionists. Their cultural activities took place in the "Hatechiya" hall, which also served as the library. A new spirit began to spread in the town, and youths who would occupy the benches of the Yeshivas would abandon their learning, to the distress of their parents. They would only come to the Beis Midrash on festivals, in particular on the Days of Awe. On the evening of Simchat Torah, [5] the youths would compete with their parents for the purchase of "Atah Hareita". Even the richest of the householders could not stand up to this competition. When the young people won the auction, they would honor the honorable people of the town with the recital of the verses.

The youths also took part in the Hakafot, and the joy on Simchat Torah eve was exceedingly great.

In 1924, a group of Hechalutz members of Stawiski made aliya to the Land of Israel. The older youths could not obtain certificates, and many of them had no choice but to leave Poland, and ended up through various routes in the United States. Two of my brothers were among these, who joined their eldest brother who had immigrated several years previously to America. My brother Yitzchak of blessed memory died there at the early age of 45. His good soul – as he was known by all of his friends and acquaintances – left him in an untimely fashion.

Aharon Eliezer Zak spent a great deal of time at our home in those days. He loved to have discussions about various matters with my father. These discussions would continue until a late hour in the evening. He would read the long feuilliton style letters that my brother Nechemia would send to us from the United States. He would not skip out anything, and he would enjoy reading these letters greatly. He would eat lunch with us every Passover eve. Once Aharon Eliezer revealed to us the secret that we have a poet in the family – Chaim Leibel wrote songs that were beautiful and well received by his audiences. Chaim Leibel, the youngest of our brothers, had an artistic soul, dreamy eyes, black curly hair, and a sweet pleasant face.

Aharon Eliezer Zak was the driving force of the members of Hatechia. Unlike most of them, he still wore a long black coat and wore a small hat, as was the custom of the Orthodox in those days. One day his friends decided that the time had come that he too should wear modern clothes. The matter was prepared secretly. On the first day of Passover, the door of our home opened with great noise, and Aharon Eliezer Zak entered accompanied by a group of youths. He was wearing a modern suit, and on his hat was a nice hat. We were shocked, but the joy of the youths influenced our household, and father did not say anything.

The difficult winter that overtook Poland in 1929 did not pass over Stawiski. The elders of the community did not remember anything like it for the previous fifty years. There was an unusually harsh cold spell for three days. People did not venture outside except for urgent matters. It was impossible to draw water, for the well had frozen so much that it was impossible for water to enter the pipe. The school was closed and the children sat imprisoned in their homes. When the cold spell snapped, the villagers that had begun to come to the town said that there had not been such a cold spell for decades, and they told of incidents where people and animals froze from the deep cold.

As far as I remember, for almost all the summer there was a fierce wind in the town. In the middle of a clear summer day, the sky would suddenly cloud over with black clouds. A strong wind would suddenly blow, which would stir up high whirlwinds of sand, which would dance about and sweep up anything that was standing in their path. With difficulty, people were able to flee from the marketplace and take refuge in the nearby houses, as they left their merchandise to its fate. The stalls overturned, and the merchandise scattered in every direction. As the storm abated with the same suddenness that it had started, an eerie quiet prevailed. Only after the heavy gray clouds broke up and the peaceful sun began to appear, did people return to the marketplace to gather up what the storm had left behind.

I remember another unusual natural phenomenon that took place in our town. This was on one of the hot summer nights. As usual in the evenings, there were many people strolling along the wide sidewalk that was at the side of the road, as well as people sitting on their porches. Suddenly, bolts of lightning began to flash. There was not even one small cloud in the sky, and one could see stars scattered around. The lightning was of a unique nature, in that it was not accompanied by thunder, and the bolts intersected each other, as if two people were fighting unceasingly with flashing swords. People froze in their places, with their heads turned upward, watching this strange vision in awe and fear. This vision lasted for a long time, and then slowly people began to scatter and hurry to their homes.

The following day, everyone was discussing this event. Nobody knew how to explain this strange evening, and even the elders had never seen anything like it in their lives. The villagers also discussed this event in fear, for they interpreted it as a bad omen – a difficult war that was about to break out. A few years later, their frightful prophecy was fulfilled.

My Parent's Household

There were always many fires in the town. Most of the houses had been destroyed by fire and rebuilt. Our house, which was passed down as an inheritance from the parents of my mother of blessed memory was an old house, and was one of the few in the market plaza which had not been burnt down. It was a corner house, with its front facing the market plaza. From there it turned rightward to Biczki Street (on that wall, there were worrisome cracks), and its two other sides created a long narrow courtyard by the house, which lead to the back doors of the residences. There was a cowshed in the yard, as well as a shed for firewood, and a large storehouse for grain that was owned by Uncle Chaim Kabakowicz of blessed memory.

As was customary, the ceilings were built out of criss-crossed planks. In the large room of our house, the short widthwise planks rested on one long plank which went the entire length of the room. This plank was square and so large that it impressed anyone who saw it. People did not understand how, with the building conditions that prevailed in my great-grandparents' era, they were able to lift such a plank to the height of the ceiling.

This plank was the source of suspicions – once by the German invaders during the First World War, and once after the war as I have told previously. The suspicion in the first case was aroused by a thick rope that was tied to one side of the door of the baking oven, since one of its hinges had broken. At that time, there was no possibility of fixing the door, or of exchanging it for another one. My father, who was very handy and knew how to fix broken things, had no other choice but to tie a rope to the side of the door. He tied the other end of the rope to the heavy plank – and this enabled the door to turn on its one hinge without difficulty. That rope, which innocently fulfilled its duty, aroused suspicion in the hearts of the Germans who encamped in the city at the time they invaded Poland in 1914. They thought that this rope served as a wireless connection to the Russian enemy. It took a great effort on the part of my father to assuage their suspicion.

Our town was not blessed with a multitude of means of livelihood, however there were artisans of all types. The Jews provided for their households through a great deal of backbreaking work. They also ensured that they would be able to teach their children Torah, and provide a dowry for their daughters when they reached the appropriate age. There were very few wealthy people in Stawiski. The few that were there were mainly lumber merchants, and one cloth merchant. The rest were of the middle class, storekeepers for the most part. The majority of the population were poor, and worked in various trades – shoemaking, tailoring, porting, glassmaking, etc. There were also wood choppers and water drawers. Almost all of the barbers were from one family, and they also served as the band players at weddings.

Menachem (Mendel) Lewinowicz of blessed memory

The bakers had a special place in our town. Most were scholars. Father of blessed memory had studies in the famous Mir Yeshiva, and he was known as an illustrious scholar. Moshe Goelman of blessed memory told me this. After he got married, he decided to support himself by the work of his hands, and he went to work in the bakery of his father-in-law. Work in the bakery was free work, which was done by all the members of the families. My brother Yitzchak of blessed memory, who was a wheat merchant, would provide the flour that was needed by the bakery. The baking of bread and rolls of all types for weekdays, and braided challas for Sabbaths and festivals would commence in the middle of the night. At an early hour in the morning, the sale of the baked goods would commence. After dinner, father would go to the Beis Midrash, where he stood at the head of the group of those who studied Torah. In the cold winter nights, he would stay home and study Talmud with its commentaries until a late hour at night. These were the times of rest from his difficult work in the bakery.

Father was tall and had an upright posture. The lines on his face were aristocratic. His brown eyes exuded tenderness and good-heartedness. He had pleasant mannerisms, and he was upright in his behavior. We learnt from him not to take an oath even about something that is true. He was beloved and honored by his fellowmen. Many would come to him to discuss their troubles, to solicit his advice, and to request that he argue their case or pass judgement on their issues. Women would come to him to ask him questions about kashruth (Jewish dietary law).

Aharon Eliezer Zak of blessed memory related to father as the lion of the group. He respected his great erudition, and valued his generous personality and his straightforward intellect. Aharon Eliezer, in addition to his knowledge about a variety of subjects, was an expert in mathematics. He would often present mathematical problems before father, and solicit his expertise to help find a solution in a straightforward and logical manner.

When the Zionist activity started in the town after the Balfour Declaration, father was the head of those that addressed the community from the pulpit of the Beis Midrash, and encouraged many to collect money for the settlement of the Land of Israel. He desired with all his heart to make aliya to the Land of Israel, and he hoped for the day when his dream would be fulfilled. I once asked father how it would be possible from the medley of languages to promote the Hebrew language in the Land, and he answered me: it will be a matter of only one generation, and Hebrew will be the language of the people who settle Zion.

As his youngest daughter, in my childhood, I would accompany father to the Beis Midrash on festivals. The prayers, with their sad and heartwarming melodies, were magical to me. I especially enjoyed the style of prayer of the teacher Reb Akiva the Hassid, who had sweet melodies that were devotional without bounds. He sung the "Hayom Teamtzeinu" prayer at the end of the Musaf service with exceptional joy and enthusiasm [6]. Even though father was extremely pious, and careful about both the easy and difficult commandments, he refrained from fanaticism. Once a young rabbi, who was often at our home, asked him why he permitted me to ride a bicycle. Father answered him: "where is it written that the riding of a bicycle is forbidden for a girl?". Nevertheless, when I asked him to teach me a chapter of Talmud, he did not want to transgress the adage "whomever teaches his daughter Torah is as if he teaches her foolishness" [7]. Nevertheless, he sent me to study in the Hebrew gymnasia (high school).

Father saw an evil portent for the future in the frequent battles and hatred between men. Once he said: "a time will come, and the living will be jealous of the dead". He prophesied, and did not realize that his prophecy would be fulfilled in his generation, and in the generation of his household.

His desire to make aliya to the Land of Israel was never fulfilled. On the 18th of Tevet 5689 (1929), his pure soul left him. His body was placed on the floor of the bedroom, and candles were lit at his head. The men of the Chevra Kadisha (burial society) sat around him and recited chapters of Psalms, and I, the daughter of his old age, recited the Kaddish prayer between each chapter.

The honorable men of the town carried him on a black gurney to his final resting-place. In the open area between the synagogue and the Beis Midrash a large crowd gathered. Reb Shay Mendel Zilbersztejn of blessed memory eulogized him. He said: "We eulogize for the dead, even though his wish was not to be eulogized. For a great man of the generation was taken from us today."

A great yoke fell on the shoulders of mother of blessed memory. She would often wake up in the night prior to father and prepare the dough for the white bread and roles. In my childhood, when I woke up at night and could not sleep, I would get up from my bed, sit next to mother as she was working, and I would sing songs that she loved to hear.

In addition to the work in the bakery, mother also took care of the home. She did not concern herself only with her own home, but she helped the needy in many ways and in a quiet fashion. She would give bread on credit to poor families, knowing from the outset that they would not be able to pay their debts. I remember one respectable elderly man, who for some reason was not given sufficient food in his own house. He would come to us each morning, quietly go into one of the shelves, help himself to a loaf of bread, put it into his bag, and leave. During the entire time, mother would shield him with her body so nobody would see him in his disgrace, and no evil rumors would be spread about him or his household.

Mother had dark hair and was very pleasant. She was very pretty in her youth – so related her friends. She had long hair even in her adulthood. She became gray prematurely, but there were still strands of black hair that stubbornly clung to their black color. Her eyes were brown, and her eyelids and eyelashes were black. On Sabbaths and festivals, when the entire family would dine together at the long table, her eyes would sparkle with joy, and her beautiful voice would mingle with that of the rest of the family in singing the hymns, for they all loved to sing. She particularly loved to sing "a brivele der mamen" ("a letter from mother"), in which she expressed her longing for her eldest son, who had moved to the United States when he was still a young man.

Rashke (nee Kabakowicz) Lewinowicz, may G-d avenge her blood

On Sabbaths and festivals, the weariness that was stored up from the week suddenly dissipated. The black wig that she wore on her head and the gold earrings she wore on her ears brought her back, so to speak, to the splendor of her youth. She was slender and thin, but she was full of vigor. Her gait was quick and deliberate. It is impossible to understand from where she drew her spiritual and physical strengths throughout the difficult travails of raising a family. She was very occupied in the raising of her family and the running of her home. As their strength waned, my parents liquidated the bakery and opened a small grocery store.

Toward twilight on Sabbath, we would sit – mother, my sister, and myself – in the darkness of evening and wait until three stars would appear in the heavens – the sign that it was now permitted to turn on the lights. Like all Jewish mothers, mother would recite the prayer "G-d of Abraham, Isaac and

Jacob", and with the turning on of the lights, the atmosphere of Sabbath suddenly dissipated, and the difficult and wearisome week took its place.

On occasion, I would accompany father as he went to the Beis Midrash after the third Sabbath meal. The sun began to set. Slowly darkness fell, and the windows of the Beis Midrash appeared scary due to their darkness and height. The congregants recited chapters of Psalms in unison with a special melody that was reserved for that time, and as they shook back and forth in their seats, their shadows danced on the walls, as if they were part of a secret conclave.

The mysteries of the Sabbath dissipated suddenly as Reb Yaakov the Shamash (sexton) lit a candle and made the "Hamavdil" [8] blessing over a cup of wine in his pleasant voice. We children would surround him, and respond Amen with the rest of the worshippers.

After father passed away, the splendor of mother's face darkened, and her posture became bent. It was difficult to get used to the emptiness and gloom that suddenly descended upon the house. The three of us – mother, my sister and myself, for our brothers were in the United States – did our best to look after each other, to ease the pain and loneliness, and to continue with the customs which we were used to while father was alive. I loved to kiss mother's forehead, which showed the difficulty of her life and the toil of the years. I did not want to leave mother and my sister alone in the house, in particularly when the sky clouded over and a thunderstorm was about to break out; it was difficult to weather the fear all together.

For a certain time, prior to my aliya to the Land of Israel, mother would scream n her sleep. I was worried about this strange symptom, which was happening too frequently. When I heard the strange scream, I wanted to wake her up. Her breathing was heavy from the effort of the scream that strangled her throat. She was always happy when I woke her up and saved her from her nightmare. When I asked her for an explanation, she would tell me that in her dream, a pack of wild dogs attacked her and threatened to tear her to pieces. She wished to escape from them but was unable to do so. She wished to shout for help, but it was impossible; she tried to awaken but did not succeed.

This frightful dream was repeated until it became reality – a pack of dogs in the form of human beings, the refuse of the human species, pursued her and her family and tore them to pieces.

My sister Chana of blessed memory bore the burdens of the household from a young age. She was very dear, and had pleasant mannerisms. She related pleasantly to everyone, she tended toward righteousness and justice, and hated flattery.

Chana was tall and erect. Her head was covered with light brown hair. Her visage was pleasant, and her teeth were very beautiful, without blemish. When she grew up she was a pretty and pleasant. During the First World War, it was necessary to perform an operation on her neck near one of her ears. Father took her to a hospital that the Germans set up on the estate of the Squire Kiszlaniczki, a distance of a kilometer and a half from our house. After the operation, father carried her home on his shoulders when she was still anesthetized, and with her head bandaged. She was asleep for about three days. Due to her high fever, she would utter words that did not make sense, however she repeated one sentence over and over again: "the sheet is torn and worn out, torn and worn out – –." Mother stood by her and comforted her.

We were concerned and worried about her well being, despite the reassurance of the German physician. I remember in the afternoon of the third day – suddenly a bird flew into the house, flew around, tweeted, and left as suddenly as it came. We watched it leave with trepidation, and suddenly mother said: "good news, good news". We hurried to my sister's room, and she was lying there with her eyes open and a faint smile on her ashen face. We were happy, for it was as if our sister was reborn. Aharon Eliezer, who participated in our concern, said: "the bearer of tidings left". Indeed, this was the beginning of her recovery from her illness.

Chana (nee Lewinowicz) and her husband Yisrael Zeev Solnik,

may G-d avenge their blood

One of my sister's hands was full of moles. The German physician who looked after her attempted to remove them with various methods – but he was not successful. Once the Rebbetzin Remigolski noticed this, and was determined to cure her. She said: "it is not a fitting thing for a girl". The Rebbetzin stood for an entire day and tied many knots in a string that she brought with her, and hid it in a secret place. A few days passed, and the moles disappeared as if they had never been there. This was a wonderfully mysterious thing in everyone's eyes, and nobody knew how to explain it.

Chana desired to make aliya to the Land of Israel, but she did not succeed in doing so. She got married to Yisrael Zeev Solnik, the son of the shochet (ritual slaughterer of Nowigrod. She blossomed as a flower, and her entire being was refined and noble. Her brother-in-law Chaim said of her: "It appears to me, as her character was like one of the matriarchs".

With the ascension of Hitler to the government, anti-Semitism increased in Poland. The venomous anti-Semites in the town began to come forth, and did not give the Jews any rest, neither in the day or the night. They would set up guards in front of every Jewish store, and would not permit gentiles to enter. After the sun set, the Jews would be locked into their homes, and the shkotzim [2] would throw stones at the doors and closed windows. The ban on Jewish business reduced the already difficult livelihood of the Jews. The gates in the land were locked, and the hope to free oneself from the strangulation grew greater by the day. I was lucky to receive an "authorization" for my family, through the help of a good man, Dr. Y. Goldsztejn of blessed memory, who was the head of the national council of Keren Hayesod in the Land of Israel. Nevertheless, when anyone brought the authorization and requested a certificate, S. The head of the aliya office in Warsaw, requested a sum of money that was so large that it was impossible to pay. Aharon Eliezer Zak, who had been a friend of S. years back, made a special trip to him in Warsaw, explained the difficult family circumstances, and requested that he go beyond the letter of the law in this case. However his efforts were in vain, and his requests fell upon deaf ears. He returned empty-handed.

Even during this difficult situation, my family was concerned about the situation in the Land of Israel. On the eve of Shavuot 5699 (1939), my mother wrote to me, among other things:

"... Yesterday, all of the stores were closed, and the Rabbi gave a speech denouncing the black "White paper". – With such a lot, there is no place in the world where a Jew can rest."

One year later, I received a Soviet manufactured postcard from my sister dated June 17, 1940. In it, she expressed her fear that "your lot (i.e. in the Land of Israel) should not be like our lot". This was after the partition of Poland between Nazi Germany and Soviet Russia, in accordance with the Molotov-Ribentrop agreement. On September 18, 1940, my mother and sister wrote:

"... the news that reaches us about you worries us. We hear that the despot (i.e. Hitler) is approaching you also. – We cannot rest from the danger that is awaiting you –. "

My mother and sister were worried about my lot and did not realize, just as the rest of the Jews of Poland did not realize, that their fate had been sealed. Mother, my sister Chana, her husband Yisrael Zeev and their three children – Menachem, Nachum and Nechama – were all murdered along with the rest of the Jews of the town in the terrible holocaust that fell upon our town, the Jews of Poland, and the rest of the lands of Europe.

It is told of Yankel Nissel, the son of my Uncle Chaim Kabakowicz of blessed memory that he succeeded in fleeing along with one of his children to a certain landowner with whom he conducted business previously and who knew him. There, the two of them found refuge. They were hidden there for a long time, and the landowner provided for them, and made sure that nobody would discover them. Nevertheless, the matter became known to one gentile, and he informed about them to the Germans. An S.S. group arrived, and wanted to take also the landowner to be killed for the crime of sheltering Jews on his land. However Yankel Nissel bowed down at their feet of the murderers and pleaded with them to leave the landowner alone if he would take an oath that he knew nothing about their presence on his land. Thus did my cousin save the life of his benefactor, and he and his son were taken out to be murdered.

Translator's Footnotes :

1. Hamotzi Lechem Min Haaretz (He who brings forth bread from the earth) is part of the text of the blessing that is to be recited before eating bread.

2. Sheketz (plural Shkotzim) is a derogatory term for gentiles.

3. I am not sure what this refers to.

4. Presumably referring to Max Nordau, one of the original founders of Zionism.

5. The recitation of special Simchat Torah liturgy, of which the honor of reciting is often auctioned off. Hakafot are the processions made around the synagogue with the Torah scrolls on Simchat Torah.

6. "Hayom Teamtzeinu" ("May He strengthen us today") is a prayer recited toward the end of the Musaf (additional) service of Rosh Hashana and Yom Kippur.

7. Traditionally, it was frowned upon to teach a woman theoretical aspects of Torah, particularly Talmud. Nowadays, in more modern Orthodox circles, where women have equal educational opportunities to men in the secular world, this has been relaxed significantly, although Talmudic study has

generally remained for various reasons in the domain of men. The reasons behind this tradition, and the various applications of it in different streams of Orthodoxy nowadays, are quite complex, and beyond the scope of this footnote.

8. "Hamavdil" ("He Who differentiates" between sacred and profane...) is the main blessing of the Havdalah service which marks the conclusion of the Sabbath.

On the steps of the Post Office stands Tova Brikman (murdered)

A vista of Stawiski as one arrives from Szczuczyn

Standing next to the stream: Golda Zweibek and Cherna Suralska

Members of the "Halutz" (Pioneers") in 1926

"Shomer Hatzair" (The Young Watchmen"), Trumpeldor group

"Hadassah" group of the Shomer Hatzair on the occasion of the aliyah to Israel of the head of the group, Yissacher Zilbersztejn

Meeting Place: (right to left): Meir- Hershel Rubinsztejn, of blessed memory (murdered); Chmielewski (lives in the United States); Chaya Sarah Goelman, of blessed memory, Zeledka Ladelski,of blessed memory (both murdered); Rachel Goelman, of blessed memory (died in Canada); Gittel Rubinsztejn of blessed memory, Leibke Ladelski of blessed memory (both murdered). At the top of photograph: Avrehmel Mark of blessed memory (passed away).

{193}

The First Steps of Modern Hebrew Education in our Town
by Moshe Goelman of blessed memory
Translated by Jerrold Landau

With respect to modern education, or as it was known in those days, "improved" (metukan) education, our town, like all other towns in Poland and Russia prior to the First World War, was very conservative. Jewish children studied in cheder, and when they grew older, many were sent to continue their education in Yeshivas, some close by and others far off. This was with respect to boys. Regarding girls, most of them learned to read and write for one hour during the day in a cheder, separate from the boys, and their period of study was very short. When Reb Berl Siemienowicz sent his eldest daughter Sarake to Warsaw to study courses for kindergarten teachers with Yechiel Halpern, this was an extremely exceptional occurrence in our town.

The majority of the Zionist maskilim in town were able to understand and speak Hebrew, and they would read "Hatzefirah" or "Hazman", the Hebrew dailies that were published in Warsaw and Vilna. With regards to education, they relied on the "Cheder Hametukan" whose curriculum was based on the study of Hebrew language and its grammar, bible, and Jewish history. They also improved the physical environment of school – that is to say, that it was not a group of students sitting on benches on two sides of a long table, but rather separate school desks along the length of the schoolroom, as was customary in the government schools.

A revolution in the field of Hebrew education did not occur at that time, but nevertheless, there were two attempts in that direction that are worthy of noting.

a) Approximately two years prior to the First World War, Chuna Mondensztejn, the son of Yechiel the baker, returned to Stawiski and established the Cheder Hametukan, consisting of a kindergarten and grade 1. It was a "metukan" (improved) cheder in the full sense of the word both with regards to its physical appearance and its curriculum. The room was rented from one of the rich farmers who lived on the outskirts of the city, on the way to the post office, behind the civic court building.

The students were mainly girls, with a few boys. Only a few parents would permit their sons to study in a cheder that had a mixture of girls and boys, and where the teacher taught without a head covering. Furthermore, the course of study was different from that which was traditional in the cheders. The power of Chuna was in his song. He had a pleasant voice, and his enthusiastic singing of Hebrew songs would draw the hearts of his students. At that time, I was studying in a Yeshiva in a city far away from Stawiski, and I would come home for Passover. I remembered visiting the Cheder Metukan of Chuna prior to the holiday, and I recall that the students were singing songs of Passover and sections of the Haggadah <u>ut.</u> The Cheder Hametukan of Chuna lasted about two years, until the outbreak of the First World War.

b) During the First World War, our town was conquered twice by the Germans: at first for two weeks before Rosh Hashanah of 1914, and the second time in the middle of the winter, in February, 1915. Our town was literally on the front line during the first year of the war. The front itself was at the forest on the route to Lomza. During the time of the occupation, Jewish youth were conscripted for various tasks, such as paving the road between our town and Jedwabne, fixing up other roads around our town, as well as sanitary work such as cleaning the houses and inoculating the residents against influenza and typhus, illnesses that were very prevalent in those days.

At the beginning of 1916, the front moved in the favor of the Germans, with the conquest of Lomza, Warsaw, and the surrounding regions. The occupying army in Stawiski was composed of reservists. A German captain oversaw the town, and he had various guards at his side. Chaim Zebulon Bramzon was appointed by the captain as the mayor of the town, and several other prominent residents were appointed to the town council.

The Jewish youth, for want of anything to do, began to organize. The Hatechiya meeting place was set up, which served as a location for meetings and various cultural activities. A library was established, consisting mainly of Hebrew books. On Sabbath eves, there were lectures. Members of the army and the German guards would come to the lectures. We received permits from them to engage in cultural activities. This detail is worthy of noting in the historical annals of our town during the First World War.

At that time, there were two centers of Jewish life in Stawiski: The Beis Midrash for the adults and elderly in the town, and the Hatechiya hall for the youth. The cheders fulfilled their role faithfully in imparting knowledge of Torah and fine traditional education to the Jewish children.

Moshe Aryeh Brzostowiecki was regarded as one of the finest teachers in the town, and excelled particularly in the teaching of Talmud. When Chaim Zebulon Bramzon sent his oldest son, of about ten years old, to study in the Cheder of M. A. Brzostowiecki, he mad a condition that he would dedicate a few hours of the day to the study of Hebrew language, Jewish history, and bible.

At that time, I was occupied with private teaching to small groups of individuals, and Moshe Aryeh and Chaim Zebulon turned to me and asked me to teach those subjects in the cheder. I accepted this request happily, for I saw in it a chance to change the customary teaching methodology, and take the first steps toward the founding of a Cheder Metukan in town. For two semesters, summer and winter, I taught the students in the Cheder of Moshe Aryeh five days a week, for about an hour and a half a day. This was during the time that the Rebbe ate lunch and took his afternoon rest.

Relations between us were excellent. Moshe Aryeh was happy that the number of his students grew, and due to the variation in curriculum, the students displayed greater interest, and paid attention better even during the study of Talmud. To my sorrow, this partnership only lasted for one year – 1917 – due to the opposition of the teachers in the city and their supporters. The teachers feared that as time would go on, they would be left without students, so they spread rumors that we are turning away from the true path, and setting up a generation of heretics [2], Heaven forbid.

I recall the graduation party that took place in the month of Elul, at the end of the second and final semester. A public quiz took placed in all of the subjects that the students had studied during the semester. Chaim Zebulon Bramzon, Aharon Eliezer Zak and David Dobrzyjalowski were the examiners. The emotions of both the students and the examiners ran very high. When Chaim Zebulon heard his son answer one of the questions in history, and explain the details of the era of Ezra, Nechemia and the return to Zion – his eyes welled up with tears. He kissed his son as well as the second student Zelig, the son of the teacher Moshe Aryeh, who both excelled in their knowledge.

After the quiz, a party took place, and presents were distributed to the teachers and the students. I received a set of 5 machzorim for all of the holidays [3] inscribed with a special dedication. I still have them to this day.

From among the students, two in particular stood out. These were the sons of Moshe Aryeh. One of them, the first born Chaim, was a well-known teacher for many years in New York. He authored several textbooks. He died while still in his prime. The second, his younger brother Zelig, changed his family name to Broshi. After some time, he immigrated to Antwerp, where he served as a teacher. He was in Belgium at the outbreak of the Second World War. He survived, and lives today in New York. He wrote two books – one on Rabbi Saadia Gaon and the second on Rabbi Eliezer ben Horkonos [4]. Aside from these books, he published articles in Yiddish and Hebrew in New York newspapers, and also articles on explanations of books of the bible.

Footnotes :

1. The Haggadah is the text of the home ceremony conducted on the first two evenings of Passover (the Seder). Its main content is a relating of the story of the Exodus from Egypt, interspersed with songs and prayers.

2. The word used for heretic here is Apikorus. It derives from the Greek philosopher Epicurus, whose philosophy was to enjoy this life because there is nothing thereafter. It is the traditional Hebrew word for a heretic or non-believer.

3. A machzor (plural machzorim) is a holiday prayer book. A set of 5 machzorim includes a volume for each of Rosh Hashanah, Yom Kippur, Sukkot, Pesach, and Shavuot.

4. Saadia Gaon was a famous philosopher and leader during the late Babylonian
   period (around 900). Rabbi Eliezer ben Horkonos is a Talmudic sage.

{198}

The Founding Meeting of the "Hacherut" Organization
October 1, 1921
by Chaim Leibel Goelman of blessed memory
Translated by Jerrold Landau

Members:

Imiol M. Tz.	Madrykamien Litman
Imiol Sh. G.	Marek E.
Ipkowski Yaakov	Marek Sara
Ejmanska Etka	Morus Y.
Bursztyn E. L.	Morus K.
Berkowicz Elka	Markus Y.
Goelman Ch. L.	Mejzner Pinchas
Golombek Gutka	Milberg Chaim
Goldsztejn Gittel	Siemion Rachel
Goldsztejn Natan	Sachnowicz Zerach
Golombowicz Leib	Sachnowicz Aharon
Golombek B. Z.	Sachnowicz Leib
Denenberg Z.	Stolnicki Yaakov
Deneberg Y.	Salomon Lemel
Horowicz Reuven	Perlowicz Feiga
Zarocki Moshe	Finkiel Ch.
Chmielewski Z.	Zipkowska Sh.
Chmielewski Nechemya	Kalinski Y. M.
Cheslok Rachel	Kaminski Chipa
Jakubcyner Gutka	Kreplak Chaya
Linsberg Feiga	Sztern G.
Lejbik Rivka	Szpiler Libe
Lew Menachem	Szwarc Natan

Charter of the "Hacherut" Organization

1. The union is an impartial, independent organization.

2. The organization will conduct enlightened activities for the youth in a
   Zionist Socialist spirit.

Substantiation

Zionism: Taking into consideration that the abnormal situation of the Jewish people is a result of the their lack of a homeland for almost 2,000 years already, Zionism strives to raise the level of the Jewish people to that of all peoples, and to base the life of the people in its historic land, the Land of Israel, and thereby to heal the wounds that they accumulated during their long exile. This organization sets as its goal to educate its members in the Zionist spirit, to strengthen the national feeling, and to raise a nationally conscious youth, who will fulfil the deposit in the appropriate epoch.

Socialism: Taking into consideration that Socialism strives to liquidate the existing order, in which injustice and exploitation prevail, leading to wars and bloodshed – its lofty aim is to rebuild human society on a basis of freedom, justice, and collectivity. The organization sets as its goal to educate the youth in a socialist spirit, and to awaken in them a social consciousness so that they will ready for the social struggle.

In order to actualize the above mentioned goals, the organization will base its activities upon the following points:

1. It will arrange frequent readings on various topics. There will be a particular emphasis on the development of Zionism and Socialism.

2. There will be lectures on Jewish history, politics, economics, etc.

3. In order to combat illiteracy, the organization will open courses to study Yiddish, Hebrew and Polish, in accordance with individual desires.

4. A reading hall will be opened in the existing library.

5. Special funds will be raised for the library and the organization through flower days, evenings, and the like.

6. It will work for all of the Zionist funds, especially for the national fund.

7. It will support the Socialist movement, professional unions, sick funds, and the like.

Election Rules

1. Elections will be secret and will be conducted in the following manner:

2. Every member has the right to nominate candidates in writing.

3. The candidates with the greatest number of ballots will be selected.

4. There will be: a) a management committee of 7 members; b) a house committee of 6; c) an audit committee of 3; d) a reading hall committee of 3.

5. Each member can be elected to one committee.

6. Calling new elections requires the approval of two thirds of the members, or alternatively, elections can be called by the audit committee if they find errors in the work or the managing committee. They must bring their opinion before the general meeting, which will make a decision based on a majority vote.

Management Duties

1. The management committee of 7 people selects a permanent chairman.

2. The management committee sends a member to each committee, and also selects a secretary and a treasurer.

3. The management committee appoints a librarian and a library committee of 4 people.

4. The librarian, with the agreement of the management committee, can remove or accept a member to the library.

5. The management committee has the duty to administer the program. They can also accept a motion by a member during their meetings.

6. The management committee has the right to make decisions on all questions related to the ideological activity of the organization; technical matters must be brought to a general meeting.

7. The management committee sets recreational activities, evenings, etc.

8. The management committee has the duty to designate required material for public readings, etc., and the engage lecturers.

9. The management committee has the rights to accept a new member.

10. The management committee has the right to change the membership fee, in accordance with the needs of the organization.

11. Meetings of the membership committee take place once every two weeks.

Member's Duties

1. Each member must take interest in all that the organization undertakes, and frequently visit the organization.

2. For not visiting the organization for the duration of a month, the member will be called before an honorary judiciary committee.

3. Each member must ensure that an exemplary decorum prevails at reading events and meetings.

4. Each member must submit himself to the discipline of the organization, and must fulfill exactly his assignments based on the decisions of the management committee or the other committees.

5. For not coming to the general meeting – after receiving an invitation – a member will be strongly penalized.

6. New members will be accepted upon the recommendation of two members and the payment of 500 Marks.

7. There will be reductions for those who do not have the means.

8. The membership fee must be paid by the 10 th of each month.

9. Members will be not accepted if they are younger than 17 years of age.

10. One member cannot transfer his ballot to another.

11. For not paying the membership fee for a period of two months, a member will be excluded from the organization.
Remark: There will be exceptions for those who do not have the means.

Auditor's Duties

1. The audit committee has the duty to issue a warning so that the organization does not overstep its charter, to audit the work of the organization, to oversee financial matters, etc. Remark: There will be exceptions for those who do not have the means.

2. The audit committee must document every audit. Remark: There will be exceptions for those who do not have the means.

3. The audit must not be less frequent than once a month. Remark: There will be exceptions for those who do not have the means.

4. If it finds a bad ordinance, the audit committee has the right to call a general meeting to remove the protocol.

General Statutes

1. This charter, or a portion thereof, can be changed by a vote with a majority of two thirds, at a general meetings called by the management committee or the audit committee. Remark: There will be exceptions for those who do not have the means.

2. All polls (excluding elections and removing a member) are open.
Remark: There will be exceptions for those who do not have the means.

3. The reading events will be free for members. For non-members, there will be a charge. (Changes can be made at the discretion of the

management committee.)Remark: There will be exceptions for those who do not have the means.

4. A member who refused to fulfill a statute or a protocol from a general meeting can be removed by a decision by two thirds of the attendees of a general meeting. Remark: There will be exceptions for those who do not have the means.

5. General meetings will be held regularly four times a year; and extraordinarily based on a decision. Remark: There will be exceptions for those who do not have the means.

6. A general meeting can make decisions with the participation of two thirds of the members; if there are fewer, the meeting will be postponed. Remark: There will be exceptions for those who do not have the means.

7. The chairman: at the general meetings, he will be elected by the assembled. For reading events, he will be decided upon by the managing committee.

Rights of the Chairman

1. The chairman directs the meeting. All members must relate to him with respect and trust. For insulting or expressing mistrust in him, one can be removed. Remark: There will be exceptions for those who do not have the means.

2. The chairman issues a warning that the speaker should hold to the topic under consideration. After three notices, he can remove the right of speaking. Remark: There will be exceptions for those who do not have the means.

3. Prior to removing the right of speaking from a speaker, the chairman must clarify why he is doing this.

The General Meeting

1. Elects all committees. Remark: There will be exceptions for those who do not have the means.

2. Considers the report of the audit committee. Remark: There will be exceptions for those who do not have the means.

3. Confirms those matters that the management committee does not have the right to decide on its own. Remark: There will be exceptions for those who do not have the means.

4. Can remove a member. Remark: There will be exceptions for those who do not have the means.

5. Can change a point or a statute. Remark: There will be exceptions for those who do not have the means.

6. All votes (except for elections, and removing a member) are open.

Library System

1. A librarian and a 4-person committee will be chosen. Remark: There will be exceptions for those who do not have the means.

2. The librarian and his committee will be subordinate to the management committee. Remark: There will be exceptions for those who do not have the means.

3. The initiative to purchase new books belongs to the librarian, with the approval of the management committee. Remark: There will be exceptions for those who do not have the means.

4. The library is open to borrow books two times a week – Monday and Thursday. Remark: There will be exceptions for those who do not have the means.

5. Each leader pays monthly dues and a zalog [1] for the book (except for those who do not have the means). Remark: There will be exceptions for those who do not have the means.

6. Removing and accepting members to the library committee can only take place with the approval of the management committee. Remark: There will be exceptions for those who do not have the means.

7. The timeframe for borrowing a book is 14 days. For each overdue day, there will be a payment of 5 Marks.

Statutes of the Reading Hall

1. The reading hall is an independent entity. Remark: There will be exceptions for those who do not have the means.

2. Daily newspapers, periodicals and brochures will come into the reading hall. Remark: There will be exceptions for those who do not have the means.

3. The reading hall is open from 7:00 to 10:00 in the evening. Remark: There will be exceptions for those who do not have the means.

4. The entry fee is 10 Marks. The weekly fee is 50 Marks. For members: 5 Marks per reader, and free entry for non-readers.

Footnotes :

1. I am not sure of the meaning of this word. It is some sort of fee, obviously.

{203}

Hechalutz in Stawiski
by Yitzchak Kotton
Translated by Jerrold Landau

Muli Wingrowicz, Mattityahu Liberman, Choronziski, Shimon Kagan, Chaim Pesach Kulawski, Avraham-Pesach Goelman -- Translator's note: the photo is entitled "Members of Hechalutz in Stawiski", and is dated 18 th of Nissan, 1922, April 16, 1922

Approximately fifty years ago, a chapter of Hechalutz was founded in our town by a group of youth. The founding of Hechalutz was a significant occurrence in our town. This was the fruit of the vision of a few, who did not find satisfaction in the realities that surrounded them, a reality without aim and purpose. They were brazen enough to see into the future. Hidden in their bosom was the realization of the desire of their hearts – a group of young people dreaming, struggling, and making aliya to the Land of Israel to work it and protect it.

The founding of Hechalutz did not arouse any opposition or negative reaction from the Jews of the town, most of whom were well rooted. Even though they were faithful to traditional Judaism, they accepted the change that was taking place amongst the youth with full understanding, for they realized that there was no future for the Jewish youth in the town, and life in the town was not going to provide them with a goal.

At first, we were few, and our work was confined to a room that was the size of a door squared. However, within a short period of time, other boys and girls joined the small group, and a new life, vibrant and full of content, was infused into the Hechalutz organization of our town. We devised an interesting and practical program of work, and, through this; we succeeded in instilling the pioneering idea to the majority of the Jewish youth in town. Only a small number of the youth chose different movements.

As new members joined, we became the center of pioneering Zionist publicity in the town, a center that could take credit for much successful activity. We succeeded in implanting the pioneering Zionist idea into the Jews, who up to that time were quite distant from this mindset. Through our educational programs, we showed the youth ways to serve their nation and their Land, and to prepare themselves to a free life in their Land. We served not only as an ideological center, but also as a practical center for hachsharah (preparation) towards aliya and labor. Until we were able to fulfil our objective [1], we were practically the only pioneering youth movement in town. Youth continued to join us; and, from our side, we did what we could in order to take them under our wings in order to prepare them for realizing their aliya. It seems to me that we fulfilled this objective in a non-trivial manner, and the number of natives of our town who made aliya testify to this.

<u>Translator's Footnotes</u> :

1. I assume that this means until the time that the majority of the leading members actually made aliya themselves.

{205}

Hashomer Hadati [1]
by Elazar Goelman
Translated by Jerrold Landau

The Secret Meeting

It was an unusual weekday evening. A small group of young people waited until the last of the worshipers in the Chevrat Kass Beis Midrash went home. Outside, an autumn wind blew, an Elul wind saturated with the awesomeness of the time of year, the first days of Elul.

The lights of kerosene lamps were flickering from the windows of the houses. The Shul Gasse (Street of the Synagogue) was already empty of people. A few people were passing by. These were the last young people who were hurrying to the spring to fill their pitchers with the water that flowed from the iron pipe that was fixed into the rock. This water flowed day and night without stop. This well had a special status, in that it rested against the eastern wall of the Beis Midrash. It was as if the water flowed from under the Holy Ark – pure, cold, refreshing water.

The spring flowed from the vicinity of the Great Synagogue, which was like an old fortress that instilled a feeling of awe to its surroundings.

All of the communal buildings were centered in this area. It was like a plaza, in that everything was there: the Great Synagogue, the Beis Midrash, the Talmud Torah on the eastern side – these were wooden buildings that were built in the style of homes, with rooms in the attic. On the southern side of the plaza was the rabbi's home, which was communally owned. The horse stables of the wagon drivers were next door to the rabbi's house.

Across from the rabbi's house were the civic properties. There was a fire station, and a large hall that served as an auditorium for concerts and performances – like a town hall. Next to this hall were the wooden sheds that housed the fire engines, which were the pride of the town.

On that evening in the month of Elul, groups of youth, boys and girls, came to a large meeting in the Talmud Torah, in one of the rooms of the attic, in order to found a local branch of Hashomer Hadati.

The room that was chosen for this purpose had its windows facing the fields and marshes that were adjacent to the river. The bridge over this river led to Szczuczyn. We were sure that the light that issued from these windows would not give us away, for there was no worry of anyone noticing us from that direction.

We had the courage to gather together in secret in the Talmud Torah, but we were not so brazen as to request permission to hold this meeting. We were afraid. For what and from whom were we afraid? I don't have an answer.

We gathered together in the room at the appointed time. Our guest was Moshe Lufgass from the Moshava [2], who came specially to help us found the branch of Hashomer Hadati in Stawiski.

How was it that a delegate of a Moshava of Hashomer Hadati ended up coming to Stawiski?

It happened like this. During the summer, a summer convention of the national Hashomer Hadati movement took place for more than a month in the forests of Chmielewo. Chmielewo was a village surrounded by pine forests. Nearby, there were ponds of water for bathing and swimming. There was a flourmill nearby that was owned by a Jewish family, which lived in a lone house next to the mill.

For us, the young people of Stawiski, this summer camp was an unusual event, for until that time we had not experienced the happiness and effervescence of youthful communal life.

It was told to us that, at the Moshava, a delegate from the Land of Israel would participate. He was a young man with a black beard, in the style of Herzl. This delegate, Mr. Ben Nun, stayed at the summer Moshava for a few days. We, the children of Stawiski, stood by the gate to observe what was happening at this Moshava. We caught the attention of this guest from the Land of Israel who then invited us in to participate in the dances. We quickly became enamored by Hashomer Hadati. One of the leaders of the summer Moshava promised to come and establish a branch of Hashomer Hadati in our town. He promised, and indeed kept his promise.

The room in the attic was filled to the brim. An organizational committee was chosen. The life force of it was Buchi (Baruch Zilbersztejn) who, if I am not mistaken, was the only one of us who was present with the knowledge of his father (Reb Yeshaya Mandel). This increased his importance to us and also his self-importance, for he studied in the Tachkemoni School of Bialystok, and most of the students of Tachkemoni were members of Hashomer Hadati in Bialystok.

We rented a room for the group. We were interested in the cheder room of the teacher Reb Gedalia Rubensztejn of blessed memory, who had closed his cheder during that time frame. This room had many attractions. It was in a self-contained structure next door to the house of Cybulki – a family whose children had left Stawiski due to their business ventures in the outside world. The windows of the room faced the far side of the Market Square, toward the route to Jedwabne. However, to our dismay, the room also had windows that faced toward the market, and we needed camouflage in order to hide the existence of the group.

This writer had the task of being the first counselor for the girls' group. This was a large group, and was not divided by age. The girls gathered for activities twice a week. We had a large lamp at our disposal, however we were afraid to light it lest its light give away our existence. Instead, we used small kerosene lamps. They only lit up the room a little bit, and the shadows were more than the light.

It did not enter our minds at all that the song that broke forth from the room would give away our location, and the half-lit room would serve as a pretext to accuse us of gathering together in the dark.

The Religious "Shomer Hadati" (Religious Watchmen) group.

The First and Last Crisis

It was the eve of Hoshanah Rabba [3]. We stayed late at the synagogue to recite the special Hoshanah Rabba evening ceremony. As did all of the children, we generally busied ourselves with the preparation of the Hoshanot bundles on the eve of Hoshanah Rabba, and went to the synagogue with our fathers. However this time, we agreed to meet at our headquarters and go together to the synagogue.

Apparently, we did not watch the clock, and did not realize that time was passing. Near midnight, we were still sitting in our dimly lit meeting place, singing songs of Zion. Suddenly, the door burst open and a group of parents from among the honorable citizens of the town broke in. They had discovered our hiding place. They broke into the room and honored us with the rods that they carried in their hands. They were not satisfied with merely administering the beatings, for they also confiscated our large lamp and the small kerosene lamps. We fled to the synagogue, chastised and beaten though we were guiltless.

However, this also turned out for the best. After the invasion of the meeting place by our parents, its existence became known and it received its due recognition. Some looked kindly upon it and others did not; however the game was over. Hashomer Hadati in Stawiski became an indisputable fact, and it no longer had to exist in secrecy.

I described the story of the beginnings of the organization at length. We were innocent youths. We did not trod on the path of rebelliousness, and we had no intention of forging a new path. We had difficulties and internal struggles. Everything came suddenly, like thunder that deafens the ear on a clear day; however this passed. The difficulties lasted for a long time. The worst of all was the slander. They spread rumors about us. The rumor was heard in town: These "Tzatzkes" ("young devils"), Yeshiva students, meet in a dark room behind closed doors. We were quiet; we were confused, for these were difficult things to bear. We had to forge the path for hundreds of boys and girls, for whom the meeting place was like a home. The members of Hashomer Hadati of Stawiski integrated successfully into the religious nationalist youth movement. The movement gave them a communal outlook and lofty ideals, most important of which was the desire for aliya to the Land of Israel.

The Activities of Hashomer Hadati

These were normal times. The activities of the organization were conducted on weekdays and Sabbaths. There were discussions and meetings. The struggle for existence was difficult. We moved from location to location, not for reasons of comfort. Two reasons forced us to wander from place to place.

   a. The neighbors were not happy with the noise that came from the
       meeting place, which continued until late in the night;

   b. We could not afford the rent, so we stopped paying, resulting in eviction
       from the location.

The branch of Hashomer Hatzair was founded prior to Hashomer Hadati. It conducted well-organized educational and social activities. Until this day, I do not know the reasons why Hashomer Hatzair disbanded.

The Zionist activities of the town were conducted, so to speak, by the aristocratic members of the community. The meetings and activities took place in the library, the "Bibliothek". The local activists regarded the Bibliothek as an important cultural organization, through which they maintained their connection to the world of "culture". These activities were conducted by the intelligentsia, who were mainly honorable members of the community.

Additional activities were conducted on behalf of the Keren Kayemet (Jewish National Fund), such as emptying the charity boxes and other work connected with the collection of money. All of these activities were in the domain of the "parlor Zionists" who guarded their control of these activities.

On the other hand, Hashomer Hadati opened up its gates to all of the local children, without concern about status. Its membership included children of workers as well as children of merchants. After a short period, some of them became known as people of ability, who attained an honorable place in the organization. This positive development had an influence on the self-worth of the youth, and caused a revolution in the status of the young people, in that they were valued for their abilities. Hashomer Hadati was extremely successful in this area in Stawiski, and served as a means for increasing the abilities of the outstanding youth, who when they became older joined Hachsharah kibbutzim and made aliya.

The Hashomer Hadati branch in Stawiski played an honorable role within the map of Hashomer Hadati of Poland. It was regarded as one of the most dynamic and active groups in the Lomza-Bialystok region. Members of the leadership committee continued with their nationalistic activities, played an active role in regional conventions, and a few of them were chosen for national positions.

The branch in Stawiski organized regional gatherings and meetings, as well as a roving Moshava. The flourishing of the Stawiski branch began with the start of the active role of Patricus of Bialystok, who took upon himself the role of the head of the branch after the writer of these lines made aliya.

The selection of Patricus for this position was beneficial and successful. He was beloved by the youth, and he loved them in turn. Even after I made aliya, I remained in contact with him by letter. The correspondence between us only stopped with the conquest of Poland by the armies of Hitler, may his name be wiped out. May these lines serve as a memorial for the member Patricus. His students who survived will always remember him with gratitude and thanks, for the man was precious. He was an outstanding teacher who loved the youth and brought the poor of the nation close to the religious Zionist idea.

May this article serve as a monument of memorial for the members of the group who perished in the holocaust during the days of wrath, fury, and tribulation. May it be G-d's will that we should suffer no more.

Youth Group, 1924. Standing (from right to left): Y. D. Imiyal, of blessed memory; Gershon Funk, of blessed memory (both murdered); Dr. Yonah Rubensztejn (lives in France); Professor Avraham Yitzchok Katz (Kac) lives in the U.S.; Zelig Broshi Bzostowiecki, lives in the U.S.; David Friedman, of blessed memory (died in Paris). Second Row: Yissachar Zilbersztejn, of blessed memory (died in the United States); Yechezkel Rubinsztejn, of blessed memory (murdered); Third Row: Nechka Stolnicki, of blessed memory (died in Israel); Avigdor Goelman (lives in Canada).

The Religious "Shomer Hadati" (Religious Watchmen) group.

In the forest on the way to Lomza: On the occasion of the aliya of Nechama Kotton to the Promised Land. From right to left: Pinchas Mejzner, of blessed memory (murdered); Gittele Rubinsztejn, of blessed memory (murdered); Rachel Olchowski (lives in Israel); Yosel Mondensztejn (lives in the United States); Fruma Zak (nee Zilbersztejn), of blessed memory (murdered); Nachem Kotton-Bizounsky (lives in Israel); Leiba Ladelski (murdered); Chemda Lewinowicz-Kantor (lives in Israel); Chaya Sarah Goelman, of blessed memory (murdered); Meir Hershel Rubinsztejn, of blessed memory (murdered).

Flour Mill Sokolicha (Trans. Note: four men pictured in boat, no names given).

———

Footnotes :

1. Hashomer Hadati (literally "The Religious Guard") is a religious Zionist youth organization. (Note: the "Ha" in Hashomer is a definite article meaning "the". Hashomer Hadati is sometimes interchanged with Shomer Hadati (without the definite article in this translation.

2. A Moshava is an agricultural settlement in Israel. In the context of this article, it refers to a 'model' summer settlement in the Diaspora, similar to a summer camp, for Zionist training.

3. Hoshanah Rabba is the 7 th day of Sukkot, prior to the full festival days of Shemini Atzeret and Simchat Torah. Hoshanah Rabba is the fifth of the intermediate days of Sukkot, when labor is permitted (as opposed to the first two and last two days, when labor is prohibited). On the eve of Hoshanah Rabba, there is often a special study ceremony at the synagogue. The following morning, there are 7 circuits with the lulav and etrog (the palm frond and citron, which are Biblically mandated to be used as part of the Sukkot rituals), and a special bundle of willows, known as the Hoshanah, is beaten on the ground.

{213}

A Bundle of Memories from my Town Stawiski
by Shifra Zwiliczowski (nee Liberman)
Translated by Jerrold Landau

It has been nearly fifty years since I left my birthplace, and some of the memories are clear, while others are cloudy and obscure. I will attempt to present a few of them – and this will be my contribution to the monument which we are erecting to the memory of this Jewish community, which was small in population but rich in a life full of content and energy.

One of the important places of Jewish life in Stawiski were the fairs and market days, on which farmers from the neighboring villages came to sell their produce and to purchase their needs in the Jewish stores. However it is not about that fairs and market days that I wish to write, but rather about one certain person whom I knew, who used to take opportunity of the days of the fair, and would come to town so that I could write a letter for her to her cousins in America. The most interesting thing was that each letter was written in the same style: how many cows and pigs she had on her farm and how much income they brought in. The letter was simple and naïve, however it was full of the joy of creativity of a woman who worked the land, who was tied to the land with all strings of her soul. I remember that as I wrote the simple words and the banal content of her letters, I was jealous of that gentile woman due to the close connection that she had to her own land, and the great satisfaction that she derived from her work.

On Sabbath afternoons, at the time that the fathers gathered in the synagogue for the third Sabbath meal, the road to Lomza was full of youths, boys and girls, who took a stroll on that street. They walked in groups along the length of the street, as was the custom of young people during their romantic age, and there were many love relationships formed between the girls and the boys. Nevertheless, I do not remember very many weddings in our town. I attribute this to the difficult economic times of the Jewish population. The youth did not see a future in the town or in Poland in general. Everyone desired to emigrate, to America, to the Land of Israel, or to other lands. There was no inclination to set up a family when everyone was sitting on their suitcases. A portion of the youth, who saw no possibility in making aliya to the Land of Israel, and to whom the gates of America were also locked, became engaged in Communist ideology due to their despair. Some traveled to Russia, and we lost trace of them.

The suffragist club in our town was a one-of-a-kind phenomenon. From rumors, I knew that a group of girls was formed who decided not to marry, and if it would happen that one of them would marry, they would judge her harshly, and see her as a traitor to the sublime idea. Among the suffragists there was one pretty girl, Chaya Zelda Wilamowski, who got married, and the entire group castigated her for treason to the ideal. Rozka, the daughter of Rabbi Remigolski, was at the head of the group. She eventually made aliya to the Land of Israel, and lived in a collective. She eventually died under mysterious circumstances.

My aunt lived in a large, shaky, wooden house. For many years, there were no improvements made to the house. She rented half of the house to a family with children. The head of the family was a carpenter, who was called Srulka the Staliar. His workshop was in his home. He worked hard all his days. He earned a meager livelihood through the sweat of his brow. My uncle, who was a teacher of children, died young, and my widowed aunt did all sorts of work privately in order to subsist, and she also helped her daughter who lived in Lomza. Her other two daughters and her son left Stawiski, and immigrated to America and Lithuania. My aunt was goodhearted, and she would put up guests who required lodging for the night in her poor house. There was a girl in our town who was not of sound mind. My aunt brought her into her home, and concerned herself with her livelihood. When the neighbors would say to her: "Chaya Zelda, the girl is disturbing your sleep", she would answer: "This poor girl is a human being as myself and yourself, and what right do I have to deny her a roof over her head?"

Mindel Liberman of blessed memory, the mother of Shifra and Tzvi Liberman.

My father would often travel and give lectures in synagogues and study halls, however he earned his livelihood with difficulty. One day I heard that my mother decided to close the store and to travel with neighbors to the fair that was to take place in a village not far from Stawiski. I begged my mother to take me to the fair. My mother got up early in the morning, and when she saw that I was still asleep, she did not want to wake me, so she went with the neighbors. When I awakened and saw that my mother was not in the house, I became very troubled. I got dressed very quickly, and decided to catch up to them. I set out on the journey. It was easy to guess the direction of their travels, since everyone was traveling in the same direction. I was a young girl, and many people offered me a lift on their wagons. At first I refused, since it was a very nice day, the weather was pleasant, and I was enjoying walking by foot. However, after I walked some distance, I became tired, and I accepted the offer of a wagon driver to give me a lift on his wagon. When I arrived at the village in which the fair took place and my mother saw me, she became very troubled, for she suspected that some disaster happened in the house. However, when I told her the reason for my arrival, she was very happy that I had arrived in peace.

I did not feel bad about my mischievous activity, since I was very happy in the village.Jews came to the fair only to sell their wares, but for the gentiles the day of the fair was a holiday. On that day, they took off work, became drunk in the pubs, and rejoiced in their customary manner. In the evening, we returned home, all tired out. My grandmother became angry with me, for she worried all day that something might have happened to me on the journey.

Shifra was the sister of my grandmother Chana Zelda, and her husband was Zeev Denenberg. She ran an inn in the square in the center of the town, and her husband supplied the Russian army. It is related that Denenberg once saved a young Polish man from hanging. One day, Turkish soldiers came to their inn with a Polish young man. They accused him of spying, and they were about to hang him on a gallows near the tavern. Denenberg negotiated with the Turkish soldiers, paid ransom for the young man's life, saved him, and put him up for some time in their house.

Years passed.Once Denenberg took it upon himself to provide merchandise to the army for a specific period of time, and for various reasons, he was unable to obtain the merchandise.He traveled to Warsaw to request a deferment.When he entered the army supply office, a young man came to him, bowed down before him and kissed his hand.Denenberg was startled, and he did not know why a stranger would bow down before him.In a few moments, the matter was clarified.It became clear that this young man, who now was an official in the supply office, was the same youth that Denenberg saved from the Turkish soldiers. When Denenberg entered the office, that man recognized him immediately, and related the story to his co-workers and superiors how this Jew had saved him from the gallows.Needless to say, the requested deferment was granted immediately.

I studied in "Ort" school.Once I returned home from Warsaw and I had to sleep over in Lomza. In Lomza, a woman from Stawiski, Chaya Beilka, had a guesthouse, and people from Stawiski would stay with her.I arrived in Lomza at night, and I did not find the way to Chaya Beilka's guesthouse. I was afraid of wandering the streets for fear of the people of the underworld. Since I had no other option, I returned to the train station. I sat between the tracks all night until dawn. There was one deranged woman there who cried and sang all night, and several homeless drunken gentiles found a place to rest between the tracks. I was afraid to fall asleep, and the stationmaster promised me that he would watch out that no bad person would hurt me. The night passed somehow, and I set out for Stawiski the next day. I kept this adventure secret from my parents for a long time.

I have brought down several episodes from my memory of my town of over fifty years ago. These episodes remind me of the days of my youth, and of a world that was mercilessly destroyed. May these lines serve as a modest contribution to perpetuation the heartwarming and beautiful way of life which once was and is no more.

{217}

In the Paths of My Youth
by Chemda Lewinowicz
Translated by Jerrold Landau

From times of yore, the same difficult, critical question faced the Jewish youth of the Diaspora – "To where?" A small town in Poland was poor in opportunities and challenges, since it was entrenched in its narrowly focused way of life. From the age of five, Jewish boys would start to study in Cheder. Not infrequently, when they left the Cheder, and their parents, who were for the most part quite poor, sent them as apprentices to various artisans in order to learn one of the trades that was popular in the town, including: shoemaking, tailoring, woodworking, tin-smithing, etc. A few of them trained in their parents' occupation. The most intellectual of the youth continued their studies with the best teachers in the town, and some of them went out to a place of Torah to study in a Yeshiva far from their parent's home.

When the news of the national awakening reached the town, a different, refreshing spirit blew through the town. The pining for Zion that had been absorbed in the parents' home, in the Cheder and Beis Midrash – broke out at this propitious occasion with the currents of the time, and the youth searched out ways to actualize and realize this path. When news of the Balfour Declaration reached the town, joy broke out among all the residents of the town, who saw this as the beginning of the redemption. On a peaceful winter day in December 1917, the news arrived. Light snowflakes blew around the air and melted before they reached the ground. Next to the Hatechiya Hall (at the corner of the homes of Kopelowicz and Bramzon, near the road to Szczuczyn) a large crowd gathered. Pelet (Paltiel) Remigolski of blessed memory, the son of the rabbi of the town, was standing at the podium. He delivered an enthusiastic Zionist speech. After a public assembly in the Beis Midrash, the community, led by the older youth, escorted Rabbi Remigolski of blessed memory to his home.

It can be said that from that time, Zionist activity commenced in Stawiski. Zionist lectures were delivered on occasion from the podium of the Beis Midrash by heads of the city and representatives from the Land of Israel who visited the town on occasion and shared the image of the realization of the dream of the return to Zion which was taking place in the Land of the Patriarchs. Collections of money were conducted. In addition to money, many people donated valuable objects for the rebirth of the Land of Israel. The blue box of the Keren Kayemet LeYisrael was displayed prominently and with pride in every Jewish house. It served as a symbol of the connection of the Jewish soul to Zion that was being redeemed from its desolation.

Nevertheless all of these activities were not sufficient to address the problems of the older youths, and certainly not of the oldest youths who had already finished their studies with the best of the teachers in the cities. As well, they could not address the problems of the students who had finished their studies in the Polish primary school. The town was not blessed with institutions of higher education, and whoever desired to study Torah had to go far off. Only few had the opportunity to take this route. In order not to waste their time, they would study with teachers who came to Stawiski for set periods and would teach Torah to groups or individuals in private lessons conducted in the Polish language.

The first Hebrew primary school in Stawiski was founded by Chuna Mondensztejn. After a period of time, Gedalia Rubensztejn of blessed memory set up an additional school. He founded the "Cheder Metukan" where boys and girls studied together. After some time, Moshe Goelman returned from the Yeshiva. Moshe, who was a dedicated Zionist and faithful to the Hebrew language, set up as his holy goal the introduction of the living language to the youths and adults. The studies were conducted in Hebrew. Aside from the younger people, older students also studied with him, who wished to acquire knowledge of spoken Hebrew, along with its grammar and literature, over and above the written Hebrew which they had already learned from the best of the local teachers. Thus did Moshe Goelman train a generation of Hebrew speakers, who did not embarrass us even when they moved overseas. A few of them who live in the United States would correspond with their revered teacher in beautiful Hebrew, which was still known to them after decades. This is an example of the adage that what is taught to children is not easily forgotten.

Despite all of the good intentions, there was no practical possibility of obtaining organized and comprehensive education in Stawiski. The parents, who wanted to impart Torah to their children, had no other choice than to send them off to a place of Torah far from their homes. The first stop was

Lomza, where there was a Jewish-Polish gymnasia founded by Dr. Goldlust. From Lomza, they would go to Lodz or Bialystok, and finally to Vilna, the Jerusalem of Lithuania, where most of the youth from Stawiski who continued on with their studies ended up. Some of them studied in the Tarbut Hebrew gymnasia, and others in the Jewish-Polish gymnasias (which were accredited by the government). One person (Yosele Mondensztejn) studied in a professional school, two studied in teacher's seminaries – one in Hebrew and the other in Yiddish – both of which were housed in one courtyard. Many of the Orthodox youth studied in Yeshivas.

As is well known, youth groups covering the entire spectrum operated among the Jews at that time. The Zionist groups included Hechalutz, Young Hechalutz, Hashomer Hatzair, Hashomer Hadati, Beitar, and others. The non-Zionist groups included Bund youth, and the Communist youth group that operated underground. Most of the youth of Stawiski who studied outside the city joined the Hashomer Hatzair movement. When they returned to Stawiski at the conclusion of their course of studies, they founded a branch of Hashomer Hatzair in Stawiski.

The headquarters of the organization was in an attic in the old, abandoned house of the Cybulki family, which had previously served as a pig-hair workshop for its owners. The stairs that led to the second floor creaked under the feet of those that climbed them, and it seemed as if they were buckling under the weight of those that were going up and down. Nevertheless, they served their purpose honorably.

The Hashomer Hatzair branch was the first organization of Stawiski that attracted the majority of the youth and children of the town. The children of the well to do, apprentices of artisans, tailors, as well as students of the primary school – to all of them, the vibrant Hashomer Hatzair organization was like a home which bestowed meaning, warmth, and recognition of self-worth upon them. The meetings for cultural activities and the celebrations with song and dance lifted them out of the monotony of their small-town lives.

The leaders of the chapter were burdened with work – joint meetings, deliberations regarding various topics, conducting day-to-day activities, training younger counselors, and other such activities. The financial situation of the chapter was for the most part quite tight, due to the many expenditures and meager income. The decoration of the room was done by volunteers, its cleaning was done by a rotation system, and members brought jars of kerosene from their homes for heating. However the dues paid to the headquarters in Warsaw, the rent, and other expenditures were not completely covered by the dues that were collected from only a portion of the members of the chapter.

Leadership of "Hashomer Hatzair" Stawiski, 27 Tammuz, 1925 [July 19, 1925].

In order to cover the chronic deficit, soirees were organized on occasion. Among other activities, lotteries were conducted for valuable prizes. One day, the leadership decided to arrange a soiree with an organized program. The decision to put on a presentation on the stage of the fire-hall and to sell tickets was a daring step, and imposed a great responsibility on the organizers. The preparatory work was divided up among several members – one person arranged the choir, and another trained a group of girls from the older group in various dances with a unique style of choreography. Boys were not brazen enough to join the group of dancers, for who among the boys would dare to appear as a dancer dressed up as a girl? The problem was solved as follows. A group of girls agreed to appear dressed as boys. Someone agreed to take care of the technical work that was connected with such a performance. The rewards were great. The soiree was one of the most successful in Stawiski. The program included songs of Zion sung by a choir, various readings, and lovely dances. One of the girl and "boy" dancers so entertained the audience that the calls for an encore lasted a long time. The troupe accompanied her in a second dance.

The lot of Hashomer Hatzair in Stawiski worsened when the principal of the primary school, who like most of the Poles was a venomous anti-Semite, made his presence known and began to search for pretexts to interfere with the existence of the organization. He made use of the ban on primary school aged children from participating in a political organization. Only sport and scouting organizations, which were very common in Poland, were permitted for the younger people. Incidentally, the well-known Sokol Polish sports organization was known for its anti-Semitic leanings in the Andak spirit.

The Hashomer Hatzair organization registered itself officially as a Jewish scouting organization with an orientation toward encouraging aliya to the Land of Israel. It was recognized by the Polish government. Nevertheless, the branch of Hashomer Hatzair in Stawiski was, as has been stated, like a thorn in the eyes of the anti-Semitic principal of the primary school. During one of the teachers meetings, I was accused (at the time, I was formally registered as a teacher of religion to Jewish students, as was required by the education ministry of Poland; in actuality I taught Jewish children about Jewish history) of conducting damaging political activities, that is to say Communist activities. They claimed that I and my associates were damaging the characters of the children who came to the Hashomer Hatzair activities in the evenings and remained their until very late hours, where they would imbibe to the point of drunkenness and become involved in a bad crowd. It was necessary to contradict this libel and to prove that the children who came to the movement in the evenings came there to learn the language and Jewish history.

To our ill fortune, that day was a school vacation, and the counselors took advantage of the opportunity to go out on an excursion with several of the groups of youth into the nearby forest. After the meeting of the teachers, I quickly hurried out to the forest on my bicycle, and I told the counselors about the accusations of the principal. We brought the children back to town in a roundabout manner, and sent them straight to their homes.

The Hashomer Hatzair chapter breathed a breath of life into the town. I remember that on one Lag Baomer, all the members of the chapter went out on an organized excursion into the forest on the route to Kolno. Provisions for setting up of camp, and food for one entire day, brought by the members from their own homes, were laden on wagons. This was an organized camping day with planned activities. Food was prepared on a campfire, and a communal meal was organized, according to the best of Hashomer Hatzair tradition. We heard lectures about the history and meaning of Lag Baomer, and there was also singing and dancing. Toward evening, the group returned to town, with every group marching in formation with its own flag and singing songs of Zion. Members of the chapter spread out to all four corners of the Town Square and marched toward the headquarters. Crowds stood on the sides of the paths and greeted the returnees with cheers. Yisrael Eli Shapira was distraught. He told me that had he only known that we would return home in this manner, he would have spread flowers in front of our path.

The Hashomer Hatzair movement conducted a regional convention in our town. One summer day, the Shomrim from all nearby cities and towns gathered in the town, and the town was crowded with joyous and bubbly young people, attired in the khaki outfit of this youth group. The convention took place in the Sokolicha forest and lasted an entire day. Kuba (Yaakov) Ryftyn led it.

Every representative from the Land of Israel who came to our town would visit the Hashomer Hatzair headquarters, meet with the youth, and discuss what was going on with the building up of the Land. Members of the older groups were active in the Brigade for the Keren Kayemet LeYisrael, which was headed by Pinchas Mejzner of blessed memory. Once a month, pairs of members would make the rounds to the houses and empty the blue boxes, which were found in every Jewish home, rich and poor. The Jews welcomed the pairs with respect. Some people would add a sum over and above what was collected in the box, if they felt that the amount as too small.

The Hashomer Hatzair chapter was active for quite a long time in our town; however, with the passage of time, its activity began to dwindle. This was caused by the fact that the older youths did not see their future in the town, and whoever was able looked for a means to go to the wide world. The gates of the Land of Israel were almost closed, and without possibility of making aliya to the Land, people began to immigrate to any place that was possible. In the late 1920s, immigration to the United States was almost impossible, unless it was for family unification reasons. Only a few managed to make way to the Land of Gold or to nearby Canada. Those who had the means, and these were few, went to France or Belgium to work or continue their studies. The only girl who succeeded at that time to arrive in the Land of Israel as a tourist for the first Maccabia that took place in 1932, and to remain there, was Nechama Bizounsky (nee Kotton). When most of the leadership of the Hashomer Hatzair had left the city, its activities ceased. The older group opened up a branch of Hechalutz Hatzair with the hopes that they would thereby succeed in making aliya to the Land, but Hechalutz Hatzair functioned in Stawiski for only a brief period.

One of the most important institutions of Stawiski was the library. It contained the best of Yiddish literature as well as books in Hebrew, original works and translations. Many of the translations were of classic world literature. The library had sections of Hebrew books for children and youth. Most of the youth in the town knew how to read Hebrew, and the library was a place of gathering for those who thirsted for a Hebrew word, in particular for the young people who perfumed themselves with the aroma of books such as "Remembrances of the House of David", "Achsa the Daughter of Caleb", as well as "Ahavat Zion" and "Ashmat Shomron" of Mapu, as well as others.

The readers would pay a monthly fee for use of the library, however this income was not sufficient to acquire new books, pay the rent, repair worn out books, etc. The income needed for the larger expenditures was obtained by arranging evening programs. There were lotteries for items of value that were donated by residents of the town, in particular by the storeowners. A special committee, headed by Pinchas Mejzner of blessed memory, ran the library.

When even these sources of income were not sufficient to cover all the expenditures, the committee decided to obtain income by putting on a bona fide performance. This matter was discussed at length by the older groups, who carried the banner of culture and Haskalah in our city, and it was decided to begin activities in that vein.

The family of Moshe Zilbersztejn moved to the town after the First World War, after the head of their family, who served as a Rabbi in a town of Lithuania, died. Moshe was the oldest son. Yisrael, the second son, worked for a short period in directing the youth. The oldest daughter Frumka married Aharon Eliezer Zak. The youngest daughter Chaika studied in the Yiddish teachers' seminary in Vilna and later served as a teacher in Harobiszow after she married an honorable person from that town. The Zilbersztejn house was a meeting place for the older and maturing youth. Aharon Eliezer Zak served as their spiritual leader. A. A. Zak stood at the head of the committee that decided about the performance. The other members of this committee were M. Zilbersztejn, Pinchas Mejzner, Yosel Mondensztejn, and others. They decided on the play "Gott, Mentch, Un Teivel" (God, Man, and the Devil) by Jacob Gordin based on the advice of M. Zilbersztejn, who stage managed this play with a troupe in Lithuania, and played the role of the Satan. He was chosen as the producer of our play.

An amateur play was a rare occurrence in our town. From the time of my youth, I remember that the adults put on the play "Yankel der Schmied" ("Yankel the Smith") by David Pinski. The play took place in the large granary of one of the rich farmers of the town. We children were forbidden from entering, and I was indeed vexed when my friend Gittele told me the next day that she had sneaked in and seen the play.

It was the summer of 1926, the year that many people finished their studies in Vilna. One day we, a group of boys and girls, were invited to a meeting in the home of the Zilbersztejn family, where we were informed of the decision to perform Gordon's play and to include us in the performance. The preparations began with the reading of the play. The narrator and expositor was A. A. Zak. He gave us thorough lectures about the content of the play, and the various social ideas contained in it. He participated in every rehearsal as a viewer, and he attended diligently to every detail that seemed not to go smoothly in our acting. He clarified any matter that was not clear enough to us, and he never tired of explaining again and again, until we understood our role clearly.

The diligence of A. A. Zak is shown by the following incident: During the time of the first dress rehearsal, which took place on the stage of the fire hall a few days prior to the first performance, A. A. Zak turned to us and said: "Children, perhaps you are not yet sure of the tasks that you have to perform? If so, it is better that we push of the date of the performance for two or three weeks, so that we can study more until we understand everything to its full depth. As you begin to feel and understand your parts more, you will be more complete in your acting." Indeed, we worked with enthusiasm and endless dedication. We made our nights like days with endless rehearsals. Even though everyone filled his task to the utmost of his ability, we were afraid to hear his comments – lest despite all this we would not be ready enough for this most serious and important experience in our lives.

The only one who was fully self-confident was M. Zilbersztejn. This was due to the fact, as has already been pointed out, that this was not his first performance. He played the role of the Satan expertly and infected us with his confidence and freestyle acting. The others roles were played by Kaplan, Yosele Mondensztejn, Yisrael Morus, Gucha Morus, Feigel Niedzwiadowicz, Gittel Kac, and the author of these lines. Hershel Rubensztejn was the prompter, even though everyone knew their lines very well by heart.

The first performance took place on the first intermediate day of Sukkot 5687 (1926). The hall was full to the brim. Many knocked at the doors and had to return empty handed since there was no free space. The performance was more successful that we would have ever imagined, and the audience thanked us with hearty applause. The second performance took place on the following night – this was something that had never occurred in our town, for no troupe had ever been successful – and indeed various troupes did come to Stawiski – putting on a performance two nights in a row.

A. A. Zak was moved and awestruck due to the greatness of our success. We did not let him down. Of course, we were all happy, and the happiness knew no bounds. It came to expression with the hearty song that burst forth from our mouths at the conclusion of the performance, when we were still behind the stage. The income from the two performances also did not disappoint us. The library acquired new books, and the community of readers benefited from numerous good books that were added to the library.

It was the 1930s. Anti-Semitism in Poland increased daily, and the Jews began to feel more and more as if the ground was being pulled from under their feet. Many of the residents of the town, first and foremost the artisans and small business owners, again saw no future for themselves and their children in Poland. They desired to make aliya to the Land. However the few certificates which His Majesty's government granted to the Jewish agency were given primarily to pioneers who spent a long hachsharah (training) period in the hachsharah farms. (Indeed one group of pioneers did their hachsharah on the farm of a Jew named Denenberg, who lived on the route to the summer village of Chmielowo, on the secondary, unpaved road to Kolno.) There were also certificates that could be obtained for large sums of money, however most of the families who were of modest means could not afford the fee or the travel expenses. Only a few families made aliya to the Land via various means, after overcoming countless difficulties. Years previously, a group from the Hechalutz organization, which was founded around 1922, made aliya.

One of these was Reb Yaakov Leib (Lip) of blessed memory. He was a scholar, an upright and G-d fearing man, modest in his ways and his manner of living. He would spend a few hours a day in his small haberdashery store, which was one of six stores that were located in the building that was adjacent to the fence that surrounded the courtyard of the church. He would assist his wife in running the meager business. He was a friend of our family. One day, he appeared at our home and informed us that he was taking leave of us, for he said that he was going to the Land of Israel. It was told about him that he traveled from city to city and from country to country – in fulfillment of the adage that the Land of Israel is only acquired through tribulations.

Some time later, after I had made aliya, I visited Reb Yaakov a few times. As always, he was good hearted, modest, and upright. The Book of Books was always opened before his eyes, to fulfill the verse "This Book of Torah should not depart from your mouth, and you shall engage in it day and night..." [1].

As time passed and no solution appeared on the horizon, despair overtook the masses, and many good people, for lack of other options, moved into the Communist party, which up until that time had only a small influence in the town. Overnight, the chapter of Hechalutz Hatzair became a Communist group. Nevertheless, their abandonment of the Zionist idea due to despair did not stand the dear youth in good stead during the days of wrath.

The bitter and violent day was not long in coming, and the lot of the Jews of the town was determined decisively when Hitler's armies invaded Poland. Men, women, children, scholars and Maskilim, workers and effervescent youth who had desired to be numbered among the builders of the Land, students of the Cheders and Torah schools, working women, grandmothers, young mothers, and newborns – all of them perished in the holocaust at the hands of the Germans with the assistance of non-Jewish citizens of the town and the area. They murdered, burned, and destroyed the members of our nation in cold blood and out of their own freewill.

The Jewish town of Stawiski was cut off along with the other holy communities of Poland, large and small. The few who escaped with the Red Army as it retreated from this area of Poland with the Nazi invasion died of hunger in the plains of Siberia, where they were exiled by the Soviet authorities. Only a very few succeeded in escaping from the vale of murder and found their way to the homeland.

Translator's Footnotes :

1. Joshua, 1, 8.

"Hashomer Hatzair" Organization in Stawiski Av, 1926 [August, 1926]

Happenings and Personalities

{235}

The Sabbath in Stawiski
by Rabbi Chaim Leib Bernsztejn
(Memories from my childhood)
Translated by Jerrold Landau

The Holy One Blessed Be He gave a precious gift to the Jewish people – the Sabbath. This gift was accepted by the entire nation with great joy. The joy of the Sabbath was particularly great in the Jewish towns.

There were two things for which a Jew was willing to mortgage half of his house: to pay tuition costs to the teacher and to prepare for the Sabbath in honor and glory.

The Jew basked in the splendor of the Sabbath for all the days of the week. Until Tuesday, he still felt the sweet taste of the past Sabbath, and from Wednesday he already started to prepare himself to greet the coming Sabbath. On Thursday, provisions for the Sabbath were already taking place in the house, such as baking, cooking, cleaning, putting things in order, and spreading fresh sand on the floor. On Friday morning, when you went out to the Jewish street, it was already perfumed with the aroma of the Sabbath delicacies coming out of every house.

The preparations for the Sabbath were like preparations for a wedding. On Friday afternoon, fathers and their children streamed to the bathhouse. In their hands were a pail and a broom made of twigs, and a bundle of white sheets. This was all in honor of the Sabbath.

Mothers washed their young children hurriedly. They shampooed their heads and dressed them in their Sabbath clothes. They did this all in haste, so they would not be G-d forbid late in greeting the glorious Sabbath.

As the sun was setting, Reb Yoel David, the Shamash (sexton) of the Great Synagogue appeared on the Jewish street with his thick cane. In a joyous and festive voice he declared: "Jews, prepare yourselves to come to the synagogue!" As soon as his low voice was heard, the shopkeepers closed their stores and the artisans closed their workshops. The Jewish population began to prepare themselves to greet the Sabbath queen.

The first stop of Reb Yoel David was in the vicinity of the bathhouse. It is impossible to describe the flurry and confusion that took place that overtook the bathers at that moment. From there, he continued along other streets of the town, declaring that the holy Sabbath was about to arrive. He went from one end of town to the other.

As magic, the weekday worries and concerns were set aside as if they never existed. The holy Sabbath had arrived. Fathers and their children, attired in their Sabbath clothes and with splendorous faces streamed in joy to the synagogues and Beit Midrashes to welcome the Sabbath queen.

In the large Beis Midrash where the rabbi of the town and the important people of the town worshipped; in the high synagogue which had a splendid holy ark; in the two Beis Midrashes of Chevra Kass the scholars worshipped; and in the Talmud Torah where the ordinary people worshipped – all of them were lit up with candelabras. Candles were burning in the old bronze chandeliers and spreading bright light. The Jews who came in joy clearly felt the additional soul, which filled every place with light and joy. The Jews welcomed the Sabbath queen with song and jubilation.

What was the situation in the Jewish home? It was clean, orderly, decorated and sparkling. It spread its light and warmth to the environment. A white tablecloth was spread on the table. Two braided challah loaves were covered with the Sabbath challah cover. The flames of the candles were dancing from the candelabras. The mother had recited the blessing on them. They spread the beams of the mystery of the Sabbath to all corners of the home. The Sabbath delicacies were giving off their pleasant aroma and whetting the appetite.

The father returned from the synagogue and blessed the household with a hearty "Shabbat Shalom" ("Peaceful Sabbath"). The children lined up and waited for the blessing of the father. With eyes exuding devotion, the father placed his hand upon the children and blessed them with the traditional blessing: "May G-d make you like Efraim and Menashe, Sarah, Rivka, Rachel and Leah".

When he finished blessing the children, the father walked around the house and greeting the angels of peace that accompanied him from the synagogue back to his family with "Shalom Aleichem". He then recited "Eishet Chayil Mi Yimtzah"[1].

And the mother – who could recognize her? She no longer had to worry about the housework. She had abandoned the worry and concerns of the burden of housework. The signs of toil and fatigue were hidden away. The smell of pickled foods and pitch that accompanied her all week were forgotten.

The mother sat down satisfied, beaming, and glorious in the modesty of her Sabbath attire. In her hands was the "Korban Mincha" prayer book, and her lips silently whispered the Sabbath prayers and supplications. She exuded an inner complacency, and thanks to the Blessed G-d. She gazed at her husband and young children who were sitting around the table as "Olive saplings" [2].

After her husband recited Kiddush over the wine and washed his hands, the tasty Sabbath delicacies were served to all of those at the table. Between each course the father sung the Sabbath hymns, and the children accompanied him with their young sweet voices, as a choir.

It was the holy Sabbath today, and in every Jewish home, the Divine presence dwells...

Translator's Footnotes:

1. Jewish tradition states that angels accompany a man home from the synagogue on Sabbath evenings. The "Shalom Aleichem" hymn is sung welcoming these angels. The "Eishet Chayil" hymn, in praise of the Jewish women, is then sung. It is taken from the final chapter of the Book of Proverbs, verses 10-31.

2. A reference from Psalm, 128.

{238}

The Rabbi and the Cantor by Pesach Kaplan of blessed memory
(A bit of family chronicles)
by Avraham the son of Isser Chalofowicz of blessed memory
Translated by Jerrold Landau

The cantor Binyamin Noach looked around the town and suddenly felt somewhat of a feeling of strangeness and not being at home. It seems as if the same Jews are conducting themselves a bit strangely. They are not Hassidim, they worship in the Ashkenaz prayer mode [1], they study a page of Talmud, they speak Yiddish in a non-obscure manner as in deep Poland – however they have an accent and intonation of words that is different than that of Lithuania. There is a sweetness in their mouths when they chant with the melody, and their dry and sharp expression exudes a sort of coldness and distance. There was nobody in the entire town who spoke with a hardened Lithuanian Yiddish, and he himself felt as if he was lost somewhere on an island. He had no friends or acquaintances here. He felt alone and lonely.

Quickly, he realized that also his sole friend and protector, the rabbi Reb Leibele, himself does not sit securely on his seat, for he is surrounded by detractors.

Why was it like this? Binyamin Noach perhaps understood the reason. However, he never talked about it subsequently.

Reb Leibel was a great scholar, well versed in Talmud and halachic decisions, and pious without any ulterior motives. Until this day, one can find at the home of his grandson in Bialystok Reb Yaakov Meir Rakowski the Talmud from which he studied. The margins are annotated with his glosses, written in minute letters, which attest to his great breadth and depth of knowledge. However, the modern ways overtook his family. His son Avtcha (Avraham Abba Rakowski), who at that time was a young man in his father's home, studied Bible and grammar, peered into little books [2], and was known as being a Maskil. The rabbi himself loved the cantor for his lovely, flowery letters, which shone a light into his intimate inclinations.

From cut off words that he heard from the congregants during the time of prayers, Binyamin Noach realized that a cold atmosphere prevailed around the rabbi, and at times it seemed to him as if they were quietly plotting against Reb Leibele...

Jews of the small towns (shtetls) would often love to talk quietly and secretly, looking around to see that nobody was listening. It was close to the Prussian border, and in the town, they often used to talk about the Prussian towns of Elk (Lyk) and Johannisburg, delivering greetings from the other side. At that time, after the failure of the uprising, the flow of Polish youth across the border strengthened, and the Jews probably had regarding this enough to exchange secrets about... However, in the town, "Obizdszikes" [3] would wander about, the ones with green belts, who had a habit of looking a person in the eye and eliciting a shiver with their glance. Binyamin Noach already noticed this in the first days, and therefore he probably didn't pay attention to this, so he thought that they were telling secrets about the rabbi, and thought that they were also against him, the new cantor and shochet, he kept his distance...

The cantor continued with his singing, and was ready for his "debut" on the first High Holy Days. He selected a few young helpers and sang with them a few pieces. He gave a special "job" to the base, Feivel the doctor, a tall, yellowish young man with long, threadbare eyebrows. In every melody, he had to interject his heavy "bom bom bom" or "tom tom tom". The cantor took great pleasure when he would sit in his house in the evenings around the with the young singers, as he held the tune with his hum, and hear that outside the window there gathered a crowd of curious people who were engaged in cheerful conversation. He was certain that he would excel in the synagogue on the holidays.

Indeed, that was the way it was. During his Musaf [4] renditions a strange sort of intimacy prevailed between him and the crowd. All restraint disappeared. Jews worshipped with heartfelt devotion [5], and the cantor created that mood.

However on the second day of Rosh Hashanah, right after the service, something took place that felt as if a thunderbolt fell upon his head.

As the cantor and his singers were finishing the singing of "Hayom Teamtzeinu" [6], as the members of the congregation were removing the tallises from over their heads and placing them back over their shoulders [7] and looked about with excited faces, Yankel the soldier ascended the bima (prayer leader's lectern). He was a tall Jew with a wild, black beard, and a brass plate over his heart. He ordered the shamash Berl Velvel to knock with a board upon the pad, and then, holding a paper in his hand, declared that this was an decree from the governor of Lomza. The content of the decree was as follows: the authorities obtained trustworthy reports that the rabbi, Leib Rakowski, had secretly become involved with the Polish "Miaczenikes" [8], and therefore he was ordered to leave the city voluntarily within 24 hours. Otherwise he would be bound in chains and put into jail.

A storm broke out in the synagogue. Reb Leibele, who worshipped in his own nook near the Holy Ark, was immediately surrounded by friends, including also Binyamin Noach the cantor. Other worshippers stood in groups and conversed. An oppressive secret hovered over all the murmuring. Slowly, everyone separated and the cantor, who was tired from the rendition of Musaf, felt his knees buckling under him, and felt as if the ground was tottering beneath him...

For the next year in town, they did not cease to talk about that bizarre event. Children heard about it from their mothers, and one told it over to another. Later, the story as clarified as follows: That same night Reb Leibele packed up and left town along with his family, and the next day, on the Fast of Gedalya [9], it was verified that the entire story with the governor's document was a pretext by several members of the community, leaders of Hassidic circles, who wanted to get rid of the rabbi. They chose to do this by frightening him with a concocted order from the authorities...

Binyamin Noach felt as if he had been shot from beneath. His sole refuge was gone, and what would be with he himself? Who knows what those same Jews are capable of doing to him?

In the coming days it became clear that his fear was not for naught. On the intermediate days of Sukkot a meeting of the gabbaim (trustees) took place regarding a new rabbi and also regarding kashruth.

With regards to the latter question, the gabbaim decided that one shochet who also works as a cantor is not sufficient. Therefore they certified as a second shochet a young Hassidic man, Reb Leizer from Radzilow. Therefore, both shochtim would slaughter together, one opposite the other, and he must not hold the slaughterer's knife [10] ...

After the decision was taken, they sent for the new cantor Binyamin Noach, and told him to sign a note that he agrees that there will be a second shochet, and that he would go together with the new shochet to the slaughterhouse and slaughter only under his supervision.

Bent and broken, Binyamin Noach signed the note, as if he was signing a verdict.

They later chose Rabbi Meir Noach Lewin as the rabbi. He later became the town preacher in Vilna, and many years later, a rabbi in New York, America.

Translator's Footnotes:

1. There are various styles of prayer structures or modes, depending upon the community. The main division is between Ashkenaz (European / Germanic), and Sepharad (Spanish / North African / Middle Eastern). The Hassidic prayer mode is called Nussach Sephard, which bears some similarity to the true Sephardic prayer mode, even though it is European (this is due to the fact that is based on the prayer mode of Rabbi Yitzchak Luria of Safed, in the Land of Israel, who was a precursor to Hassidism). There are many more nuances that I can mention in a brief footnote.

2. Seemingly an inference to modern books. The term here for books 'sfarimlech' seems to have a mildly derogatory tone to it.

3. I am unsure of the meaning of this word. Probably some sort of local ruffian gang.

4. The latter part of the Sabbath and festival morning service, which is conducted with special pomp and circumstance on the High Holy Days.

5. The word really means "a sense of being broken", reflecting the humility and broken heart that is supposed to be felt during the prayers of Rosh Hashanah and Yom Kippur.

6. "Strengthen us today", a hymn at the end of the Rosh Hashanah and Yom Kippur Musaf service.

7. It is customary to wear the tallis (prayer shawl) over the head at various parts of the prayer service. Some people do it more, some less, and others not at all – depending on custom.

8. Possibly the Mencheniks, a Russian minority party at the time in opposition to the Bolsheviks.

9. The day after Rosh Hashanah is one of the 4 minor fast days of the year, the fast of Gedalya, commemorating the murder of Gedalya the son of Achikam, the governor of the Kingdom of Judah installed after the destruction of the first death. With the murder of Gedalya, the remaining Jews of the land fled, and the destruction was complete.

10. The exact meaning of this phrase is unclear. It may be incomplete, with the word 'alone' missing from the end. It seems to impose some form of slaughtering restriction on Binyamin Noach.

{241}

"Tefilla Zaka" [1] in Poryte
by Avraham the son of Isser Chalofowicz of blessed memory

On the highway between Stawiski and Kolno, about five kilometers from Stawiski, the village of Poryte spreads out for about 1.5 kilometers along the two sides of the road. About 10-12 Jewish families lived there. The Jews of Poryte were engaged in various trades. Some of them earned their livelihood from labor, others from business, and a few tilled the soil. From a spiritual viewpoint, they were part of the Jewish community of Stawiski. If a boy was born, he would be brought into the covenant of Abraham by a mohel from Stawiski; if someone had to slaughter a chicken, he would bring it to the shochet in Stawiski; if there was a question of kashruth or a Torah litigation case, they would turn to the rabbi of Stawiski; if a woman required ritual immersion [2], she would fulfil this commandment in the mikva of Stawiski.

It seems to me, if I am not mistaken, that if the Jews in the city were living in exile, the exile of the village Jews was sevenfold more severe. At least the former lived with their co-religionists in their own area of town; whereas the villager lived in the heart of exile, that is to say, the exile pervaded literally in his own house.

In the following lines, I wish to describe an event that took place on the eve of Yom Kippur 5675 (1914) in the village of Poryte. I was eight years old. The matter began with the outbreak of the First World War, on Thursday, two days prior to the Sabbath of Chazon [3]. A fair took place in Kolno every Thursday, and on that Thursday, at 6:00 p.m., decrees of the Kaiser were posted. The background was red and the letters black. These decrees informed the population that war had broken out between Russia and Germany, and that all of the reserve soldiers up to the age of forty were required to present themselves on the Sabbath of Chazon at the enlistment center in Lomza. The confusion and screaming in town were very great. However, it seemed to me that the cries of my grandmother Tzipa were the greatest of all, for of her four sons, three were required to go out to a war whose causes and meaning were strange and unknown to her. They told her about some crown prince who had been murdered, whose name she had never heard before, and of whose existence she was unaware.

The marketplace emptied out speedily. The gentiles and merchants who had come to the fair fled while they still could. Only the residents of Kolno remained, and the sounds of the weeping and wailing of my grandmother grew greater from moment to moment.

The border with Germany was speedily shut, and the Jews of Kolno who conducted business with Germany and were present there on the day of the outbreak of the war were stuck in Prussia. These included my eighty-year-old grandfather, Reb Moshe Zeev of blessed memory. The next day, on Friday at 3:00 p.m., approximately ten wagons appeared in the outskirts of the town, and all of the enlisted Jews up to age forty were transported to the enlistment station in Lomza. They traveled on Friday in order to prevent the desecration of the Sabbath. The screaming and weeping at the time of parting was literally heartbreaking. My grandmother Tzipa was spared the pangs of parting since her three sons who were enlisted were not in Kolno. My father Isser was not in Poryte. Uncle Pesach lived in Finland and had to enlist in his place of residence. Uncle Shaul was serving in the army at the time.

That Sabbath eve was particularly sad and full of fear for the future. On Saturday morning, representatives of the government appeared in the buildings of the liquor monopolies and confiscated the products. All of the reserve soldiers up to age forty were enlisted from the neighboring villages. Some with song and others with weeping, they were transported in covered wagons to the darkness, to Lomza.

My mother Rivka was in Poryte with four young children. I and my brother Yisraelka studied in Kolno with Yudel Nachum the Talmud teacher. We lived in the home of grandmother and grandfather. According to my mother's strategic military understanding, my brother and myself were in greater danger than our enlisted father was, since Kolno was closer to the German border. Therefore, on Sunday morning, the day that Tisha Beov was observed, my mother hurried to Kolno as fast as a disturbed bird whose nest is endangered and who does not know the fate of her nestlings. When she found us in a normal situation, she was placated and began to plan what to do. Finally, she reached the decision that myself, my brother Yisraelke and grandmother Tzipa must leave Kolno for Poryte, which was a bit farther from the border.

The war became a reality. The enlisted soldiers went along all of the routes towards the border. The Jews were particularly afraid. The Russians accused them of spying, and many, in particular the Jews of the border regions, were exiled to Siberia.

With the enlistment of my father, mother remained with six children and five rubles in her pocket. Yet, we had to live! My mother and grandmother began to bake baked goods out of white wheat in order to sustain the family. We children would sell the baked goods to the soldiers, and that is how the family earned its livelihood. After some time, news reached us from father that he was being sent to the front. Uncle Shaul had already been there for some time.

The Days of Awe approached. As usual, prayer leaders from Stawiski were invited to Poryte – Nota Mendel as the leader of Shacharit and Michael Goldkirsz as the leader of Musaf. The well-to-do Jews from the nearby area – Alter of Poryte, Avrahamel of Rostki and Meir of Zaskrodzie, who were owners of flour mills, as well as a few families of Dzierzrbia and the Jews of Poryte, arranged a minyan (prayer group) in the Rostki flourmill, since this was the central spot of the entire region. On the Days of Awe, the flourmill was converted into a small synagogue. Three Torah scrolls were brought, and the aliyas [4] were distributed in a democratic fashion among the worshippers, without discrimination.

The two days of Rosh Hashanah passed as usual, almost without change from prior to the war. The only family that stood out was ours, since father, who had been drafted, was absent. The weeping and screams of my mother and grandmother ascended Heavenward from the women's area. However, on Yom Kippur, the heartrending weeping of daughters of Alter of Poryte was heard as well, since the Russians imprisoned their father on the eve of Yom Kippur. He was the richest and most honorable Jew in the village of Poryte. They tied him to the tail of a horse with a long rope and dragged him to an unknown place.

During the Ten Days of Penitence [5], the German army conquered the villages, however the Russians chased them out two days later. On the morning of the eve of Yom Kippur, as we returned from the morning prayers at the Rostki flourmill, we saw an infantry division next to the flourmill of Poryte. The Jews of Poryte spread out in all directions in order to avoid the soldiers; however Alter of Poryte and his family, having no choice, continued onwards towards their house. I was accompanying them by chance, since I had no fear of the soldiers due to my business dealings with them...

When we were near the mill, the captain asked: "Who is the owner?" Alter answered that he is the owner. The captain immediately began to beat him on the head with a whip, as he shouted very loudly: "Despised Jew, you brought Germans to Germany, do you not know that they are our enemies?" Without waiting for an answer, he asked his soldiers: "Who volunteers to transport him?" Immediately, five soldiers came out of the line.

The wailing and screaming of the family were to no avail. They took Alter, and tied him with to the tail of a horse with a long rope. Four soldiers walked two by two on each side. They dragged him to some unknown place. It is easy to imaging the feelings of despair that afflicted the Jews of the village and the entire region on that eve of Yom Kippur. In addition, a rumor spread that a similar fate was in store for all of the Jews.

The time of Kol Nidre came and went. The public recitation of Kol Nidre was incalculable. My G-d fearing mother, as she was reciting the blessing over the candles after the final meal, wept so much that I felt that all of the wellsprings of tears that had been stored up throughout the long Jewish exile had opened. She was not content that my brother and myself, two young Jewish boys, would stay at home on the night of Kol Nidre, so she sent us to our neighbor Yankel of Poryte to say Kol Nidre and to recite the evening service of Yom Kippur together with him. She told us that we should direct our prayers, not only for the merit of our father at the front, but for all of the Jewish people who are in great danger [6].

Yankel of Poryte, a Jew whose long white beard flowed over his robes, dressed in his kittel [7] appeared to me as the High Priest at the time of his service. When we arrived at his house, there was still a bit of light outside, and the time to recite Kol Nidre arrived. As was customary, he sat down to recite Tefilla Zaka. Fifty years have passed since that Kol Nidre night, and I can still hear the echoes in my ears of the gloomy, heartrending whisper in which Reb Yankel recited Tefilla Zaka. Similarly, I cannot forget the morning of that Yom Kippur eve, when they dragged Alter of Poryte away in such a cruel manner, tied to the tail of a donkey.

Yom Kippur night passed in peace. The next morning, the Jews of the village were not content to worship privately on the holiest day of the year, not being able to pour out the bitterness of their hearts together to the One and Only who was able to help. One by one, they streamed to the impromptu synagogue. The morning service (Shacharit) went as usual, but during the Musaf service, during the recitation of the Unetane Tokef prayer [8], the prayer leader and the entire congregation together with him broke out in bitter weeping, as they pleaded with the Creator of the world to have mercy upon his people of Israel and to open up the gates of mercy. The weeping and wailing from the women's section reached to the heights of the Heavens.

A few weeks later, thanks to various actions that were taken in this regard, Alter was freed and returned to Poryte. We all believed that Alter was freed thanks to the merit of the prayers that came out of the depths of our hearts on that Yom Kippur, and reached the Throne of Glory.

Alter died in 1929, and was brought to eternal repose in the cemetery of Stawiski.

Translator's Footnotes:

1. Tefilla Zaka (the Prayer of Merit) is a long, confessional prayer recited in private prior to the Kol Nidre service at the beginning of Yom Kippur.

2. This refers to the ritual immersion at the conclusion of the 'nidda' period, the period of time that includes the menstrual cycle and the seven following days. A couple is not permitted to engage in marital relations until the wife immerses in the ritual bath (mikva) at the conclusion of this period of time. This tends to be a monthly immersion, although it varies with the length of the menstrual cycle.

3. The Sabbath of Chazon is the Sabbath immediately prior to Tisha Beov, the fast of the 9th of Av that marks the day of the destruction of the two Temples in Jerusalem and many other calamities throughout the ages. This is always the Sabbath that the Torah portion of Devarim is read, and is about seven weeks prior to Rosh Hashanah. In Jewish tradition, it is considered to be no coincidence that the First World War (which in a sense set the stage for the Second World War) broke out in close proximity to Tisha Beov. Indeed in that year, Shabbat Chazon itself was Tisha Beov (when Tisha Beov, the 9th of Av,

falls on the Sabbath, the observance of the fast is postponed to Sunday). Thus, the first world war did indeed break out in immediate proximity to Tisha Beov.

4. The honors of being called up to the reading of the Torah.

5. The days between Rosh Hashanah and Yom Kippur, inclusive.

6. The two youngsters were probably too young to make the long trek to the synagogue in Rostki. The neighbor was probably too old and frail to do so.

7. A white cloak worn during the prayers of Yom Kippur.

8. A prayer that describes the holiness of the days of Rosh Hashanah and Yom Kippur. It contains the statement: "On Rosh Hashanah it is inscribed, and on Yom Kippur it is sealed: how many shall pass away and how many shall be born, who shall live and who shall die, who in a timely fashion and who in an untimely fashion, who by water and who by fire, who by sword and who by wild animal..."

{248}

Fragments
by Nechemia Lewinowicz

(Memories from Childhood)

Pale pictures of my town of Stawiski prior to the First World War arise in sections. The poverty was great, and the life of toil was the lot of the Jews in the city – a subject about which we can write a great deal, but here is not the appropriate place. Therefore, I will describe only a few isolated incidents that are guarded well in my memory, events that thrilled the hearts of children and filled them with joy and sweet longing.

I recall the joy and emotions that stirred our hearts at the time of the preparations for the holiday of Passover; the longing and thrill of a new set of clothing that was being sewn in honor of the holiday, a new pair shoes with squeaky soles and a new hat – all of these were moments of inestimable joy within the poverty that pervaded in town. There was great effort to remove the chometz and to "bring in" the Passover [1]– the joyous, clean, and sparkling festival – this also added moments of joy and happiness for the children, who shared the burden of the cleaning and polishing efforts, the purging of the dishes, the removal of books from the closets and placing them on the long table, which exposed them to the fresh spring air as they were aired out by leafing through the pages. I remember the volumes of the Talmud and Chovat Halevavot [2], dear holy books that our father of blessed memory purchased with boundless love and sparse coins, the fruits of toil, sweat, and the steadfastness of heart.

The preparations for the baking of the matzos – where is the ink to describe this? They began with long discussions regarding the price of the flour, an endeavor that was generally fraught with frustration. Once the flour was purchased, the preparations for the baking began. The baking was a collective endeavor. It is interesting that in this regard, they used the modern American manufacturing methodology – albeit for reasons of religion – of dividing up the tasks to different people. Each person had his job. He who kneaded the dough did not pour water into the flour, and he who perforated the matzos did not do another task, etc.

The most famous of the matzo bakers in our town was Shalom the melamed (teacher) of blessed memory. He was also an excellent Torah reader, and blessed with a sharp sense of humor. Regarding his many daughters, he would explain the verse: "I am weary of my life because of the daughters of Chet" [3]. (There is a play on words here, for the letter Chet has the numeric value of 8.) This was the style of humor that circulated in our town, originating from Reb Shalom, who was an interesting, multi-faceted personality.

We had two grandmothers: One was from Stawiski, the mother of our mother, who was known as "Itka Chaya Leahs". Her many grandchildren were called by her name – "The grandson or granddaughter of Itka Chaya Leahs"). Our second grandmother, the mother of our father, lived in the town of Wasosz near Szczuczyn. The two grandmothers were different in their character and temperament. The common denominator between them was that both of them were stronger than their husbands, our grandfathers. I remember the grandmothers very well, but the image of the grandfathers is clouded in my memory. As were most of the women in that era, our grandmothers were very prolific, and bestowed upon us a bounty of aunts, uncles and cousins.

We had many uncles. Two of them were named Chaim. One of them, Chaim Kabakowicz of Stawiski, and the other was Chaim Lewinowicz of Wasosz. They had the same name, but were different in character. Uncle Chaim Kabakowicz, who was closer to us because he lived in our neighborhood, was known in town as "Chaim Kasztan" (chestnut) on account of the chestnut color of his hair. He was tall, proud, and solid backed and he loved life. His wife, Aunt Miriam, was an exemplary housewife. Her house was the cleanest and shiniest of all of the houses in the neighborhood. We children used to enjoy visiting the house of Aunt Miriam.

Uncle Chaim, in partnership with his firstborn son Yankel Nissel, conducted business with Prussia. That is to say, they would purchase grain from the Polish landowners and neighboring farmers and export it to Germany. Due to their contact with the world at large, their status of life was higher than that which was customary in the town.

Uncle Chaim was known as a joker, and his tricks elicited waves of laughter. He would have fun at the expense of the schlemiels [4] and the fools, who were not spared from his sharpened tongue. A lazy person merited a special nickname: "the prachownik", that is to say "the working person".

Uncle Chaim had children from his first and second wives. Wonderful Aunt Miriam raised the orphans from the first wife with the same dedication that she raised her own children. In order to remove any sign of difference between the first and second groups of children, they all called her "aunt" instead of "mother". I remember Aunt Miriam as one of the most noble of the women of Stawiski.

Of all of the children of Uncle Chaim, only three that immigrated to the United States survived. All of the rest, sons, daughters and grandchildren, perished during the Holocaust at the hands of the Nazis.

Uncle Chaim of Wasosz was an entirely different character. We would wait impatiently for his visit to us on every Chol Hamoed of Passover [5]. He was tall, handsome, ruddy cheeked and red lipped, and his face always had a heartwarming smile. Without doubt, all of the girls in town loved him. He dressed impeccably, clean and shiny. We children were very proud of Uncle

Chaim, and we were sure that Uncle Chaim was the most handsome of all of the uncles in town.

Out of six children, one son Yehoshua was literally saved from the conflagration. (The oldest is alive in Argentina.) He was serving as a soldier in the Polish army at the outbreak of the war. When Poland was conquered, he went to Vilna and from there to the Land of Israel. Here, he fell in the War of Independence at Gush Etzion.

Regarding the Passover Seder and the holiday in general, it seems to me that there is nothing to add. Here, I wish to tell of one event that is etched in my memory from the days of my childhood. One of the closest friends of our father of blessed memory was Reb Gedalia Goelman of blessed memory. Reb Gedalia, who was an emissary of one of the Yeshivas of Poland, was away from home for most of the year. However, he would return home for Passover in order to celebrate the festival with his family. To us children, Reb Gedalia was a greatly beloved and desired guest. He was a jolly Jew, and spread his good spirit to his surroundings. Furthermore, he would always bring a present to our family for the holiday, a very pleasant present for which we awaited impatiently. He would bring a quarter of a liter of grapes. Each child would receive 2-3 grapes. After the blessing of "Shehecheyanu" [6] the great experience of holding the grape in the mouth would take place. It was hard for me to swallow such a wonderful present – a round, sweet grape, the fruit of a far-off land, which in addition came from the generous hand of Reb Gedalia, who brought with him the aroma of the wide world when he returned from afar to the small town, as well as the aroma of grapes and oranges. In order to lengthen the experience, I held the grape in my mouth for a period of time and did not chew it, until the warmth of the mouth overcame the will and the grape was chewed and swallowed. I am not ashamed to confess that my disappointment was great when the sweet-sour grape was chewed up and was no more, for now I would have to wait an entire year in order to merit a tasty, beautiful, splendid, appealing grape!

The center of "the celestial Stawiski" [7] was, in my opinion, the large Beis Midrash. There my father Reb Mendel of blessed memory shook off the dust of the bakery and turned into a new man. There, in the Beis Midrash, Reb Mendel turned again into the brilliant student of the famous Mir Yeshiva. Around the table of the "Magen Avraham" [8] study group was Reb Velvel Zak, the leader of the group. If my memory serves me correctly, the Magen Avraham study group was the spiritual height of Stawiski, a part of the celestial Stawiski.

Prior to the First World War, practically all of the Jews of our town were Orthodox, observant of the commandments, taking care to worship three times a day – Shacharit (the Morning Service), Mincha (the Afternoon Service), and Maariv (the Evening Service). If that was the case every day, on Sabbaths and festivals it was moreso. With regard to that group, who I refer to as the

Celestial Stawiski, they had special privileges, such as: receiving the "eighth aliya" on the Sabbath, reciting "Maftir Yonah" at Mincha of Yom Kippur [9], and those who knew how to lead services in a pleasant fashion would have the privilege of leading the services in the large Beis Midrash on the High Holidays – someone for Shacharit and someone for Musaf, not to speak of Kol Nidre and Neila.

Reb Velvel Zak, the father of my childhood friend Aharon Leizer, was ordained as a rabbi. However, like our father of blessed memory whose inclination was to occupy himself only in Torah but was forced to be a baker in order to sustain his family, Reb Velvel, the great scholar, saw the need to do business in a store that sold metal objects. In truth, his righteous wife Rivka, the mother of my friend Aharon Leizer, conducted the business. She became known for her great abilities.

The image of Rivka Zak is etched in my mind as a woman who exemplified the best of Jewish traits. One would never hear a bad word from her about anyone. She was a modest woman, almost bashful. The honor of every person was dear to her. It once happened that Chaim Zebulon Bramzon, a young, strong man, opened up a business in metal objects, and the livelihood of Reb Velvel was impacted in a significant fashion. One of the women of Stawiski who admired the Zak family once cursed Chaim Zebulon in the presence of Rivka. This refined and righteous woman literally trembled from the words, and with tears in her eyes urged that woman not to spew forth venom about any Jewish person. It is forbidden – she said, as she placed the palm of her hand on the mouth of that woman so that she would not sin with her lips.

The way of life of the Jewish of Stawiski had very little influence upon the Polish population. In that era, the G-d of Israel still ruled all aspects of Jewish life, and the cultural and ethical level of the Jews was incalculably greater than that of their Polish neighbors. I remember very well Friday afternoons towards evening, when the shamash (sexton) quickly spread through town, declaring "it is time to go to the synagogue"! Every word echoed in the air and reached all corners of the town. This was the time that the mundane disappeared, and the Sabbath queen drew near.

My mother of blessed memory hurried to place the last pots of hot foods into the large oven. She wiped the sweat off of her face with her apron, and gave to the Good L-rd that the cooking had come to an end.

If you wish to know what was the most valuable merchandise to the Jews of Stawiski – it was torah. At the age of ten or eleven, the boys would be sent off to different cities to study in Yeshivas. There they would "eat the days"[10] with families who valued Torah students. They would prepare themselves to serve in the rabbinate or in other professions connected to the Jewish way of life, in the same manner that Jewish parents today send their children to universities to study free professions. As I have already stated, the spiritual life was centered around the large Beis Midrash, the Great Synagogue and the Hassidic shtibels. The most important "bank" to them was in the upper spheres, where all Jews gathered great and small mitzvahs (commandments) for the World to Come.

The main source of livelihood of the Jews was from doing business with the farmers of the nearby villages. The most important day was Thursday, the market day. The market took place in the large square in the center of the city. The Catholic Church rose up from one side of the square. From its midst, the "holy mother" and her godly son looked upon those who believed in them, with the hope that they would leave in peace the sons of the nation from whose bosom they emerged. However, their hope was in vain. With their "eyes", they saw how their believers afflicted the Jews of Stawiski with cruel and unusual deaths.

My town of Stawiski, you no longer exist. Your memory has been erased from under the heavens of G-d. They razed the synagogue and large Beis Midrash to the ground. The graves of the great rabbis of Stawiski have been ploughed over; the cemetery has become a pastureland. The "holy mother" and her son – who was born as a Jew and died as a Jew – witnessed from the windows of the Catholic church how their believers from amongst the Polish nation, adorned with crosses, went out and murdered the Jews of Stawiski, and they are silent. Perhaps they shed a tear? Perhaps they wept silently when nobody who hear, just as the Divine Presence weeps at the bitter fate of the six million Jews, the children of Abraham, Isaac, and Jacob [11].

Miami, Florida

Translator's Footnotes:

1. Chometz is leavened food that is prohibited from being eaten on Passover. This sentence probably refers to the changeover of dishes and cooking vessels from the year round chometz dishes to the special Passover dishes that never came in contact with chometz. Some dishes that are used year round can be cleaned or 'purged' for Passover (the halachic details of this being beyond the scope of this footnote). The removal of books refers to the checking of books that might have been brought to the table during the year for particles of bread.

2. A medieval volume on Jewish thought by Rabbi Bachia Ibn Paquda.

3. A verse from Genesis, where Rebecca describes to Isaac that she is tired of the Hittite women (daughters of Chet), and would prefer if Jacob marry someone from her own family. The word Chet (Hittite) is a homonym for the eighth letter of the alphabet, that has the numeric value of 8 (each Hebrew letter has an associated numeric value).

4. A well-known Hebrew / Yiddish term for a good for nothing or an inept person.

5. Chol Hamoed is the term for the intermediate, non-festival days of Passover and Sukkot, between the first and last festival days.

6. Shehecheyanu (Who kept us in life to this time) is the blessing made upon eating a new fruit which has not been partaken of for a period of time. It is also made at other occasions.

7. A term for the spiritual side of Stawiski. The term comes from the "the celestial Jerusalem", which is the heavenly, spiritual Jerusalem that is supposed to exist along with the "earthly Jerusalem".

8. The Magen Avraham is one of the commentators on the Code of Jewish Law.

9. There are seven aliyas on the Sabbath morning. Additional aliyas are allowed to be added. If one additional aliya is added, it is called Acharon, and this is what the eighth aliya is referring to. Maftir Yonah is the reading of the Book of Jonah during the afternoon service of Yom Kippur.

10.   This refers to the Yeshiva students taking their meals on a daily rotation basis at different host homes.

11.   The animate references to the statues of the "holy mother" and son here are not meant to literally attribute life to the statues and images, but rather to illustrate a graphic point about the behavior of those that believe in them.

———

{257}

What Hassidim Are Capable Of
by Puah Rakowski of blessed memory
(A chapter from her book "Memories of a Jewish Revolutionary")
Translated by Jerrold Landau

My grandfather Reb Leibele Rakowski was then (in 1873) the rabbi in Stawiski, which is in the Lomza Gubernia.

My grandfather was a great Misnaged (opponent of Hassidism)... He hated Hassidim deeply, and they, the Hassidim, caused him broiling troubles. In Stawiski, for example, where he was the rabbi, on one Friday – my grandfather was then still a young man at the time – they put nails with the points up in the bath that was prepared for the rabbi.

Fortunately, had a sick child at home, and therefore he did not leave the house that day, so he had no need of that bath.

After this story, grandfather went to Plock, where he was a rabbi for a full 17 years, even though he always wanted to get away from there due to the standard battles between the Misnagdim and Hassidim.

After Plock, he accepted the rabbinical seat in Mstsislaw (in Yiddish Amtchislav, in the Smolensk Gubernia.)

Between Mincha and Maariv
by Rabbi Chaim Leib Bernsztejn
Translated by Jerrold Landau

I left Stawiski at a young age, but my memories of it are among the best and most beautiful in my memory. It was a city of Torah, service and good deeds[1]., and it was famous for its rabbis, gaonim and tzadikim, starting with Reb Chaim Leib the Great, and including Rabbi Yehoshua Lang, Rabbi Doborcki, Rabbi Remilgoski, until the last of its rabbis, Rabbi Wasserman of holy blessed memory, who perished in the Holocaust.

The large Beis Midrash, replete with its erudite scholars and students, stands before the eyes of my spirit as if it is real. At one table, they studied the Shulchan Aruch (Code of Jewish Law) with its commentators: the Shach, the Taz and the Sema[2].. At another table they studied Talmud; at a third table, near the oven, the simple folk studied Ein Yaakov[3].; and in a special room on the side was the fortress of "the common folk" – the Tehillim group[4]..

Fluttering before the eyes of my spirit is the Great Synagogue, four stories high, with thick walls and square pillars. The pinnacle of its glory was the Holy Ark, made of fine craftsmanship, known throughout the entire area for its splendor and glory.

The Holy Ark in the Great Synagogue

On the right hand was the room of Chevra Kass (The purchasers of books)[5]., where the people who would debate as well as those who studied individually would congregate. On the second side was the Talmud Torah. A precious Jew by the name of Muncki would teach and expound before the common folk from the book "Menorat Hamaor". All of the tables were filled up, with no space, as the Jews would toil and drink with thirst the sweet words of the expounder. At times, due to the great weariness from the toil of the day, the eyes would close...

I remember that, as evening approached, between Mincha and Maariv, all of the Jews of the town would leave their pursuits, including the tailor, the shoemaker, the wagon driver and the shopkeeper, the well-to-do and the poor – all of them shook off their concerns, as they made way to the synagogue or the Beis Midrash to spend an hour in pleasant pursuits. One would study a page of Talmud, another a chapter of Mishna, someone else the homilies of Ein Yaakov, and those who did not study recited Psalms in a group or privately. Everyone did what he could according to his level, and according the group that was fitting for him. Scholars and simple folk refreshed themselves and restored their souls during this time. If there would be a lecture by a rabbi or a preacher that evening – the enjoyment would be multiplied.

Along the streets that led from the marketplace to the synagogue, primarily on the alley near "Shia P.", groups of people streamed in one direction – toward the synagogue. How wonderful was this sight!

As has been said, Stawiski excelled in its Torah and service. There are two implications to the word "service" – the service of the Creator and regular work. Stawiski was a city of laborers, of whom can be said "You shall eat your bread by the sweat of your brow"[6].. Everyone worked hard, and sustained their families through the work of their hands. They earned an honest and proper living.

And the last is the dearest: good deeds. In Stawiski, individuals and the community took interest in the well being of their fellow. Various organizations existed to offer aid to the needy: The Talmud Torah, Hachnasas Orchim (insuring that guests were taken care of), Somech Noflim (sustaining those who had fallen), Gemillus Chessed (offering assistance), Matan Beseter (giving of charity in secret), etc.

There was an interesting and characteristic situation in Stawiski: almost all of the bakers were men of stature: Reb Chuna the gabbai of the large Beis Midrash; Reb Mendel the Baal Shacharis[7].; Reb Yaakov Chatzkel the gabbai of the Chevra Kass; Reb Shalom the shofar blower; Reb Matel the gabbai of the Talmud Torah, Reb Meir Katz the cereal maker, and others. It is worthwhile to make mention of Reb Yosel Shaya (my Rebbi), Reb Moshe Leib, Reb Gadalia Goelman, Reb Akiva – all of whom were Baalei Mussaf[8]., Reb Zawel, and Meizner the water-man – all of whom were expert teachers and outstanding and important people.

It was not only the elderly and the adults who occupied themselves with Torah. Many of the youth left the city to places of Torah. They studied in the Yeshiva in nearby Lomza, as well as places farther away. They even reached far off Slobodka[9].. During the Yeshiva breaks in the months of Nissan and Tishrei, when the students came home to Stawiski for the festivals[10]., the benches of the large Beis Midrash would be filled with the Yeshiva students, and the sweet hum of Talmud study would fill the hall of the Beis Midrash.

All of this once was and is now no longer. The Amalekite Nazis[11]. and our Polish neighbors destroyed and murdered everything. Oh would it be that we, the survivors of the sword, should merit to see the fulfillment of the words of the Torah: "Unto Me is vengeance and recompense, at the time that they shall stumble, for the time of their punishment is near, as vengeance shall be visited upon your enemies, and the Land shall atone for the people!"[12]..

Translator's Footnotes:

1. These three attributes, Torah, (divine) service and good deeds, are mentioned in the chapters of Pirke Avot (the Chapters of the Fathers, a Mishnaic tractate dealing with moral adages) as three pillars upon which the world stands.

2. Three well-known commentators on the Shulchan Aruch. Their commentaries appear on the folios of the work, on the sides and below the main text.

3. A book of excerpts of the homiletic (aggadaic) material of the Talmud.

4. A group of people, who were not at the scholarly level to study the deeper works, who spent their time reciting chapters of Psalms (Tehillim). The meaning here is that, what they lacked in their scholarship, they made up in their piety.

5. A group of people who raised funds to purchase holy books. Kass (an acronym with the letters kuf and samech), stands for Keniat Sefarim – the purchase of books.

6. A quote from the book of Genesis, where G-d tells Adam after the expulsion from the Garden of Eden that he must earn his bread with the sweat of his brow.

7. The leader of the morning services (shacharis) on the High Holy Days.

8. The leaders of the Mussaf (additional) service on the High Holy Days.

9. One of the most illustrious Yeshivas of the time. Slobodka is a suburb of Kovno (now Kaunas) Lithuania.

10. Nissan being the month in which Passover falls, and Tishrei being the month of Rosh Hashanah, Yom Kippur and Sukkot.

11. A reference to the biblical tribe of Amalek, the first tribe who attacked the Israelites as they left Egypt, and considered from then on to be the paradigm of anti-Semitism.

12. The final verse of the farewell song of Moses (Haazinu) near the end of the book of Deuteronomy.

{260}

The Deeds of the Fathers are a Portent for the Children
by Zelda Holtzman (nee Funk)
Translated by Jerrold Landau

As I retell the history of my family, memories come before me of a blossoming, many-branched family upon which destruction came. Only I out of all the members of the family merited to retell its history, after I actualized the secret dream of many of its members – the establishment of the Jewish homeland.

My paternal grandfather, Reb Avraham Zelig, whose name I bear, made aliya to the Land of Israel in the year 5661-1901. He possessed fine character traits, loved his fellow man. Brotherly feelings toward his fellow beat in his heart all the days of his life. He was one of the dedicated worshippers of the Chevrat Kass synagogue. At home they would tell that, during the time that he served in the army of the Czar, he was extremely careful about Kashruth, and subsisted only on water, salt and bread.

His love of Zion was very great, and he always pined to live in the Holy Land. As I stated, he fulfilled his desire in the year 5661. His letters from the Land of Israel flowed with love of the Land, and through his words, he stressed its uniqueness. Every letter was concluded with the phrase "May our eyes merit to see Your return to Zion"[11]. When he died, he was brought to eternal rest on the Mount of Olives in Jerusalem.

The aliya of my grandfather to the Land, and his letters, influenced my father greatly. However for various reasons, it was impossible for him to join his father in the Land of Israel. He was active in various organizations that worked for the Land of Israel. In his naivete, he fell into a trap that was set for him and others by a Jewish group that called itself "Nachalat Achim" and sold "properties" in the Land of Israel. My father purchased a plot in the Land of Israel from that organization, and received a "document" attesting, so to speak, to his ownership. Many people fell into the trap of that organization, which succeeded in dishonestly "selling" hundreds of dunams of land in the Land of Israel. When the scam was uncovered and many people were overcome by wrath, my father's reaction was as I expected. He said: "It is forbidden to mislead Jews", and he comforted himself with that. To his friends and neighbors who also fell into that trap he said: "At least the money went into the hands of Jews, they should be ashamed of themselves".

The Funk Family- most were murdered in the Holocaust.

    The will of my grandfather regarding aliya to the Land of Israel never left
my father's heart. He never ceased to hope that one day he would merit to live
in the land, and if Heaven forbid, his desire was not to be realized, he hoped
that at least one of us would fulfill this hope. He was not only an enthusiastic
lover of Zion, but he also loved his fellowman, and was concerned about other
people. His home served as the address for many charitable institutions, not
only for our town of Stawiski, but also for other neighboring towns, as well as
for the capital city of Warsaw. They also knew of him there. During the course
of his business, father would travel to Warsaw on occasion. Whenever he
arrived there, there would be several communal activists as well as people who
were in need of his spiritual and physical support waiting for him. In addition
to his work for the various charitable institutions, my father ran his own
charitable organization. How did he conduct it? Once every four or five weeks,
he would travel to Warsaw to purchase merchandise for his textile store. He
would finance the activities of the "cassa" with the money that he accumulated
from selling the merchandise between his trips. He would provide loans of
between 1,000 or 2,000 Zloty without interest, without documents, and
without guarantors to whomever was in need. Many people depended upon
loans from my father's private charitable organization. When a borrower
defaulted in paying back the loan, my father would comfort him and say: "My
son, nothing happened"), and he would push off the repayment of the debt.
His borrowers included food merchants. If it was difficult for the grocery store
owner or the butcher to pay the loan back in cash, he would accept repayment
in foodstuffs. The helping of other people was the most important goal of his
life.

We children helped in the establishment of this charitable organization. We served as emissaries for the good deeds, that is to say we would bring the money to the needy person, who sometimes was embarrassed to ask my father directly for a loan. We would also return the debt to father. Our payment was that we received sweets from both sides.

We had a large house, and we would rent out apartments. The tenants, such as the Bramzon widow and her children, as well as the ritual slaughterer and his three daughters did not wish to move to other dwellings, even though rooms for rent were plentiful in Stawiski. For why would they want to change dwellings? Father never pushed for the payment of rent, and in certain cases he satisfied himself with a token payment. Furthermore, he rented out the dwellings with no lease and no obligation. Who would want to leave such a landlord? With his motto was "Jews should benefit", he continued along his path of helping others. He would always say: "Livelihood comes with the help of G-d."

My mother Bilha of blessed memory was a pretty woman, who dealt well with her fellow and was acceptable to everyone. My mother enjoyed reading books, and knew how to conduct business. She was very vigilant and intelligent, and loved to express her opinion not only regarding family matters, but also regarding to the communal matters of the time. My mother died early and left eight children – four girls and four boys. From that time, my father had to fulfill the role of mother and father simultaneously, and he filled that role with unbounded dedication and love. He sent us to the Hebrew school of the town. My brothers studied holy subjects (Bible, Mishnah, and Talmud) with expert teachers. Some of the children were sent to study in schools outside the town, and most of my brothers completed academic degrees, which enabled them to conduct business, perform accounting, etc.

After I made aliya, I learned a few more details about my father and my family of blessed memory from the few Stawiskites who survived. After the Germans entered Stawiski, my father moved to Bialystok, where he continued in the textile business. He continued to assist refugees and conducted joint business ventures with them, which only rarely realized profits. He did what he did for the sake of Heaven. My father merited to die in his bed in exile of Bialystok, and was brought to burial in the Land of Israel on Tisha B'Av 5702-1942. May his soul be bound in the bonds of eternal life.

My brother Gershon of blessed memory, the first born of the brothers, was a member of the leadership council of "Hechalutz". He went through Hachsharah on a Kibbutz, and received a permit to make Aliya to the Land of Israel. However, his luck turned bad, and at that time, he was drafted into the Polish army. My brother Betzalel was also active in a Zionist pioneering organization, Hashomer Hadati. He also desired to make aliya to the Land, but his desire was never fulfilled.

My brother, the lawyer Avraham Funk, who was named after my father, immigrated to the United States. He established his family there; however in his inner heart, he always hoped to make aliya to Israel. On his last visit here a few years ago, he told me a bit about the thoughts of his heart. However, due to his illness, he was not able to realize his heart's desire. He died in the year 5729 (1969) in a foreign land. He left behind a wife and a son named Pinchas, who is a university student in Boston. He is the only one who carries on the Funk name.

We absorbed a great deal of fine traits from father's home, which I have tried to instill into the hearts of my children whom I raised in Israel.

I met my husband Avraham Holtzman in 1932. He was a Zionist activist, who was active in the Keren Kayemet Leyisrael (Jewish National Fund), Keren Hayesod, and Hechalutz. He carried with him the credentials to obtain a certificate for aliya to Israel, which was for us a prime factor in setting up a Jewish home. Before I made aliya, I took leave of my large family – from my three sisters Reizel, Zlatka and Sheindele, and from my young brother Dov Berele. The words of my father Reb Pinchas, which he said to me at the time of our parting, are engraved upon my heart: "May our eyes merit to see Your return to Zion" – words which were always on the lips of his father. Father further told me: "You are the only one who merited to actualize the desire of your grandfather with respect to making aliya to the Land of Israel". On November 2, 1933, the anniversary of the Balfour declaration, I and my husband Avraham Holtzman arrived in the Land of Israel on the ship Polonia. After many trials and tribulations we arrived at the port of Kantara on the Suez Canal, from where we continued by train to Tel Aviv. I am the only descendent of the large family who was able to actualize the will of my grandfather Reb Zelig of blessed memory.

Footnotes:

1. A quote from the daily prayers, expressing the hope that our eyes should merit the return of the Divine presence to Zion.

———

{263}

Personalities and Characters from my Hometown of Stawiski
by Chaim Aryeh Lewinowicz of Miami, Florida
Translated by Jerrold Landau

The Jewish towns of Poland, with their populist-traditional way of life, were well endowed with personalities of lofty spiritual levels, as well as simple folk. Both types forged their way in the exile of Poland, which was full of tribulations.

These personalities and characters arose and were nurtured in the unique Jewish environment in which they lived. They inhaled its atmosphere, and soaked up into their souls the traditions and customs that had been passed down from generation to generation, which forged their personalities, and bestowed color and content to their lives, gracing them with an exceptional Jewish charm.

Stawiski did not stand out in the wide spectrum of cities and towns of Poland. Even though it was a small town – it only had a population of about 3,000 people – it was influenced by various personalities and characters, like a kaleidoscope of personalities. I will attempt to describe some of them who are etched in the depths of my memory, and who in combination form a wide tapestry of various different types of Jews.

The first whom I member, different from all the others, who had a special aura surrounding him, was the town's Tzadik Reb Velvele Zak. He had a generous personality. His righteousness, uprightness modesty, and spiritual nobility rendered him heads and shoulders above anyone else in the community.

Every generation has its own righteous people. In the previous generation, there was Reb Chaim Leib, the Tzadik of that generation who lived in our town. A few people of our town, myself included, merited to be named after him. The Jews wished that their children would grow up to be G-d fearing, and they saw it as a good omen to name their children after Tzadikim who had been dear to them. More than once I heard my mother of blessed memory utter the name of the Tzadik Reb Chaim Leib with holy awe. She added afterward a supplication that he should be an intercessor for us in the world of truth [1].

Reb Velvele Zak was an outstanding personality, who served in our town as a rabbinic judge. He was the only one who the Jews of Stawiski referred to with the endearing title of Tzadik. When the name of the rabbi was uttered, they would say "The rabbi, may he live long", however they related to Reb Velvele as if they would relate to the holy G-d. They saw him as the additional soul of Stawiski.

Indeed, Reb Velvele was unique in town. He had rabbinic ordination, and if he had wished, he could have sat on the rabbinic seat of Stawiski, however he refused to accept this position because he did not want to make Torah as a spade to dig with [2]. He earned his living from his metal goods store. His occupation in business was a trivial matter to him, for most of his time was spent in studying torah for its own sake. Reb Velvele sat in the Beis Midrash day and night, and occupied himself with the debates of Abaye and Rabba [3].

The patriarchal image of Reb Velvele stands before my eyes to this very day. He was tall and erect, and his large sad eyes exuded good heartedness, uprightness, and spiritual peace. We were neighbors and our families were friends. Often I went to Reb Velvele's house, and I can testify that I never heard him raise his voice to anyone, neither in his home nor in the Beis Midrash. He presented a class in Gemera to the erudite of the town in the Beis Midrash. They sat around a long table, and he stood on his feet during the lecture. In my imagination, I see him as one of the sages of old who spread Torah to their students in the famous Yeshivas of Israel and Babylon. Reb Velvele conducted the question and answer period that followed the lecture quietly and serenely, as it says, "the words of the wise are heard in serenity." [4]

His wife Rivkele was also righteous. She was short in height, and a woman of few words. Her good heartedness and refinement glowed from her melancholy face. When she came to our house, her footsteps were barely heard. My mother would listen to her words with awe and respect. When she was shopping, she never haggled over prices, as did the other women of the town, and on Fridays she never touched the challas with her hands as did the other women of the town. She came quietly and left quietly, and when she exited, she left behind an atmosphere of calm, which lasted for quite a while, and affected the rest of the purchasers in the store.

She would visit us on Sabbaths. If someone uttered something bad about a person, even justly, she would put her fingers in her ears and say in a whisper: "It is forbidden, it is forbidden to speak bad about a Jew". This was the noble and refined character of Rivkele, the wife of Reb Velvele.

Their son, Avraham Leizer Zak studied in Yeshiva, and was given the nickname "the genius of Stawiski". He was also an unusual person. He was blessed with a wonderful memory. It is said of him that he remembered every page of Gemara by heart (this was surely and exaggeration, however there is no doubt that he possessed an exceptional memory). Not only this, but he was also able to read an upside down page of Gemara by heart, that is to say from bottom to top. When he read a book, he would merely flip the pages, and he would know the content better than someone who read the book for many days would. My father of blessed memory, the pious Reb Mendel, always sat at the right side of Reb Velvele when he gave his class in Gemara. He always kept quiet about the freethinking ideas of Aharon Leizer, and he did indeed suspect that he was somewhat of a heretic; however due to his respect for him he never let on what he was thinking.

The youth of the town literally revered Aharon Leizer. We saw him as our spiritual guide. He was short and also stuttered slightly; however, when he appeared before a group or a gathering of youth, he words flowed like an overflowing spring. On such occasions, he was freed completely from stuttering. He was a wonderful orator. He never prepared himself for a lecture or presentation. His words flowed without stop, and his influence on his audience was so great that he would often bring them to tears. On joyous occasion, he would jest and joke as he described those present, and the audience would be rolling with laughter. He was not a good-looking man, and he was bald; however he had sharp black eyes which added charm to his visage.

Reb Akiva

Reb Akiva, the prayer leader at our Beis Midrash, was a Hassid. The question was asked: In our town, where most of the population were Misnagdim (non-Hassidim), why was it such that a Hassid led the prayers in the synagogue? There is no real answer to this question, but one thing is known to me: the Misnagdim also enjoyed his style of prayer and his pleasant voice. He would lead the prayers on the High Holy Days, and his pleasant voice and melodies are remembered by me to this day. His style of prayer and enunciation were filled with grace. The young people particularly enjoyed hearing his Hassidic melodies and songs. Even today, when Rosh Hashanah arrives, my heart pines to hear "And therefore instill your fear", or "Let our supplications arise" in the style and melody of Reb Akiva, the prayer leader of our Beis Midrash, as he would pour out his heart before the Blessed G-d on the Days of Awe.

Reb Shalom the Teacher

Reb Shalom the Teacher was a unique character in our town. Reb Shalom was the Gemara teacher, and he was graced with a fine and sharp sense of humor, which often strongly affected his "victim". To be honest, he himself was often the object of his own sharp barbs. He did not withhold the staff of his mouth from his students who did not pay attention to his lessons. For example, once he told a particularly bright student who was graced with a long nose: "Your problem is that you exchange your good head for your long nose, however withhold your nose, lest it grow even longer."

On occasion, he would reprimand a student with in the style of Gemara: "There is no immodest matter with less than two people. What does that teach us? That a cow flies from the rooftop and lays an egg, that will take you into the darkness." The poor, confused student would then answer in the same Gemara melody: "That he will take you to the darkness." The answer caused the students to laugh, for in the end the barb came back to Reb Shalom the teacher.

He also baked the Matzo Shmura [5]for the Orthodox Jews of Stawiski. For this endeavor, he hired many women to roll the matzos. It was interesting to see how he urged them on that they should role faster. He would bring an image of the exodus from Egypt and declare in a loud voice: "Hurry up women, work faster, do not delay the redemption". The matzos were rolled with haste and enthusiasm.

A Jew for the Whole Year

Itche Leizer the innkeeper was without doubt one of the colorful Jews of Stawiski. There was one inn in the village, on the road to Lomza, and he, Itche Leizer, was the proprietor. He was not a great scholar; however he had the ambition to be perceived as a learned person, and he loved to converse with the scholars of the town. On the Sabbath after the meal, he would come to our home to converse with my father and with Aharon Leizer the son of the judge, who was in our house every Sabbath. My father of blessed memory, Reb Mendel the baker, was considered to be the sharpest scholar of Stawiski. After the death of Reb Velvele, he accepted the responsibility of giving a class in Gemara to the scholars of Stawiski. Reb Itche Leizer the innkeeper would say: "and why should I not go into the home of Reb Mendel?". He would then make a deduction according the style of Tevye the milkman: [6]"Harav et riveinu, hadan et dineinu – A rabbi goes to a rabbi, a judge to a judge, and I go to Reb Mendel. And where do you expect me to go? To the ignoramuses, to the wagon drivers?"

The adage "Leolam yehei adam" [7]was explained by Itche Leizer as follows: Always be a man, and fear G-d in private". He loved to quote, as it were, Ben Sira [8]. He would say: "Ben Sira says: A person should always be what he does." Who would argue with him and say that Ben Sira did not say this? In general, people listened to his interpretations with patience, and they even enjoyed his pranks.

Once, an event occurred which aroused the ire of Itche Leizer against his neighbor Paltiel the shopkeeper. Paltiel was a very poor Jew, however, he satisfied himself with little. He was a modest, G-d fearing Jew, and he would not even hurt a fly. His store was tiny, and his income was small change. It is hard to understand from where this Jew earned his livelihood. His honesty was without bounds. They would say of him that he would even cut a peppercorn in half, so that they would not suspect him, Heaven forbid, of taking merchandise into his store in an incorrect measure.

It happened that Itche Leizer took out his anger upon that Jew. One day, he met Aharon Leizer Zak on the street, and told him in these words: "Aharon Leizerke, you surely know this scoundrel, this despicable person, this denier of the G-d of Israel". Aharon Leizer asked him in surprise: "Who is such a Jew?" Itche Leizer answered him: "Aharon Leizerke, I am surprised how a person such as you does not know who it is. It is Paltuska the storekeeper."

It is further told of Itche Leizer: Once he took a loan from a well to do man in the town, with the condition that the loan should be paid back in one year. As was customary in those days among the Jews, no surety was given for the loan. A word and a handshake were sufficient. The well to do person visited Itche Leizer often in his store, and he was always greeted pleasantly, and offered a glass of whiskey and biscuits. He was even on occasion invited for a meal. The food was very good, and the well to do person enjoyed the tasty delicacies. Obviously, he was certain that the storeowner was doing this out of gratitude for the money that was lent to him. However, Itche Leizer did his own accounting, and when the time for the payment of the loan arrived, he opened up his "book of accounts". In it was written in black and white a list of all the good food that the well to do person ate at his store. At the end of the accounts, he explained that the loan had already been repaid for some time, and that the well to do person even owes him several dozen silver rubles over and above the original amount of the loan.

Wagon Drivers

The wagon drivers were considered among the haughtiest and coursest people of Stawiski. They were also known for being willing to step over each other; not physically, but through curses and boycotts. In this area, there were no other people equal to them. More then once, when I would be going to the Beis Midrash, I would hear their lengthy curses that they would pour onto each other. These curses and swear words would not be found in any dictionary. In truth, they were experts in Yiddish swear words.

The wagon drivers of our town were not strong men, with one exception – Hershel the wagon driver. Hershel was a strong, hot-tempered man, who instilled his fear upon anyone who saw him. Even the gentiles were deathly afraid of him. Due to his "fine character", he was the ruler of the marketplace of wagon drivers, and he had a monopoly on the transit to Lomza, the capital of our district.

All year long, Hershel the wagon driver ruled by force, by instilling fear in everyone. However, when the Days of Awe drew near, this man would change significantly, as if he shed his skin and wore a new skin. This was seen as a wonder, how this coarse man, who spewed out curses and swear words from his mouth like a volcano, all of a sudden turned into a quiet and modest Jew, who walked modestly among his fellow man, was very polite, and barely uttered a word from his mouth.

He was the first to arrive at the Selichot service [9]. He was also the first to arise when he heard the knocking of the shamash as he declared: "Jews, arise for the service of the L-rd!". On the eve of Yom Kippur, Hershel the wagon driver requested that the shamash have no mercy on him during the administering of the flogging him, and give him the full number of 39 lashes. On Yom Kippur, he did not budge for one moment from his place, which was in the row right behind us. He worshiped with great devotion, and when he came to the Al Chet prayer, he beat his chest with such force that the entire Beis Midrash shook.

On Yom Kippur, I had the opportunity to study Hershel the wagon driver very closely. His countenance did not show at all that he was a coarse and strong Jew. Just the opposite, he appeared as a fine Jew, whose heart was open to the service of the Creator. There was a small smile on his face, which looked almost ethereal. I remember that as a child, I was not afraid of him at all on Yom Kippur. On the contrary, I wanted to go up to him and ask him: "Reb Hershel, how is your fast going?", and to wish him that he might be sealed in the Book of Life.

Here lies the secret of Jewish spirituality, in that even the coarsest person could, for a period of time, attain a lofty level and turn into a refined and modest person.

All of these characters and personalities, who could be found in any Jewish city and town, were annihilated and murdered by the murderers while the world looked on silently. We are the surviving orphans of most down to earth and vivacious portion of our people. We are witnesses to the destruction that was greater than any other destruction that our people endured throughout its history.

Translator's Footnotes:

1. The world of truth referring to the life of the soul after death.

2. A statement from the Mishnaic tractate of Ethics of the Fathers, saying that one should not make use of the Torah to earn a money (the metaphor used is not to use the Torah as a spade to dig with).

3. Two sages who are frequently quoted in the Talmud.

4. A quote from the Book of Proverbs.

5. Matzo prepared with special meticulousness for Passover.

6. This is the Tevye from Fiddler on the Roof. The following quote is a play on words. The phrase 'harav et riveinu, hadan et dineinu' is a segment of the blessing recited on the festival of Purim following the reading of the book of Esther (the Megilla). It literally means "He who fights our cases, and who judges our judgments". 'Rav', here meaning to fight, is a homonym with the work 'Rav' meaning rabbi, although there is absolutely no relationship between these words. The deduction made here is a meaningless one.

7. A segment of the morning prayers, quoted only in part here. The translation is: A person should always fear G-d in private and in public.

8. Ben Sira is an author of an apocryphal book of adages, similar to the book of Proverbs, but not often studies in traditional Jewish circles.

9. Selichot (Penitential Prayers) are special services conducted every weekday morning from approximately one week prior to Rosh Hashanah up till Yom Kippur. The first Selichot service takes place around midnight on the Saturday night preceding Rosh Hashanah (or one week earlier if Rosh Hashanah falls early in the week). There is a custom, not often practiced nowadays, but frequent in Europe, of the shamash of the synagogue administering a symbolic flogging to the members of the congregation. Al Chet is the confessional prayer of Yom Kippur that enumerates the sins that people are guilty of.

Top: Stawiski Porters, bottom: Stawiski Butchers
No names given

(Left to right): Mordechai Chaver (Kotton), fell in the Philippines in World War II serving in the U.S. Army, Eliyahu Chaver (Kotton), of blessed memory died in the U.S.

Isaac Lewinowicz, of blessed memory, died in the U.S.

{273}

Hershel the Wagon Driver
by Moshe Goelman of blessed memory
Translated by Jerrold Landau

At the beginning of this century, more than sixty years ago, before there were automobiles and busses, our town did not even have one carriage to transport people to Lomza, the district capital, or to other nearby villages. There was only the covered wagon of Hershel the wagon driver.

He had a long wagon with two long ladders on each side of it. It was upholstered inside with two half of baskets that were woven from branches. On top, it was covered by large wooden rings with spaces between them, connected to each other by ladders. A tarpaulin was spread out over the rings, which in the summer served as protection from the sun or rain, and in the winter from snowstorms and cold winds.

There were two sections in the wagon. The back section was for transporting merchandise that the local merchants ordered from Lomza, such as barrels of kerosene, herring, cases of tobacco and cigarettes, as well as sacks of sugar, flour, salt, and other such items. In the front section, there were narrow ladder-like planks covered with wheat sacks, which served as seats for the travelers. Two or three people would sit on each plank. There were sacks filled with oats and fodder for the horses in the front near the horses. The wagon driver himself sat on these sacks.

This was the "boyd" (wagon) which traveled daily to the large city of Lomza. There were smaller wagons that traveled to the neighboring villages such as Kolno, Szczuczyn, and Grajewo a few times a week. There was another large wagon in Stawiski, with boards on all sides and covered by a thick tarpaulin. It was driven by Niedzwiadowicz once a week to the capital city of Warsaw in order to bring in merchandise that was ordered by the local merchants, in particular various types of cloth and material. Niedzwiadowicz left Stawiski on Saturday night after the Sabbath and returned on Thursday with his wagon laden with merchandise.

In our town, they baked matzo for the Jews of Warsaw. The matzo for export was baked by Michael the baker, who commenced his baking on Tu Bishvat and continued until Purim [1]. These matzos were sent to Warsaw via Niedzwiadowicz immediately after they were baked.

Hershel the wagon driver was a well-known character in our town. When anyone found it necessary to travel to Lomza to arrange various matters, in particular the merchants who went to purchase merchandise from the wholesales, Hershel was the man who would transport the merchandise to town. There were certainly other wagon drivers who drove to Lomza; however Hershel was heads and tails over them all due to his trustworthiness and importance. Hershel was a person whom one could trust. On frequent occasions, a merchant would give to Hershel the list of merchandise he required, and Hershel would arrange the purchase and deliver the merchandise to the person who ordered it the same day.

Hershel was tall, strong, with wide shoulders, and red cheeks. A small yellow beard adorned his face. He was known for his great strength. If a wheel would break while on the journey, Hershel would lift up the wagon with his shoulder and replace the broken wheel.

A story circulated around the children regarding the source of Hershel's strength. It was said that he had wide rings of blood around his waste, from which he drew his strength. We all had a great desire to find him in the town bathhouse on the eve of the Sabbath, in order to verify this story. However our desire was not filled, for Hershel was always the last of the last to come to the bathhouse, and he left there when the shamash had already issued his declaration: "Jews, come to the synagogue!" His voice was strong and loud, and his tongue was different from the tongues of the other wagon drivers, in that he often uttered verses of Psalms and other prayers that he remembered by heart.

The order of his day on weekdays was as follows: He woke up at dawn and hurried to the small Beis Midrash, Chevra Tehillim, where he worshipped. This Beis Midrash was located in the anteroom of the main Beis Midrash. He hurriedly recited his daily Psalms, worshiped, hurried home for breakfast, and then took out his wagon to road, near the street of the butchers. He would slowly collect his travelers at that location, and then travel onward to his final stop, which was next to the inn of Itche Leizer. From there he would ascend to his platform on the wagon and go on his way.

When he tired of waiting for a traveler who was slow in going out from his house to the wagon, he would hurry him along with his loud voice: "Nu, move already and come out to the wagon. The east side [2]is already occupied, and you will not have any place to sit." (The "east side" of his wagon was the two first planks next to him, where the most honorable travelers, who did not wish to sit with the woman, would sit.)

His voice was so strong that it could be heard throughout the Market Square, particularly when he was arguing with one of his fellow wagon drivers, when he was negotiating shipping fees with a merchant, or when he was urging a traveler to hurry up and leave his house. He did not go to beg for the shipping fees from his customers; rather, they had to go to him, to the wagon, to discuss the price and pay. His strength and loud voice instilled fear in everybody. He would not hesitate to use physical strength when a dispute broke out with another wagon driver. If it came to pass that a merchant could not agree on the freight fee with him, the merchant would run home and send out his wife to finish the business. He spoke calmly and quietly only with women. Hershel was a trustworthy and honest man. He kept his word and fulfilled his promises exactly. In short, one could trust him.

He lived in an alley on Bicki Street, in the eastern part of the village. It was a long walk from his home to Chevrat Tehillim, however he went there every morning at dawn, in any weather, summer and winter, in order to recite his daily Psalms and to worship.

On Sabbath mornings, in the summer and the winter, the worshipers of Chevrat Tehillim would gather together one hour before the prayers to study the weekly Torah Portion, and a section of the Code of Jewish Law. My father of blessed memory was their rabbi for all the years that he lived in Stawiski. The worshipers were wagon drivers, porters, smiths, and other workers. They would come to wake father up with a strong knock on the window shutter. The small room of Chevrat Tehillim was always filled to the brim, especially on Passover and Sukkot. On these festivals, the workers came to celebrate together with the Song of Songs and Kohelet [3]. They would be sitting and standing, listening with complete concentration, in particular to the stories and legends, and to the special melody which father used to give his lesson on the words of our sages.

Hershel was particularly diligent in two commandments, which he kept with all his might. One was between man and G-d, this was the recital of the daily Psalms which he recited every morning, and the attendance at the class on Sabbaths and festivals. The second, between man and his fellowman, was that he always expressed honor to scholars.

As is known, many of our townsfolk studied in the Yeshiva in Lomza. As was customary with all Yeshiva students, they would eat two meals a day on a rotation basis with different householders, and they would receive 3 kopecks for their evening meal – bread and a glass of tea that they purchased from the shamash of the Yeshiva. There were a few students, not many, who were lucky and had a rotation arrangement for all the days of the week, but most of them were missing a few days. These students would sustain themselves on those days with dry bread and a glass of tea. Thus, it was very important for these students to receive care packages of food at least once a week from their home. Hershel was the emissary for this holy duty, and he brought the packages and letters to these students from their families. He fulfilled this commandment with love and dedication.

There were set times during the week when the students would go out the courtyard where the wagons that arrived from neighboring areas would park. They would come to Hershel and receive their packages and letters from him. In this manner, they would also send letters back to their parents, for who would be able to permit himself to spend 3 kopecks for postage? Hershel would greet each student in a friendly manner, and if there were no package for a student that day, he would comfort the student and promise to speak to his mother to insure that a package would be sent the next day.

His son Michael was not as kind hearted as his father. He would chase the students, shouting: "Go on your way, why are you bothering me?" When

Hershel heard his son telling off the students, he would reprimand him for this. He would say to his son: "You know Michael, this is a great mitzvah, and you do not know whom you are yelling at. Perhaps he is destined to be a rabbi, and certainly a scholar."

That "brave Samson", as the children would call him, changed completely when the month of Elul arrived. When he heard the first shofar blast, he would immediately lower his stature, go around with his eyes facing downward, and speak slowly and calmly. He would address everyone in a respectful manner [4], including his fellow wagon drivers whom he normally related to with scorn and cursing. In the month of Elul, he would speak to them calmly, in particular to the chief porter. He would say: "Reb Moshe Ber, be well and healthy, hurry up a bit, for my horses also have to have a bit of rest after a hard day of work. Beware of harming the animals...". To the merchants who would be negotiating prices with him, he would say: "Give me one more guilden (15 kopeck coin), and may you be blessed with a good year!" He himself would spend more time in his Beis Midrash, and lengthen his daily recital of Psalms as well as his prayers. On those days, his son Michael would take out the wagon to the street.

On Rosh Hashanah and Yom Kippur, the Chevra Tehillim synagogue was closed and the worshipers went to various other synagogues, including the large Beis Midrash, Chevrat Kass, and the Talmud Torah. Hershel and his son Michael worshiped in the Beis Midrash, in the bench just behind us. Hershel would stand during the prayers, with his tallis (prayer shawl) over his head and he would recite the prayers and liturgical poems with a heart filled with emotion. He would weep with actual tears. On occasion, a sigh would come out from his heart, accompanied by "Oy, Merciful Father!". He would not exchange a word with anyone else, even during the breaks in the prayers. Rather, he would read from his book of Psalms. He only answered when someone wished him a good year. After the conclusion of the services, he did not hurry to go out. Rather, he waited until some of the worshipers passed by him and wished him a good year. He would especially wait for the worshipers of the eastern wall to pass by him and bless him with a good year "immediately". He did not understand the import of this word; however he would listen to it with special concentration, as if there was a great secret hidden in it. He valued the blessings of the scholars.

On Yom Kippur, he stood on his feet all day, including the breaks. The beating of his breast during the Ashamnu and Al Chet (confessional) prayers resounded throughout the entire Beis Midrash, especially during the silent Shemone Esrei prayer. During the break in the services, he would recite chapters of Psalms, and review the liturgy of the day.

One Yom Kippur, when I was eight or nine years old, I had already begun to fast for part of the day. I only ate once during the day, between the Shacharit and Mussaf prayers, and then I fasted for the remainder of the holy day. During the Neila prayer (the concluding prayer of Yom Kippur), when the congregation was standing on its feet, I no longer had the strength to stand, and I sat on the bench behind my father. Suddenly, when the cantor called out with a loud voice "Open for us the gates", the bench moved and I fell to the ground. Father looked behind me, however he did not want to interrupt his prayers, so I stood beside him until the conclusion of the service.

After the evening service at the conclusion of Yom Kippur, when all of the congregation went out to sanctify the moon [5], Hershel stood beside father and recited the blessing of sanctification of the moon by heart, hearing it from father word by word. Father attempted to say it slowly so that Hershel could recite it after him.

As we walked home, father asked Hershel: "Reb Hershel, why did you shake so much during the recital of 'Open for us the gates'?" Hershel smiled and answered: "Reb Gedalia, what do you think, that the gate should open by itself? One has to assist it with a strong push...!"

Translator's Footnotes:

1. Tu Bishvat is a minor holiday that falls two months prior to Passover (three months prior in a leap year). Purim is one month prior to Passover.

2. The east side of the synagogue is considered the most honorable place to sit.

3. The Song of Songs is read in the synagogue on Passover, and Kohelet (Ecclesiastes) is read on Sukkot.

4. Literally, in the plural form, which is considered a formal respectful mode of addressing one's honorable fellow.

5. The ceremony of sanctification of the moon is a blessing and accompanying verses that are recited once per month when the new moon is in view. It can be recited any time during the first part of the month, when the new moon is waxing. For the month of Tishrei, it is customarily recited at the conclusion of Yom Kippur, which falls on the 10th of the month.

{281}

Yossel Joreder the Rabbi of the Thieves
by Pesach Kaplan of blessed memory
Translated by Jerrold Landau

The story of Yossel Joreder, who was hanged in Stawiski after the Polish uprising of 1863, eight years before my birth, has remained in my memory for decades, due to my mother's frequent retelling of it.

A few years ago, I found the history written in an edition of the "Der Farband" journal, the organ of the federation of Polish Jews in New York. Then, the story again floated around in my head, thanks to the Stawiski native, writer, and party activist A. W. Rabinowicz.

I will attempt to restore the story, as it is recorded in my memory.

My mother was already an old woman when she told me the story. She would speak in an easy going manner, reciting the words, the entire time wiping off with two fingers of her left hand the small streaks of foam that accumulated in the corners of her mouth. Apparently, she, as I at the time, could scarcely estimate the moral level of the Jews of Stawiski. This is what she told me, and this is what remains with me.

Yossel Joreder came from the small village of Jurowce, not far from Stawiski. He was reckoned as an outstanding householder in the town, although they knew that he earned his living through robbery, and that he was the "rabbi" of the thieves.

I was amazed by strange expression – how could it be, a rabbi, not of the Hassidim, not for students, but for ... thieves? My mother explained to me that a rabbi of thieves is not someone who goes out himself to rob, but rather who dispenses advice, takes the stolen objects from them, sells them, and divides up the earnings among the group – in short, someone who does not have a very fine profession, but who could himself be a fine person.

Indeed, Yossel was a very fine person. He was a middle aged Jew with a long yellow beard, with an atlas style long frock [1], slippers, white socks and a red kerchief hanging from his back pocket. He would walk with deliberate steps. He would never miss a service at the Beis Midrash. He would get a fine aliya [2] and give a fine donation.

They used to say that thanks to him, Stawiski and its surrounding region were careful regarding thieves. He would "work" only in far off places.

Often, he would be away for a week. In town, they understood that somewhere, a large piece of work was transpiring. However, he would return, and again become the calm, sedate, fine householder. Never did they catch or punish him.

His own house, in which he lived, was not far from the church. He rented out a portion of it to the chief of the guards, as well as the subordinate thieves and drunks who were not lacking from any town.

At that time, when heaven and earth were being swept in Poland, when people were afraid to travel for fear of the Russian and Polish soldiers, Yossel was away for several weeks, until they brought him back beaten and in chains. They placed him with the chief guard, in his own house.

One can conceive of the terrible cries of his wife and children. In town, they said that they arrested him at an armed robbery at a landowner's (Poretz's) estate near Suwalki, and he was sentenced to the death penalty. Therefore, everyone was very amazed when they quickly let Yossel go to his wife. What took place? There were no secrets, and very soon, everyone had something to tell to his fellow.

Yossel worked as a middleman in conducting the armed robbery. They let him out on bail so that he would bring his accomplices. Then his sentence would be lightened.

He was absent again. His first absence was for a few weeks. Then he returned and brought a victim with him, who was imprisoned alongside Yossel. The entire town wept for that victim. He was a young man who had sung with the cantor in the Great Synagogue during the previous High Holy Days and who ate on a daily basis [3] with several householders. Whether that singer was indeed dragged into the band of thieves, or whether he a free victim of Yossel's provocation, this is a mystery which is covered in the earth.

Later they arrested a third partner, a gentile. They tried him, and his sentence was hanging.

The hanging was to take place behind the town, on the left of the Lomza Highway, not far from the Jewish cemetery. The two Jewish convicts were first taken to the mikva [4]. Drums were drumming in the ears during the entire duration of their immersion, so that they could not hear the lamenting of Yossel's family, and of the entire town for the singer. Afterward, they led them to the gallows. After the execution, they buried them near the gallows.

I myself saw that hilly ground.

I knew Yossel's son. He was a small Jew with a yellow beard, named Zeligel. He was a furrier by trade, as well as a professional informer. One used to see him in the Beis Midrash sitting near the door, wearing his dirty tallis. He informed about military conscription, and about contraband. Thus did all the years pass by.

Finally, something ugly took place to him. On a winter night, someone placed a sack on his head, took him to the Lomza Highway, and drove him to the Narew. In the spring, the river spat him out. They conducted a large trial against Jews of the town, which lasted for several years and resulted in nothing.

Translator's Footnotes:

1. I am not sure of the reference here.

2. An aliya is the honor of being called up to the public reading of the Torah in the synagogue. At each service where the Torah is read, a certain number of people are called up for an aliya.

3. This refers to the daily rotation system used to sustain Yeshiva students from out of town, who are assigned to a different house each day to partake of their meals.

4. A ritual bath.

{283}

Three Personalities
by Meir (Meitshak) Bogdanowicz
Translated by Jerrold Landau

Chaya Shlia of blessed memory

Her name was Chaya, but the people added to her name the nickname Shlia. Why Shlia? There is no explanation. Perhaps because she always dragged her feet in a large pair of shoes – men's shoes – and wore two dresses, one on top of the other. One was long and reached the ground, and the other was shorter than the first.

Chaya Shlia was not born in a golden cradle, and she did not have much happiness and comfort in her life. Chaya also had a heart and soul that was in need of its share of comfort, and without any other source, she got her pleasure in the following manner.

Every day, before dawn, Chaya would already be dragging her feet through the alleys of Stawiski. Where would she be going at such an early hour? To the Beis Midrash. She would come to the vestibule, wash her hands, and then enter into the Beis Midrash, place herself before the holy ark, and say in her simple language: "Good morning, Master of the World, your servant Chaya is here." She would say her piece, and then leave the Beis Midrash. She would then go to the vestibule, stand in a corner, and wait until the Jews would come to pray in the first minyan (prayer quorum). After each blessing, she would answer Amen. During the recital of Kedusha (the sanctification prayer), she would jump up a bit as did the men. Chaya Shlia would then return home happy.

The entire town knew about Chaya's morning visits to the Beis Midrash. One day, one of the town jesters decided to play a practical joke at the expense of Chaya, in such a manner that the entire town would be rolling with laughter. Given that Chaya wakes up before dawn, our hero woke up that night in the latter part of the night, and immediately hurried to the Beis Midrash. He hid there in a corner, so that nobody would see him, and waited patiently for his victim.

Chaya arrived at the Beis Midrash, and said as usual: "Good morning Master of the entire world, your servant Chaya is here". A voice was heard in response: "Good morning to you, my servant Chaya Shlia".

Due to her great naïveté, she believed that the voice that was speaking to her was the L-rd's. Her face shone with joy. She forgot that she was standing in the Beis Midrash of Stawiski, and her imagination carried her to the celestial worlds, the worlds of splendor and purity. Her ears heard song and joy. This is the son – she said to herself – of the angels singing each morning in honor of the Creator of the world. Chaya looked around and saw the closed door; however she believed that at any moment the door would open and G-d in His glory would enter and appear before her eyes. After she attained her first "victory" – hearing the voice of G-d – she had the strong desire to attain her second and final "victory". She called out enthusiastically: "G-d, now that I have merited to hear Your voice, please show me Your being." Our hero did not hesitate, he came out from his hiding place, placed himself face to face before Chaya and showed her his true identity.

Chaya was distraught. In a split second, she fell from her lofty heights to a deep pit. She again saw herself in the Beis Midrash of Stawiski. Her face was enveloped with gloom. With great travail, she dragged her feet to the door and went outside. The freshness of the morning restored her soul, and only then did she begin to understand what had happened to her, and whom she had seen – her closest neighbor. Tears of anger and disgrace rose up from the throat of Chaya. That morning, she returned home crushed and in agony.

Itche Leizer Horowicz

Itche Leizer Horowicz though very highly of himself, and took pride in his pedigree. What was the greatness of his pedigree? It was that there were no mere working people in his family; everyone was a merchant. He himself was an innkeeper. Itche used to say that a working person is like a dog.

Itche Leizer was afraid of three things: G-d, death, and the police. If he saw a policeman on the street, even from a great distance, Itche Leizer would immediately flee. If it happened that someone died in town, Itche Leizer would be so perplexed that he would hide under his bed. On the other hand, he went three times a day to the Beis Midrash to pay his debts to the Creator of the world with all his heart.

The Jews suffered greatly in anti-Semitic, Fascist Poland, however they also had some "benefits", such as high taxes and the requirement of army duty. Of course, the young Jews of Stawiski were among those who possessed these "rights", and every year, when the time came, a group of them were required to present themselves before the army induction committee.

The night before the enlistment, the conscripts did not sleep. That night was dedicated to various pranks. The most popular prank was always the parking of the "carriage" (that is the hearse which transported the deceased to the cemetery) in front of Itche Leizer's door. As usual, Itche Leizer woke up early in order to be one of the first to arrive at the Beis Midrash. However, when he opened his door and saw the "carriage", he let out a scream that would pierce the heavens and called for the assistance of his wife Shifra. (Itche Leizer always interchanged 'r' with 'l'.) He would say: "Shiflinka, what has happened to me? I still want to live; I will send them to jail for a week". Itche Leizer uttered his bitter shriek every year, when he gave release to all the fear that was stored up in his heart as he saw the "carriage" standing in front of his door.

In truth, he Itche Leizer never "sent" anyone to jail, and hi himself was barely spared from the great fear which accompanied him all his days, which, when expressed, made him into a laughing stock not just in the eyes of the town pranksters, but also in the eyes of serious people.

Hillel the Hat Maker

Who did not know Hillel the hat maker? He toiled all his days, traveled to fairs, and was only able to sustain his family in a meager fashion. However Hillel was blessed with one fine trait – he was happy with his lot and satisfied with what he had.

One Friday, when he was going with his hats to the marketplace, Hillel saw an unusual piece of paper lying on the ground. He bent down, lifted up the notes, and was full of wonder at the nice looking people who were illustrated on the paper. As he was still walking along in wonderment, he met one of the young men of the town. Hillel showed him the "note" and told him that he found it on the street. That person took advantage of Hillel's naïveté and told him that he had just lost that note. Of course, Hillel returned the note to "its owner".

When the matter became known to people, they explained to Hillel that this note was a five dollar bank note, that the money did not belong to the man who took it from him deceitfully, and that with the amount, he would be able to purchase a new pair of boots. Hillel answered them: "Well, it looks like I won't have a new pair of boots".

"Buntze the silent" (the mighty man of Peretz), did not withhold himself from a bun spread with butter, and he also did not feel that he had to purchase it with his own money; while he, Hillel, passed over a new pair of boots that he could have had without toil. One must toil and work hard for a pair of boots, for only then would they have value. If one finds a note that one could exchange for a pair of boots – this was not the business of Hillel the hat maker of Stawiski. Boots such as this would not be worthy of their name.

**Next Six Images are from Memorial Meetings
No names or dates given, location probably in Israel**

{289}

For Those Who Passed Away
by Chemda
Translated by Jerrold Landau

Yisrael Eli Shapira of blessed memory

Yisrael Eli Shapira of blessed memory was an exceptional personality. He had great capabilities and a sharp intellect. He was pleasant in his ways, and pleasant in his conversation. He would analyze any topic with great clarity and ironclad logic. He lived in the home of his father, Menashe Shapira of blessed memory, near the road. His father, who was a widower, lived in the attic, and took his meals at his son's table. The "Young Chalutz" group had its headquarters in one of the rooms of the attic for a certain time.

Yisrael Eli was a member of the town council. No small amount of civic matters were decided by him. As P. Kaplan pointed out in one of his articles, he was set to be elected as the mayor, however the rabbi dissuaded him since serving in this position would lead on occasion to the desecration of the Sabbath. The gentile mayor was narrow-minded, and enjoyed to tipple. He was not chosen for this position due to his capabilities or his plans, but rather because he was the lesser of the evils, for he was the least anti-Semitic of the candidates for that position. Even though the Jewish vote was assured to him from the outset, prior to the election he would stand next the his office window, invite Jewish passers by in for a friendly chat, and give them a good quality cigarette. This was his way of insuring the Jewish vote.

Yisrael Eli Shapira prepared the financial accounting for the mayor. He knew Polish very well, and wrote with a fine style. He would often help Jews with their written requests to the authorities in Warsaw regarding the many weighty taxes that the Polish regime imposed upon them. He would chain smoke as he worked at his desk. As he said, this sharpened his mind, and he was then able to produce good and clean work with his hands.

His only daughter Salcha was a pretty brunette. Here eyes were like plums, decorated with black eyebrows and eyelashes, displaying a silent melancholy. She inherited her grace from her mother and her exceptional abilities from her father. When I was already living in Israel I heard that she had completed the Polish gymnasia in Lomza with excellent grades.

Yisrael Eli's brother-in-law was the landowner Denenberg, who was married to his wife's sister. His brother was a pharmacist in one of the towns. This was quite rare in Poland, for there was a "numerus nullus" clause in effect in the faculties of medicine, that is to say that for the most part, Jews were not accepted to those faculties.

Yisrael Eli served for many years as the secretary of the communal council, and he headed the popular bank that was founded in Stawiski. He was an enthusiastic Zionist. He participated in all the events that were connected to the Land of Israel. When the opening of the Hebrew University of Jerusalem in 1925 was celebrated in the city, he marched at the head of the large parade, as he carried with pride the large banner of the university building. He saw in the establishment of this institution of higher learning one of the wonderful manifestations of the spiritual life of the nation on the land of the fathers. He desired to make aliya to the Land with his family, but he did not have the necessary means to overcome the difficulties of aliya during that time period.

Yisrael Eli Shapira did not merit arriving at his desired destination, and he was torn up by the human beasts. As Yisrael Eli once said when a splendid automobile passed through quickly, and left smoke and a bad smell in its wake: "Thus is civilization…"

{290}

Chaim Kadysz Kolinski of blessed memory

Chaim Kolinski, the eldest son of Reb Avraham Ber of blessed memory, was a tailor by profession. He serviced the farmers primarily, and he would travel with his sons to the fairs in order to sell his merchandise. If a gentile measured the coat and the sleeves were too short – Chaim Kolinski would tell the gentile that he is guilty, for his arms were too long; and if the sleeves were too long – he would claim that the arms of the gentile were too short.

Chaim Kolinski was a good person, with a warm Jewish heart. He lived with his extended family in the second floor of the large house of Hershel Mark, may G-d avenge his blood. His economic situation was tight, however one never heard him complain. He always found a reason to joke. He was also always prepared to help his fellow. On Purim, he would dress up in the clothes of a Russian captain, with "golden" shoulders, wear an army cap on his head, cover his face with a mask, and go from door to door to collect "mishloach manos" for the poor of the city[1].]. They greeted him with joy and friendliness everywhere. During my childhood, I was afraid to look at the mask on his face, and when I saw him from afar, I would hide "until the trouble passed". Chaim K. knew my weakness, and did not let me be. He searched after me until he found me, and he forced me to look at his masked face. Later, in order to calm me, he would remove his mask so that I can see his real face, that it was the same face as yesterday, and he would laugh with his usual hearty laughter.

At the end of the First World War, when postal service was renewed with the outside world, he was appointed as the postmaster. This was the first and only time that a Jew from our city was appointed to that position, and even that was for a short period only. One day he came to us with a letter from my brother Nechemia: "Your son is the first one of our townsfolk in the United States, who 'broke through' the path from New York to Stawiski" – he said half jokingly, half seriously, full of reverence for the dedicated son.

His oldest daughter was quite talented. She studied everything that came her way. She swallowed up books ravenously. She eventually moved to Vilna to study and work. She saved her money until she succeeded in bringing her younger sister with her, and she helped her acquire Torah and knowledge. When she visited me once during her vacation, I was surprised at what I saw – before me was a beautiful girl full of grace and delicacy.

(Note: an article by Chaya Kolinski on Stawiski is included in this book.)

{290}

Solarczyk of blessed memory

Solarczyk arrived to town one day, and was hired as a Hebrew teacher for the daughters of the miller in nearby Rutki. He came into town for the Sabbaths and festivals. Our home was always filled with the tumult of youths, friends of my brother. A day that Solarczyk came would be an especially joyous day. He was an intelligent young man, happy and full of humor. He knew how to tell stories and jokes with grace and good taste. He also sang nicely, and once participated as a soloist at one of our evenings of song, readings and dance, which we would organize from time to time for the benefit of the library. That evening, he sang with great feeling his beloved song: "My L-rd, my L-rd, why have You forsaken me?" [2]..

He had an artificial leg. I heard him tell with great agony that he was wild during his childhood. Once, as he was climbing a tall tree, he fell to the ground, was seriously injured, and it was necessary to amputate his leg. He never forgave himself for being handicapped, and he saw in this the source of his difficulties and setbacks in life. He often thought that if it were not for his injury, he might have a future as an actor in the theater --a childhood dream of his. Indeed, he had such talents. Nevertheless, this did not detract from his joyfulness, and he was always a pleasant guest.

One winter day, he sat in our house with a number of friends, including another guest who was a competitor with Solarczyk in the realm of jokes and humor. That guest told about his period of study in Berlin, and the life of deprivation that he lived due to the lack of means. In order to "ease" his situation somewhat, he switched his room every month, and told the new landlady about this "birthday" that falls in that month. As was customary, the landlady would bake cakes in honor of the "birthday" and give him presents – which would benefit him for several days.

Story continued after story, and joke after joke, until suddenly a group of Germans approached in order to conscript the young men for paving roads among the high piles of snow that were heaped up in the streets. The youths were alert to the situation, and disappeared into the yard via the back door. Solarczyk fled to a nearby room and hid in the clothes closet.

Once, Solarczyk told about the stinginess of K., even though he was a man of means. K. had two daughters. As usual, the daughters supervised the household. One Sabbath, Solarczyk along with a number of friends visited the house of K., and the girls served them tea. The father made haste and divided the sugar cubes into four smaller pieces. Usually, one would sweeten a glass of tea with two sugar cubes. Unsweetened tea would be drunk with a half a cube, or at most one cube, placed in the mouth. Solarczyk, who understood the motives of the stingy father, decided to teach him a lesson. He placed a sugar cube in his mouth, crushed it with his cheek, and swallowed it with each sip of tea. Thus did he use up many sugar cubes with one glass of tea. K. saw this and begged him to sweeten the tea. "I don't like sweet tea" – answered Solarczyk, and continued doing what he was doing.

From that time on, whenever Solarczyk came to K.'s house, the homeowner would slink into another room so that he would not witness Solarczyk's gluttony.

Solarczyk studied in the Hebrew teachers' seminary in Vilna, and then served as a teacher in one of the nearby villages. He got married there. Every Friday, a satire page would appear in the Jewish newspaper of Vilna entitled "Di Bomba" ("The Bomb"). This page was given that name after a frightening incident that took place in one of the Polish gymnasia of Vilna. Several students, who were angry because the failed a test, tossed a bomb at their teachers. Two professors and three students were killed. As a result of this event, a decision was made to make the matriculation exams easier in all of the gymnasia, including the Hebrew "Tarbut" gymnasia. His column was very successful, and it appeared in the newspaper for many years. Solarczyk did not sever his connection with Stawiski, and he visited on specific occasions.

{292}

Fishel Cybulski of blessed memory

Fishel Cybulski of blessed memory was one of the youths of our town who was successful at his endeavors. He was a pork merchant, and owned a brush factory. Even though he was successful and entrepreneurial, the town was too small for him, and he went out to the outside world. Within a few years, he became one of the largest merchants of valuable pelts. Fishel settled in the free city of Danzig, and from there he conducted his flourishing business endeavors in the lands of Europe, and particularly in Germany. After some time, he brought his two younger brothers to him and involved them in his business.

His elderly mother, as well as his sister who was married to the teacher Gedalia Rubinsztejn, remained in the town. The family lived on meager means for many years. Rubinsztejn had difficulty supporting his family from his teaching salary. They had four sons and one daughter. The youngest son, Yoel, was a hunchback. As he became older, his condition worsened, and he became a dwarf. Yoel was blessed with a clear, sweet, and exceptional voice. When he would sing, his melodies would pour out like the sounds of a violin. His rich uncle spent a fortune to cure him. He brought him to the expert physicians in the country, however all the effort was for naught. To augment to the anguish, Fishel did not have satisfaction from his two younger brothers as well.

After he attained greatness, Fishel decided to do something for his family. He purchased a two-story home from the widow Naszelski, and renovated it beyond recognition. One day, trucks laden with modern furniture came to the home. Within one night, the area was turned into a palace. He settled his mother in that house. He settled his married sister into the upper floor, and looked after their livelihood. He would come to Stawiski for the festivals, to celebrate among his family.

After all of the renovations in the house, he opened the doors wide, and the townsfolk came to see the wonders – new and splendid furniture. A large chandelier decorated with crystal candleholders hung from the ceiling of the large guestroom. A large lion skin, with regal eyes sparkling from the head, covered the floor of the room, and softly cushioned the footsteps of those who trod upon it. The kitchen was embellished with vessels of porcelain and expensive glass. The beautiful beds with their soft, springy mattresses caught everyone's eyes. Who ever saw a springy mattress, and who ever felt its flexibility? A mattress in Stawiski was a wide sack filled with straw, which would be changed once a year on the eve of Passover, resting on a sodden box. Sleep on such a mattress was not particularly restful. Often, one would arise from sleep with "streaked", aching ribs[3].. If one of the wooden planks would break in the middle of the night, the straw mattress would sag, and the noise of the broken planks would wake up all the family members in a startle.

Fishel Cybulski honored his elderly mother greatly, and did the best he could to insure that she would be able to enjoy of her good fortune in her old age. He gave her every good thing, and protected her to the best of his ability. Once she took severely ill, and they thought that the end had come. They called Fishel from Danzig, and he brought the best doctors with him. She regained her health – one can even bribe the Angel of Death with money.

Fishel also did not forget his native town of Stawiski. He paid for the repair of the leaky roof of the Beis Midrash, and for the installation of beautiful electric chandeliers. Thus, the light in the house of prayer and the joy in the hearts of the worshippers increased. His hand was open to charitable needs.

Fishel was a friend of my brother Yitzchak of blessed memory. Fishel would visit us when he came to Stawiski even after my brother immigrated to the United States, for he enjoyed father's company, and loved to chat with him.

As the Holocaust drew near, he looked for ways to escape from Danzig. He attempted to reach the United States with the help of friends, but he was not successful. Fishel perished in the great conflagration that engulfed the House of Israel in Europe.

Nissel of blessed memory

Nissel was a great good-for-nothing. Pity was aroused for him also for his short stature, which on occasion served as a pretext for all sorts of pranks and jokes. Nevertheless, Nissel was a clean boy, who dressed nicely.

He was not fit for any work, and he had no work in the town. He also understood that he had no future in Stawiski, and since at that time America enchanted anyone who was concerned about his future, Nissel thought that he should immigrate to the land of endless opportunity. It is not known how he found his way to the United States.

As was customary, all of the arrivals to the borders of the United States disembarked at Ellis Island, and there the destiny of each immigrant was decided – who would merit to remain, and who would be sent back to the land from whence he came. The officials examined the case of Nissel and decided to send him back to Poland. For Nissel, this was too much to bear. He could not understand why the Americans invalidated him. Broken and crushed, he returned to his mother's house.

The scoffers in the group, who accosted him on occasion, did not leave him alone, and they would often mention the incident of the United States to him. Poor Nissel poured out stream of invective against the Americans.

One day, they decided to put him to a test. They told him that he would not succeed in carrying a sack of flour from one corner of the room to another. Nissel could not tolerate the embarrassment, and he assured them that he could do so. The youths loaded a sack of flour on his shoulder – not one of the smaller ones – and he carried it on his back, although he was bent over so much that he almost fell down. However, he succeeded in the test. After this exercise, they treated him to some food, however Nissel was also week with regard to the act of eating. "He ate like a bird" they would say about him.

Indeed, the lot of Nissel did not improve in the world of G-d.

Translator's Footnotes:

1. On the festival of Purim, it is customary to dress up. Gifts of food "mishloach manos" are delivered to friends, and charity or food is distributed to the poor.

2. A verse from Psalm 22, which is quite well known for its Christological connotations, obviously not intended here.

3. Referring to the red rashes that occur when pressure is placed on various parts of the body for prolonged periods.

{294}

Those of Ill Fate
by Bat Menachem

As in every city and town, in Stawiski there were also people who were not
of full mind. One of them was a young lad, Alter the orphan, who lived at the
home of his grandmother. People called him "Alter-Keili Yomtov", on account
of the song that was always on his lips, with his own special melody, with the
nonsensical words "Eini Keili Shabbas Tadi-Risa-Bom; Eini Keili Yomtov, Tadi-
Risa-Bom". The meaning of these words was "Enjoyable Sabbath, Enjoyable
Yomtov (Festival)".

A little older than him was someone they called Zelig Bonk. Nobody knew
why he had such a strange nickname. He would wander around the streets
aimlessly, with his hat hanging over his forehead, its visor pointing to the side.

Among the not completely sane girls was one who would spend the entire
summer at her parents' home, swaying endlessly without saying anything. Her
picture, with her hand outstretched to receive charity, was perpetuated by the
Germans during the First World War on one of the many pamphlets that were
printed regarding the happenings of the town.

A. B. was different than the rest. It was related that she was a very pretty
girl during her youth. Many rumors circulated as to the reason for her
insanity, however nobody knew the real reason. When her family moved to a
nearby city, A. B. would maintain her connections with Stawiski, and she
would visit it at sent times, primarily on Passover and the High Holy Days.

She knew the prayers like an experienced elder. She grew up in an
observant household and thoroughly knew the customs of the Sabbaths and
festivals. She would usually carry a regular prayer book (Siddur) or festival
prayer book (Machzor) with her, and she would study them. At times, she
would go up to the women's gallery of the Beis Midrash on festivals, look out
through one of the windows and shout loudly to the worshippers. The women
were not able to quiet her. Without any other choice, several men would have
to go up and forcibly remove her.

Chana Zelda was a righteous woman. She sufficed herself with a morsel of
bread and a small measure of water. She was always satisfied with her lot.
She never uttered a complaint about her ill fate. Thus was the will of the
Master of the World, and who was she to complain about it? She spoke
reasonably, with a pleasant voice and sparkling eyes, and a smile on her face.

Kind hearted Chana Zelda could not accept the fact that A. B. was
wandering around outside, especially on cold and rainy days. She worried
about how she could wander about without a blanket to warm her body, and
without a pillow for her head. Chana Zelda brought her to her home, put a
roof over her head and shared her meager morsels with her. However, a
person such as A. B. was not happy with a permanent place, and she also did

not want Chana Zelda to share her meager morsels with her. Her spiritual unrest did not permit her to live and rest in the house of her benefactress. She continued to wander on the streets of the town for most of the hours of the day and the night. She would sometimes begin to run, and then suddenly stop. On the Sabbath she would often sit on the bench in front of the pharmacy in the center of the city. She would pray quietly, talk to her herself, or lose herself in her thoughts. She generally avoided conversation. As was often the case, the children did not leave her be, and if they tormented her too much she would chase after them in anger

On occasion, she would peer through the windows of our house at night. People would say that she was searching for her beloved in the hiding places. She would come to our house on festivals before my parents returned from the Beis Midrash. With difficulty, we urged her to eat something. Once she engaged me in a conversation for a longer time than usual, and I was surprised at her intelligence and lucidity. It seemed to me at that time that if she only had the will, she could become healthy like a normal person. I told her that. She was silent for several moments as she tried to find the words.

"My daughter, you should not know from this agony", she answered with sadness, and then she was silent.

One Sabbath eve, I visited with my cousin Devora some acquaintances who lived near the Beis Midrash. The sounds of the worshippers could be heard from all of the houses of prayer. As we were conversing with each other, we did not realize that time was passing, and when we left, we saw to our fright that the houses of prayer were all dark, and there was no living soul on the streets. This meant that the prayers had already concluded some time ago, and they were waiting for us at home for the Sabbath meal. We hurried home.

As we passed the dark synagogue, a strange voice broke out from it. In the silence and stillness of the night, the mysterious voice instilled fear in us. We ran with all our might due to our fear, as the echo of the mysterious voice chased after us. We reached our home out of breath. When I told my parents what had happened to us along the way, the told us that this was a vain fear, and they attempted to placate me. I did not calm down for some time. I remembered the frightening stories that we children would whisper to each other. According to one of those stories, at night the souls of the dead would enter the women's gallery to worship together, with one of them serving as the cantor. Before dawn they would disappear and return to from where they came. There was no doubt that this frightful voice from the synagogue was the voice of that cantor, with the souls of the dead surrounding him...

Years passed. When we, the group of gymnasia students, returned to Stawiski at the end of the study term, we organized courses to teach Hebrew and Jewish history to youth groups. The courses were conducted at night, three times a week, in the cheders that were close to the synagogue, after the time that the students finished their studies. Once I arrived at the cheder before the students entered, and I waited outside for their arrival. It was a dark night, and silence pervaded everywhere. Suddenly a black figure approached from afar, ran quickly, and with one sharp turn approached the entrance to the great synagogue. Even in the darkness, I recognized that the mad running was that of A. B., and I figured out that she used to sleep there.

After many years, when I met Dr. Leibele Remigolski of blessed memory in Israel, she told me that A. B. ended up in the hospital that was under his direction, after she caught a severe cold. He took care of her with great dedication, but could not cure her. Thus did A. B. return her disturbed soul to her Creator.

During the Days of the Holocaust

{299}

For These do we Weep [1]
by the lawyer Chaim Wilamowski

(Words of memory presented at the Organization of Stawiski Émigrés on July 14, 1968.)

We have gathered together to unite ourselves with the memory of our dearly beloved who did not merit to arrive at safe shores and to be together with us here in our land. Without doubt, they also – the unforgettable ones – have a hand and a portion in the establishment of our land.

Enveloped in deep mourning, we join ourselves together with our dear ones who were murdered with frightful cruelty by Hitler's soldiers, the shame of humanity that forever stamped the German nation as the source of bands of murderers. Until the last moment of our lives, the terrible visions of millions of innocents being taken out to their deaths, men, women and children, will never move from our eyes and our memories.

Indeed, other nations also sinned and acted with iniquity, in particular during the time of the war; however in the bloody annals of world history, the Germans were the only ones who prepared strangulation chambers, crematoria and speedy trains ready to transport myriads and hundreds of thousands to the death camps.

Hitler slaughtered and the world was silent. The power and brazenness of the Nazis flowed forth from this silence that enshrouded the enlightened world. Therefore, the nations of the western world are not able to wash their hands in innocence and to say that they are not guilty in what the Nazis did to us. Even the Soviet Union bears no small share of the guilt, for omission is also a deed. The world kept silent because the victims were Jews. The silence that enveloped the world served as a green light for the Nazis to perpetrate without concern their iniquity, which has no equal in world history. There are plenty of proofs of the silence of the western powers. I will only mention a few of them.

The American vice consul in Bern sent a telegram to Washington on January 21, 1942, relating that every day the Germans are murdering 6,000 Jews in Poland. He requested that his telegram be transferred to Dr. Stephen Wise, and the content be brought to the attention of the government of the United States and its allies. Three weeks later, he received a reply from his superiors, saying, "we advise you that in the future, private messages will not be accepted from you, unless unusual circumstances make this activity necessary". The explanation of the matter is that the daily murder of 6,000 individual worlds [2] was not regarded as sufficiently "unusual circumstances" for the government of a mighty power to transfer the message to an "private individual" who happened to be the president of the World Jewish Congress and the recognized head of American Jewry.

The allied powers, Britain, the United States, and the neutral states of Europe refused to lift a finger to protest the murder. The allied governments were requested to bomb the gas chambers and crematoria in Auschwitz and other death camps, as well as the railway lines that led to the valley of death – such bombs could have saved myriads and hundreds of thousands; however eyewitnesses testified that the allied aircraft bombed precise targets near Auschwitz and deliberately avoided the railway lines, gas chambers, and crematoria. The governments of many nations, large and strong, were fighting a victorious battle and had the power to save, but they avoided doing so without any concern of conscience.

Not only this, but also the thundering silence of the spiritual leaders of western Christianity, Pope Pius XII and his assistants, can be considered to be one of the causative oversights that expedited and encouraged the murder of European Jewry. The guilt of genocide rests on them as well.

We cannot ignore the guilt of the Poles, in whose midst we dwelt for hundreds of years and on whose behalf we worked. They aided and abetted the deeds of murder and extermination. A large majority of the millions of Jews that were killed were killed on Polish soil. This was no coincidence, for when the Germans looked for a "fitting" place to erect the death camps, although they had a large choice of countries since most of Europe was in their hands, they chose Poland and set up most of the death camps on her soil. The Jews were brought to these camps from all corners of Europe, and in Auschwitz, Treblinka, Sobibor and others they were strangled with gasses and incinerated in crematoria. It is a sign of disgrace for the Poles that it was their soil that was chosen as the site for the worst crime in history, for the Germans knew that the Poles would see the extermination of the Jews as their chance to free themselves from them. Furthermore, these Poles also gained benefit from the murder of Jews – they "inherited" their houses, took over their businesses and pillaged their belongings.

Furthermore, the most well known Polish and Russian partisans murdered in the forests the Jewish partisans who had fled from the ghettos. When the surviving Jews returned to Poland after the war, the Poles conducted pogroms with the frightening motto: "Behold, another one has fled from the furnace".

It was not only the gentiles who closed their ears from the cries of the nation being slaughtered, but the Jews also did not enough to raise the frightful alarm. The leadership of the Land of Israel and the Diaspora hid the frightful details from the Jews of the free lands and the people of the free world for many weeks. They were not strong enough with respect to the allied powers. Nevertheless, this matter will be finally decided by the historian who researches the archives of the Jewish agency in the Land of Israel, England, and the United States, which are still closed to the public. The president of the Jewish Congress and the Zionist Organization already admitted the shortsightedness and dearth of action on the part of the Zionist and Jewish leadership to limit the bounds of the Holocaust.

With respect to the Jews of Europe themselves – they were left without leaders at the time of the Nazi occupation, for at the outbreak of the war all of the Zionist and non-Zionist leaders, from the extreme right to the extreme left, fled to countries outside of the Nazi occupation, and the masses of the House of Israel were left like sheep without a shepherd.

Despite all this, the annals of Jewish history from this tragic era also have chapters of might and resistance; bright chapters that illuminate the darkest paths of our history, the days of confusion, destruction, and hopelessness. For in those gloomiest of days, those sentenced to death rose up with great bravery against the murderers. In the ghettos, forests and inside the wire fences of the concentration camps, Jews obtained weapons and fought against the murderers. This was the first time in Jewish history that in days of darkness, during a time of destruction and annihilation, Jews rose up on a strange land and fought with weapons against their oppressors. Partisans and ghetto fighters went out to fight the Nazis; one against a thousand, ten against a myriad, a Molotov cocktail against a tank, a grenade against a cannon, and a rag dipped in benzene against a conflagration. With these simple weapons, the Jewish fighters felled many victims from among the Nazis and took revenge for the honor of the downtrodden Jewish people.

Among other factors, the Holocaust contributed in a significant way to the establishment of the State of Israel. The compass that pointed for some time toward the nations of the west for their abandonment of the Jews of Europe, the fate of the Holocaust survivors, and the fight for the settlement of the Land – all joined together and pushed for the establishment of the Jewish State.

Not only in the War of Independence, but also nineteen years later, during the dramatic days that preceded the Six-Day War, the Holocaust played a prime role in the preparedness of the nation to conduct a fitting battle.

The European Jewry that was exterminated was the spiritual future of the entire nation and of the community in the Land. With the deaths of six million, Israel did not only lose a physical potential, but also the powers of the victims to contribute to the spiritual renewal of Jewry in our time. The loss of European Jewry is an irreplaceable loss.

———

Translator's Footnotes :

1. A paraphrase of a verse from the first chapter of the Book of Lamentations.

2. Based on a traditional Jewish adage that every human being is the equivalent of an entire world.

———

{301}

The Holocaust in Stawiski
by the lawyer Chaim Wilamowski

The town of Stawiski lies on top of the hills on the highway from Lomza to Szczuczyn. Prior to the Second World War, the town had approximately 2,000 Jews, very few of whom survived the holocaust.

The Gathering Area

The Second World War broke out with the invasion of Hitler's army into Poland. When the Germans arrived at Stawiski, they gathered all the men at the memorial monument, brought them into the church, and transported them by vehicle to the gathering area (Stablage) in east Prussia, about 50 kilometers from Grajewo. The aim of the Germans in exiling the residents from their homes was to prevent resistance to the invasion. The Poles were also exiled from Stawiski. In the camp, the Polish soldiers were separated from the civilian exiles. People who succeeded in escaping from Stawiski while there was still time and were later caught in various places were also brought to this camp.

My late father David Wilamowski and my late brother Moshe, as well as men from the Dobrzyjalowski family: Avraham, Moshe Yankel, Moshe Chatzkel and 13 year old Chatzkel Berel were among those who were captured and brought to the camp. Many of those incarcerated in the camp died from various illnesses, primarily dysentery as well as hunger. There was a German physician in the camp; however the remedies he had at his disposal included only absorbent cotton and iodine. In reality, the physician was only present in order to fulfil the obligations to the International Red Cross. My father David Wilamowski became ill with dysentery and rested in the tent that was set aside for the ill until he died without having received any medical attention at all. The Germans requisitioned ten men from among those imprisoned to come and bury his body. Twenty people volunteered. In the absence of burial shrouds, my brother Moshe took off his outer cloak and covered the body in it prior to the burial. This was the tragic end of my father, after he had succeeded in escaping with his family from Stawiski to Lomza during the first days of the German occupation of our town.

My late sister, Babcha Wilamowski, describes the details of the escape to Lomza in a letter dated May 5, 1940: "No person can imagine how much he is destined to suffer. As I write these lines, pictures of the past come before my eyes: the flight from Stawiski, the bombardment of Lomza, and the escape from there as well. We fled along with father last Friday. Shells exploded above our heads. As we shut our eyes due to the sound of the bombardments, we awaited death at any moment. We were starving in the barns. I held father in my arms for the entire time, but I was not able to prevent his capture by the Germans. How difficult is it to live in this world!!!"

In accordance with the Molotov-Ribbentrop agreement, the area of Bialystok was transferred to the Russians. Only then did the Germans permit the many people imprisoned in the camp to return to the Russian occupied sector. Avraham Dobrzyjalowski was in the first group who were freed, and my brother Moshe in the second group.

On June 22, 1941, the German army overcame the Soviets, and the section of Poland that had been under Russian occupation fell to the Germans after heavy bombardment. Jewish young people retreated along with the Russian army. The German airforce bombarded the retreating group, and many were killed. My brother Moshe of blessed memory was among those who were killed in the bombardment. He met his death in the forests of Bialystok.

{302}
The Day of Blood

The Russian army retreated from Stawiski a few days after the beginning of the war between the Germans and Soviets. Even before the Germans entered the town, the local ruffians demonstrated what they were able to do, and what was to take place to the Jews not only at the hands of the German murderers. The first victims of the local Polish neighbors included 24 year old Fruma Walder and Zeidka Gelbord. Both of them were stabbed with knives by the murderers, who gashed their flesh and spread salt on their wounds. Overcome by fear, the Jews of Stawiski hid in their homes and waited with fear for the arrival of the Germans. On Friday, June 27, 1941, the first German representatives entered the town. The German murderers immediately made a brotherly connection with the local Polish fascists. They were unified in their common hatred of the Jews. The local ruffians had only one request, that the Germans permit them to pass judgement on the accursed Jews. The Germans were deeply pleased when they realized that they had faithful assistants in this filthy war, and they gladly gave their assent to the Poles. It was later related among the Jews that the Germans "limited" the number of Jews whom it was permitted to kill to seventy. They granted a short reprieve of life to the majority of the Jewish population. Be that as it may, the open murder of the Jews began at the hands of the Polish gangs, often headed by members of the intelligentsia, most of who had only recently been released from Soviet jails.

On the first Wednesday in July 1941, known as "the day of blood", an edict was issued in the morning that the Jews, from young to old, were to appear in the marketplace at noon for work. The atmosphere in the town was very tense. The Jews felt that a great tragedy was imminent. They did not know how to greet the face of the evil. At around 11:00 a.m., gentiles from all of the surrounding villages arrived in town with iron bars and wooden rods in their hands. Before noon, the ruffians broke into the homes of the Jews and chased them out with the warning: "Jews, to work!". Anyone who did not hasten to leave was beaten. Women with their children, as well as the elderly, were forced to bend down on their knees and clean the marketplace from weeds. The men were harnessed to wagons laden with rocks. They had to transport these wagons from the post office to the bridge over the Biebrza River and back, accompanied by the hooligans. Cruel blows were administered to anyone who could not move the wagon at the required speed. During the time that the Jews were busy dragging the wagons, the evil people went through the empty Jewish homes and took anything that they wanted. At around 6:00 or 7:00 pm, all of the Jews were gathered together at the "Pomnik" (a memorial monument). There, the head of the murderers and leader of the ruffians, Jozef Wietszork, who was personally responsible for the murders of dozens of Jews, gave a lecture to the Jews. He concluded his incendiary speech with the well known Polish motto: "Attack the Jews!". Incited by the motto "dawajcie fury, zabierajcie skory" ("bring wagons and take the corpses"), the hooligans fell upon the homes of the Jews, took out men and women, and beat them with murderous blows. They also used their iron bars and wooden rods against any Jew who attempted to escape, for Stawiski was completely surrounded by bands of ruffians, and there was no place to escape. Only very few managed to evade the hooligans. When they returned home, the beaten Jews found empty closets and beds. The ruffians pillaged everything. The Jews realized that evil would come that night. Many recited Psalms and the confessional prior to death, for they had a premonition that their end was near.

At 11:00 p.m., farmers from the neighboring villages arrived on wagons. Approximately an hour later, the screams of the victims could be heard. The farmers broke into the houses and chased out the Jews with the shout: "Jews, to work!". However, when the Jews came out, they were beaten with wooden sticks and metal rods until they were murdered. Those that were killed, along with those that were hovering between life and death, were loaded upon wagons, and brought to a place outside the town where they were buried. A few Jews who had only been wounded succeeded in digging their way out of the pits and returning to their homes. In the morning, they began to search for one another. There was great sorrow when it was discovered that so and so was missing a child, someone else was missing a brother or sister, and another person a mother or father. Dismembered limbs rolled about on the streets of Stawiski, and pools of clotted blood could be seen everywhere.

The Germans allotted the farmers twenty hours to execute judgment upon the Jews, and they helped them a bit with their iniquitous work; however for the most part they were busy with photographing the riots. This was not sufficient for them. On that day of blood, the Germans organized a "performance". They brought Rabbi Shmuel Nachman Wasserman, the rabbi of the town, to the synagogue, put a Torah scroll in his arms and ordered him to sing "Hatikva" [1]. Then they set the synagogue on fire and sent the rabbi into the burning synagogue. A miracle took place: the flames did not engulf the whole building at one time, and after the Germans left the place, a noble hearted Pole, a builder by the name of Antony Nawieci, led the rabbi out through the back door of the burning synagogue. He brought the rabbi to his own home, where he spent the night. The next day, Antony accompanied the rabbi to the Lomza ghetto, where he lived until November 1942, when the Jews in the region of Bialystok were liquidated. The rabbi was brought to the Zambrow Camp and it is not known what his fate was.

The first victim on the day of blood was a Jew who took his life in his hands to save the Torah scrolls from the synagogue that had been set on fire by the Germans. The second victim was a Jew who attempted to save his property from the hands of the rioters. The following were among those murdered that day: Yitzchak Piekarewicz, a 75-year-old smith and his son Zelig, who had been hiding in the home of their neighbor Rozensztejn at the time of the pogrom. Their heads were cut off after they were murdered; Rachel Niedzwiedzka, 24 years old, who was in her final months of pregnancy. She was brought out from her home and taken to a place near the bathhouse, where her stomach was slashed open and the fetus was taken out. With her fetus beside her, she suffered the pangs of death until she died in a pool of her own blood; They cut off the head of the fifteen month old child of her sister Chawa, and they forced the mother to take her dead child outside the city, where they murdered her with sticks. In the nearby village of Poryte, an entire family was murdered and their bodies were tossed into a dry pit. In the village of Zanklewo, near the flourmill, six members of the Calecki family were murdered and their bodies were tossed into a potato field. The cruel murders in the town inspired many Jews to search for refuge in neighboring villages; however the villagers also murdered them.

The sisters Chaja and Bryna Czapnik, the Morus family (a father, two sons, and an eighteen year old daughter), as well as many others were similarly murdered.

{304}
Prior to the Establishment of the Ghetto

The pogroms and murders continued for more than a month prior to the establishment of the ghetto, when the remaining Jews were imprisoned. Those who were not murdered were taken out for backbreaking labor. On the way to work, they were beaten with deathblows and brought low. Their situation was dependent on the mood of the work supervisors. If the supervisors were in a bad mood, work did not even save from death. Many were shot as they were working in cleaning the streets of the town. Herschel Mark and others were murdered as they were working. Jozef Wietszork, known for his cruelty, murdered with his own hands the Jews who worked in the village of Skroda near Stawiski. He murdered the 26-year-old shoemaker Avraham Yitzchak Fenik and Moshe Czerwinski, a 24-year-old baker from Grabowo. 18-year-old Velvel Goldman was injured so badly from his beating that he died one day after he was transferred to the Szczuczyn Ghetto. It should be pointed out that the murderer Wietszork requested from Hasoltys, the mayor of Skroda, that he provide people to help murder Jews. Hasoltys refused the request, and fled from the village along with other farmers.

A young lad named Velvel, the son of the smith Avraham Shlomo Piekarowicz, was in Grajewo at that time. The Germans ordered him to jump out from the window of the synagogue onto the street. The hooligans from Grajewo waited below for him, and murdered on the spot anyone who attempted to flee. After Velvel jumped out from the synagogue, he ran toward the Jewish cemetery. He was caught by the Polish murderers who were pursuing him. He was tossed into a lime pit near the synagogue.

The hell of the Jews of Stawiski did not last for long. Death redeemed them from their afflictions and great suffering. On Saturday, August 15, 1941, the mass murders began. The entire town was surrounded by the Gestapo men. The executioners broke into the homes of the Jews with wild screams. They chased everyone out to the marketplace, where they were ordered to line up. The young people, those from ages 15 to 40, were commanded to walk along the road to Poryte. From there they were to go on a death march toward Nowogrod. Near Miechowo and the village of Nienowice, the Soviets in their time had dug anti-tank trenches, 6 meters deep, 3 meters wide, and 15 meters long. These pits were destined to serve as mass graves for the young Jews of Stawiski. The children who were not able to move quickly enough were caught by their legs by the Germans and tossed onto the transport trucks. The old people and children were brought to the Kisielnica Forest, where they were shot in their necks and placed into pits that had been dug. About 500 people are buried in this communal grave.

{305}
The Stawiski Ghetto and its Liquidation
After most of the Jews of Stawiski had been taken out to be murdered, a few professionals whose services were in demand by the Germans remained alive. These Jews also assisted the local farmers. About 20 professional families, numbering 60 people, were gathered together on August 17, 1941. These professionals included a doctor, shoemakers, sewers, tailors, carpenters, smiths, etc. were included among them. The place of the ghetto was set around the Great Synagogue, and after some time it was transferred to the area behind the homes of Jeleniewicz and Zalman Leibel. The area of the ghetto was surrounded by a few simple houses in a place that was known as "the bent wheel" (Krzywe Kolo) behind the Wilamowski homes.

The Jews in the ghetto worked for the Germans for no payment; however life within the ghetto walls was relatively free. There was no guard posted next to the ghetto, and the entry and exit was unimpeded. The Germans and local farmers gave various tasks to the people of the ghetto. The remnants of the

Jewish community of Stawiski who lived in the ghetto hoped that their lives would be spared because of the benefit that they provided to the Germans in their work. A few Jews who succeeded in escaping to the villages and forests during the time of mass murders came to visit the ghetto on occasion; however these visits were fraught with severe danger for them and for the people of the ghetto. The Germans set a bounty for every Jew that was given over to their custody, and the work of snatching Jews and turning them over to the Germans was very fruitful. The farmers would receive sugar in return for the Jews that they turned over to the Germans.

Life in the ghetto continued for a little over one year. It was a life of work and want, and the thin ray of hope that perhaps they might be able to survive provided them with the strength to remain alive. However, on November 2, 1942, a drastic change of the situation occurred. The Gestapo men surrounded the ghetto at night, and removed all of the residents from their homes with shouts and beatings. The residents were concentrated together and marched to the Bogusze Camp with their sacks and children on their shoulders.

The Bogusze Camp had served previously as a concentration camp for Russian prisoners of war, where myriads of prisoners were tortured to death. The forests surrounding Bogusze were strewn with giant communal graves of prisoners. The camp occupied a very large area, and was surrounded by a barbed wire fence. It had trenches covered with simple roofs that served as living quarters for the residents of the camp.

Jews from Grajewo, Szczuczyn, Trestina, Augustow, and other villages of the area were brought to this camp. It was clear that the Germans intended to liquidate all of the ghettos in the vicinity of Bialystok. The residents of the camp did not receive any food at all for three or four days, and then they were given a daily allotment of 100 grams of bread per day, as well as portions of potato soup a few times a day, totaling ½ liter per day. The famine was great, and those imprisoned in the camp would gather around the kitchen to grab potato peels, which they would swallow without even cooking. The death rate among the residents of the camp was very high on account of the hunger and filth. Every evening, they would gather the bodies of those who died during the day and toss them into a pit. In the morning, they would bring the bodies to the cemetery where they buried the Russian prisoners of war the year before. Those injured and ill were shot immediately by the Gestapo men, and the rest of the residents of the camp lived in the conditions that were described above (if this can be called living), until December 15, 1942.

On that day, the liquidation of the Bogusze camp began. The inmates were sent to the gas chambers of Treblinka, Birkenau and Auschwitz. The inmates were ordered to leave the trenches in which they lived and were brought to the train station, accompanied by beatings and shots. The path was muddy, and the feet of those walking the path sunk in the mud as they were being sent out from the life of hunger in the camp. The journey was difficult for them, and anyone who lagged behind was murdered by a shot. The entire path was strewn with corpses. Those that reached the train station were pushed onto the wagons that transported them to the death camps. When they arrived at their destination, they were commanded to leave everything on the train and exit. There, a few of the younger men were selected to assist the murderers in their task of murder prior to meeting their own bitter end. Everyone else ended up at the crematoria. On that day the furnace in the death factory burned endlessly. This was the end of the Jews of Stawiski.

{306}
Those That Escaped

There were a few incidents were Jews succeeded in escaping from the ghetto. The Indurski brothers, Velvel and Zeinwil, along with Zeinwil's wife Golda and their child, escaped from the ghetto and found refuge with a farmer until 1944. One day, the farmer rose up and murdered them all. Their bodies were found in the forests of Zawila (near Stawiski). Feivel Chonkowicz and his family and Feivel Kadysz with his two children also met tragic fates. At the time of the liquidation of the Stawiski Ghetto, they succeeded in finding refuge with the farmer Ridzowosky in Bajdy, near Stawiski. One farmer turned them in, and they were all shot along with the farmer who saved them. Alter Brom and his son met the same tragic fate. They hid in a village until 1943, and were murdered by the German gendarmes after being turned in by a Pole. Mietszak Chonkowicz, his wife, son, and daughter, as well as the grain merchant Perelowicz and his two children were also turned in by the Poles and murdered by the German gendarmes. All of them had escaped from Stawiski and hid in the forests. Luck did not shine upon them and were exposed by the Polish fascists, who turned them in to the Germans.

From the Rozensztejn household, former owners of the flourmill, Yaakov Rozensztejn, his wife Liba, and their twelve-year-old son, as well as thirty-year-old Avigdor Zalecki, the husband of Feigel Golombek, perished. Feigel hid with farmers for four months after the liquidation of the Stawiski Ghetto. Then she went out into the forests, where she lived until Stawiski and its environs were liberated by the Red Army on January 24, 1945. Guta and Sima Stryjakowski fell on August 15, 1944 at the hands of Polish partisans.

{307}
The Following Remained Alive

Avraham Rozensztejn

Feigel Golombek (nee Rozensztejn)

Yudel Kiwajko, 19 years old

Itshe Meir Siemon, 24 years old

Piekarewicz, 17 years old

Chawa Fuks (nee Rozensztejn), 13 years old

Hertzki Cheslok

Avraham Dobrzyjalowski

Rivka Yaffa remained alive in Auschwitz

Noshe Chizda

Bibliographic Notes

1. "The Life and Death of the Jews of Stawiski and environs during the German Occupation" by Feigel Golombek (nee Rozensztejn), published by the Woywodit Jewish Historical Committee, Bialystok, June 24, 1946.

2. "The Destruction of Stawiski", Chapter 17 from "The Destruction of Bialystok and Environs" by Dr. Shimon Detner, published by the Woywodit Jewish Historical Committee, Bialystok, November 28, 1946.

3. "Over Stones and Sticks"   by M. Zanin – a travel through one hundred destroyed communities of Poland – page 164, published by "Letzte Nies", Tel Aviv, 1952

4. A letter regarding the destruction of the Jews of Stawiski, by Helena Laskowska, a Christian teacher in the elementary school.

5. a) Wednesday, the day of blood. b) The Stawiski Ghetto, by Yehuda Kiwajko.

6. The Concentration Place, by Avraham Dobrzyjalowski

7. A diary, by Chawa Fuks (nee Rozensztejn)

8. The Grajewo Yizkor Book

9. A letter regarding the escaped from the bombarded Lomza by Babcha Wilamowski.

{308-316 – The Yiddish version of the above section.}

————

{316}

The Destruction of Stawiski
by Rivka Zilbersztejn

It is hard for me to find the name of my birthplace Stawiski on a current map of Poland – my town is near the regional town of Lomza, surrounded by forests with tall trees that cover an area of several kilometers square. There were also many orchards there, and when the spring comes and the trees blossom, the pleasant aroma fills the entire town.

The Jewish population of Stawiski was small in number, but very rich in its institutions: religions, cultural, and communal. Before the eyes of my spirit stands the splendid Great Synagogue with its engraved Holy Ark; the Beis Midrash, the shtibels, and the cheders in which the Jewish children studied Torah, the Zionist organizations, and the libraries where the youth would come to read books or to discuss books and authors until late in the evening. Plays were performed in my town by the Zionist organizations, and furthermore, there was even once a play put on in the Beis Midrash by the students of Beis Yaakov, the Orthodox girls' school that was founded in Stawiski in 1935. It is superfluous to say that the Jewish populations enjoyed these plays very much and gave the youth and the children – the actors – wild applause in return for their entertainment.

In 1936, anti-Semitism heated up in Poland, and took on an aggressive form. A large part of the blame for the incitement of anti-Semitism lies with the priest. For on Sundays, when the priest would deliver a venomous sermon against the Jews, the influence was immediately felt outside. The Jewish merchants and artisans felt its influence. When the incited Poles left the church, the oppressive atmosphere was immediately felt on the streets. Guards were immediately posted next to the Jewish stores, and big signs were posted in Polish: "Don't buy from Jews". If a Christian would stealthily enter a Jewish store to purchase some provision, the guards would pour kerosene on the merchandise immediately as he left.

The path of the Jewish students who studied in Polish schools was not paved with roses. In accordance with the course of study, the Christian students would hear a lecture on the Catholic religion from the priest once a week. This class in religion was turned into venomous anti-Semitic incitement. After this class, it was difficult for the Jewish students to return to class, for every Christian child saw in the Jewish child, who was his classmate, a child and descendent of those who crucified their god.

It was also difficult for the Jewish children in that they were excellent students. The principal of the school, the anti-Semite Kotarski, could not make peace with this fact. On the other hand, I remember with reverence my Polish teacher Helena Laskowska, who was a woman of noble spirit, honorable, and regarded every child, without exception, as a student and a human being.

Life became more difficult by the day, and the skies covered with clouds. Passover approached. The Jews were baking matzos, and in the streets, a wartime atmosphere pervaded. There were draft notices and many Jewish young men were called up to the Polish army. The Jewish parents were worried. Nobody knew which route to take – to leave Stawiski or to remain. In 1914, during the First World War, Lomza was more secure than Stawiski, for Lomza was known as a fortified city. Nobody imagined that the Germans would come along with such a plan of annihilation. People still remembered the proper German from the First World War.

In the interim, the Second World War broke out. Jews packed whatever belongings they could, and fled in wagons and automobiles to the large cities. The home of Herschel Mark resembled a way station. My father of blessed memory and other Jews attempted to pack up their merchandise in order to send it to Ostrowiek (Ostrow-Mazowierka). They felt that it would be more secure there, however my mother of blessed memory decided to remain in Stawiski. She still remembered what it was like to be without a house in 1914. Very few Jews remained in Stawiski.

The first airplanes crossed the skies of Stawiski. Bombs fell upon the town. The yard of the poretz (town owner) was on fire. The Germans shot three young "shkotzim" who were standing on the bridge. The town was swarming with Germans. They immediately began to seek out Jewish men, and gathered them in the church. All of the Jewish stores were broken into. The Germans took the choicest merchandise and loaded it onto their cars, and the Poles took the remaining merchandise and loaded it into sacks. When they left their prayers in the church, they felt that there first "mitzvah" was to pillage and steal the merchandise of the Jews.

The Jews who were gathered by the Germans into the marketplace near the church were commanded to crow like chickens and howl like dogs all night. The next day they were taken off to somewhere, to a place from where Wilamowski and others never returned.

The Germans captured the small towns one after another, but they met serious resistance in Lomza. Lomza was bombarded from the air and the fires that that broke out from the bombardment could be seen all the way to Stawiski during the night. Many of the Jews of Stawiski had fled to Lomza, thinking that there, in a large city, they would be able to save their lives. The battle of Lomza lasted for eight days until the Germans conquered the fortifications of the city. The Jews of Stawiski returned to their homes. Some were captured by the Germans and shot on the spot, and others succeeded in evading the eyes of the Germans as they returned to Stawiski at night.

Dark fear pervaded in the city. A gentile would go through the streets, ring a bell and declare: "Jews to church!". A German official issued the order. The Jews who still remained in Stawiski, blackened like the bottom of a pot, left their homes open and went to church. The Jews and a small number of gentiles stood in the front, Germans wearing helmets stood behind. The priest delivered a venomous sermon and accused the Jews of concealing weapons and shooting Germans at night. This was not the first libel that was made against us Jews. The Germans ignited the town from all four sides.

That day, in the afternoon, we returned home. From our windows we could see the Germans standing next to the synagogue, removing the Torah scrolls and setting them on fire. A blue flame ascended from the burning scrolls, and they were not consumed. The parchment of the holy scrolls burned for a long while. Until a late hour in the night, when we peered out from cracks in our covered windows, we could see the burning scrolls before our eyes. We saw in them a portent of our destruction.

The next day, Chaim Kadysz-Kolinski came to me and told me that the German official ordered us to open an office to register all of the Jews who returned to Stawiski. In the Rywicki School, I registered all of the Jews who had returned to the town broken and oppressed. Who could have imagined at that time that this would be the beginning of the murder of six million Jews, those dearest to us among them.

The German regiments pillaged the town. My sister and I wore long dresses and hid in the cellar, and my mother of blessed memory would bring us some food on occasion. Moshe Niska the wagon driver returned to his home in Stawiski with his family. The German murderers captured his two daughters and tortured them all night. Oppressed and downtrodden, they returned home and took refuge in their grandmother Rodka's home. A rumor spread through town that girls were being sent off to Germany for hard labor.

The gentiles took us to work in the yard of the poretz. They commanded us to clean the lavatories with our hands. The famine was great.

In the meantime, the political situation changed. Whoever was able to left Stawiski on the horses that had belonged to the former overseer of the poretz' estate. The Germans left the town and the Russians entered in their place. The Jewish communists danced outside from joy – our liberators were arriving. We children asked about the reason for this rejoicing. One of the people explained to us that now the road has returned to us. The men were still in German captivity, and the Jews were still suffering the disgrace of famine in the town. Businesses were closed. The Russians opened a few stores, and long lines formed in front of those stores in order to obtain a piece of bread, a measure of salt, sugar or kerosene. Everything was very expensive.

The town was full of Russians. They confiscated rooms from wealthy homeowners. A few days later the prisoners returned – at first the foresters and estate owners (poretz) of the neighboring region returned, and later the

Jews returned, including my father, Horowitz, Lejbik, Chonkowicz, and others. All of them had been imprisoned in the prisons of Lomza. Six months later, we were exiled to Siberia.

When I returned from Siberia, I thought that I would find my town as I left it, perhaps as it was before the outbreak of the war, and that my eyes would again see Jews dressed splendidly for the festival days, young children hurrying off to school, and the adults – some in their stores, others in their workshops, some on the platform of the wagon to Kolno, Lomza or the "fairs"; that the fairs of Monday and Friday would again be full of life; that I would meet again my friends from the past, with whom I maintained correspondence from Siberia until the middle of 1941; that my legs would again take me to the cemetery to visit the graves of my holy grandfather of blessed memory, of my grandmother whom I had never met, of the mother of my father who was blind and who lived in hour house for nine years, and that I might perhaps again see Chaya Shlia [2] who used to sleep in the cemetery.

However, it was not to be, all of these things were no longer there. They were only a dream. I never saw Stawiski again. I was in Poland in 1946, however Stawiski was muzzled before me. It was dangerous to travel there. I was not able to see my orphaned town of Stawiski, and the homes of the Jews that were murdered by the Poles. The ruffians Wietszork and his comrades who murdered Jews, who cut open the bellies of Jewish women in public, who shot Jews who were hidden in bunkers. One of the three Jakubcziner sisters, who hid in the home of a gentile on the street of the smiths, was murdered after the war by the gentiles.

Jewish life in Stawiski was no more. Crosses hung in the homes of the Jews. Jewish boys and girls no longer bathe in the Sokolicha River, they no longer congregate in the forest to read books and enjoy themselves, and the Zionist organizations have disappeared. A small number of young Jews survived the terrible Holocaust, chosen by G-d himself to tell how the Jews of Stawiski were murdered with unspeakable cruelty.

{319-324 – The Yiddish version of the above section.}

A Brand Plucked From the Fire
by Herzl (Hertzke) Cheslok of blessed memory [3]

Standing from right to left: 'Iche Leizer's grandchild; Bluma Indurski; Rifka Laska (Zilbersztejn) lives in Israel; Lazar Goldsztejn's daughter. Sitting from right to left: first-unknown Lewinski; Ritsha (Rifka) the bagel baker's daughter - lives in America; Stern, Beile Kadysz

As much as a person attempts to relate the horrific events that took place to him under the dominion of the Nazi murderers, it is not completely possible. For it is impossible to describe the tribulations, fear, oppression, and spiritual and physical torture that was the lot of these people. I will go out on a limb and state that a person who did not experience the atrocities of this tragic-cruel era with his own body is not able to comprehend it. It is even impossible for him to believe that such events could take place, and that a human being can experience all of the seven levels of hell and still remain alive. Even though I know how difficult it is to transmit these ideas – I will nevertheless attempt to describe to some degree those frightening days that were my lot during that era that was full of atrocities.

Our town Stawiski was small in area and in population; however it was large in spirit, and he righteousness of its way of life. Its children loved their town as one loves a loving and dedicated mother. Whenever its residents found themselves in a foreign place, they would take pride in Stawiski and exult its virtues.

Herzl (Hertzka) Cheslok of blessed memory in Auschwitz

Pages of memories that were never written down are turning over in my head, memories of joy and sadness, until the page of that cruel and frightful era opens up. In the eyes of my spirit, I see realistic images of Sabbath eves filled with light and happiness; Sabbaths and festivals; long awaited Passover Seders that brought joy to hearts; the afternoon hours of Sabbaths and festivals, when, after the toil of the six work days, the parents went after the conclusion of the festive meal for a sweet Sabbath nap, and the youth spread out in the roads in a joyous crowd – some going for a walk and others going to the meeting places of one of the cultural organizations. A mighty stream of exuberant youth poured out all over town, and spread out on the streets of Lomza, Kolno, and Szczuczyn.

The pages turn with lightning speed, and before my eyes stand the cruel and oppressive scenes of destruction, and the images of the martyrs. Trembling trees with their tips bent to the ground, a stormy wind uprooting them; and the terrifying cries that accompanied the Jews, men, women and children, along their final journey. The souls of our ancestors come down from heaven and hover over the heads of those condemned to death, and cry with an otherworldly agony over the lives of their children that were being cut off.

The pages of this bloody era continue to turn, and we stand before unmarked communal graves of fathers and mothers, sisters and brothers, children and babies who had not yet had a chance to live and had not sinned, whose only sin that condemned them to death was the fact that they were Jewish children. The stare of the toddlers was frightful as the fear of death stared them in the face, as they embraced the cool cheeks of their mothers. The tearful eyes of the Sarales, Chayales, Mosheles, and Shlomoles were full of fear, innocent questions, and pleas.

May these lines serve as a flask for the tears over the communal graves of the dearly beloved, which our eyes do not behold and our feet cannot take us to visit.

In accordance with the Molotov-Ribbentrop agreement, White Russia and Ukraine fell under Soviet rule after the partition of conquered Poland. Stawiski fell under Soviet rule already in September 1939. When the war between Russia and Germany broke out in June 1941, the town was attacked and panic ensued. Nobody knew what to do. Men, primarily youth, decided to escape. However, to where does one escape? And how? I was not able to personally participate in the various meetings that took place regarding this subject, due to the position that I had held with the Soviet authorities; however through my brothers Leizer and Moshe and my brother-in-law Yisrael, I found out that we would be fleeing to Bialystok. I turned to my supervisor and requested that I be permitted to join the flight. He answered me with the following words: "No, you will flee together with me, and you don't have to worry." Since there was no choice, I remained.

The next day, many young men arrived in our town from Kolno, including some Russians. Then my supervisor told me to prepare to leave Stawiski. I immediately went home, took leave of my parents and sisters, and left my birthplace.

On the way to Bialystok, we had to cross the Radzilowa. There I met all of those who fled Stawiski the previous day, and we decided to continue our flight toward Osowiec. When we were some distance from the town, we saw it go up in fire, and we continued forward on side paths. We decided to rest a bit after we crossed the forest. However, just as we entered it, German airplanes bombed us. When I got up from the ground, I saw that the bombs killed many of those who fled. There was not time to care for the dead. I myself was not sure if I was alive or dead. We had to continue onward.

When I reached the road that led to Bialystok, I saw two or three dozen wagons laden with families of Soviet army personnel who were leaving Stawiski. The wagon drivers were farmers from Stawiski and the neighboring villages. The Soviets forced them to transport the wives and children of the Soviet army personnel to Bialystok.

I joined up with this retreating transport. With them, I reached a half destroyed bridge, which had apparently been severely damaged by the bombs from the air raid on the forest. One by one and with great difficulty, we crossed the bridge on foot. In Bialystok, I found my brother and brother-in-law as well as other Stawiskites. My brother Leizer and my brother-in-law Yisrael informed me that they were about to return to Stawiski, since in any case, the Germans were approaching Bialystok. They felt it was better to be together with their wives and children. My brother Moshe and myself decided to remain in Bialystok.

The confusion in Bialystok was even greater than the confusion in Stawiski. On the Tuesday following the outbreak of the war, it was impossible to obtain a loaf of bread anywhere in the city. The family with which I was staying did not have a slice of bread on that Tuesday. By chance as I was walking, I found a bakery in the city which still operated and which intended to distribute bread the following morning.

At 10:00 p.m., I arrived at the wooden fence that surrounded the bakery. With great effort, I climbed the fence and approached the bakery. I saw the workers engaged in their work through a closed window. Some were working near the machine and others near the oven. The aroma of fresh bread penetrated my nostrils and reawakened my appetite. I knocked on the window. A man approached and asked with astonishment who I was and what I wanted. Even though he spoke Russian, I immediately recognized that he was Jewish. When I showed him my work permit, which was similar to the certificate of that company, he opened the door and let me in. I told him that I was a Jew, that I fled from Stawiski, and asked that he permit me to help them bake bread. He told me that all of the workers were Jews, and that in the morning, 1,000 kilos of bread would be ready.

I heard them debating among themselves as to how to distribute the bread in a manner that the bakery would not collapse due to the large crowd. I advised them to turn to the captain of the city who would send soldiers to keep the order during the time of the distribution of the bread. The captain of the city sent only two soldiers. We prepared notes, distributed them among those waiting and told them that whoever would come tomorrow with that note would receive a kilo of bread.

As I went out to distribute the notes I suddenly heard a voice calling my name. I turned around to see who was calling me, and to my joy I met several Stawiskites: Fishel Mickucki, Fruma Wloder, Chaim David Koplowicz, the two sons of Abba the porter, and others. From that time, we met every day until the Germans entered Bialystok. A few days later I again met Fruma Wloder and Chaim David Koplowicz. They told me that they were preparing to return to Stawiski.

The Germans conducted their first aktion already on the first Sabbath after the conquest of Bialystok. They captured 500 Jews and took them to an unknown place. This first German action became known as "the Sabbath aktion".

When the Bialystok ghetto was established, my brother Moshe, myself, and the uncle of my brother-in-law lived together in a two-room apartment. Moshe decided to bring his friend Anna Liba Goldsztejn from Stawiski (her father was the brother of Hertzka Goldsztejn). She came to Bialystok along with her mother and her younger brother.

My brother and I worked in a clothing factory in the ghetto. After some time, they began to send the men out to various work camps. One day, we both received a notice to present ourselves at the work office. We went to Mendel Goldflam who worked in the Judenrat and asked for his advice as to what to do. He immediately prepared for us two certificates with various names. We did not present ourselves at the work office on the designated day. As we were eating breakfast, a guard suddenly appeared accompanied by the person responsible for the house and asked for my name. I showed him my certificate, as did my brother Moshe. The guard asked about the Cheslok brothers and there whereabouts. The aunt of my brother-in-law was surprised and was not able to utter a sound from her mouth. Nevertheless, Anna Liba did not lose her composure and she answered: "Indeed the Cheslok brothers did live here, but they left and we do not know their whereabouts." To our good fortune, the owner of the house was silent about the fact that he knew us, and he did not turn us in.

Thus did we succeed in eluding the Gestapo and remaining in the ghetto. However, this was not to be for a long period. The time for the liquidation of the Bialystok ghetto was rapidly approaching. I succeeded in being counted among the workers who were sent to work in the Bialystok prison.

Herzel Cheshlok's family

I was not present when the revolt broke out in the ghetto, and I do not know what became of my brother Moshe. After a few weeks of working in the prison, the Germans decided to send us to a camp. We were brought to Lublin, and from there to Treblinka. From Treblinka we were sent to the Blazin work camp near Radom. My joy was great when I found my brother Moshe of blessed memory in the work camp. We then remained together for close to a year. We were sent to Auschwitz when the camp was liquidated. There we were separated, for we were each sent to a different block. When a transport was being sent out for another camp, my brother Moshe volunteered to be included in it. They accepted him but not me. We were again separated, and I again lost track my brother. When the Germans began to liquidate Auschwitz, they transferred me to a camp by the name of Liba Roza in Germany.

A few weeks later, they brought additional transports to that camp, and my brother Moshe was on one of them. We remained in Liba Roza for three months, and from there we were transferred to Grossrosen. There I was again separated from my brother, and I never saw him again after that. They sent me to the well-known camp of Mauthausan in Austria.

On one cloudy day when we did not go out to work, we saw through the barbed wire fence that separated us from the women's camp that a group of women had portions of food in their hands. Many of them ate the bread and other victuals with a great appetite. We knew that this was their final journey. They went in peace to the gas chamber without being accompanied by a kapo or by an S.S. man. The scene was frightful, and tears welled up in our eyes. They looked at us, and to our great surprise we did not notice any emotion on their faces, even though they knew that this was their final journey. They made peace with their fate, and realized that tears and sighs would not change their verdict. Until this day I can see before they eyes of my spirit this group of women going in stoic peace along their final journey.

I was liberated from Mauthausen by the Russian army. When the Russians left Mauthausen and the Americans came in their place, I decided to return to Poland, hoping that perhaps someone of my family would have survived. To my great sorrow, I discovered in Poland that my entire family had perished.

I remained in Poland until 1957, and then made aliya to Israel. On the ship en route to Israel, I saw that one of the emissaries was wearing a kippa. I had an idea: perhaps through him I would be able to make contact with Elazar Goelman. He told me that he knew him, and he gave me his address. I immediately phoned Elazar when I arrived in Israel, and on that day he came with his brother to greet me. Elazar informed Yoel Ciechanowicz of my arrival, who told Chana Wiener of blessed memory. She came to see me the next day.

Thus did I renew contact with the natives of my hometown who were living in Israel. From the first moment, they received me graciously and enthusiastically.

Only very few natives of our town survived. In agony and worn after the long path of agony in camps in various countries, they merited to remain alive. After they were liberated, and after a period of acclimatization, they regained their spark of life and their hope to reestablish their broken lives.

Translator's Footnotes:

1. Hatikva (The Hope), is the national anthem of Israel. It predated the state, and was a Zionist theme song.

2. See page 283.

3. "A brand plucked from the fire" is a quote from Zecharia III, referring to a small number of survivors of a calamity.

{335}

Upon Your Ruins Did I Sit and Weep[1]
by Yehuda Chiwicho
Translated by Jerrold Landau

It was June 1941. On Sunday morning, the Germans arrived in Stawiski, and toward evening the entire population of Jewish youth retreated toward Bialystok. We were bombarded by German bombers throughout the entire journey. We reached Bialystok on the second afternoon, as the Red Army was beginning its retreat. The Jewish youth followed after the Red Army; however the Russians did not behave particularly sympathetically toward us.

The group of Jewish youth from Stawiski separated in Bialystok, and whoever could set out toward the Russian border. Fires were breaking out everywhere from the bombardment. Food could not be found. All of these towns were in a state of confusion. We continued our journey for an entire week until we reached the village of Amszecziwow, not far from Volkovysk. When the Germans arrived there as well and continued toward the Russian border, we decided to return to Stawiski.

A Jewish council was set up in Stawiski. Its members included my brother, Meir Hershel Rubinsztejn Wladalski among others. On occasion, the Germans would arrest its members and request a ransom for their release – large quantities of jewelry and gold.

The Zhimni bakery baked bread for the Jews only, and it was distributed by ration.

The Bloody Wednesday

On Wednesday morning, Roszczik, the town administrator, rang his bell and decreed that all of the Jews must gather in the Market Square by noon. Any Jew who would be found in his house at that time would be shot on the spot.

My entire family went out to the Market Place. Only I remained at home alone. At 12:30, non-Jews from all of the surrounding villages streamed into town and forcefully chased out all of the Jews who remained in their homes. One non-Jew found me and chased me out to the Market Square.

In the market, all of the Jews were sitting stooped over, plucking weeds from between the stones. The Poles walked among the Jews with sticks in their hands. If any Jew lifted up his head for a moment he would be savagely beaten. A few youths and middle aged Jews were tied to wagons laden with rocks and forced to drag the wagons from the post office to the train, that is to say from one end of the town to the other.

Hershel Mark of blessed memory was murdered on that day. When he saw from afar that the hooligans were pillaging his store – Hershel, as is known, owned the largest store in town – he hurried toward his home, and he was shot by a German as he was on his way.

That day, the Germans set the Great Synagogue on fire. When Aharon the shamash ran to rescue the Torah scrolls, a non-Jew hit him over the head with an axe and killed him. The murderers grabbed Rabbi Wasserman, the rabbi of Stawiski, and threw him into the burning synagogue, which was miraculously not burned completely.

Toward the evening, Wiaczork, the chief of the anti-Semites and the head of the ruffians of Stawiski, gathered together all of the Jews who were in the market place at the freedom statue (commemorating the freedom of Poland), and delivered a venomous speech against the Jews. He accused all of the Jews of Communism and hinted that the war broke out because of them. As is customary for a murderer of his ilk, he concluded his words of incitement with the well-known anti-Semitic motto: "Attack the Jews!".

Then a frightening scene took place in front of my eyes – all of the Jews started to flee and the gentiles chased after them and struck them over their heads with sticks. The entire Market Square was full of pools of blood. The beaten and injured Jews returned to their homes, finding them empty and pillaged of every item of value.

I wish to point out that there were some decent people from among the Jews who advised the Jews to seek refuge and informed them that the ruffians would be conducting a frightful massacre of the Jews that evening. Adding to the calamity, the town was surrounded on all sides, and nobody could flee from the murderers. In order to calm the Jews so that they could lead them out to be pillaged, they promised them that mercy would be shown to all of those that had suffered at the hands of the Russians.

Many families gathered in our house. At 5:00 a.m., the builder Nowicki arrived, accompanied by a woman. When the woman took off her outer clothes, we were astonished to see our rabbi, Rabbi Wassermann, without his beard. The gentile Nowicki, one of the righteous gentiles, saved the rabbi by removing him from the burning synagogue. All of the Jews recited Psalms. The next day, the rabbi, dressed as a gentile, was taken to Lomza.

That same night, non-Jews from the nearby villages again streamed into Stawiski, wearing festive garments with white shirts. Some of them were carrying sickles, and others were carrying sticks. Close to midnight, frightful screams reached our ears, and the cries of men and women pleading before the murderers – "Take everything, but leave us alive". That entire night, the bodies of those murdered and those injured badly were taken out of the city by wagons.

The next morning, when those who remained alive ventured outside, a frightful scene was appeared before their eyes – crushed body parts were rolling around in the pools of blood that covered the streets. If my memory serves me correctly, 360 Jews were murdered that night.

The Frightful Friday

When the storm abated slightly, word spread that youths between the ages of fourteen and eighteen would be sent to hard labor camps in Germany. My parents sent me to a gentile in the village of Grabowo. I found there a few Jews from Stawiski – Avrahamcha the son of Riva the butcher, and Alter Brau with two other children. Jews hid in other villages as well.

That year, Tisha Beov was pushed off [2] and fell out on a Sunday. I came to Stawiski that day, and again on Thursday. This was a more or less calm week. When my brother took me back to the gentile, we met the head of the village who told him that the situation was very dangerous, and it was not appropriate to be wandering around outside. When I left the house, my parents requested that I return for the Sabbath. The next day on Friday at 10:00 a.m. I was struck with a deep longing for my home, and I decided to return to Stawiski. I grabbed some fruit from the fields and ran home. When I was near the village of Budne, the gentile Ridzwoski, who had returned from Stawiski, met me.

"Where are you going?", he asked me. "Return to where you came from quickly, for they are killing Jews in Stawiski."

I stood dumbfounded, but I did not feel any fear at all. I wanted to be with all the Jews of Stawiski during their frightful moments on their final journey. I did not listen to the gentile, and I continued on my route to Stawiski. A shegetz[3], a friend of mine from school, suddenly stopped me along the way and said:

"Stand still, do not go further!"

Closed trucks passed along the way. The shegetz told me that the Jews who were able to stand on their feet were being made to run along the Kolno road, and the closed trucks were transporting the children and the elderly.

I returned to Grabowo and told the Jews that were there about everything that I had seen and heard. When they all heard the frightening news, we all broke out in bitter weeping. That day, we left the village and sought refuge in the forests of Lomza. We found the Chonkowicz brothers in the forest and they told us about the slaughter in Stawiski.

After the terrible Friday, a number of families and youths managed to flee from Stawiski and take refuge in the villages and forests. The Germans left a number of artisans in the town, such as tailors, shoemakers, stitchers, smiths, wagon drivers, etc. They concentrated them in one area near the synagogue. Later, they brought them all to the ghetto that they had set up in the vicinity of the houses of the Wolinewicz and Marchawki families.

Zweiback and his wife Ana, of blessed memory.

Zweiback, of blessed memory.

Freidel Blankensztejn and her daughters Tzippa and Feigel of blessed memory.
(Side caption: murdered in the holocaust – applies to all on this page)

Right: Niedzwiadowicz Family, from right: Zelig, Bluma, Yaakov, Gabriel and the mother Beila, of blessed memory (standing around the grave of Zeev the son of Yaakov Nizwadowicz[4] – translator's note, not in caption.)

Left: Zeev Niezwiadowicz (died)

Right: Pinchas Piekarewicz, of blessed memory.

Left: Chaim Piekarewicz and his wife Sheyna, of blessed memory.

———

Jews from the nearby villages were also brought to the ghetto. The artisans did various tasks for the Germans and also for the non-Jews of the town. Their situation was relatively not too bad. The Jews received our visits to the ghetto with bitterness from fear lest they be swallowed up on our account. There was a large ghetto in Lomza, and there were also ghettos in Grajewo and Szczuczyn.

As the winter neared its end, the wanderings from village to village began. I was in Grabowo with some local Jews, and an owner of a flourmill from Kosakowow was also there. In the Lomza ghetto there were, along with other Stawiskites, Rabbi Wasserman, Liba Kadysz, and Zhimni. Rabbi Wasserman told me to leave the village and to come to the ghetto so that I could be among Jews.

At the beginning of 1942, news spread that the Jews that had fled to the villages were about to be transferred to ghettos. I moved to the Szczuczyn ghetto. I wore gentile clothing and traveled to Lomza. I stayed in the Lomza ghetto for a few months, and I was close to Rabbi Wasserman the entire time.

When I found out that some members of my family were in the Bialystok ghetto, I went there. My Aryan appearance eased my dangerous travels along the roads. I found some members of the Niedzwiadowicz family in the Bialystok ghetto.

I remained in Bialystok for three months and then returned to the Lomza ghetto. From there I returned to Grabowo and found some work with a gentile. Several Jews were taking refuge in Grabowo. I, Avrahamchi Kadysz and the brothers Moshe and Yitzchak Kolinski lived together dressed up as gentiles, and we assisted a gentile in bringing potatoes and flour to the Lomza ghetto. We gave out potatoes to the residents of the ghetto, and we sold the flour to the bakers who baked black bread. We remitted the payment to the gentile.

We would visit the Lomza ghetto every Sunday. The Stawiskites maintained contact with the Jews of Grabowo, and they intended to flee to that village if the situation in the Lomza ghetto were to worsen. On one Sunday at the end of 1942, the liquidation of the Lomza ghetto began. As my luck would have it, I found myself there that Sunday. In the evening, Michael Kadysz and his father-in-law came to us and told us: "flee for your lives for they are about to liquidate the Lomza ghetto." We fled to the forests. News of the liquidation of the Lomza ghetto spread very quickly. The gentiles in the village no longer wished to employ Jews, and they sent us to the city to be registered there.

We hid in pits that we dug in fields during the winter of 1942 [5] . During the nights, we went out to scavenge for food from wherever we could find it. Zhimni and Liba Kadysz were with me. Zhimni took ill as he was residing in the pit and he died. Liba Kadysz was murdered. Those of us who remained alive were jealous of those who already died.

By the end of 1943, almost all the Jews who had fled were killed. According to what I later heard from the gentiles, all the Jews of Stawiski who were killed were buried in the vicinity of Maly Plock. They also told me that in a school in the village of Wysokie, on the route to Lomza, ten Jews of Stawiski were hidden. The Germans found them late at night and murdered them all by candlelight. The Chonkowicz brothers hid in a bunker in the field of the farmer Ridzwaski. At the beginning of 1944, a number of Germans went out to hunt in the fields and chanced upon the hiding place of the Chonkowicz brothers. They ordered them to vacate their shelter, and when they received no answer they tossed grenades into the shelter and the brothers were killed.

I hid in villages until the beginning of 1945. I returned to my town one week after the entry of the Russians into Stawiski. I worked in the police force for three months.

I remained as a sole Jewish lad, persecuted and wandering. Filled with endless pain and grief, I sat on the ruins of Stawiski and wept – – – .

Translator's Footnotes:

1. A paraphrase of the opening verse of Psalm 137: "By the rivers of Babylon, there we sat down and wept as we remembered Zion.

2. Tisha Beov is the somber fast day on the 9th of Av (in late July or early August) that marks the day of the destruction of the temples in Jerusalem, as well as other tragedies that befell the Jewish people through the ages. If it occurs on a Saturday, it is pushed off ("nidche") to the next day, Sunday the 10th of Av, so as not to conflict with the Sabbath.

3. A derogatory term for a non-Jew.

4. The caption on the grave reads: Here is buried a distinguished man, who excelled in fine character and good deeds, and set aside times to study Torah. All of his deeds were in faith. Reb Zeev the son of Reb Yaakov Niedzwiadowicz. Died with a good name on the 3rd of Tishrei 5684 (Oct 23, 1933), in the fifty sixth year of his life. May his soul be bound in the bonds of eternal life.

5. Based on the chronology of the narrative, I suspect this means the winter of 1942 going into 1943.

{343}

A Visit to my Birthplace
by Rabbi Baruch Zilbersztejn
Rabbi of Heichal Emanuel Synagogue, Brooklyn, New York.

There were two large houses of prayer in my town of Stawiski: the synagogue and the Beis Midrash. This was aside from a number of smaller houses of prayer, including: Chevras Kass and Chevras Talmud Torah in the anteroom of the synagogue, and Chevras Tehillim in the anteroom of the Beis Midrash.

The synagogue was a large, tall building. It exuded splendor with its solid framework and its internal decoration. It was only used for prayer on Sabbaths and festivals, and for gatherings on special occasions. During the hot summer months, they also worshipped there on weekdays. Its worshippers were not known for their exceptional piety, and they were not numbered among the "face" of the city[1].

In contrast, the Beis Midrash was a more modest structure, as were its worshippers. It was always filled with people and bustling with life. After the first quorums (minyanim) for the morning service finished, the scholars remained in the Beis Midrash to study their page or chapter. After the prayers, some Jews stayed behind to recite Psalms. Others stuck around simply to pass the time, as they enjoyed discussing affairs of the wide world, exchanging news with each other, etc. When it was not the time of services, it was also permitted to smoke cigarettes in the Beis Midrash, and many took advantage of this privilege. Some people would say that there were those who tarried in the Beis Midrash on Sabbath eves until the early risers, that is to say those who recited the morning service at the earliest possible time, began to arrive for the first minyan. It can be seen that the candle of the house of the L-rd never went out, and the voice of Torah was never silent in the Beis Midrash of Stawiski.

The synagogue courtyard, which separated the two houses of prayer, was paved with smooth stones. Next to the wall of the Beis Midrash, a spring arose from the ground. Cold, fresh water flowed from it day and night without stop. (This well was a gift from the German soldiers during the First World War, who remained in the city for four years, and called it "the well of Moses".)

During the times of prayer, this courtyard served as a noisy and vibrant meeting place for the townsfolk. Children played there, youths met there, and Jews who were expert in the affairs of the world discussed and debated various topics. Even the elderly people went out to the courtyard to enjoy the fresh air, to smoke a cigarette on a festival[2], or to quench their thirst from the clear, cold waters of the well. The non-Orthodox people would often stroll around the courtyard, especially during the times of the reading of the Torah on Sabbaths. It was a frequent occurrence to see an angry father pulling his son back into the house of prayer, or the shamash calling out the crowd to come back in for the Mussaf[3] service. There were times when the important men of the city would surround those gathered there, and not allow them to escape entering the house of prayer.

My father and I left Stawiski in 1929. For all my days, I pined to see my birthplace again. My dream only came true in 1969, after forty years elapsed. I went to visit Poland. The Polish government severely restricted my itinerary, and forbade me from visiting my birthplace. I arranged my visit to Stawiski clandestinely. I hired a special taxi, and we reached the town in two hours. The town itself had not changed much over the years, and even the wartime years did not affect it for the worse. I recognized every road, alley, house, corner, and tree.

However, my visit to the courtyard of the synagogue and Beis Midrash was very tragic.

I stood again on the synagogue courtyard "shulhof". The memories and impressions of my youth were deeply engraved upon my heart, so that the elapsed period of forty years was almost erased. I again felt myself as a child who escaped from the eyes of my father, and went out the courtyard to play with his friends and to drink from the flowing well. I was again a child who walked from the Beis Midrash to the synagogue, the place where grandfather worshipped, in order to get a candy from my uncle, or a present from grandfather himself. At times, I ascended to the women's gallery to get a kiss from grandmother, who would be surprised by my visit.

I recognized the Beis Midrash immediately, but it seemed to me that it was much smaller than it was in my imagination. However the building appeared cleaner and neater, due to the new color on the outside. I recognized a few changes in its structure, but not so much so as to change my childhood memories of it. When I attempted to enter through the main door, I caught sight of a large sign in Polish informing of the government offices that were located therein. I immediately went out.

But where was the synagogue? Where was the solid, beautiful building? Was the synagogue not a short distance away from the Beis Midrash, a distance of 30 cubits, not more[4]? I lifted up my eyes and saw a large area of broken stones and scattered bricks. These were the remnants that remained from the large synagogue that was the glory and splendor of our town.

Indeed, I had already known what had happened to the synagogue before I saw the Beis Midrash that was opposite it, and therefore I first turned my gaze to the Beis Midrash. One of the few Holocaust survivors from Stawiski told me about this in a hotel in Tel Aviv several years before my visit to Poland. The story was very tragic.

One night in 1942, many Jews were expelled from their homes by the Germans and Poles together. They were concentrated in the synagogue, and the Germans and Poles surrounded them from all sides, in order to prevent any Jew from escaping. The Germans and Poles ate and drank gluttonously all night, and then set the synagogue on fire with all of the Jews inside. The large area covered with stones speaks with a thunderous silence about the atrocities that took place in this holy place.

I could not find the cemetery of my town. It was ploughed over and planted with wheat. The Stawiski forest on the route to Lomza also no longer existed.

I did not speak to anyone. Indeed, people came out of their homes to stare at me and the taxi, but I was afraid to speak to them. I was even afraid to leave the taxi. We drove through the streets that I recognized, through the market square, and then we returned to Lomza, and from there to Warsaw.

{345}

Stawiski after the War
(Yiddish: The Modern Stawiski)

Eliahu Nissel at the Monument on the communal grave in Stawiski forest.

The market place and a lawn. (Yiddish: The market place after the war.)

This photograph and those on the previous page were taken by Eliahu Nissel of blessed memory during his visit to Stawiski in 1966. Here he is standing at a monument next to the route to Szczuczyn.

<u>Translator's Footnotes:</u>

1. I am not sure about the meaning of this expression. It seems to indicate that the worshippers of this synagogue were not the defining element of the Jewish community.

2. Smoking is forbidden on the Sabbath, as it is forbidden to make use of fire, but is permitted on weekday festivals, when the use of fire is allowed, but the kindling of a flame is forbidden. On festivals, a cigarette would have to be lit from a pre-existing flame or pilot light.

3. The additional service on Sabbaths and festivals, which takes place after the reading of the Torah.

4. A cubit is a biblical measure, equaling approximately 18 inches.

{348}

Lest I Forget You, Oh My Hometown...
by Chana Wiener of blessed memory

Our town was small in area, but rich and deep were the wellsprings of its life. Its population was not large, and its people were not blessed with wealth, but who can enumerate their character that was dearer than gold! The dearest characteristic of the Jews of Stawiski was their satisfaction with their meager lot in life. They were always happy with their lot, and faith, trust and joy dwelt in their midst.

The joy on Sabbaths and festivals was particularly great. How can I forget the atmosphere of holiness that enveloped every house and family in Stawiski on Sabbaths and festivals? Before the eyes of my spirit, I see the splendorous image of my father, with my modest mother beside him, and the children surrounding the table "as olive shoots"[1], all washed up and wearing their Sabbath clothes, with the candles lit. The Sabbath meals were festive family gatherings. The hymns sung by my father and the children still ring in my ears as a family choir.

In my memory, images float by of the final era of our brothers and sisters in my town – images saturated with joy and images saturated with suffering that I will never forget forever.

The memory of the youth is dear to me, for the Zionist nationalist spirit enlivened their spirits and served as their guiding light. I remember how on Sabbath afternoons, as the parents were still enjoying their Sabbath in accordance with the adage "sleep on the Sabbath is a pleasure", the youth would leave their homes and go out, some on the road to Lomza, others on the road to Kolno and Szczuczyn, and others to various youth groups including Hechalutz and Hashomer Hadati. However, these images turn over very quickly, and are replaced with a different horrifying image, the image of holy martyrs – young and old going along the route from where there was no return.

How awesome is it to think about parents, brothers, sisters, friends and acquaintances, among them babies who still suckle from their mothers' milk, with the elusive question in their eyes: Why? Why did fate choose this end for us? Where are the Avrahemeles, the Sarahles, the Rivkeles, and the Shlomoles, who are dearer than gold? Where are all of the people of our town? Where is Polish Jewry in general, this splendid Jewry?

The memories of my townsfolk are dear to me. You are all etched in my heart. To all of you I am bound with bonds of love that cannot be severed.

It is fitting for our pure and upright forbears, as well as the young people of our town who did not merit to live with us in our Land, to perpetuate them with this Yizkor book, which will serve as a monument to their holy memory, for us and our children forever.

We are orphaned and bereft of our children. Our brothers, sisters and relatives died in unnatural deaths at the hands of the Nazis and their assistants, may their names be blotted out, and they did not even merit to be buried in a Jewish grave. Therefore, we are duty bound to inscribe in a book the stories of bravery and sanctification of the Divine name of men and women, young and old, students at the school with the Rebbi, infants and toddlers, so that their memory should be bound up in this memorial book, so that our children and grandchildren should know about the rock from which they were hewn, about their grandparents and relatives who were murdered and destroyed at the hands of the enemy. Our children should take this book into their hands and unite themselves with their family members. This book should serve as a link in the chain of generations that is never to be severed, and should remind us and our children about the ancient command – "Remember that which Amalek did unto you…" [2].

Translator's Footnotes:

1. A quote from the book of Psalms, describing the blessings of having one's children around the table.

2. A quote from the book of Deuteronomy, and one of the 613 commandments of the Torah. It is incumbent upon the Jewish people to remember how the tribe of Amalek (considered to be the archetypal anti-Semites) was the first to attack the Jewish people after they left Egypt. This command is formally fulfilled once a year on the Sabbath of Zachor (The Sabbath of Remembrance), on the week prior to the Purim festival. A special public reading of the Torah on that day makes the proclamation of remembrance, as a fulfillment of this commandment.

{351}

The Two
by Tzvi Lieberman

The boy was ten years old and the girl eleven.

He witnessed the murder with his own eyes,

She wandered from village to village,

She saw a world filled with frights as if in the netherworld.

On what merit where they saved? – From the designed of humans –

On their own merit? Certainly not. There was not found in them

Any deeds that were not found in others.

In the merit of their fathers? Much fault can be found in them

They did not live according to the rules, and their ways were not pleasant.

Perhaps in the merit of the generations, in the merit of Abraham

Isaac and Jacob, and Sarah and Rachel the mothers.

They uttered their names with voices of pleading

In the silence of the Sabbath, at Havdalah over a cup of raisin wine

Or a cup of sweet tea.

Surely in their merit; our fathers heard voices

So awesome, so frightening, wondrous, stubborn.

Someone with great splendor whispered without end.

Someone with wonderful strength whispered and promised,

That in the Land of Canaan their children would multiply as the stars in
the heaven,

And as the sand on the seashore.

The voices were clear,

Promising, and not ceasing. They knew the Land of Canaan,

Left forlorn at the time of its siege, and they returned and returned again.

Inside themselves, they bore a desire made impure by blood.

The children who will inherit, will inherit with the blood of the protectors.

And these two, the wind carried them like

Red Currant seeds. Far, far away from the land of Poland

To the Land of Canaan, they were saved, for the sake of the generations

And for their own sake, so that they will relate

How the gardens blossomed, and the people were treasonous,

How the fields were emptied, and the young girls rejoiced

At the sight of blood. At the sight of young girls who were slaughtered.

———————

{352}

The Battle for Life
by Chava Fuks (nee Rozenstejn)
Memories from the time of the Holocaust
Translated by Jerrold Landau

{Photo page 352a -Upper right: Mitshak Chonkowicz and family, of blessed memory Upper left: Avraham Yitzchok Barbanielski of blessed memory Lower right: Yechezkel Goldsztejn, of blessed memory (standing); parents Hertzke and Miriam, of blessed memory. Lower left: Chaim-Leibl Barbanielski, of blessed memory. (Side caption to the photographs: murdered in the holocaust).}

These memoirs were written in a notebook in France in 1947, when she was 15 years old. They were written in Hebrew after she had studied the language for six months. The memoirs are published with small amendments to the language by the editors.

It was a warm summer day in 1941. Our town was conquered immediately at the outbreak of the war between Russia and Germany. The period of tribulation for the Jews of Poland began, our town included. At first, they began to kill individual Jews, and later they ordered a "march". The majority of the Jewish residents of the town were gathered on that day, and were brought, accompanied by the cruel Germans, to the anti-tank ditches that were dug by the Russians, and there they all met their deaths. My sister Antsha was among those murdered. For several days, the earth trembled from the blood of the pure people of my town. Even though the town was small, the anti-Semitism was great. The gentiles made enthusiastic requests to kill "a few" Jews, and the Germans permitted them to conduct a pogrom, which broke out suddenly in a bloody night. Hundreds of Jews were killed in that pogrom.

It was night. The town was in a deep slumber. Only the sound of the frogs and various night birds could be heard, as well as the voices of weeping and pleas for mercy of those who were condemned to death.

The cruel gentiles came armed with knives and sticks with sharp nails. Many Jews received deathblows from them. Small children were torn to pieces and tossed onto the electricity posts or the asphalt. Pregnant women had their bellies ripped open, and children's heads were chopped off and given to their mothers to hold. Not one gentile slept that night, some were there by their own free will and others were forced by other people. Everyone participated.

The bloodshed ceased only with the break of dawn. The blood that was spilled was cleaned up by their wives, so that the Germans would not know the difference between the number of Jews that they had permitted to be killed and the number that were actually killed.

Left: Avraham Yitzchok Barbanielski of blessed memory

Right: Mitshak Chonkowicz and family, of blessed memory

Left: Chaim-Leibl Barbanielski, of blessed memory.

Right: Yechezkel Goldsztejn, of blessed memory (standing); parents Hertzke and Miriam, of blessed memory.

Side caption to the photographs: Murdered in the Holocaust

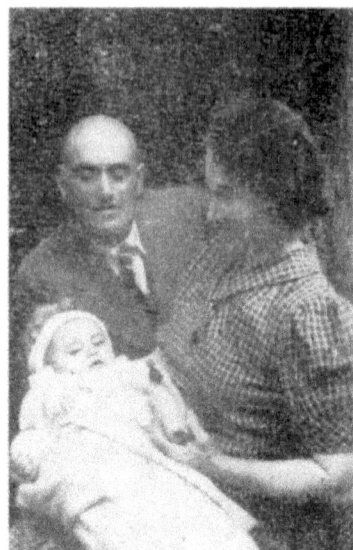

Left: Gutscha Mark (nee Morus) and her son Simcha, of blessed memory

Middle: Simcha Mark, Elka Mark and Simcha (son of their brother Avraheml, of blessed memory).

Right: Rifka and Hershel Mark and their grandchild Simcha, of blessed memory.

Left: Avraham-Yitzchok Brikman of blessed memory

Middle: Malka Kreplak of blessed memory

Right: Moshe Brikman of blessed memory

My family and myself were in a village with various farmers who knew us. We worked and hid from the death that came that night. One day it became known to us that the Germans wished to lock up all the Jews in a ghetto. At that time, we stopped working, and we began our period of hiding with one farmer in the village of Skruda. The conditions were very difficult, almost unbearable. Twelve people were hidden in a small cave in a barn, without sufficient food, without air, and most importantly, without hope. Nobody knew what tomorrow would bring.

Yitzchak Rozenstejn of blessed memory, the grandfather of Chava Fuks

When the persecution and searches ended, all of the Jews lived in the ghetto. The Germans permitted the farmers to use the Jews for backbreaking work.

After several months of hiding, we went out free – if we could indeed use that term. We again spread out among the farmers. I was with a farmer that knew me. I worked very hard despite my young age. I was ten years old at the time. He related to me as a Jewess, and he completely ignored the fact that I was young. (In fact, I was never really young.) As a result of the hard work I got a fracture[1], and I was forced to continue with the work despite great pain. Nobody carted if I was in pain or not, or if I was close to death.

On a day in the summer during the afternoon, I was tending to the cows, and I was rolling in the field due to the pain. I turned my head and saw my grandfather. He took me to the farmer who hid us before we went to the ghetto. His wife gave me a pill, and the pain was alleviated. I got better after a long time. In return for her good deed, I tended to her 200 goats.

In the meantime, my father, mother and younger brother lived in a town call Waski. My father built a flourmill for the mayor, and my mother sewed. Their situation was reasonably good. The family decided to bring me to them. I was quite ill and thin at that time. My mother began to take care of me as was appropriate for a young girl, and I began to live a domestic life. I became friendly with the daughter of the farmer. We worked together in all tasks, and I was thought of as their daughter. However our relatively peaceful life did not last long. In the fall of 1942, the ground was covered with a golden blanket. The trees were sad with the onset of the winter, and the entire areas took on the image of winter.

We gathered together on a fall evening – my parents, my brother and my uncle – with a certain farmer, and we deliberated on our fate in the future. My parents decided to send me to the farmer with whom my uncle had stayed during the time of the ghetto. This was the first tragic moment in my life.

The time for separation from my parents had come, without knowing if we would ever see each other again, or what indeed would be our fate. My mother, who was extremely religious, took a crucifix from the gentile woman and tied it to my neck with eyes filled with tears. I wept all evening, for I had a premonition of what was awaiting them and myself.

It was night. It was dark all around. My uncle and myself walked through abandoned fields we that we would not meet any Germans along the way. On occasion we stumbled and fell on clods of ploughed earth. Finally, we had completed the journey. We reached the stable of the farmer successfully. We had a roof over our heads, and we were waiting for somebody. The farmer finally came and brought us food. I suffered greatly, since I realized that my uncle would leave shortly. My uncle returned already that night, and I took the role as cousin of the farmer, and I called the master of the house 'uncle'. It was difficult for me to get used to this!! Aside from this, I was afraid lest the neighbors realize that I was a Jewess. With hard work, and internal pain that I had to hide my Jewishness, I stayed there for half a year until the maid, who was illegal herself, a Pole, informed about me to the residents of the village, and I was forced to leave the place. By a miracle, I was saved from the hands of a German who came to the mistress of the house, for her husband was in jail, and when it became known to him that I was Jewish, he wanted to kill me. However, he had mercy on the mistress of the house, since she loved me and did not want to cause me any pain, but he ordered her to expel me. This was all discussed in my presence. She sent me to her relatives in a certain village, which was nearby. This village was called Penza. I could not live openly in Penza. I hid in a closet for three months, without light, without proper food, forlorn and in constant danger. Every day, I heard the voice of August, who saw himself as the master of the house. Once, he wished to open the closet, but he was prevented from doing so at the last minute.

On Easter, they hid me in a sack so nobody would see me, and put me in a wagon in order to return me to the farmer in Waski with whom I had stayed until the liquidation of the ghetto.

The journey was very difficult in the sack. It was a beautiful day, the beginning of spring, and the sun shone on the surroundings. The fields were covered with green grass. The world had a happy appearance. We passed through towns, and I saw that children and old people were sitting on porches, and were happy. However, for me there was not one ray of light to brighten up my life. We reached the mountain that was known as Wilcza-Gora. They brought me down, as a parachutist, near the village. I turned my head, bid goodbye to the people who brought me, and disappeared into the stream that leads to the barn. There I dug a hole in the hay and fell asleep. The farmer came to the barn. He rejoiced when he saw me, however his face immediately froze with worry. He did not know what to do with me.

They brought me to a small side room, known as the "palace of the mice", and I lived there in the company of the mice for half a year. The village began to suspect them, for the door of the room in which I lived was never opened. They were forced to send me to relatives who were very poor. This was at the time of the harvest. They again put me into a sack, and I again played the part of a cousin by the name Erica. When the time of harvest and its difficult work concluded, they sent me back to the farmer from which they took me.

We arrived in the village toward evening. I remained in the field. I hid between the sheathes, so that nobody would see me, for here everyone knew me. Night fell. It was dark all around and all of a sudden, I heard steps. My heart melted with fear, however I immediately realized that this was the farmer who came to take me. On the way to his house, he stopped suddenly and asked: "Do you know who is with us?" It was difficult for me to guess, since I did not know if anyone in my family was still alive. I came to the barn, and I saw my father and my uncle standing as shadows. After all the tribulations overtook them, my father was already almost blind from the darkness of the cave where he lived in the forest.

It is hard to describe our joy in words ... however not long lasting. In the evening, my father spoke to the mayor of the village, asking him to take me in and look after me. He agreed, on condition that I would remain with him as a daughter after the war. My father did not disagree. He did not know what my fate would be. He desired that at least someone of our large family should remain alive. After the discussion with the mayor, they arose and continued along their way under the cover of the cloudy skies. I will never forget that night for the rest of my life, for that is the night that I parted from my father permanently.

Grandmother Chava Rozenstejn of blessed memory and her children –
most of them were killed in the Holocaust.}

In the morning, I sat under a roof that was burning with heat, at the home
of the mayor, forlorn, abandoned, under inhuman conditions, and my heart
was filled with fear. After a number of months, the Germans suspected that he
acted in collaboration with the partisans.

The mayor and his family left the place, and I was left without any means.
His wife brought me to another village, to the family of her maid, where I hid
together with that family from the Germans, for they also suspected them.
However, they suspected them for a different reason. After one week of
despair, I decided to go out on my own, for life or for death. All of my bridges
had been burnt behind me. I had only one means before me: to turn to a
farmer who does not know me, as an Aryan.

This was in the summer of 1943. I boarded a fishing boat and crossed the
river. I went across planted fields, and I reached a large forest. I passed
through it and I saw a small white house, surrounded by chickens. A farmer
stood by the well and was giving water to the horses. After I made a plan, I
approached him and said that I had heard that he needed help. He looked me
over from head to toe and smiled. Finally he said: "Do you know how to eat
bread? It is okay." I played the part of Krystyna Riviczka from Bialaszewo
(the village of Bialaszewo was indeed not far from my native town).

"My father was captured killing a pig, and was imprisoned in a jail in
Grodzisk. The Germans persecuted us, and we were forced to leave the village.

My mother and brother are in Szczuczyn, and I came here to find work." He believed my story. The farmer brought me into his home, and I carried my weight in all farm activities, even though he was had the largest farm in the town. The master of the house purchased shoes for me, and his wife sewed me clothes, for I did not even have a cloak for my body, and the lice were affecting me greatly. Each Sunday, I went to the church in Lomza to pray, however I never forgot that I was Jewish. The "Shema Yisrael" prayer was always on my lips. On occasion I had to confess before the priest, as was the Christian regulations. I realized this, and I was afraid. On the day of confession, I went to forest for a day, and I told the master of the house that I went to my own district to confess before the monk whom I was accustomed to confessing before.

I got up each morning at 3:00 AM to milk five cows. For a certain period, when the cowherd left us, I also served as cowherd. Aside from this, I ran the entire farm, for the mistress of the house complained that if she had a maid, she did not have to work at all. I worked from early in the morning until late at night. Aside from the work on the farm, I also wove. This work was done in the dark, and I almost damaged my eyes. However, who would care?!

On hot days during the harvest, I worked in gathering wheat stocks from behind the sickle; in the fall I gathered potatoes and spread fertilizer. My life was full of backbreaking work and fear lest the people of Penza, who would come on occasion to our village, would recognize me. Indeed, one boy from Penza recognized me, and he told the matter to his friend from the village of Jednaczewo. I became very confused when they greeted me by name, with the name that I was known in Penza – Barbara. I did not answer him, and I went to the porch, and watched how he told his friends. I immediately went to that boy from our village, and with a few heartrending words, I succeeded in getting a positive answer from him. It was difficult for me to believe that he would keep his promise, however he did not break it.

Liba, the mother of Chana Fuks (in black) and her family – most of them were killed in the Holocaust

Days and months past with deep suffering and longing. It was fortunate that I did not have too much time to ponder and think. In the meantime, the battlefronts were approaching our village. We were in the first line of the western front. They bombed the village nightly, for there were many Germans with heavy arms there. The Germans oppressed us. The situation was bad for the girls. In general, they all stayed at home; however, I was not able to permit myself such a luxury. The Germans conscripted the farmer to dig trenches, and the mistress of the house was pregnant. I herded the flock and the cattle far from the village. I had to travel several kilometers three times a day to milk them, with the danger that the cows would fall into German hands. The entire farm stood up through my own weak efforts. The mistress of the house was not able to work; she only cared for her children. I ran from one task to another. One morning, I took the cows to pasture, and I left them in the hands of a friend of mine to look after them. As I returned home through the forest, a 38-year-old German approached me. He began to speak German to me. I pretended that I did not understand, however I understood that he warned me not to go to the village, for there I would be conscripted to dig trenches. I answered him that I was not afraid, for I was only twelve years old, however he did know how to say in Polish 'wszystko jedno', that is: "it doesn't matter", and he began to caress me and say amorous words to me. I tried to flee, however he stopped me, and stepped on my wounded foot. The blood that came from the wound spurted all the way to his face. I asked that he let me go since I am ill, however he continued saying the phrase 'wszystko jedno'. He finally pushed me to the ground, and even though I did not understand very much at that time, I acted in his own manner and began to scream; however nobody heard me even though the place was close to the path. To my ill fortune, nobody passed by and heard my screams. He became angry and tried to kill me with the axe that was in his hands. When I stopped screaming, he thought that I agreed. My strength had dissipated. I got up from the ground, turned my head and said: "behold, girls are passing by". He turned his head in the direction that I pointed, and in the meantime, I slipped away and began to run toward the bushes. I fell several times since it is very difficult to run in the forest. I was saved miraculously, since he did not have any weapons. I was slapped on the face several times, however nothing more. I returned home in tears, and the mistress of the house thought that I had gone mad. She requested that I tell her what happened, but I was embarrassed. In the end I told her as a secret. When her husband returned, she told him as a secret, and he told his friends, and the matter became known in the entire village. From that time on, they looked at me as a brave person, and revered me.

The situation was very tense on the day of the German retreat. They gathered all of the residents of the village into one place and pillaged all the flocks. I ran with our flock to the forest under cannon fire, and I saved it from the Germans. The farmer returned in the evening with all the property, for he also did not present himself at the gathering place. We sat at the bank of the Narew River. We heard the noise of tanks. We saw the Germans fleeing for their lives. At dawn, I woke up to bring in the cows, for I stayed with them all night, so that nobody should notice us, and then suddenly the Russian army appeared before my eyes. We gathered all the property. I took the flock, and we turned toward the house, which was at the edge of the forest. I, with the animals, went first. My heart was filled with longing for my parents, for my home... the time of liberation had come... even though I realized that nothing was left. I raised my voice in weeping. I asked myself: how was I able to save all the animals, yet I was not able to save my parents? I reached the forest. It was a hot day, the air was clear and calm, the sun shone on the leaves, and a cool breeze blew in my hair. I walked with sure steps, with the though that we would meet our liberators face to face. I continued, and suddenly I heard a scream. A cow had trampled on a tired Russian soldier, who was sleeping under the tree. He cursed it in Russian, however he greeted me in a friendly manner: with a heartfelt "zdrastvoitia" and a smile. We reached our home. We met many soldiers, who cooked a variety of foods, and sang happy songs of their birthplace. Songs of Russia...

We did not have much time to rejoice in our home. The war heated up. We were again forced to leave the village. We stayed in the forest far from the village due to the bombardment. I again looked after everyone, from the animals to the children. Winter arrived in full force. Three families lived in one room. I slept in the barn all winter. One night, as I was in a deep sleep, I opened my eyes and I saw the farmer standing over me, saying: "Krystyna, wake up, for my wife is about to give birth". There was a new baby in the family. My situation became worse. From that time, I was not able to rest day or night. I had to concern myself with the farm, as well as with the battle that was nearing our village. At the end of the fall, literally under bombardment, I dug up potatoes. There was not much food, and in the spring we would have to plant.

It was a crisp winter night. The village was covered in white, and in the silence of night, we heard the tanks and artillery passing near our house.

After a few weeks, Berlin was captured. We returned home, however the home was destroyed. We lived with the farmer's uncle. We built a house in the meantime. The work was unbearably difficult. There was no food, and there was constant fear, now from the partisans. A difficult winter passed, and spring arrived. I tended to the cows, and I also spread out the fertilizer that had been left for almost a year. Due to the spreading of the hard manure, the skin on my right hand separated from the bone. There was no doctor. The pain was unbearable. I did not sleep at night, and the situation became more serious. At sunrise, I was already at work again. Thanks to a lad with whom I tended to the flocks, I went to a certain farmer whose lone cow I also tended to, and I requested money so that I could get my hand treated. There was one farmer in the village who knew a bit of medicine. He operated on my hand in a very primitive manner, however it did heal, and I became healthy.

In the meantime, I found out that two sisters and a brother of my father's had survived. I was the only survivor of my immediate family. My brother, my sister, and my mother were murdered by the Poles as they were hiding between the sheathes in Waski. Their flesh was eaten by the birds. The mayor's wife, who was left a widow, gave some vodka to one youth, who then brought them to burial. My eldest sister was killed in a cave, and my middle sister worked in a garden for the Germans, and the gentiles informed on her. She heard about this and started to flee. As she fled, she was shot to death. My father and my aunt's husband who survived to that point were killed by Poles who knew them in 1944, on the 27th of Sivan, close to the time of liberation. My father's brother was killed by Poles after liberation, and the rest of the members of my family died in the concentration camps or the forests of Poland.

Before I found out that my aunts and uncle had survived, I thought that I was the only survivor of all Polish Jewry. This thought did not give me any rest. I could not make peace with such a reality at all. I asked my friends in an indirect manner if any Jews were left in Lomza. They answered me: "to our great sorrow, there are still Jews there". From that time on I had only one thought in my mind: to meet Jews.

Several months passed. My aunt was at that time in Bialystock. She knew that I was in Jednaczewo, however she did not know the farmer with whom I lived. She spoke with a Jewish youth whom she knew from before the war, when he worked in the U.B., which was the organization for saving Jewish children from Poles. They punished non-Jews who were known to have killed Jews prior to the liberation and after the liberation. By chance, this youth was a friend of the farmer with whom I lived. He had already seen me when he came to visit him. He asked him who I was, however the farmer was afraid of him, for I knew many secrets. Therefore the farmer said that I was the daughter of his neighbor.

That evening, I had an internal battle inside of me: to approach him or not. He was Jewish... I would be among Jews... however I was afraid to do this. Several more months passed.

One day, during the time of the afternoon rest period, I was in a room, the cows were resting in the cowshed, and a car stopped in front of our house. I instinctively fled to the basement. The youths who arrived in the car asked about me, that is to say about the girl who was with the mayor. The mistress of the house was alone in the house. She became very confused, and said that I was in the field. They ordered her to bring me to the police in Lomza the next day. The farmer came back from the city, and when he heard this, he wanted to abandon the farm, and flee with me. He asked me if I knew any secrets about the mayor, and therefore they wanted to interrogate me. I did not know anything, and I had no idea at all that they had come to redeem me. If I would have even thought this, it was hard to believe that it would be true. In the meantime, the cousin of the farmer sent a notice to the wife of the mayor asking if she knew anything, for my aunt had been at his house a while ago.

This was in May. I went to pray. It is a Christian custom that all of the residents of the village go to pray in one house in May. That day we went to pray at the house where the farmer's cousin lived. I entered the room, and he smiled at me, and said: "Krystyna, how can you pretend so well? I can still not believe that you are Jewish, for you will always be Krystyna to me." I now had a dilemma on my hands: how should I confess everything to the farmer. The farmer's cousin took it upon himself to begin the conversation. We went into a room. He began to tell the story. I had endangered the farmer for two years, however he accepted the situation very well. He looked at me as he would a mighty person and said: "Krystyna, will you remember us?" He was always good to me, although his wife was not.

Several weeks passed without news. In the meantime, I became seriously ill. I took to bed with a high fever. After two weeks of illness, I got up on Sunday. Everyone was in Church, and I went for a stroll in the forest.

Suddenly the farmer came to me and said "They have come to take you, to my great sorrow, you must go". The mistress of the house packed my bags and wept, and their daughter stood and wept and said: "Krysynka is leaving me." We sat on the wagon and went to the place where we had arranged to meet. The group greeted us pleasantly. They made a small party for us. They spoke to the farmer, and he told them about me. They showed me a letter from my aunt in Yiddish, and they began to speak to me in Yiddish. They wanted to remind me of my mother tongue that I had not used in five years. I understood them, but I did not know how to speak. The youth who arranged the trip turned to me in song: "a Jewish girl, she is so pretty, dainty and refined, you have a thousand charms..." However, I did not resemble a Jewess at all, for the environment of the past six years had taken its toll.

The farmer sat silently and his eyes were filled with tears. The sun was going down. He got up, and parted from me like an actual father, and wept. This was a heartrending scene. I also wept. My dog stood there and waited for me to come. However, he was to be disappointed. The farmer called out: "Come Lelek, Krystyna is not returning to us." I was not able to calm down, I did not speak, I was very sad. However, this was the moment of intermingling of two different emotions.

The next day I traveled with one of the youths of the group. One the way to the train, I met a young man with whom I had tended to the flocks. He turned his head, and asked me to where I was going? However he did not get an answer from me. It was 1945.

We were at the home of my aunt in Bialystock. My younger aunt was in the house. I cannot describe the joy I felt at that time. My other aunt also came that day. She raised her voice in weeping when she saw me, and asked: "where are they all?". This meeting was a sort of memorial service for our family. For the next while, we sat down nightly and related to each other what had transpired to us.

My aunt lived at that time in a small house on Zamenhof Street. The deep grief had not dissipated, and the sorrow was great over the death of my uncle who had been killed a few weeks previously.

My aunt wanted to bring me into Jewish life. She brought me to a place called Minska, where hundreds of Jews from the concentration camp lived. The "Commitet" took care of them. I then realized that it was not only we alone who had survived. Those who knew us spoke to me in Yiddish. I did not yet know how to answer in my mother tongue, a matter that caused me much grief. They also angered me with their customs. I was not used to seeing such people. They sent me to a school, where a few children studied, however there they also oppressed me because I did not know Yiddish.

At that time, I wanted to study, given that I realized how much I had missed during the years of the war. I returned to my mother tongue very quickly, and I also learned to speak a little Hebrew. I passed from second grade to third grade in one year. I finished four grades when I was in Bialystock, and I became proficient in Hebrew. I did not only study Hebrew in that school, I also became enthralled with the Zionist idea, and I wished to make aliya to the Land of Israel.

My aunt got married in 1946, and after a period, she received a permit for aliya. My aunt asked her husband's brother to send me a permit to immigrate to America. She did this against my will, since my desire was for the Land of Israel. I was very young, and my aunt regarded herself as my guardian.

After the school exams, we prepared to travel to Sweden. This was in 1946.

We lived on Zamenhof Street in Bialystock. In that courtyard, there was a bakery, which was established by a group of young men. One of them served as treasurer. He was a young and serious boy. I would often go there to buy cakes, to get water, and to bake. The men became friendly with me, and we had good relations. Avrasha the treasurer liked me very much. I was fifteen years old at the time, and my aunt told everyone that I was twelve, since I was not that well developed physically. Externally, I looked as if I was seven years old. After much success in roles on stage (of the dramatic group of Bialystock), the men praised me, however they all looked at me as a young girl less than ten years old.

In 1946, I traveled with my aunt to Sweden. There I studied in two boarding schools, which were set up to facilitate youth aliya for no cost. At that time I was on a transit visa – with permission to go to the United States as a student to study archeology.

At the beginning of 1947, despite the objections of my aunt, I had discussions in Stockholm with the representative of the Jewish agency, and I traveled to France, en route to Israel.

I spent about a year in southern France, in Pug-Liso, a boarding school that prepared people for youth aliya. From there, I traveled from Marseilles to the Land of Israel on the fourth aliya.

I arrived in the Land of Israel on the eve of Purim, in March 1948. From the camp for new immigrants in Pardes Chana, we passed through other milestones together with our group. We fought, worked, and joined Nachal [2]. After concluding training for Nachal in 1949, we joined as reinforcements for the defense of the Chatzerim absorption center in the Negev. I worked as a dairy farmer, and I was active on several committees. I left Chatzerim in 1951, since I had a misunderstanding with the farm committee due to the fact that I was given a task that was beyond my physical capabilities. I moved to Tel Aviv. In Tel Aviv I studied, and I worked in all sorts of jobs in order to earn my livelihood in an honorable fashion. I got married in 1953, and I established a Jewish home. My husband is a professional army man, and we have a son and a daughter.

Translator's Footnotes:

1. The word 'shever' could denote a fracture, collapse, or hernia. It is not clear which is meant here.

2. The pre-military cadet corps of the Israel Defense Forces.

———

{362}

The Shul-Gasse (Street of the Synagogue)
by Rivka Zylbersztejn
Translated by Jerrold Landau

Foggy outside, although it is even moreso during the day,

The synagogue is full of executioners,

Torah scrolls are spread out on the ground outside,

My heart pounds rapidly inside of me.

The murderers are circled around,

Their hands are fiery;

The holy books are ignited –

Woe, the Torah Scrolls of Stawiski are being burnt.

Two eyes look

At night through the dark –

There glow the books

They do not want to burn...

On the Shul Gasse frolic about

The murderous executioners,

In fire they toss

Tallises and Tefillin.

Where are your Jews, clad in festive clothes,

Radiant faces during the Hakkafot [1] in the synagogue?

I search for them – here it is so vacant,

Only murderous faces are around here in such great numbers.

They leave us alone, burning in the Shul Gasse

Only black clouds inhabit this place today;

The executioners fly here like black birds

Our bloody enemies rejoice – – –

———

Translator's Footnotes:

1. Hakkafot are the festive processions with the Torah scrolls around the
   synagogue that take place on Simchat Torah.

{365}

Eulogies
Translated by Jerrold Landau
Nechka Stolnicki of blessed memory
By Chemda
(From a eulogy delivered at a memorial gathering to the Jews of Stawiski)

Nechka was taken from us about three months ago. He was the husband of our member Chava, may she live long. We all remember the Sokolicha flourmill, about 1.5 kilometers from Stawiski. From way back, and always, this lovely place was enchanting to me. Artists would come from afar to perpetuate it on their easels. We loved to climb the tall mountains, and to slide down the slopes that led into the valleys. Everything around was covered with sweet smelling, tall pine trees, which looked like their tips reached the heavens.

We would often visit the home of the Stolnicki family. We were amazed by the waterfall that operated the gigantic wheel of the flourmill. We bathed in the clear waters that flowed from the mill to the nearby valley, among thick trees.

Our friend Nechka was always happy to greet us, and he guarded us from the anger of the black dog, which we were afraid of, even though it was tied to a chain. Nechka explained to us the process of grinding the kernels of grain and wheat, and then he invited us in to his parents' house. On occasion he would bring out the clock, which made a pleasant melody when one wound up the machinery. We never tired of hearing it.

Nechka would seat us in a two-oared boat. After he taught us to use the oars, we would paddle around in the river ourselves. When we finished our paddling, we, the entire group, would go out to relax in the nearby forest. Nechka would bring us black bread and sour milk from the home, made by his mother and sisters of blessed memory.

Nechka was goodhearted. There was always a smile on his face, and his words were spiced with light humor. He was a true and dedicated friend. His life partner Chana is of the same character, and their hearts rang together. May she live long.

On that bitter day, Nechka went out to work. On that day, he promised to come home early. He wanted to bring her a present for her birthday.

Chava waited in vain for him to return. A fright overcame her – why was he tarrying, why does she not hear the familiar footsteps, as he ascends the steps that lead up to their house.

Someone knocked at the door, with evil tidings on his lips. Nechka did not return home.

When we visited the house of mourning after the tragedy, we felt that not only were the lovely wife Chava and the daughter weeping, but the entire house was crying out at the loss that came upon it so suddenly.

———

{366}

Miriam Friedman of blessed memory
By Chemda

Two months ago, we accompanied the native of our hometown Miriam Padorski to her eternal rest, that is to say Muncha of the Friedman family. The house of Reb Shabtai (Shepsil) Friedman of blessed memory was a house of Torah, which implanted its seal upon the entire family. Miriam was the eldest daughter. She excelled at her studies from her youth, and like all the youth in the period between the two world wars, she did not find her place in the small town, so she set out to study in Vilna, the Jerusalem of Lithuania.

Miriam was not of my age group. Nevertheless, her image is imprinted upon my memory from my childhood. I would often see her walking through the street with light steps, thin of stature, a beautiful brunette. In my eyes, it seemed as if she was floating upon the earth, and she exuded an effervescence and joy of youth.

A short time later, Miriam made aliya to the Land of Israel. There she studied in the nursing school that is affiliated with the Hadassah hospital in Jerusalem. I still remember the words of praise that were said about her in our house by A. A. Zak of blessed memory, about her lovely letters that were written in clear Hebrew, and her excellence in her studies.

She worked as a nurse in Jerusalem and other places in Israel for a few years. When she married Eliahu Padorski, may he live long, she settled in Petach Tikva, where they raised a fine family. We would visit them often. We enjoyed the pleasant manner in which Miriam and her husband conducted their household, and we enjoyed their endearing simplicity, and their three wonderful children.

Miriam continued to work as a nurse in Petach Tikva, and she continued her work tirelessly and with great dedication until she suffered from a heart attack last year. She regained her strength, and it seemed as if she managed to overcome her ailment. And then behold, one day, she went shopping, and suddenly fell down and did not rise again.

A great many people wept over her sudden demise. At the funeral, she was eulogized by the heads of the community of Petach Tikva and one of the senior nurses. All of them emphasized that Miriam served as a merciful nurse, whose work was holy to her. She fulfilled her tasks with boundless dedication, and she even assisted those in need outside of the hours of her work.

Eliahu lost his faithful partner. The children lost a dedicated mother. The nurses lost an elder nurse who was to them like the head of a family. We, the natives of Stawiski, lost one of the most pleasant and warm daughters of our town. A wonderful branch of the family of Stawiski émigrés in the Land has been cut down.

{366}

Berl Chonkowicz of blessed memory
By Chemda

The native of our town, Berl Chonkowicz of blessed memory, passed away in the Land. Whoever remembers him from our town, recalls him as the epitome of health, strength and might.

As we remember, the farmers of the surrounding villages would come on their holidays to worship in the church that stood in the center of the town, and to hear words of harm and hatred against the Jews from their spiritual pastor. On many occasions, Berl along with his brother of blessed memory who perished in the Holocaust, would stand up to the ruffians who attempted to torment the Jews of the town after having being incited by the priest, and having drunk liquor. It was sufficient that the Chonkowicz brothers to walk upright and proud among the crowd of revelers, for the bloodthirsty drunks to become afraid and desist from their plots. The fear of the Chonkowicz brothers fell upon them, and in their merit, the designs of the Jew haters were foiled.

Berl, the brave youth, was not able to stand up to the tribulations that overtook him after he saved himself from the Nazis, and arrived in the land of the Soviets. There, his spirit was broken, and his strong body was weakened.

He arrived in Israel broken and tormented. After some time he composed himself, and established a family, but he did not return to his original strength. Finally, an illness overtook him and destroyed him.

{367}

Chana Wiener of blessed memory

(Words from a memorial gathering on the 18th of Tammuz, 5728, July 14, 1968.)

It has been two weeks since we accompanied Chana Wiener of blessed memory to her eternal rest, and we are still astounded at the magnitude of the tragedy that overcame the Wiener family so suddenly, as their wife and mother was taken from them. We, the family of natives of our hometown in the Land, have lost this fine soul.

Most of us knew her, some close and others from a distance, some well and others not so well. Some of us remember her from her childhood in her parents' home, and others know her only from the Land. Some of us saw her on frequent occasions and other of us only at the memorial gatherings. Engraved in all of our hearts are the image of Chana's refined soul and pure heart, her hearty smile and the sparkle on her face, as well as her calm, quiet manner of speech. Her entire essence exuded modesty that inspired honor, esteem and love.

With Chana, many of us found an ear to listen to the heart's agony and a heart that understood their suffering, for she possessed a sensitive motherly heart to the pain of her fellow man. This heart directed her actions, and demanded of her to act beyond the call of duty, and beyond her physical capabilities. She did not spare any effort or toil to pave her way into the hearts of people and to inspire them to good deeds. Chana did wonderful things for those who required assistance, with the blessed assistance of Rabbi Bernstein, may he be spared for a long life. She did her acts for the most part discreetly and secretly, so that the people involved in the matter should not Heaven forbid be embarrassed or put to shame.

Thus did beat this rare heart, this merciful heart, during times of hard-heartedness, cruelty, and difficulties, until it suddenly stopped forever.

Her public activities were many and variegated – and only very few of them were discussed during the eulogies at her funeral. However we know very well what she did for the poor of our town. She sustained all 248 of their organs and 365 of their sinews [1]. Chana stood at the center of our activities, and she was the living spirit and inspiring power to our collective eyes. As most of us, she bore in her heart the agony of the destruction of our Jewish city at the hands of the Polish murderers, who were our mortal enemies at all times, and until this day. Her will was very strong to establish a memorial for our dear souls who perished in the holocaust, and to set up a monument in their holy memory. However, this did not come to be. We spoke a great deal about publishing a memorial book; we discussed this and continue to discuss this at every memorial gathering and at every meeting of our organizational committee. To our dismay, we are still at the beginning of the path.

I visited at her house on Monday, about a day and a half before the tragedy. We discussed the preparations for this memorial evening. She was going to help in the issuing of invitations, but this was not in her fate. During that conversation, she expressed her dissatisfaction regarding the poor attendance at these memorial meetings. She asked about and thought about the text of the invitation, that it should be such to arouse the interest of the natives of our town and to insure that nobody would want to miss this evening, so that we can all recall together that which should never be forgotten forever.

If on this evening, there are more of us gathered than usual; it was in the merit of Chana. It was as if she gave everything so that everyone would come – her life and her pure, refined soul.

Chana knew how to place a Jewish imprint upon her home, and to conduct it in the spirit of Judaism and tradition. In that manner, along with her husband, did she educate her children, may they live long.

Refined sensitivity, nobleness of soul and purity of character – these are the generous traits that she brought from her the home of her pure, upright parents, and were an inseparable part of her being and essence. These traits stuck to her in a natural fashion. In our eyes, and in the eyes of the many who knew her, Chana was a symbol of faithfulness, trustworthiness, truth, uprightness, charity and kindness. Are there any traits dearer than these are? Who can fill the empty void that she left behind?

How can we comfort her husband and her dear children, for there is no comfort to such a great loss? It is our hope, as it is the hope of the family, that our bond will not be severed.

And if after the passage of time we succeed in publishing the memorial book to the martyrs of our city, the chapters that she wrote with the blood of her heart will be included – and thus will be fulfilled one of the last dreams in the life of dear Chana.

{369}

My wife Chana
Your husband, Mordechai Wiener.

(On the fourth anniversary of her death)

Grief, pain, and agony accompany me from the time that you left us. Your noble and beautiful character stands as if alive before my eyes. You were the woman of valor the entire family, loved by all of us for your charm. You left us forever so suddenly.

My darling, I will not know rest and peace. Day by day, hour by hour, I remember your image, with your smile as bright as the shining sun; however suddenly the bitter reality returns and the light of the sun is clouded over by dark clouds, as tears accompany your memory.

Due to your merit, through your wisdom and influence, we merited to make aliya to our Land. You raised a generation of wonderful children and grandchildren, all of whom are blessed on your account. Your good deeds will stand forever as a memorial monument before my eyes, and will be kept in the depths of my heart. The stream of tears does not cease, and I am imprisoned in a world that is all pain and bitterness. With your death, the reason for my life disappeared. When I visit the cemetery, I stand like a living, mute statue beside you.

You bequeathed your wisdom to your grandchildren, and they are filled with a strong desire to progress.

My dear wife, you always concerned yourself that nothing bad should happen to me. Your dedication was boundless. You accepted the difficult moments of your life with patience, and you never complained. You always accepted life for what it was. Nothing remains except for your good and dear memory. The grief and pain will not leave us. Your memory will be stored in our hearts forever.

{369}

Moshe Zeev Goelman of blessed memory
By Yitzchak Kotton

(Words from the thirtieth day of his death – the night of the 9th of Kislev 5731, December 6, 1970)

Moshe Zeev Goelman

We have gathered here this evening, the members of the family of Rabbi Moshe Zeev Goelman, his friends, acquaintances and fellow natives in order to unite ourselves with the memory of the departed. Only a few months ago, we were together with him at a memorial service for the Holocaust victims of our town. We sat together, and reminisced about life in our town. Moshe Zeev always had a new story, a new episode about his birthplace.

As one of his students, I permit myself to determine that he was the person who established a generation of Hebrew speakers in our town. He introduced his students to the garden of Zionism, and to pioneering actualization. I remember that, a few years ago, I met him by chance at the Hebrew University, at the time that my younger son was receiving his B.A. degree. This was our first meeting in the land after many years of not having seen each other, for Reb Moshe Zeev lived in Canada for many years and I was in the Land all of those years, for I made aliya when I was still a youth. When he saw me that first time after what I believe is a hiatus of thirty years, he approached me, hugged me, and said: "I am very happy Itche (that is what they called me in Stawiski), and I am happy to see you among the fathers who raised children who are among those who are receiving their university degree." I asked him with surprise: "My rabbi and teacher, how did you recognize me after so many years?" He answered me: "The image of youth...", and continued, "I remember all of my students".

Moshe Zeev Goelman merited in arriving in the Land and living there. We, his students, knew that he would come, that he would abandon the familiar exile, and make aliya with his family and settle in the Land. That is indeed what happened.

We met at all of the memorials that we arranged for the martyrs of our town, and Moshe Zeev spoke about the town at every memorial gathering. Despite the many years that he lived away from Stawiski, he remained attached to it with all the fibers of his soul. Even at the final memorial gathering, when I asked about his health, he said: "Thank G-d, your eyes see that I have come to the gathering, and I hope to come to many more gatherings". That time, his hope was not fulfilled. With the death of M. Z. Goelman, we have all lost a distinguished teacher, a refined and noble man, who bestowed much of spirit onto his fellow natives who will always remember him with gratitude and reverence.

I hope that we, the émigrés of Stawiski, will establish a memorial for him in the Land, as is fitting for such a man.

{371}

My Brother Moshe of blessed memory
By Elazar Goelman

We have gathered together to unite with the name and memory of Rabbi Moshe Zeev – family members and friends from near and far. Our rabbis defined the relationship between teachers to their rabbi as follows: "Students to their rabbi are like children to their father". Furthermore, the connection to their revered teacher is not bound to the "landsmanschaft"[2]

His clearness of mind, and his uncanny astuteness to what was transpiring and was about to transpire, was astounding. He foresaw the future with the eyes of his spirit. He planned the course of his life with great clarity, and with his clear mind he saw the approaching end, and accepted his suffering. In his final days he was concerned about those around them, for he did not want to bother and trouble them more than necessary. As long as his soul was with him, his mouth did not cease from asking forgiveness about this. He told us how we should act after his death – that we should not stray from the path that he went on during his life. He requested that we not eulogize him, that we not scatter praises about him, for modesty and quietude – these were the expressions of his caring heart, as it is said: "And Aaron was silent"[3]. Silence is the expression of true anguish and deep mourning.

Our rabbis defined life and death using different criteria than we do. They explained the verse from Kohelet[4]: "A name is better than fine oil, and the day of death is better than the day of birth" as follows: "When a man is born – everyone is happy, and when he dies, all are sad. But this is not the way it should be. To what is this like? To two boats that are at sea: one is entering the port and the other is returning to the port. The one that is entering – people are happy about it. The observers are surprised, and ask them: Why do you rejoice at the one that enters and not at the one that goes out? They answer: the one that enters – we are happy that it has returned in peace, but the one that goes out – we do not know what will become of it in the future."

We are mortals, but the life of man in the eyes of the sprit is entirely different. The value and importance of life is measured by "what", "how", and "in what manner" – what was its content, how did the person behave toward his fellowman, and in what manner did he attach himself to the life of the generation, to the Jewish community, and in what manner did the human and the Jew intermingle in him?

The boat of Moshe Velvel[5] set out on its journey in a sea open to the winds of the time and the upheavals of life at the beginning of the 20th century. Kingdoms threatened each other; countries were caught up in the spirit of deceit and revolt; nations and peoples attempted to free themselves from the yoke of powerful kings. This was the stormiest period in the annals of history, and specifically in the history of our people. It seemed that this generation encompassed several generations in it, for the days were full of many changes. Our generation saw much change.

There were three stations in the life of Moshe: Stawiski – his birthplace; Goniodz – the place of his youth; and Canada – the place of his activity. When he lost his mother while he was still a young boy, he was taken in to the home of his grandfather Rabbi Elazar of blessed memory, where he was raised and educated. The influence of grandfather was very great upon him. He learnt from him the love of the Jewish people and of Torah, and primarily the love of his fellow man. His stories about his impressions from his grandfather's house were full of holy trembling. My grandfather of blessed memory was one of the most sublime personalities of the area, and many would come to his home to study Torah from his mouth, and to learn the ways of the world from him.

He also inherited his love of the Hebrew language from grandfather of blessed memory. He was always pained that he did not succeed to salvage the books of the bible, with the many grammatical notes that grandfather of blessed memory inscribed in the margins of the pages. Father of blessed memory sent him to study Torah in Krynki, grandfather's birthplace, where he was the student of the Gaon Rabbi Zalman Sender of Krynki, who was a comrade of Rabbi Chaim of Brisk and Itzele Blazer of Petersburg, who were counted among one of the three greats of the generation. He found favor in the eyes of Rabbi Zalman Sender, and merited to be counted among his close students.

Along with his friend Itzkowski of blessed memory, my brother Moshe founded a Hebrew school. This school did not last very long. It was closed at the time of the Bolshevik invasion of Poland. Moshe, who was included in the "black list" of the Bolsheviks, was forced to flee to Lithuania. When he returned from exile, he was afraid to go to Stawiski, for the Poles registered those who fled as Bolsheviks. He went to Bialystock, and from there he went to Goniodz.

Goniodz was the second stop of his life. He taught Hebrew in the Hebrew school there. This was the beginning of the era of Modern Hebrew, when the generation of the enlightenment began to clear a place for the renewed Hebrew language. The Hebrew revolution took place by uncovering the treasures of the language that were buried in the Hebrew language, and the pushing aside of the ornate style. This revolution drew its influence from the new Jewish settlement in the Land of Israel, which turned Hebrew into a living language. From the Land, the revolution came to the Jewish Diaspora.

Moshe was faithful to Hebrew education throughout his life. His work in Hebrew education was like the service of the High Priest on Yom Kippur – completely holy, imbued with the seal of a pioneering mission. In this manner, he was a member of the early generation, of those who saw themselves as the emissaries of renewal, and who dedicated their best efforts and strengths to the task that they took upon themselves, the task that sustained their souls.

In the Chapters of the Fathers, it is told that Rabban Yochanan ben Zakkai asked his students: "What is the proper path to which a man should cleave? Rabbi Eliezer answered: A good eye; Rabbi Yehoshua answered: A good friend; Rabbi Yossi answered: A good neighbor; Rabbi Shimon said: He who can foresee the future; Rabbi Elazar said: A good heart." I will not explain each of its traits, and their importance to the person and the group, however it was clear that all five of these fine qualities were found intermingled in Moshe Velvel, as a person, a father, a teacher, and an educator. In that same place, it is recorded the answer of Rabban Yochanan ben Zakkai: "I agree with the words of Rabbi Elazar ben Arach more than the others, for his answer included all the others." I can testify regarding my brother Moshe that in him the answer of Rabban Yochanan ben Zakkai was fulfilled, for over and above everything else, he had a good heart.

The love of his fellow Jew was the mother of all of his loves, and he set out on his life's journey graced with this fine trait. He was a member of the first generation in whom nationalism was forged, who took duties and tasks upon themselves, and served as a personal example to the realization and fulfillment of the goals.

His life's work in Hebrew education came to fruition in Canada, in the cities of Toronto, Montreal and Edmonton. Most of his working years were spent in the Jewish community of Edmonton, far away from the central Jewish communities of the larger cities of Canada.

Moshe Zeev came to Canada at a time when immigration to that land was increasing. The immigrants met with difficult conditions of acclimatization. They ignored their spiritual future due to the struggle for physical existence. Moshe Velvel was numbered among the small group of Hebrew educators who filled the gap, and alerted people to the spiritual dangers that were lurking at the doorways of the Jewish immigrants. He succeeded in setting up a center of Jewish nationalism, a center for both Jewish fathers and children in Edmonton. Even today, after Moshe has made aliya to the Land, the Jews of Edmonton still derive their love of the Jewish nation and the Land of Israel from the Torah that my brother Moshe spread in that community throughout the years.

Only educators that are filled with nationalistic feeling, whose roots are firmly planted in the depths of the land of the nation, are able to raise, educate, and establish dedicated students, as did my brother Moshe. In my eyes, I saw the feelings of love and reverence that his students expressed to him. Today they are parents and grandparents full of worth, as well as youths who have grown up and are fathers to a new generation.

Moshe Velvel served as a teacher in Goniodz for only three or four years – a relatively short period in the life of a person. Nevertheless, he succeeded during those few years in implanting a love and appreciation for his personality in the hearts of his students. Only a person graced with special talents could merit this.

During his life, he fulfilled the command: "Walk modestly". He always chose a discreet corner wherever he went, where he would sit and listen. Even though he was "hidden", he served as a fountain of influence for hundreds and thousands of students who listened attentively to his words.

In the family, he was more than a brother. He was like a second father to us. We related to him with honorable awe and propriety. We valued his great knowledge, and recognized his nobility and his fine soul.

With his death, our soul has been taken from us, but his spirit continues to exist. By strengthening ourselves with his sublime traits and by guarding his way of life – we will perpetuate his name.

His memory shall be ingrained in us forever.

{374}

My Teacher Moshe Zeev
By Chemda

Thirty days have passed from the time that the dear Goelman family lost the head of the family, and we lost a teacher and distinguished friend, whose memory we recall tonight in the company of his family and a small group of his relatives and friends. Many of our townsfolk still remember, some unclearly and some with greater clarity, Moshe Velvel, the fine young man with pleasant mannerisms. After spending several years in the halls of Torah study, he returned to our town, and made it his objectives to teach the Hebrew language and literature to children and youth, and to teach them Jewish history.

Moshe was not simply a teacher. His soul was given over to teaching, and he behaved towards his students with friendship. It is not surprising, therefore, that he was able to make the studying precious to his students, and to become friendly with his students. Testimony to the extent that his students appreciated him as a teacher can be found in the fact that Moshe Leib Bzostowiecki of blessed memory, one of the best teachers of the town, primarily in Talmud, who was known as being exacting and strict with his students, invited Moshe to teach Hebrew, grammar and bible. Moshe accepted the invitation and saw blessing in his labors. He was blessed by his students, and his students were blessed through their teacher. Until the end of his days he would receive letters in clear Hebrew from several of his students who lived in the United States. They remembered their Hebrew from the early days. Those who visited Israel were happy to visit their teacher. Others, including his childhood friend Yaakov Elfenbaum, hoped to visit him one day but did not succeed in doing so. One of his prize students, Zelig Bzostowiecki, who visited Israel recently, actually came to his house to see him – but he was too late.

During the period prior to the First World War, during the time of the war, and thereafter, he was overcome by the Zionist awakening. During that period, a Techiah hall was established in Stawiski, where social and cultural events were organized. This organization brought together the finest of the youth and young adults. Moshe was one of the activists who frequently lectured on various literary and Zionist topics in the hall.

During his youth, he stopped over in many places, about which Moshe writes in his memoirs. One of these stops was Goniodz, where he served as a Hebrew teacher, and met his life's partner Kayla. Later, the two of them left Poland and immigrated to Canada. In his new land he also raised up many students, faithful to Zion and to the Hebrew language. Faithful testimony to the heartfelt connections that he established with his students and friends in Canada can be seen by the countless telegrams and letters, saturated with grief and agony, that have arrived and continue to arrive to his family. In 1954, Moshe and his family made aliya to the Land that he had desired for all those years, but for various reasons was not able to succeed in coming to early. Nevertheless, finally, we were able to be together with him again.

Moshe was one of the prime movers in setting up the annual memorial gathering of Stawiski émigrés in the Land, to remember the town that went up in flames; and one of the first to think of the idea of publishing a book that would perpetuate for all generations the memory of our dear ones who were burnt and butchered by the Nazi enemy with the active help of the Polish Jew haters, residents of the town and the area. The plans for publication of this book kept him busy for years. He devoted much of his time, energies and powers to this task. We were astounded by the power of his memory that did not weaken in his old age. He drew up from the depths of his soul, and brought to the fore memories of various events and interesting personalities. He wrote with passion and great love about the important people as well as the simple folk.

He dealt with any matter that came to his hands with the same dedication. He was able to recall with detail things that many of us have forgotten. He dedicated much effort to the translation of articles from Hebrew into Yiddish for the benefit of those who were not fluent with the Hebrew language, as well as from Yiddish to Hebrew. He published many items himself in able to save money for the organization. He rejoiced at every new chapter and each additional article that was received from the natives of our city in the Diaspora and in the Land. He was prepared to meet with any person who had something to relate about what once was and is no longer, so that he could take notes from their oral testimony and prepare an article. He did not skimp on his labor, and he worked hard to uncover material that would deepen the subject and spread out roots into the eras that preceded him and us, to bring to life that which the terrible Holocaust consumed with fire. He portrayed characters of the old and young, of those that carried the banner of progress and culture, of people of toil and Torah, of the simple folk and people of the spirit. He perpetuated schools, institutions of Torah, charity and community, of our Stawiski and of the Jewish happenings that took place there throughout the generations.

We would often find ourselves at the home of Moshe of blessed memory and Kayla may she live long, in that house that was a sign of simplicity and pleasantness, enthusiasm and warmth, friendship and camaraderie. He did not despise small matters, but he also did not get caught up with them. He did not pursue honor and he did not want to push himself into the forefront. With difficulty, we would succeed in convincing him to serve as chairman of the memorial gatherings, and throughout the time, he only served in this capacity once or perhaps twice. The same was with the memorial book – he did not seek a crown for himself or any honor. He worked on behalf of the issue and its progress. He sat among us as an equal among equals, without lording over, as he dealt with us in a simple manner regarding matters of concern. He listened and expressed his opinion. He took advice and gave advice. How good was it to know that we had a man like Moshe, whom we could approach at any time and at any hour, in order to ask advice, to think together, and to work as a team.

As thunder on a clear day, the news spread among us of his serious illness. Even during the time of his illness he did not desist from his work. He wrote and published, prepared and edited. Even though he knew what was awaiting him, it seemed as if he hoped in the secrecy of his heart – perhaps there will be mercy, perhaps he would merit to see the book being covered with skin and sinews.

He continued on, but did not merit.

His household has become orphaned. Kayla lost her husband and faithful partner in life. The children have become orphaned from their father. His brother and sister, to whom Moshe was like a father as well as a brother, have lost their dear brother. We have lost a beloved teacher and a dear friend.

May it be so that our strength will continue so that we can continue in the same straightforward, communal spirit in the endeavor that we have started together with Moshe, so that we can bring it to its completion, as he dreamed.

Translator's Footnotes:

1. According to Jewish tradition, these are the numbers of organs and sinews in a human body.

2. A Yiddish term for an organization of people from a common hometown.

3. A quote from the book of Leviticus. After the two sons of Aaron were killed by divine visitation after offering a strange fire at the dedication of the tabernacle, we are told that Aaron held his silence.

4. The Hebrew name for what is often known as the Book of Ecclesiastes. Kohelet means "preacher", referring to the first verse in the book, which states "The words of the Preacher the son of David" – generally taken to refer to King Solomon.

5. Velvel is the diminutive for Wolf, which is the Yiddish version of the Hebrew Zeev. Thus, Zeev, Wolf and Velvel will often be used interchangeably.

{376}

Eliahu Livna (Bzostowiecki) of blessed memory
by Chemda

Eliahu Livna Bzostowiecki

Eliahu was orphaned from his father when he was still a young boy. After some time, his mother remarried. Shortly thereafter, his mother also died, and the young orphans remained in the home. There was no orphanage in the town, and Eliahu remained in the house of his stepfather. He worked at various jobs while he as still young in order to assist with the sustenance of the family. He did not reject any job opportunity, for the choice of jobs was not great for children of his age.

The difficult living conditions placed a great burden upon him, and he matured before his time. He learned to differentiate between good and bad, and was diligent in maintaining his spiritual character. Eliahu was mature in his outlook and ideas, of which he spoke with youthful enthusiasm, insight and levelheadedness. He was able to serve as an example to anyone who had a difficult childhood. He grew up out of his difficult childhood well-forged, spiritually strong, and possessing a fine and sensitive soul.

Eliahu joined the Young Chalutz organization, and later Hechalutz, from where he went to hachsharah. Upon his return to town he could not find his place. He knew that he could only build his future in the Land. The difficulties in aliya did not pass over him. Lacking means, he waited like many Hechalutz members for the redeeming certificate. He was anxious to embark upon the path of aliya, and he did not know from where his help would come.

Eliahu frequented our home. I knew of the difficulties of his life and was concerned that everything must be done so that he would not be left alone to his fate. One evening, I met with some of the leaders of the town and I discussed his situation with them – and I was answered. One day, I traveled with Eliahu to Warsaw the capital city. I came to the Hechalutz headquarters and requested an urgent meeting with one of the members. I described Eliahu's circumstances to him, and requested that his aliya be expedited. At first my words fell upon sealed ears, but I did not move from my place nor abandon my request until the desired certificate was given. When he arrived in the land, he joined up with a founding group (garin) of a kibbutz, which did their hachsharah in Raanana [1]. However, Eliahu did not find peace of mind since his young sister was not with him. Since he could not find the means for her aliya to the kibbutz, he left the garin and accepted a job at one of the orchards of Raanana. He very quickly endeared himself to the owner of the orchard, Mr. Leviathan; and with his assistance, and with his taking responsibility before the Mandatory government for the sustenance of his young sister, he succeeded in bringing her to the Land. She was accepted to the Chana Chizik women's pioneering group.

Eliahu married a woman by the name of Shulamit, may she live long, and they had a daughter. He lived an exemplary family life. Many good people would pass through his home and become good friends. However, he did not escape a bitter fate, for he became afflicted with a severe illness. He survived a difficult operation, and we hoped that his health would improve. He became ill again one year later, and there was no hope for recovery.

My last conversation with him was on the telephone on the night of a memorial ceremony for the martyrs of our town. I asked about his health and he broke out in bitter weeping. He wanted very badly to attend the memorial ceremony, for he felt that this would be his last chance to meet with the natives of our town. I dissuaded him from this, for I knew that his strength would not hold out, for his condition was serious.

The pleasant and refined Eli, faithful to his family and upright with his friends and acquaintances – went to his eternal rest before his time.

{378}

Herzl Cheslok of blessed memory
by Rivka Zilbersztejn

Herzl Cheslok

(Words at the conclusion of the thirty days following his death [2])

Mourners have gathered together, your friends who are natives of Stawiski, to join together with your memory, oh our dear Herzl, who was taken from us suddenly.

Herzke, only you survived from your large family who died in the great holocaust to tell of the tragedies and unimaginable hellish suffering that occurred to all the Jews of our town, of who only very few (less than ten) survived. You were in Auschwitz when it was liberated, and you were like a sack of bones. You stood on your feet with difficulty. You regained your strength after being taken care of for a long period, but you never returned to your original strength.

You began a new life. Your fortune brightened, and you merited the good and dedicated idea to make aliya to the Land. You hoped to live a life of happiness, but your lot was bitter – for your beloved wife was cut off in her prime, and you were again left alone and forlorn.

You began to seek out friends from among the natives of your town in order to relieve your loneliness. You were close to all of them, you visited them often. You rejoiced in their joy and you were suffered in their sadness.

I remember well my first meeting with you in the Land, in the home of Chana Wiener of blessed memory. You both had great merit in arranging the first memorial of the martyrs of Stawiski. Already at that time, you had in your heart the dream of publishing a book on Stawiski to perpetuate the Jewish life and martyrs of our hometown.

The picture of our final meeting, dedicated to the publishing of the Stawiski Yizkor Book, still stands before my eye. You extended your hand with your photo from Auschwitz to be included in the book. And behold, only a few days passed, and you were no longer alive.

Hertzke is no longer with us. Hertzke who attended the Yeshiva of Lomza, Hertzke the melancholy youth who peered out of the window of his home on Shul Gasse, Hertzke the only one of the natives of our town who was saved from the fires of Auschwitz.

In the eyes of my spirit I see your entire family: your mother Elke may peace be upon her, who was always concerned about your wellbeing; your young sister, my childhood friend in whose company I spent much time – her home was my home. They all perished, nobody remains of them, and now you have gone also. Our brethren, Stawiski natives, remain enveloped in agony, weeping over your untimely death.

Translator's Footnotes :

1. Garin (literally a seed or kernel), refers to a group of people who band together to make aliya together, or found a settlement or a kibbutz. Here hachsharah refers to preparations that such a group undertakes before actually going out to found their settlement (usually it refers to aliya preparations when a person is still in the Diaspora).

2. Shloshim (literally thirty) refers to the thirty-day mourning period following the death of a person. Children observe mourning for an entire year for parents, but for other relatives, the mourning period lasts thirty days.

Coordinator's Note: This is the original chapter included in English entitled "On The Occasion of Publication", as it appears in the Stawiski Yizkor Book. Since this chapter was published in English, the spellings have been kept as in the original, even though it is noted that there are some spelling discrepancies. The current name of the shtetl is Stawiski and it will be spelled that way in all translations, even though this chapter had it spelled the Yiddish way – Stavisk. This is the only place in the Yizkor Book translation that it will be spelled the Yiddish way, as that is how the editorial committee wrote it.

Jan Meisels Allen

{page I-V}

On The Occasion of Publication

For many years we pondered whether we should issue a memorial volume to the martyrs of our town Stavisk [sic]. There were many who argued against the idea, saying that it was a waste of effort to add one more book to the many memorial volumes already published, since all that had needed saying had already been said and there seemed to be nothing we could add to the subject. On the other hand, the proponents of the volume claimed that, in spite of the similarity of character and way of life which could be found in the Jewish communities in the small towns of Eastern Europe–the differences between such communities were as great as those between human beings, and that every community was unique in its own special manner. It was the uniqueness which they found worthy of commemoration perpetuating this memory for all ages.

The goal we set before us was difficult to achieve, the labour [sic] involved was plentiful, and time, as always, short. Most of our townspeople, both in Israel and abroad, had left Stavisk [sic] tens of years previously, and even though all of them treasured, and still carry with them, the memories of their families and friends, of the town and community as they saw it, the passage of time had done its best to erode and weaken many of the impressions, and many items of import had been completely erased from memory with time. Thus we knew that time was not operating in our favour [sic], knowing, as we did, that we were the remnants of the last generation which had lived {sic} at least a part of its early life – childhood, youth, young adulthood – in our town. Haste was of the utmost importance, if we were to succeed in rescuing from oblivion all that was still to be remembered by the few who could still do so and contribute their share to our project. So our call was "Let whoever is capable of expressing his feelings and memories do so, everyone in his own manner should pour out the contents of the depth of his innermost heart, so as to perpetuate the memory of our dear ones, lost forever in the terrible Holocaust which had befallen European Jewry in our times".

Like all the beginnings, ours had its difficulties as well. We introduced the idea and explained it at our annual memorial meetings in Israel, and in letters circulated amongst our townspeople in Israel and throughout the world. We asked everyone to write about the subject or persons closest to his heart. Years passed and the response was negligible, but we did to give up hope. Great thrust was given to the whole project and its final realization by our reverend [sic] and honored teacher and dearest friend, the late Moshe Goelman, who took the task upon himself, and put all the heart and energy at his command to fulfilling the goal. Moshe Goelman was one of the oldest among us, but his memory had not faded, and he was also the first to put into writing a number of the memories which had remained with him of the way of life in our community. In these sketches he described very faithfully some of the outstanding personalities and figures of the town of his time.

We approached the whole idea rather hesitantly. We certainly had no pretensions about publishing the memorial volume of its kind. We realized that there were practically no limitations to the possibilities hidden within this terrible and painful subject matter. However, realizing our limitations we tried to do whatever we could, utilizing our limited abilities and our even more limited material resources in order to erect a memorial to Jews of Stavisk [sic], their unique, communal way of life, their hopes and their aspirations, their failures and disappointments, their joys and their sorrows. We wished to describe, however modestly, the Jews of our town, their various social strata, how they clung to their faith in God, performing all His commandments willingly and with awe, who drew from their deep faith the hope and expectations of the eventual coming of the Messiah, and the strength to resist all the troubles of their existence. We desired to raise from the depth of our memories the hopes and dreams of the young people, who rebelled against the conventions of town life, who saw in the evils of Jewish life in the Diaspora the inescapable results of life dispersed among the nations, and who fervently desired to go back to the land of their forefathers and to take part in the building of a normal nation and the establishment of a new society based upon solid and normal foundations in the soil of the Homeland.

Thus they hoped and prayed, and thus they went up in flames – they and their hopes!!

*

The little that we have done in giving this book its shape, in organizing its contents, we owe to many, some of whom are no longer among the living,

First and foremost, to our teacher and guide, the late Moshe Goelman, one of the originators of the idea of publishing the memorial volume, and the first to give reality to the idea in writing. He contributed much of his time and energy to collecting the material from people near and far, spent days and nights writing, urging, activating his many friends and former pupils abroad, getting them to do their part in getting the book together. He also translated several of the contributions from one language to another, and typed them all up in order to reduce expenses. To his last days he worked to help further progress of the book, but his dream of seeing it published was not to be fulfilled in his lifetime.

The late Herzl (Herzke) Cheshluk was a "brand plucked from the flames", one of the nine survivors of the Holocaust from Stavisk. He arrived in Israel broken in flesh and spirit after the war. When he had finally begun to return slowly to normal existence, he found his way to our townspeople here. He was the one who originated the idea of holding our annual memorial meetings, devoted to the memory of our martyred townspeople, on the 17th of Tammuz, and it is to his efforts that the holding of these meeting for the many years must be credited. At a meeting of our Committee which was hold [sic] before the Shavouot festival in 1972 to discuss the memorial volume and its problems, Herzl announced his own personal donation to the book fund, and took upon himself the task of raising more funds from some of our townspeople living in the north of Israel. But Fate, having spared him from the death camps in Europe, turned upon him after he had finally managed to recover from all he had gone through during the Holocaust and afterwards, and broke his heart finally on the evening of the first day of Shavouot, as he was sitting with some friends in Haifa.

We also wish to remember the late Chana Weiner, who was a devoted mother to every one of our townspeople who was ever in need of help, who aided everyone so quietly and devotedly in her own special manner. Until the last months of her life, she was devoted heart and soul to everything connected with memorial projects for our townspeople, and especially to this memorial volume.

We mourn all of these dear friends, the good, honest, devoted people, who did not attain their dream of seeing the day our volume would be published,

Of those with us, our heartfelt thanks go to our "landsman", the lawyer Chaim Villamovsky [sic], who gave much of his time to gathering material for this book, especially much documentary evidence related to the destruction of the town of Stavisk [sic] and its Jews.

*

We wish to commend heartily our townspeople in the United States who aided us, each in his own way, in publishing this volume:

Jack Elfenbaum, of New York, who transferred to us, through Moshe Goelman, the funds remaining in the Landsmannshaft treasury in New York;

Charles Zweiback, who took the memorial volume to his heart, and who contributed a considerable sum of his own, as well as passing on some of his contagious enthusiasm to one of his friends, Nathan Caron, whose fine contribution was divided between the memorial volume and the Mutual Loan Fund managed by Rabbi HI. L. Bernstein. Charles Zweiback also placed advertisements in some of the Yiddish newspapers in the U. S. – a "Call to

Arms" to our townspeople in the U.S. to join the effort of publishing the volume;

Mr. Herman Levine (Levinovich) of Miami, Mrs. Channa Bramson of Chicago, and her brother Louis Bramson of New York, Mr. Zaritzki of New York, and Chaim Solel of Mexico City – all were active and activated others, contributed themselves and raised contributions from many others in aid of this volume.

We are thankful to all our townspeople, friends and acquaintances, in Israel and abroad, who answered our appeals for help and contributed in gathering the material, writing it up, and helped in every other way to get the book published. We are very grateful to them all – may they be blessed for their fruitful efforts.

*

We are adding this book of mourning to the long list of books already written, and those which will probably be written in the future – so that we and all who come after us may remember what the Nazi beast, in close collaboration with the antisemetic [sic] Poles, did to our community and town in the dark days when the Holocaust engulfed the House of Israel in the European Diaspora. Let us remember that in every era and in every generation our enemies have risen – and do still arise – trying to exterminate us. Let us remember that all Jews are mutually responsible for each other – "kol Yisrael a'reivin zeh bazeh" – and that the survival of our people depends upon the unity and strength of all its parts. Let us remember and let us never rest until the nation of Israel is rebuilt in our Homeland forever and ever. Amen.

Editorial Committee:

Hemda Levinovich-Kantor

El'azar Goelman

Zalman Hirshfield

Rabbi Shimon Katz

INDEX

The material in the appendices below were not included in this index.

Deneberg, 186
Denenberg, 126, 156, 186, 205, 213, 264
Detner, 284
Doborcki, 233
Dobrzalowski, 140, 141
Dobrzyjalowski, 130, 185, 277, 278, 284
Duras, 128
Dworcki, 43
Dworski, 17

E

Edelsztejn, 20, 107, 110, 111, 112
Efrat, 137
Egielski, 61
Eiger, 71, 72
Ejmanska, 186
Elfenbaum, 91, 342, 351
Epstein, 18, 79, 80, 125
Euwe, 128, 129

F

Farber, 105
Feivel the doctor, 219
Fenik, 280
Fett, 126
Fine, 72
Finkel, 79, 80
Finkiel, 186
Frank, 86, 87
Frankel, 47
Friedberg, 71, 73
Friedman, 73, 123, 199, 330
Frischman, 132
Frydman, 100, 101, 102, 104, 105, 106, 113, 119,
    146, 147, 151
Fuks, 284, 312, 315, 320
Funk, 199, 237, 238, 239

G

Ganichki, 111
Gaon, 185, 186
Gaon Rabbi Shlomo of Vilna, 76
Gelbord, 278
Glicksberg, 72
Gnida, 16
Goelman, 14, 58, 65, 66, 121, 124, 132, 139, 146,
    170, 182, 183, 186, 192, 194, 199, 201, 207, 229,
    235, 250, 295, 336, 337, 338, 342, 350, 351, 352
Goldfaden, 48
Goldflam, 293
Goldkirsz, 223
Goldlust, 208
Goldman, 280
Goldsztejn, 175, 186, 289, 293, 312, 313

Golombek, 186, 283, 284
Golombowicz, 186
Gordin, 212
Gordon, 75, 212
Granit, 132
Granit (Brzostowiecki), 132
Grenet, 19
Grenet (Bzostowiecki), 19
Grodzinski, 81, 98, 100, 112

H

Haller, 165
Halpern, 183
Haness, 45
Harkavi, 87
Hasoltys, 281
Hegel, 6
Heiman, 88
Heler, 147
Heller, 127
Hershel the wagon driver, 68, 245, 246, 250
Herzl, 142, 151, 195
Herzog, 60, 63, 87, 100, 113
Hillel, 131
Hillel the Hat Maker, 260
Hirschbein, 47
Hirschfeld, 43, 45
Hirshfield, 352
Hirszfeld, 147
Holtzman, 237, 240
Horowicz, 186, 259
Horowitz, 88, 288

I

Imiol, 186
Imiyal, 13, 199
Indurski, 13, 283, 289
Ipkowski, 186
Itka Chaya Leahs, 228
Itzkowski, 141, 339
Itzwowiski, 14

J

Jakobowicz, 19, 20
Jakubcyner, 186
Jakubcziner, 288
Jeleniewicz, 13, 281
Joreder, 255

K

Kabak, 132
Kabakowicz, 168, 172, 176, 228

Kac, 17, 27, 29, 78, 80, 81, 82, 83, 84, 85, 98, 102, 114, 119, 122, 146, 199, 213
Kac (Katz), 27, 29, 98
Kachan, 143
Kadish, 6
Kadysz, 13, 265, 283, 287, 289, 301
Kadysz Kolinski, 265
Kadysz-Kolinski, 13, 287
Kadyz, 18
Kagan, 97, 112, 192
Kahana, 86
Kaiser Alexander the Second, 3
Kajmowicz, 42
Kalinski, 186
Kaminski, 29, 31, 151, 186
Kantor, 201, 352
Kaplan, 32, 33, 37, 53, 149, 213, 218, 255, 264
Karmkowski, 1
Katz, 27, 29, 83, 87, 98, 105, 157, 199, 235, 352
Katz (Kac), 199
Katznelson, 137
Kejla, 20, 21, 22
Kilinsky, 154
Kiszlaniczki, 1, 2, 17, 155, 156, 162, 163, 174
Kiwajko, 13, 93, 139, 284
Kobrin, 47
Kohen, 148, 149
Kolinski, 6, 13, 16, 20, 163, 165, 265, 266, 287, 301
Kook, 83, 86
Kopelowicz, 206
Kopisker, 59
Koplowicz, 13, 293
Koszlowski, 24, 28
Kotarski, 285
Kotton, 114, 115, 117, 147, 192, 201, 211, 249, 336
Kotton-Bizounsky, 201
Kreplak, 186, 314
Kulawski, 192
Kurser, 71, 72, 73

L

Ladelski, 13, 114, 115, 147, 149, 150, 182, 201
Landau, 1, 2, 16, 20, 32, 41, 43, 53, 58, 64, 67, 70, 74, 78, 88, 94, 100, 106, 107, 114, 118, 121, 124, 126, 128, 130, 132, 139, 154, 183, 186, 192, 194, 203, 206, 215, 218, 233, 237, 241, 250, 255, 258, 264, 296, 312, 327, 328
Lang, 17, 233
Laska, 289
Laska (Zilbersztejn), 289
Lasker, 127, 128
Laskowska, 158, 284, 286
Leeitan, 79
Leib, 13
Leibel, 218, 281
Leibowitz, 88

Leizer, 220, 230, 242, 243, 244, 245, 251, 259, 289
Leizer Horowicz, 259
Leizers, 34
Lejbik, 118, 186, 288
Lelebel, 110
Lev, 128
Leviathan, 346
Levine, 352
Levine (Levinovich), 352
Levinovich, 352
Levinovich-Kantor, 352
Lew, 186
Lewin, 53, 220
Lewinowicz, 14, 122, 154, 169, 172, 174, 201, 206, 227, 228, 241, 249
Lewinowicz-Kantor, 201
Lewinski, 58, 107, 289
Lewkowicz, 18
Liberman, 2, 41, 45, 147, 148, 192, 203, 204
Lieberman, 19, 310
Lim, 84
Linsberg, 186
Lipkin, 42
Livna, 345
Livna (Bzostowiecki), 345
Lufgass, 195

M

Maaravit, 106
Madrykamien, 186
Maimonides, 109, 114
Makower, 53
Marchawki, 298
Marcus, 6
Marek, 186
Mark, 2, 139, 155, 182, 280, 286, 296, 314
Markus, 186
Meir of Zaskrodzie, 223
Meisel, 68
Meisels, 110, 349
Meisels Allen, 349
Meizner the water-man, 235
Mejzner, 186, 201, 211, 212
Meltzer, 97
Menachem, 271
Mendel, 223
Michael the baker, 250
Michelowski, 112
Mickucki, 293
Mieckiewicz, 111
Milberg, 186
Mocz, 68
Mondenstein, 144
Mondensztejn, 14, 43, 163, 183, 201, 207, 208, 212, 213
Montefiore, 3

APPENDIX-

This material was not included in the original Yizkor Book,

but deemed of interest to readers of this book.

Aerial Photographs of Stawiski

These next two photographs are from the Records of the Defense Intelligence Agency, Record 373. They are captured German World War II photographs available from the National Archives and Records Administration II Cartographic Section.

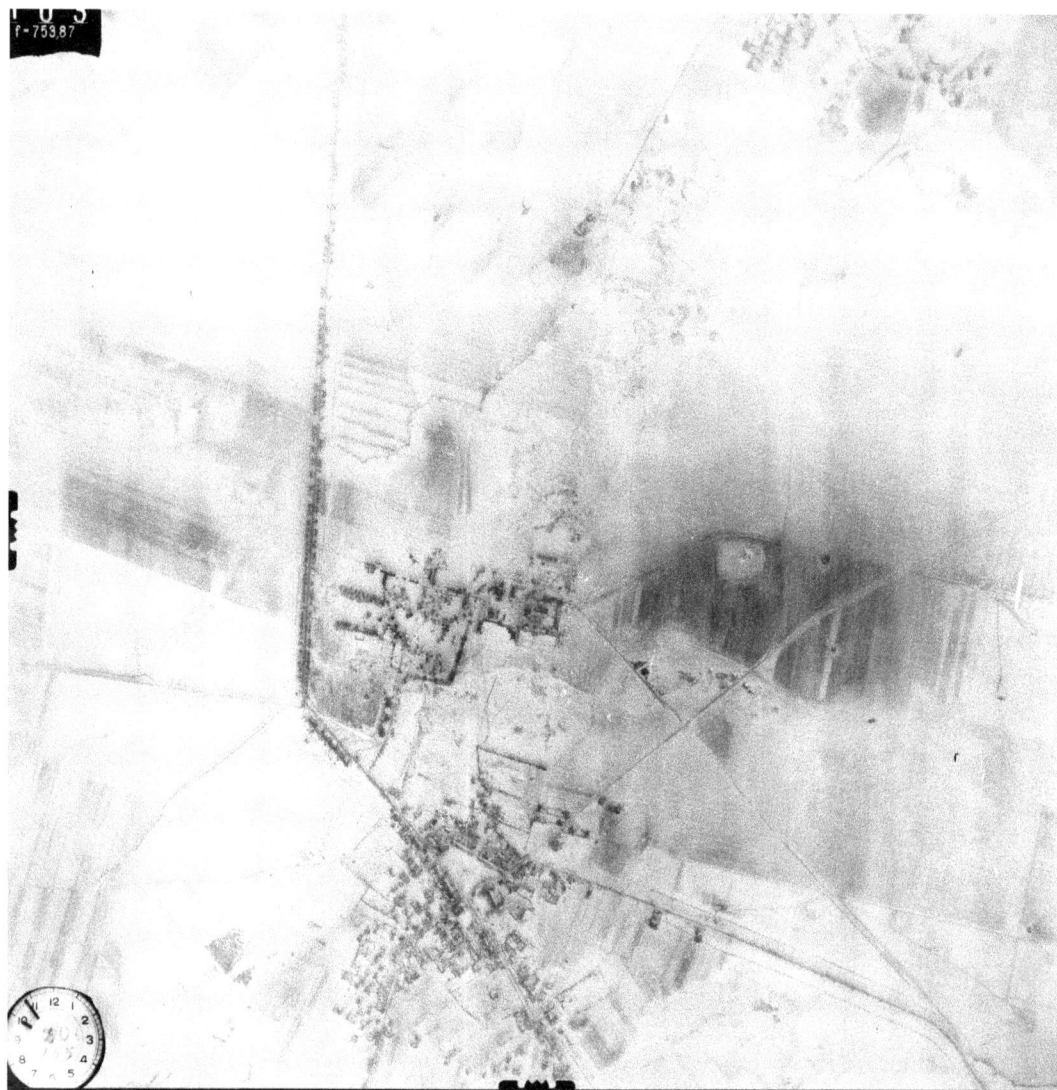

Stawiski, Poland January 20, 1945 Scale 1:12,000

Captured German Aerial Photograph

National Archives and Records Administration

Cartographic Section RG 373 ~ GX 2187 ~ SD 103

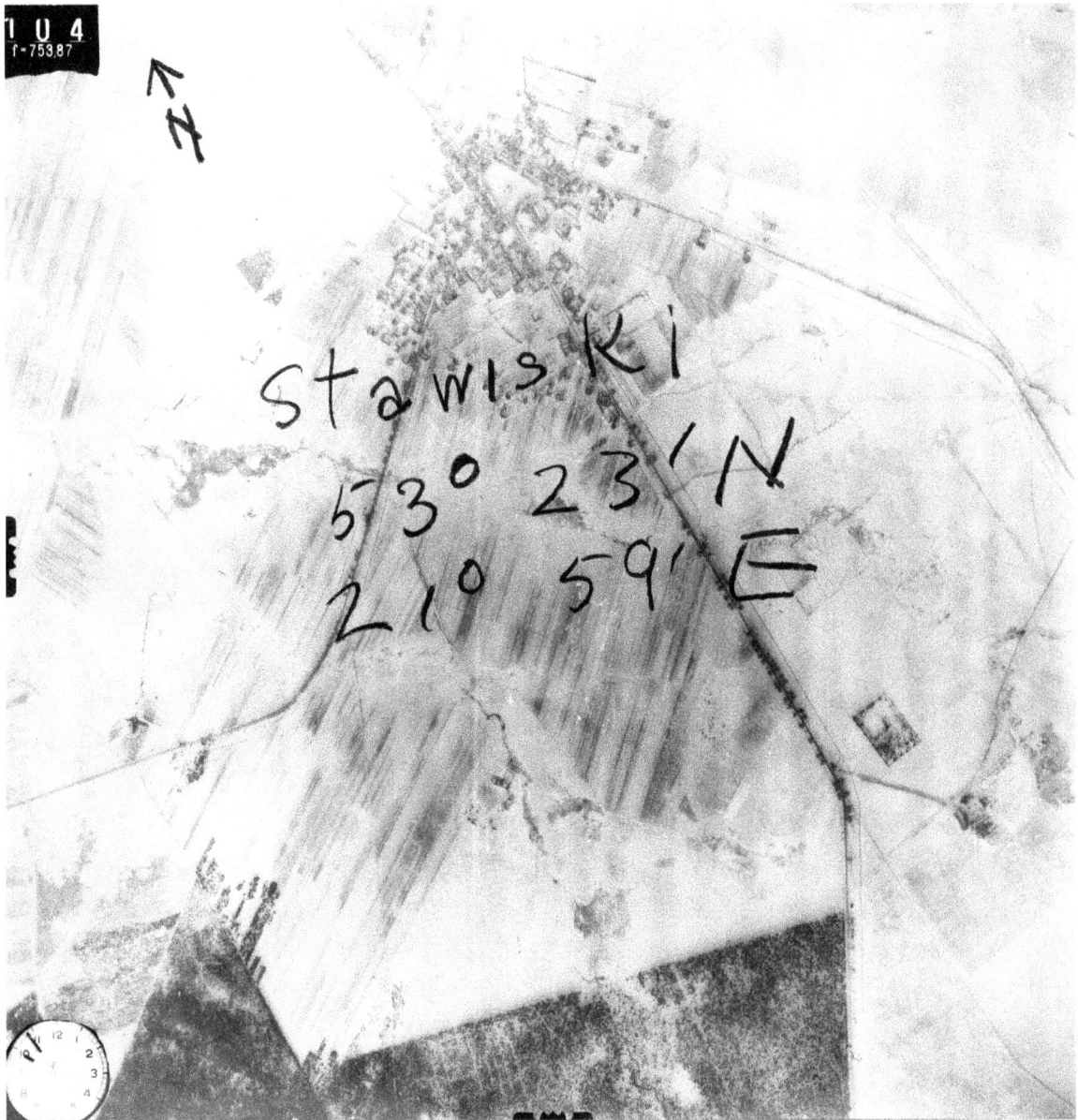

Stawiski, Poland January 20, 1945 Scale 1:12,000

Captured German Aerial Photograph

National Archives and Records Administration

Cartographic Section RG 373 ~ GX 2187 ~ SD 104

Photographs from Stawiski (1998)

Courtesy of Gene Mandel

Memorial in the woods outside of Stawiski

"This is a place of martyrdom of 700 inhabitants of Stawiski, murdered by Nazis, July 1941".

Inscription date 22 July 1964

Street scene with horse and buggy

Wooden building

Wooden building

Street scene

Market Square

Building across from market square

Catholic Church

Poland Trip 2001 (July)

Courtesy of Jan Meisels Allen

These photographs were taken in July 2001 by the Sochaczew/Stawiski Yizkor Book translation coordinator, Jan Meisels Allen, on a trip to Poland to visit her ancestral shtetls. They are representative of how Stawiski is today.

Sign at entrance to Stawiski

Farm fields

Russian style house on Lomzyska Street

Wooden house at 13 Lomzyska Street

House and farm

Fire department- former location of Synagogue with synagogue photo in front

Movie house- former location of back of Synagogue with synagogue photo in front

Town Square

Looking down street from square

Police and municipal building

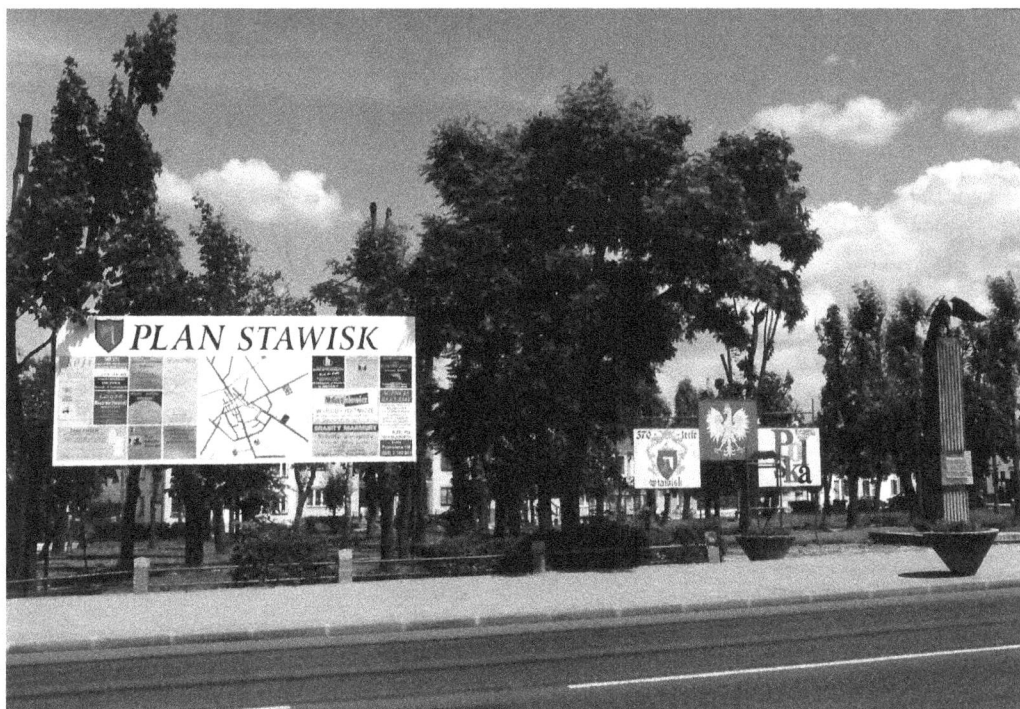

Town map and war memorial in Rynek

Local street

Looking across farmer's field to location of Jewish cemetery ruins

Plaszczatka Forest where massacre took place in July 1941

From Michael Marvin's Collection of his Father's and Grandfather's Photographs

Group in woods-Dating is Stawiski-group walks in the woods. All are about 18 years old. Dated April 10, 1928. Everyone in the group is from Stawiski except Maishe Kaplan (Szczuczyn Photographer far right bottom row)), and his Szczuczyn friend Kuberski(far right-standing). Top row middle is Sonia Wilenska (later Wilner). Next to her (left) is Dintche Kac(Katz) daughter of the famed Rabbi Katz. Sonia's father, Moses Wilenski (Wilner) was the town's Cantor, Shochet and Mohel. Maishe and Soni would marry in Canada in 1933.

Historical Note: The highway through Stawiski went to St Petersburg, Russia. Napoleon's troops camped here. The place was later THE spot for dating young people.

Stawiski, very near the German border was occupied by German troops 1914-1918. Unlike WW 11, German troops were friendly. The Stawiski Jewish community had a Kosher canteen for the German Jewish troops.

The Stawiski church c 1916 during World War I. When the occupation ended, one soldier stayed in Stawiski and married. He would go to the top of the Church each day and play trumpet solos at 5 pm.

Rabbi Katz and family in US or Israel. Several chapters about them appear in the Stawiski Yizkor book.

Soni Wilenska (Wilner-seated right) and friends. Probably 1929 before her family left for the US. Far right is Dintche Katz. One of the other girls is Elke Mark. Picture is by Maishe Kaplan of Szczuczyn, who Soni would later marry in Canada. Elke and Dintche would also leave before World War II.

School Group Stawiski c.1926. Jewish and Polish students and teachers. Soni Wilenska, bottom row far right.

Historic Stawiski Photographs Courtesy of Michael Marvins

The following photographs as well as most of the photographs in the main body of the Stawiski Yizkor Book were made by Zalman Kaplan who had an established studio in Szczuczyn (see szczuczyn.com) about 7 miles away from Stawiski. In 1926, Kaplan's son, Maishe began making the journey from Szczuczyn to Stawiski. He had previously met Sonia (Soni) Wilensky (Wilner), daughter of the Stawiski cantor, Moses A. Wilner, on a youth group exchange in about 1925. They continued dating in Stawiski until 1929 when Sonia and her family left for the US. Maishe also emigrated in 1929 and the two married in 1933 when they were both 22 years old.

Anya Lesser Kac(Katz) and Abe Katz. Anya came to visit Stawiski in 1912 from Slutsk, Russia to see her sister's (Celia Lesser Wilensky) new baby, Sonia. She met and later married Katz who had. a bakery on the town square. The Katz' and their two children were murdered in Stawiski in 1941. Abe was a nephew of Rabbi Katz.

Dintche Katz .Rabbi Katz' daughter. (See the Katz family history in the Yizkor Book)

Genia Silverstein

Elke Mark. Her family emigrated to Israel. (Note picture of her in Israel appears on page 314 in this translation of the Stawiski Yizkor Book)

Girl friends c.1925. Top row, left: Sonia Wilensky. Middle Row (marks on face):Genia Silverstein-Little girl is her sister. Middle Row sailor suit: Elke Mark.

Bottom Row on right:"Kivacki"-Father the Polish (pork) sausage maker and had a store on the square.

Friends.1927-Swimming area in the backround. It was few blocks off the square toward Szczuczyn.

Back row left: Maishe Kaplan,photographer from Szczuczyn.Bottom left: Sonia (Soni) Wilensky(Wilner)

Jewish Youth Group c. 1927-8

School Group with teachers c.1926

Friends 1927. Soni Wilensky, Dintche Kac, Elke Mark. Picture by Maishe Kaplan. Kaplan would ride his bicycle from his Father's studio in Szczuczyn, about 7 miles away to photograph in Stawiski. He kept his backdrops (see patterned cloth on the inn wall) at a Jewish owned Inn across the road from the Church. Backdrops were tacked to the Inn's outside wall. He met Sonia Wilensky in Stawiski and they later married in 1933 in Toronto, Canada.

School Group.1928. Jewish and Polish students went to school together and the teachers were both Jewish and Catholic. In some towns, like Szczuczyn, Jews and Catholics went to separate public schools.

Sonia   Wilner and   Maishe   Kaplan(Kaye   Marvins) engagement portrait,   1933, Toronto. Kaplan had to change his name to get a photographic job due to anti-Semitism in Montreal. They later moved to Houston, Texas where founded a successful portrait studio, now owned by his sons.

Moses Aaron Wilensky (Wilner) met and married Celia Lesser in Slutsk, Russia (now Belarus). He found a cantorial job in Stawiski about 1907-8. He served the town as Cantor, Shochet, and Mohel until 1924 when he found a job in Conneticut and emigrated. His family (Celia and children Sonia,Betty, Sally and Irving) followed in 1929 when immigration laws changed. He later served in Worcester, MA. Wilner served with Stawiski's famed Rabbis, Kac (Katz) and Remogolski.

Group date in the Stawiski woods. Dates usually consisted of long walks in the woods near town. The favored place was the area where Napoleon camped on his ill-fated Russian conquest. The road through Stawiski was the route to St. Petersburg.

The Stawiski Synagogue. Destroyed by the Nazis.

17 Stawiski. Juden am Brunnen.

Stawiski. Jews at the well

www.ingramcontent.com/pod-product-compliance
Lightning Source LLC
Chambersburg PA
CBHW050407110426
42812CB00006BA/1825